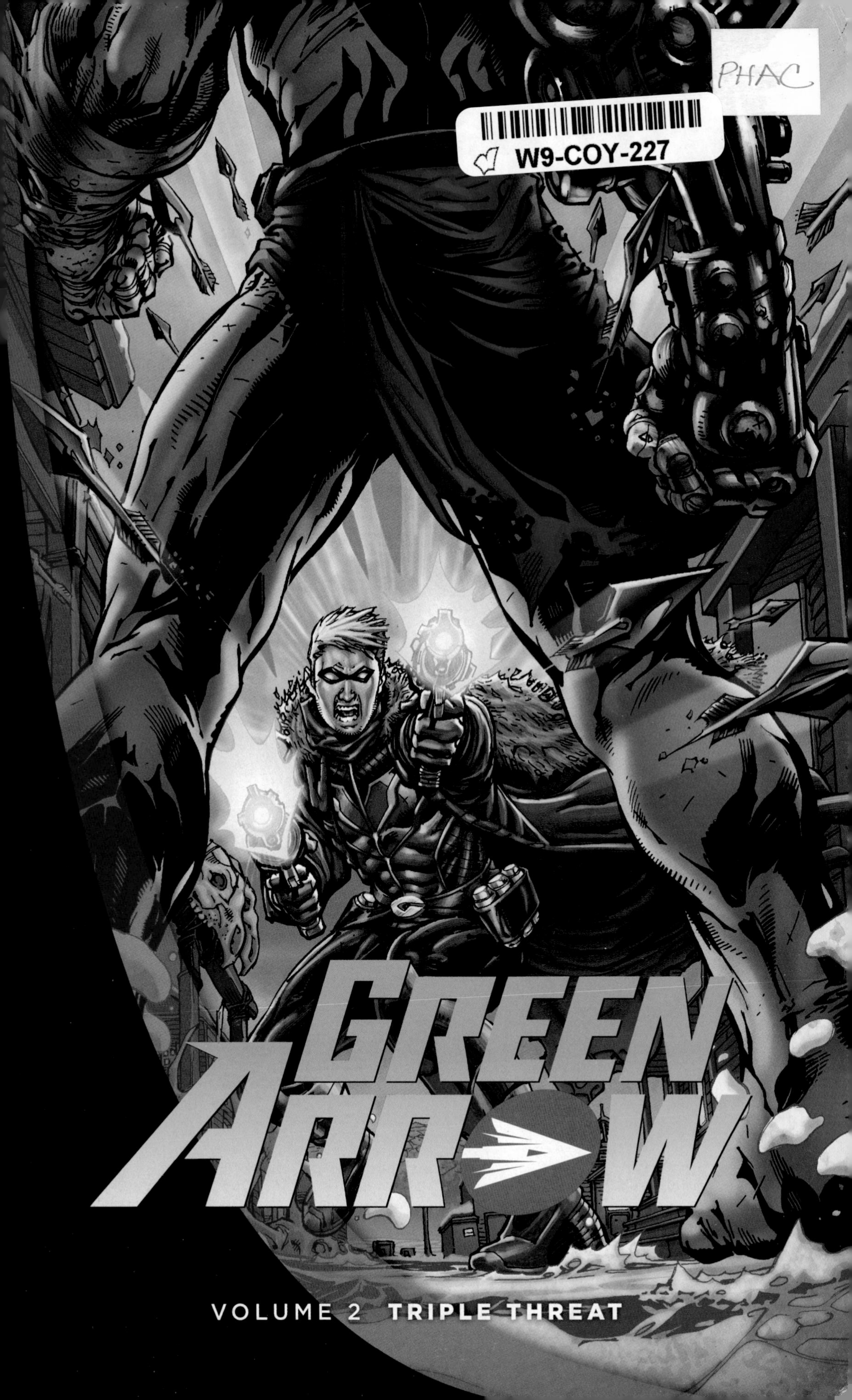

GREEN ARROW

VOLUME 2 TRIPLE THREAT

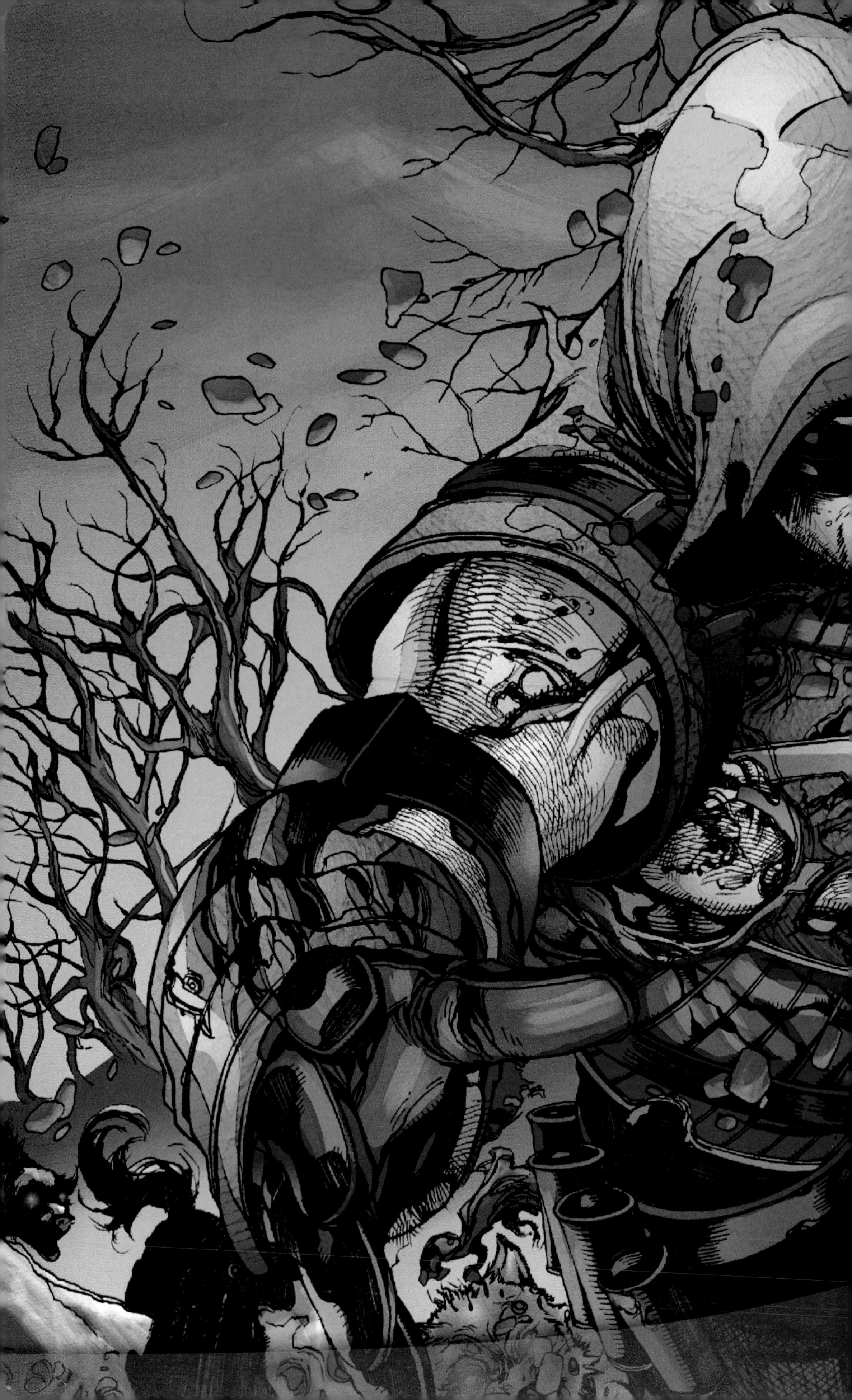

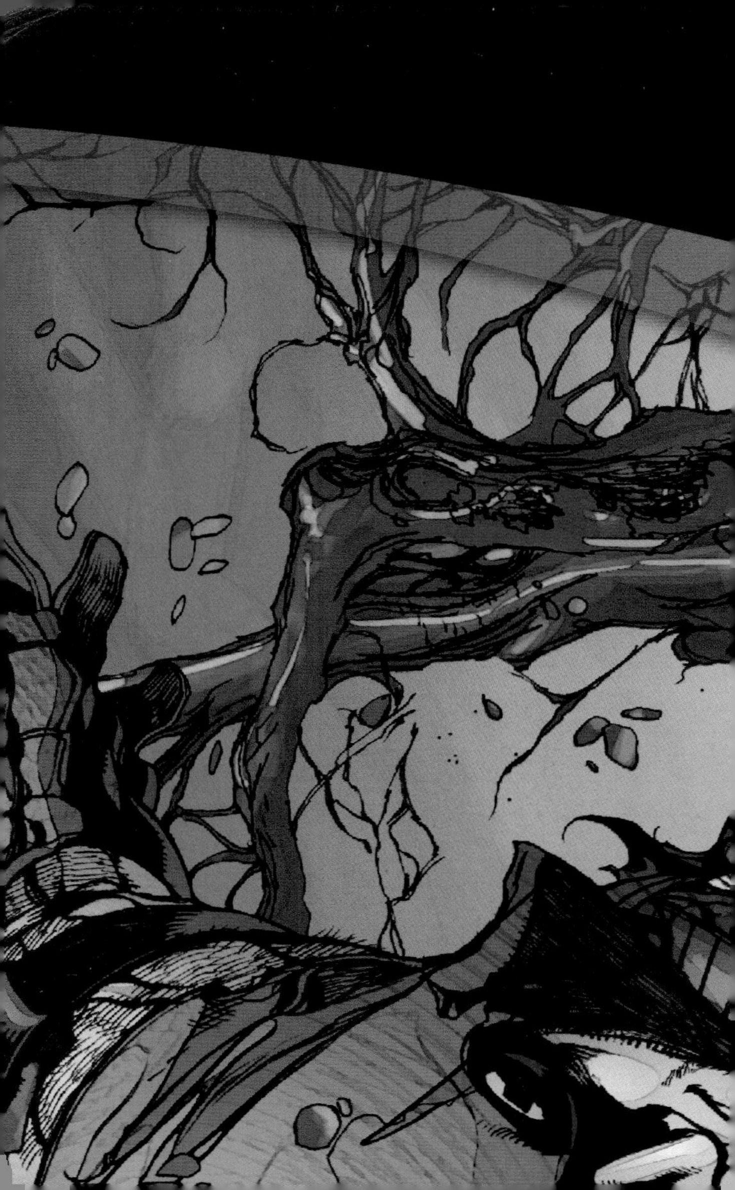

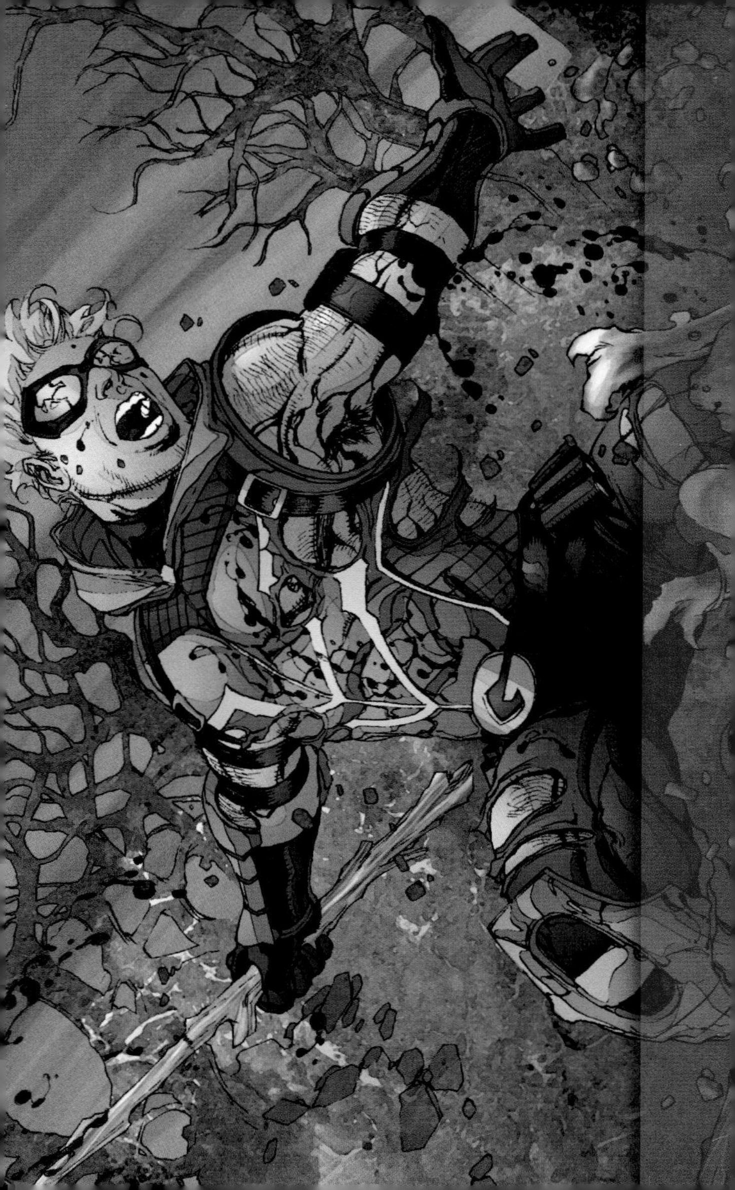

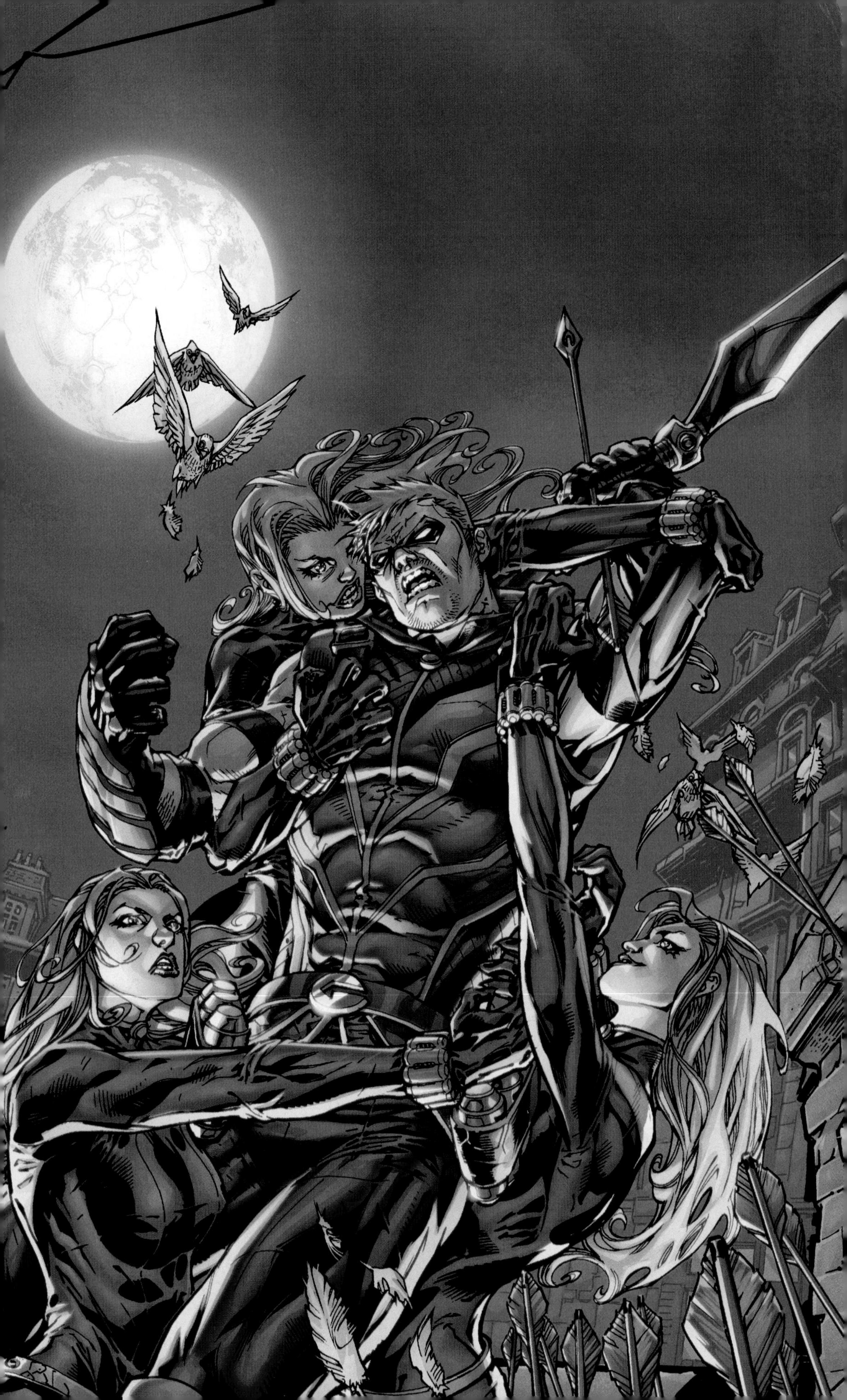

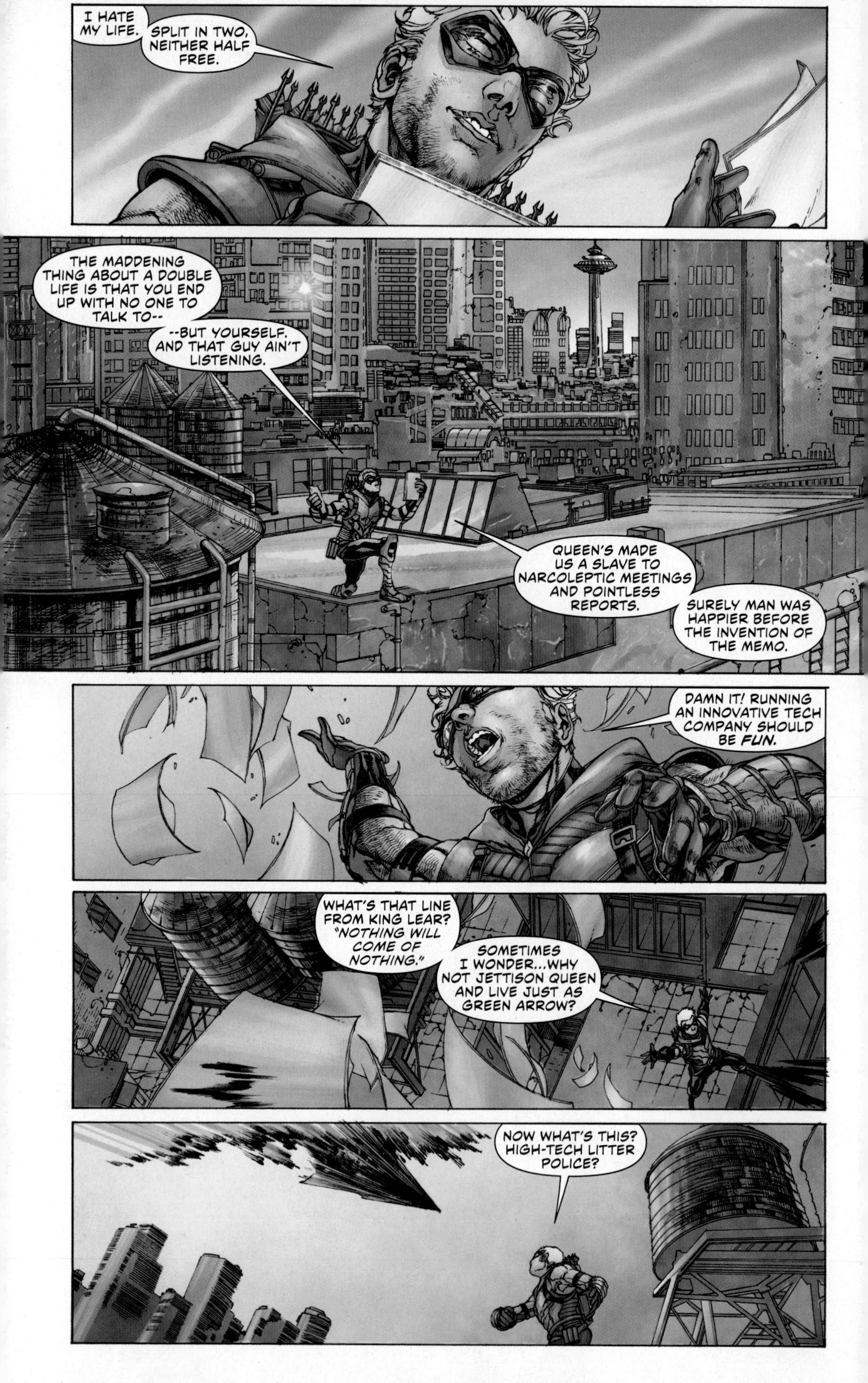
I HATE MY LIFE.
SPLIT IN TWO, NEITHER HALF FREE.
THE MADDENING THING ABOUT A DOUBLE LIFE IS THAT YOU END UP WITH NO ONE TO TALK TO--
--BUT YOURSELF. AND THAT GUY AIN'T LISTENING.
QUEEN'S MADE US A SLAVE TO NARCOLEPTIC MEETINGS AND POINTLESS REPORTS.
SURELY MAN WAS HAPPIER BEFORE THE INVENTION OF THE MEMO.
DAMN IT! RUNNING AN INNOVATIVE TECH COMPANY SHOULD BE *FUN*.
WHAT'S THAT LINE FROM KING LEAR? *"NOTHING WILL COME OF NOTHING."*
SOMETIMES I WONDER...WHY NOT JETTISON QUEEN AND LIVE JUST AS GREEN ARROW?
NOW WHAT'S THIS? HIGH-TECH LITTER POLICE?

TRIPL3 TR3AT PART 1: MÉNAGE À QUATRE

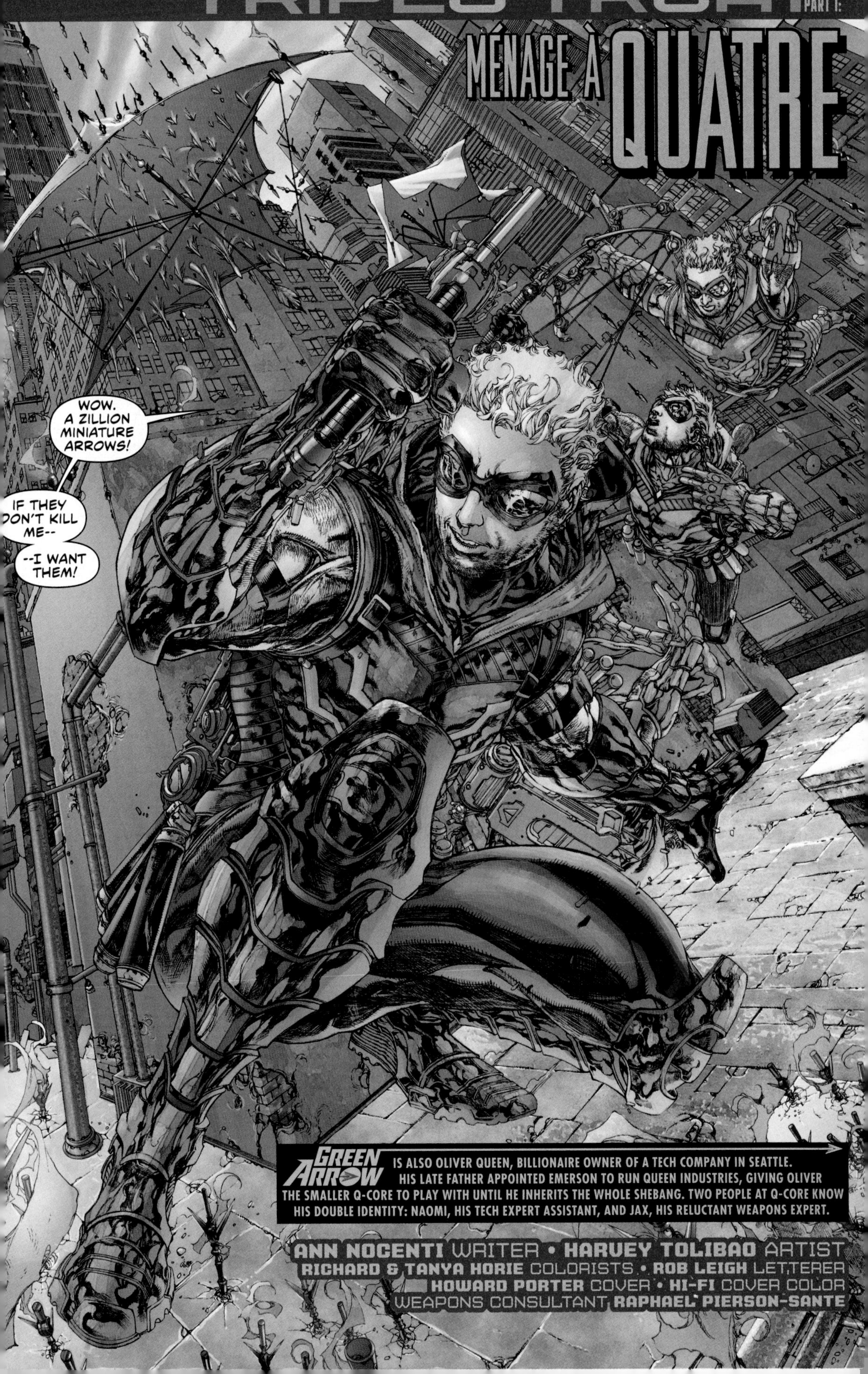
WOW. A ZILLION MINIATURE ARROWS!
IF THEY DON'T KILL ME--
--I WANT THEM!
GREEN ARROW IS ALSO OLIVER QUEEN, BILLIONAIRE OWNER OF A TECH COMPANY IN SEATTLE. HIS LATE FATHER APPOINTED EMERSON TO RUN QUEEN INDUSTRIES, GIVING OLIVER THE SMALLER Q-CORE TO PLAY WITH UNTIL HE INHERITS THE WHOLE SHEBANG. TWO PEOPLE AT Q-CORE KNOW HIS DOUBLE IDENTITY: NAOMI, HIS TECH EXPERT ASSISTANT, AND JAX, HIS RELUCTANT WEAPONS EXPERT.
ANN NOCENTI WRITER • HARVEY TOLIBAO ARTIST
RICHARD & TANYA HORIE COLORISTS • ROB LEIGH LETTERER
HOWARD PORTER COVER • HI-FI COVER COLOR
WEAPONS CONSULTANT RAPHAEL PIERSON-SANTE

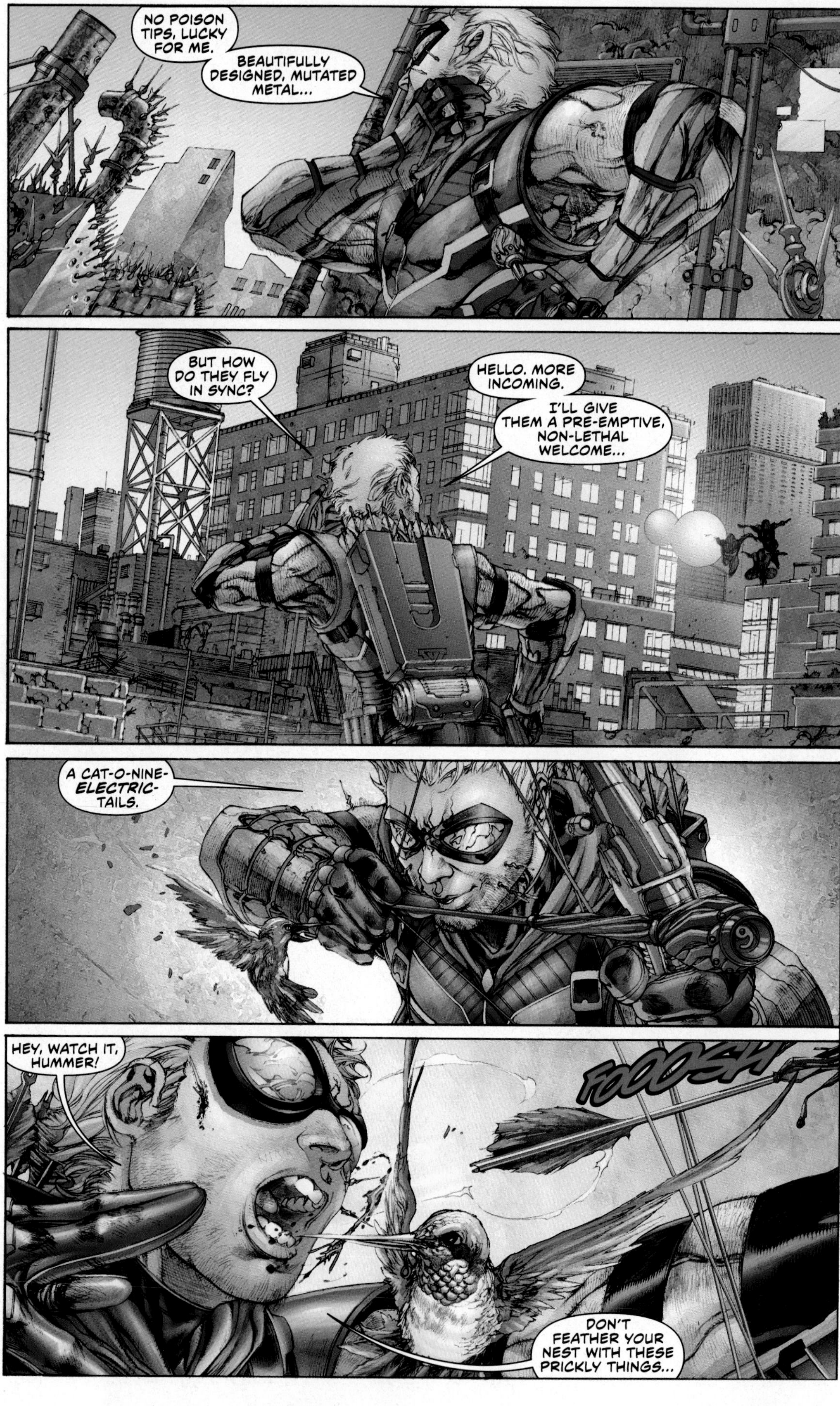
NO POISON TIPS, LUCKY FOR ME.
BEAUTIFULLY DESIGNED, MUTATED METAL...
BUT HOW DO THEY FLY IN SYNC?
HELLO. MORE INCOMING.
I'LL GIVE THEM A PRE-EMPTIVE, NON-LETHAL WELCOME...
A CAT-O-NINE-ELECTRIC-TAILS.
HEY, WATCH IT, HUMMER!
FOOOSH
DON'T FEATHER YOUR NEST WITH THESE PRICKLY THINGS...

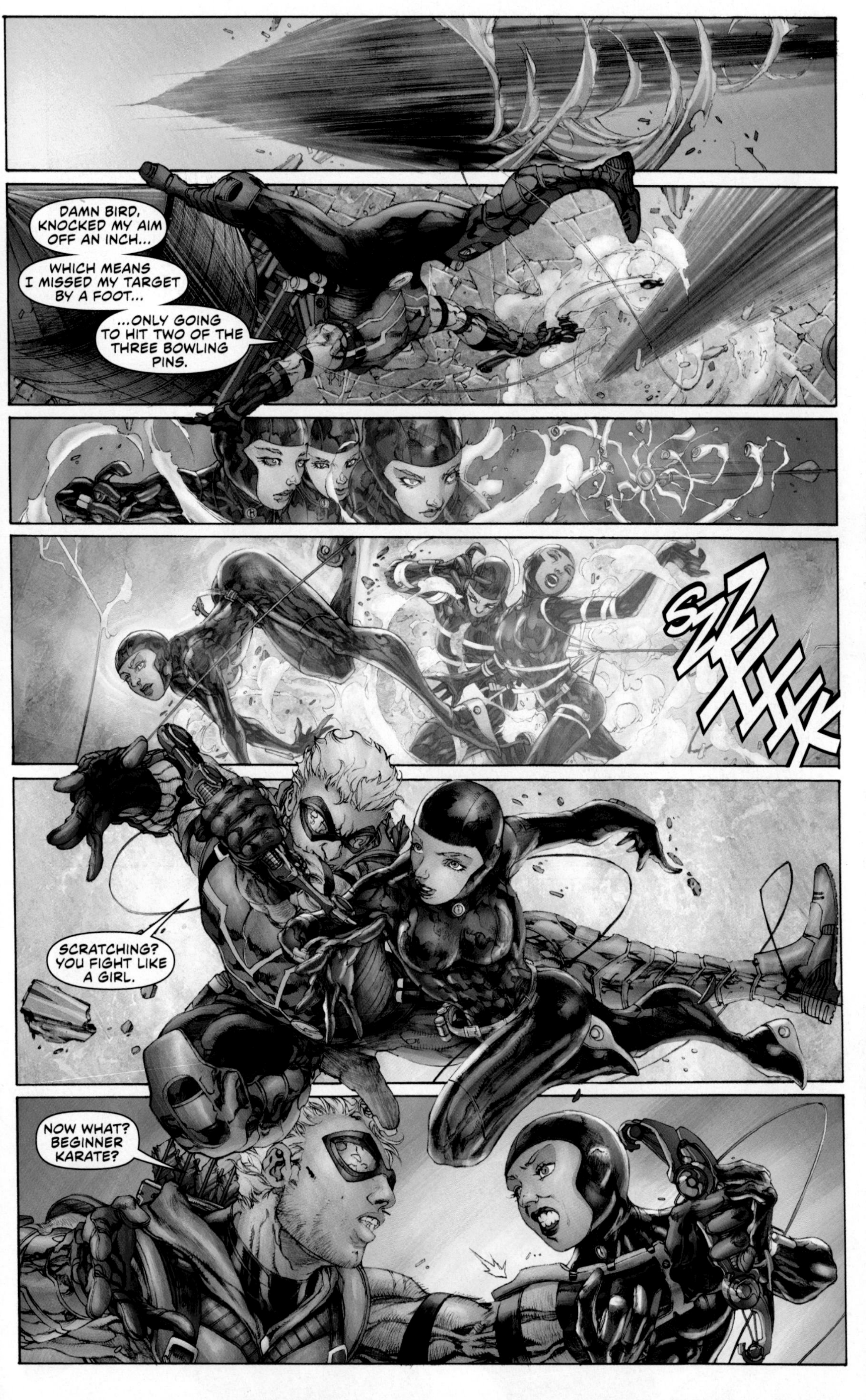
DAMN BIRD, KNOCKED MY AIM OFF AN INCH...
WHICH MEANS I MISSED MY TARGET BY A FOOT...
...ONLY GOING TO HIT TWO OF THE THREE BOWLING PINS.
SCRATCHING? YOU FIGHT LIKE A GIRL.
NOW WHAT? BEGINNER KARATE?

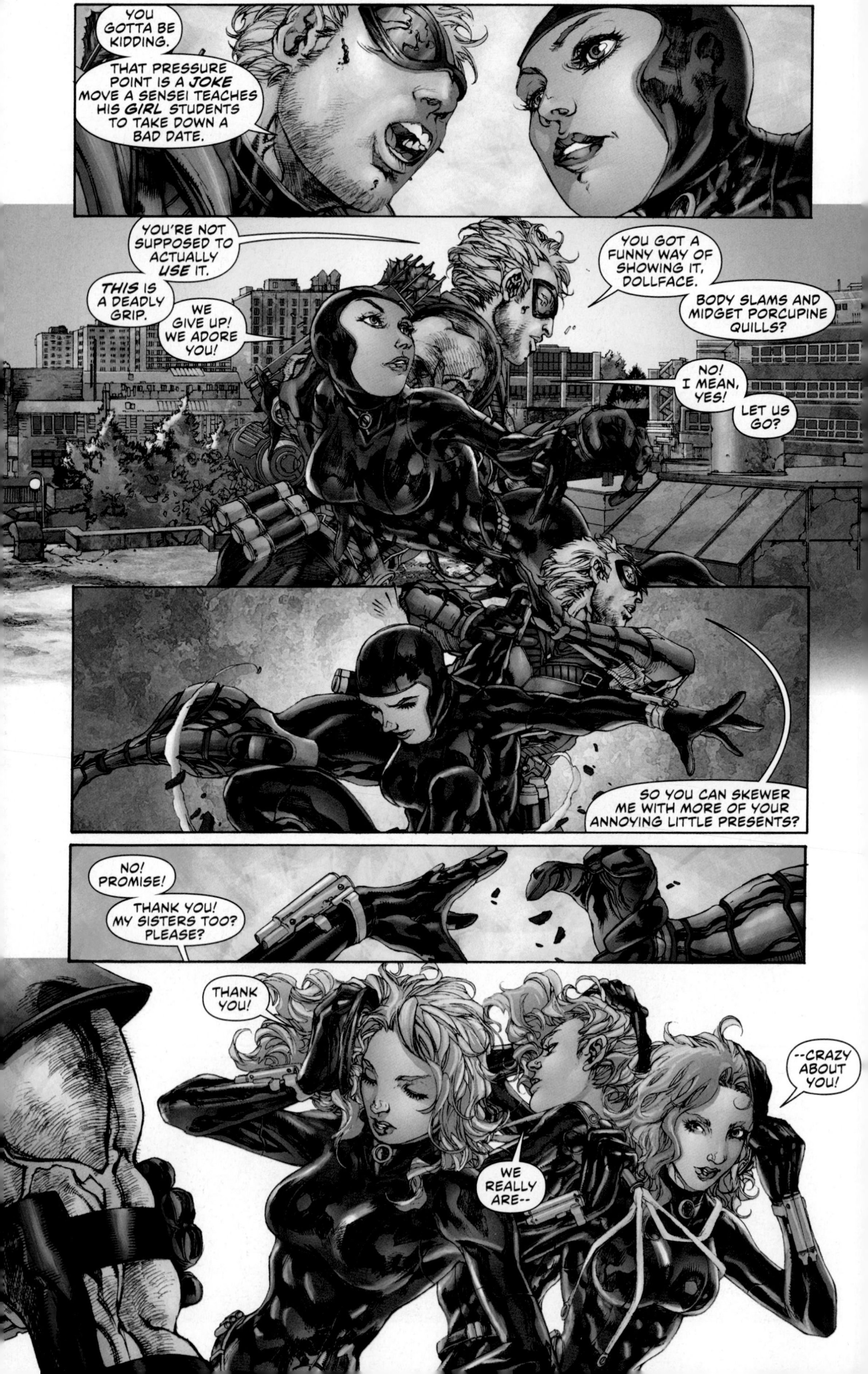
YOU GOTTA BE KIDDING.
THAT PRESSURE POINT IS A JOKE MOVE A SENSEI TEACHES HIS GIRL STUDENTS TO TAKE DOWN A BAD DATE.
YOU'RE NOT SUPPOSED TO ACTUALLY USE IT.
THIS IS A DEADLY GRIP.
WE GIVE UP! WE ADORE YOU!
YOU GOT A FUNNY WAY OF SHOWING IT, DOLLFACE.
BODY SLAMS AND MIDGET PORCUPINE QUILLS?
NO! I MEAN, YES!
LET US GO?
SO YOU CAN SKEWER ME WITH MORE OF YOUR ANNOYING LITTLE PRESENTS?
NO! PROMISE!
THANK YOU! MY SISTERS TOO? PLEASE?
THANK YOU!
WE REALLY ARE--
--CRAZY ABOUT YOU!

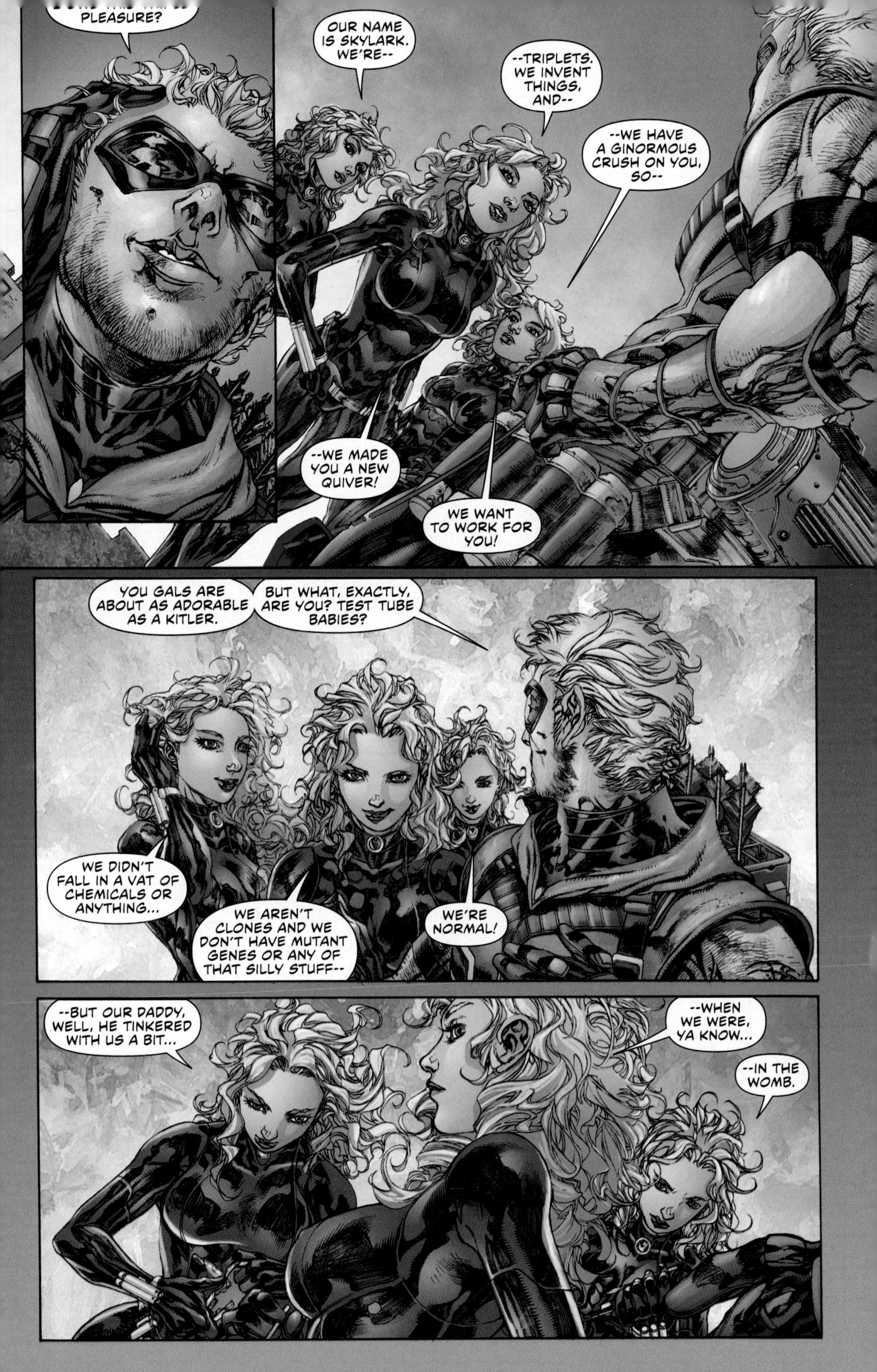

PLEASURE?
OUR NAME IS SKYLARK. WE'RE--
--TRIPLETS. WE INVENT THINGS, AND--
--WE HAVE A GINORMOUS CRUSH ON YOU, SO--
--WE MADE YOU A NEW QUIVER!
WE WANT TO WORK FOR YOU!
YOU GALS ARE ABOUT AS ADORABLE AS A KITLER.
BUT WHAT, EXACTLY, ARE YOU? TEST TUBE BABIES?
WE DIDN'T FALL IN A VAT OF CHEMICALS OR ANYTHING...
WE AREN'T CLONES AND WE DON'T HAVE MUTANT GENES OR ANY OF THAT SILLY STUFF--
WE'RE NORMAL!
--BUT OUR DADDY, WELL, HE TINKERED WITH US A BIT...
--WHEN WE WERE, YA KNOW...
--IN THE WOMB.

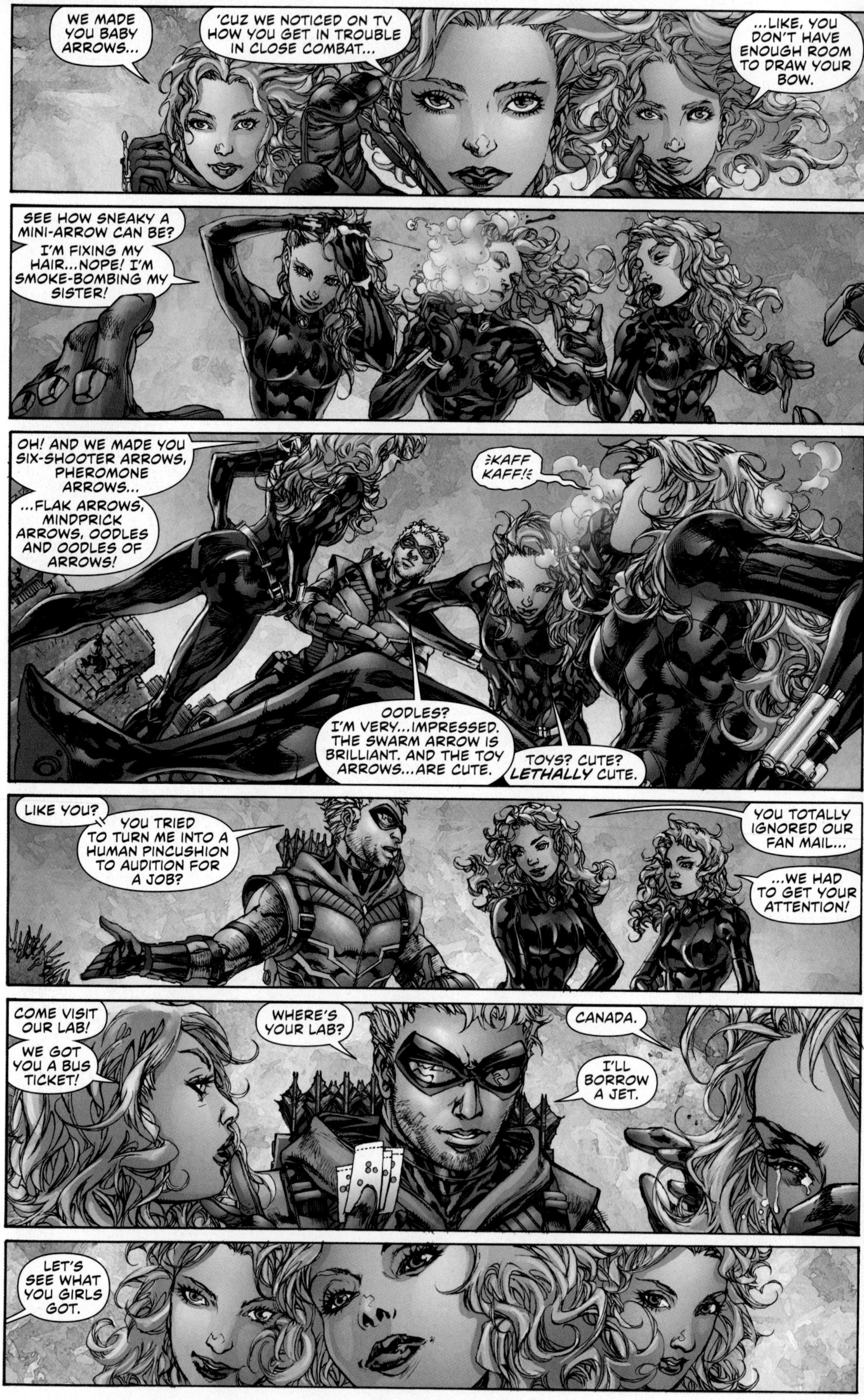
WE MADE YOU BABY ARROWS...
'CUZ WE NOTICED ON TV HOW YOU GET IN TROUBLE IN CLOSE COMBAT...
...LIKE, YOU DON'T HAVE ENOUGH ROOM TO DRAW YOUR BOW.
SEE HOW SNEAKY A MINI-ARROW CAN BE?
I'M FIXING MY HAIR...NOPE! I'M SMOKE-BOMBING MY SISTER!
OH! AND WE MADE YOU SIX-SHOOTER ARROWS, PHEROMONE ARROWS...
...FLAK ARROWS, MINDPRICK ARROWS, OODLES AND OODLES OF ARROWS!
KAFF KAFF!
OODLES? I'M VERY...IMPRESSED. THE SWARM ARROW IS BRILLIANT. AND THE TOY ARROWS...ARE CUTE.
TOYS? CUTE? LETHALLY CUTE.
LIKE YOU?
YOU TRIED TO TURN ME INTO A HUMAN PINCUSHION TO AUDITION FOR A JOB?
YOU TOTALLY IGNORED OUR FAN MAIL...
...WE HAD TO GET YOUR ATTENTION!
COME VISIT OUR LAB!
WE GOT YOU A BUS TICKET!
WHERE'S YOUR LAB?
CANADA.
I'LL BORROW A JET.
LET'S SEE WHAT YOU GIRLS GOT.

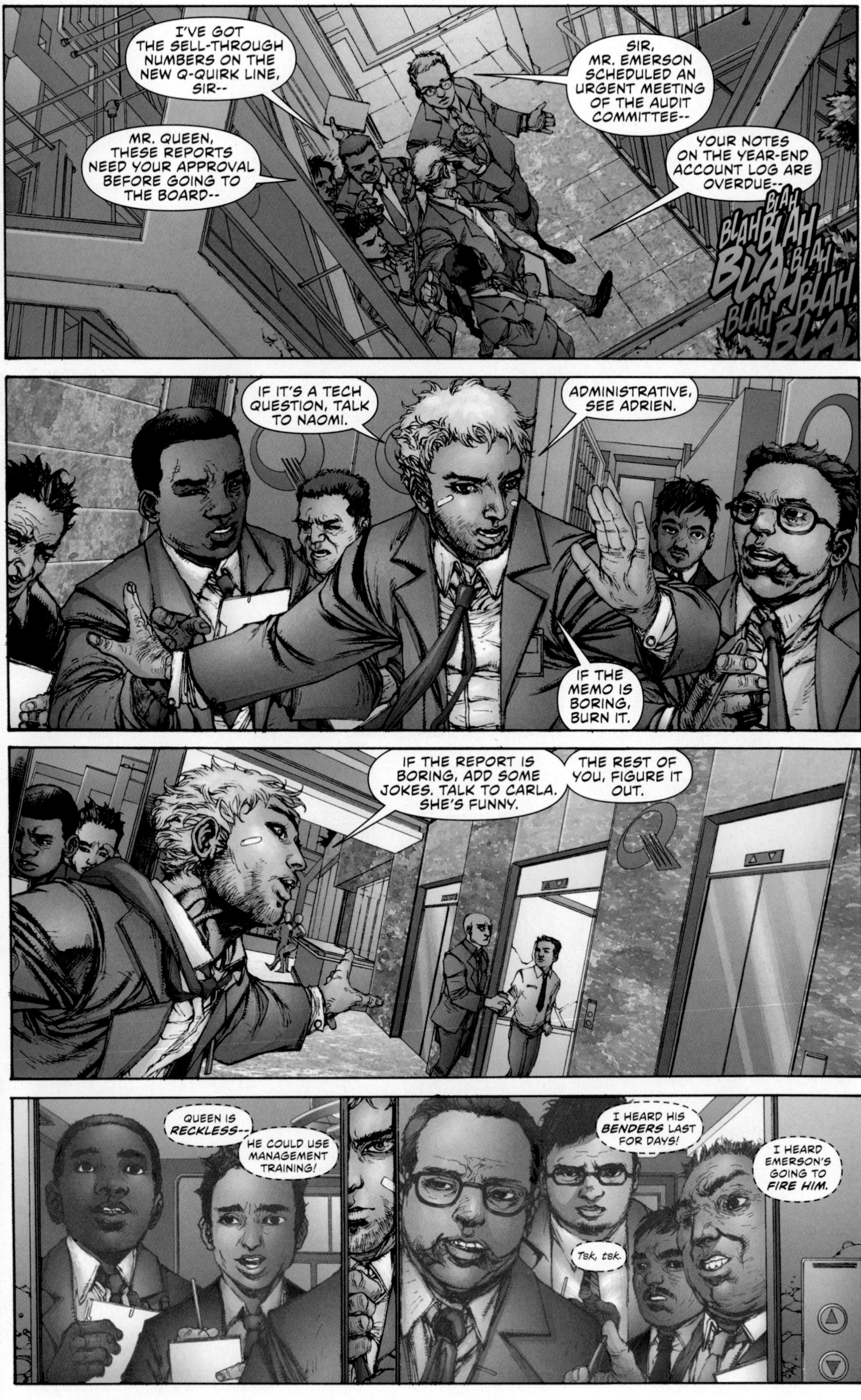
I'VE GOT THE SELL-THROUGH NUMBERS ON THE NEW Q-QUIRK LINE, SIR--
SIR, MR. EMERSON SCHEDULED AN URGENT MEETING OF THE AUDIT COMMITTEE--
MR. QUEEN, THESE REPORTS NEED YOUR APPROVAL BEFORE GOING TO THE BOARD--
YOUR NOTES ON THE YEAR-END ACCOUNT LOG ARE OVERDUE--
BLAH BLAH BLAH BLAH BLAH BLAH BLAH BLAH BLAH
IF IT'S A TECH QUESTION, TALK TO NAOMI.
ADMINISTRATIVE, SEE ADRIEN.
IF THE MEMO IS BORING, BURN IT.
IF THE REPORT IS BORING, ADD SOME JOKES. TALK TO CARLA. SHE'S FUNNY.
THE REST OF YOU, FIGURE IT OUT.
QUEEN IS RECKLESS--
HE COULD USE MANAGEMENT TRAINING!
I HEARD HIS BENDERS LAST FOR DAYS!
I HEARD EMERSON'S GOING TO FIRE HIM.
Tsk, tsk.

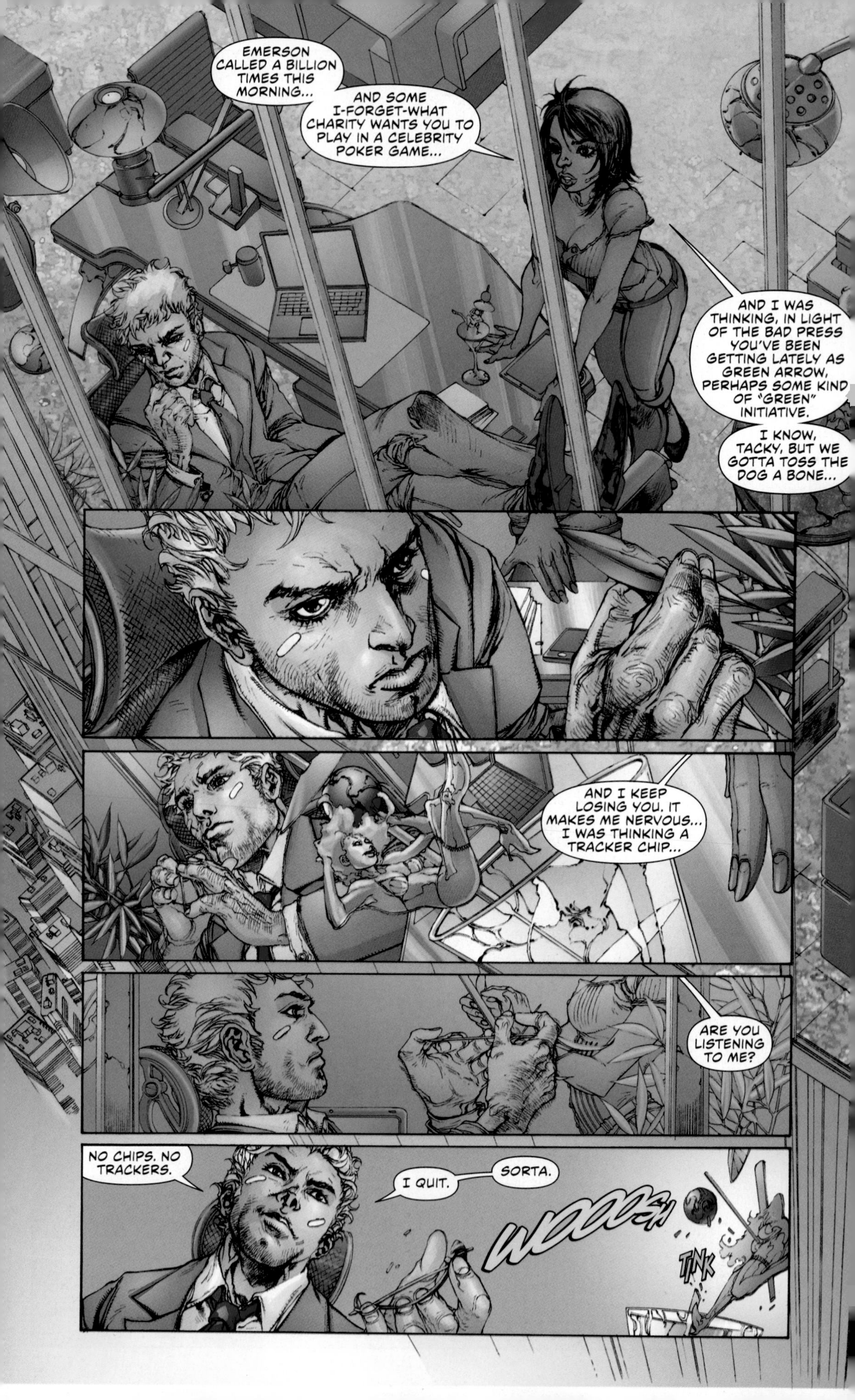
EMERSON CALLED A BILLION TIMES THIS MORNING...
AND SOME I-FORGET-WHAT CHARITY WANTS YOU TO PLAY IN A CELEBRITY POKER GAME...
AND I WAS THINKING, IN LIGHT OF THE BAD PRESS YOU'VE BEEN GETTING LATELY AS GREEN ARROW, PERHAPS SOME KIND OF "GREEN" INITIATIVE.
I KNOW, TACKY, BUT WE GOTTA TOSS THE DOG A BONE...
AND I KEEP LOSING YOU. IT MAKES ME NERVOUS... I WAS THINKING A TRACKER CHIP...
ARE YOU LISTENING TO ME?
NO CHIPS. NO TRACKERS.
I QUIT.
SORTA.
WOOOSH
TINK

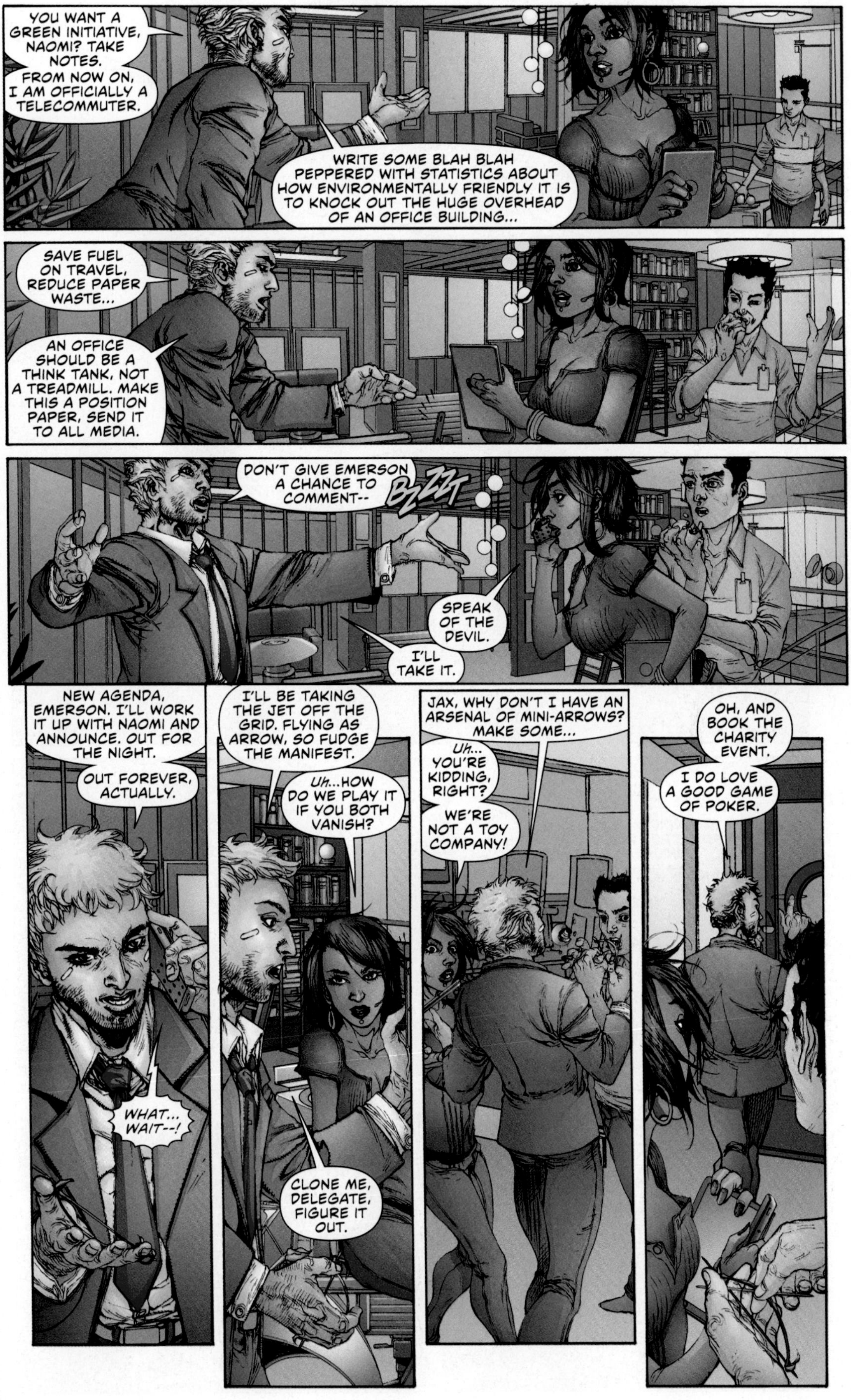
YOU WANT A GREEN INITIATIVE, NAOMI? TAKE NOTES.
FROM NOW ON, I AM OFFICIALLY A TELECOMMUTER.
WRITE SOME BLAH BLAH PEPPERED WITH STATISTICS ABOUT HOW ENVIRONMENTALLY FRIENDLY IT IS TO KNOCK OUT THE HUGE OVERHEAD OF AN OFFICE BUILDING...
SAVE FUEL ON TRAVEL, REDUCE PAPER WASTE...
AN OFFICE SHOULD BE A THINK TANK, NOT A TREADMILL. MAKE THIS A POSITION PAPER, SEND IT TO ALL MEDIA.
DON'T GIVE EMERSON A CHANCE TO COMMENT--
BZZZT
SPEAK OF THE DEVIL.
I'LL TAKE IT.
NEW AGENDA, EMERSON. I'LL WORK IT UP WITH NAOMI AND ANNOUNCE. OUT FOR THE NIGHT.
OUT FOREVER, ACTUALLY.
WHAT... WAIT--!
I'LL BE TAKING THE JET OFF THE GRID. FLYING AS ARROW, SO FUDGE THE MANIFEST.
Uh...HOW DO WE PLAY IT IF YOU BOTH VANISH?
CLONE ME, DELEGATE, FIGURE IT OUT.
JAX, WHY DON'T I HAVE AN ARSENAL OF MINI-ARROWS? MAKE SOME...
Uh... YOU'RE KIDDING, RIGHT?
WE'RE NOT A TOY COMPANY!
OH, AND BOOK THE CHARITY EVENT.
I DO LOVE A GOOD GAME OF POKER.

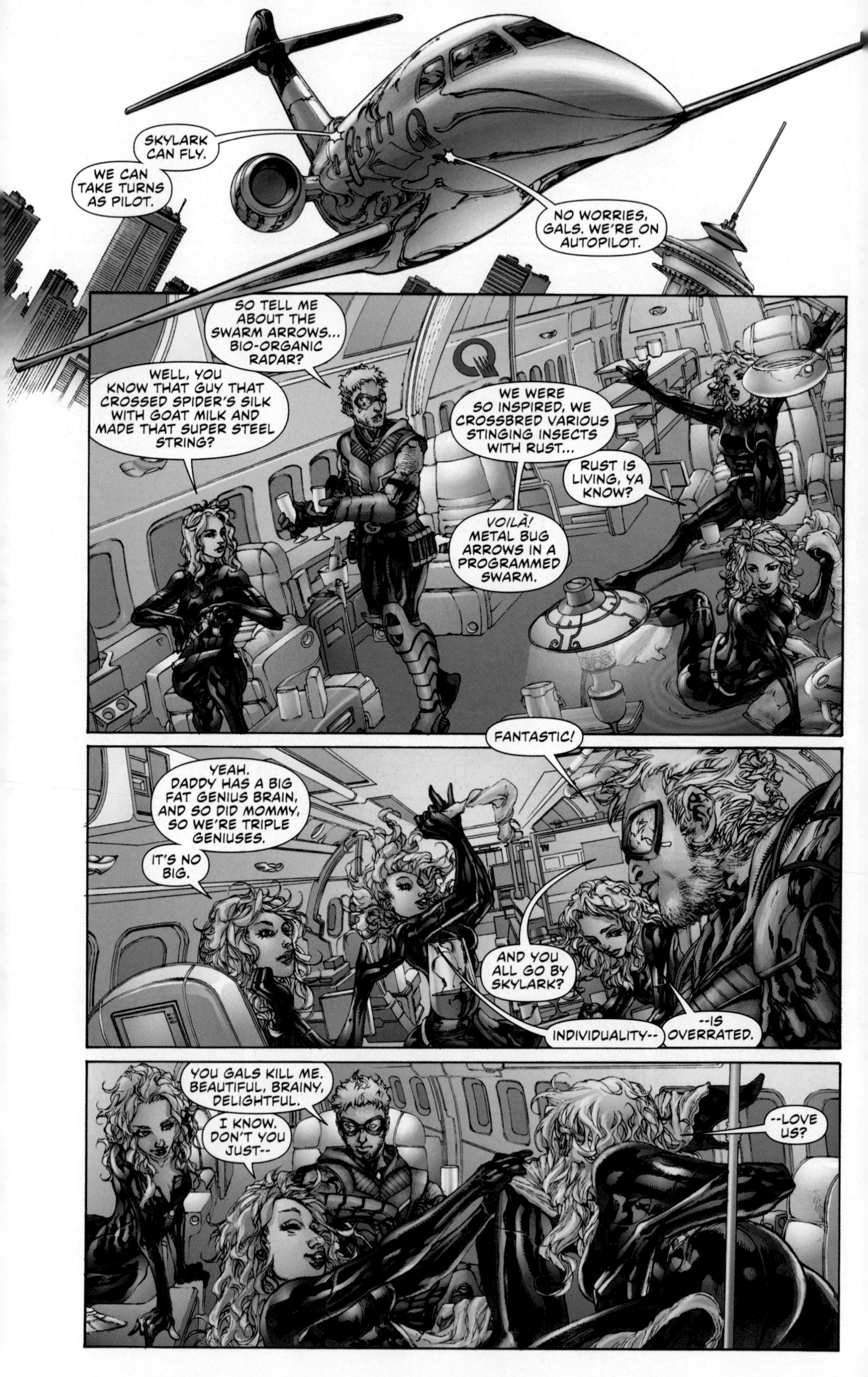
SKYLARK CAN FLY.
WE CAN TAKE TURNS AS PILOT.
NO WORRIES, GALS. WE'RE ON AUTOPILOT.
SO TELL ME ABOUT THE SWARM ARROWS... BIO-ORGANIC RADAR?
WELL, YOU KNOW THAT GUY THAT CROSSED SPIDER'S SILK WITH GOAT MILK AND MADE THAT SUPER STEEL STRING?
WE WERE SO INSPIRED, WE CROSSBRED VARIOUS STINGING INSECTS WITH RUST...
RUST IS LIVING, YA KNOW?
VOILÀ! METAL BUG ARROWS IN A PROGRAMMED SWARM.
FANTASTIC!
YEAH. DADDY HAS A BIG FAT GENIUS BRAIN, AND SO DID MOMMY, SO WE'RE TRIPLE GENIUSES.
IT'S NO BIG.
AND YOU ALL GO BY SKYLARK?
INDIVIDUALITY--
--IS OVERRATED.
YOU GALS KILL ME. BEAUTIFUL, BRAINY, DELIGHTFUL.
I KNOW. DON'T YOU JUST--
--LOVE US?

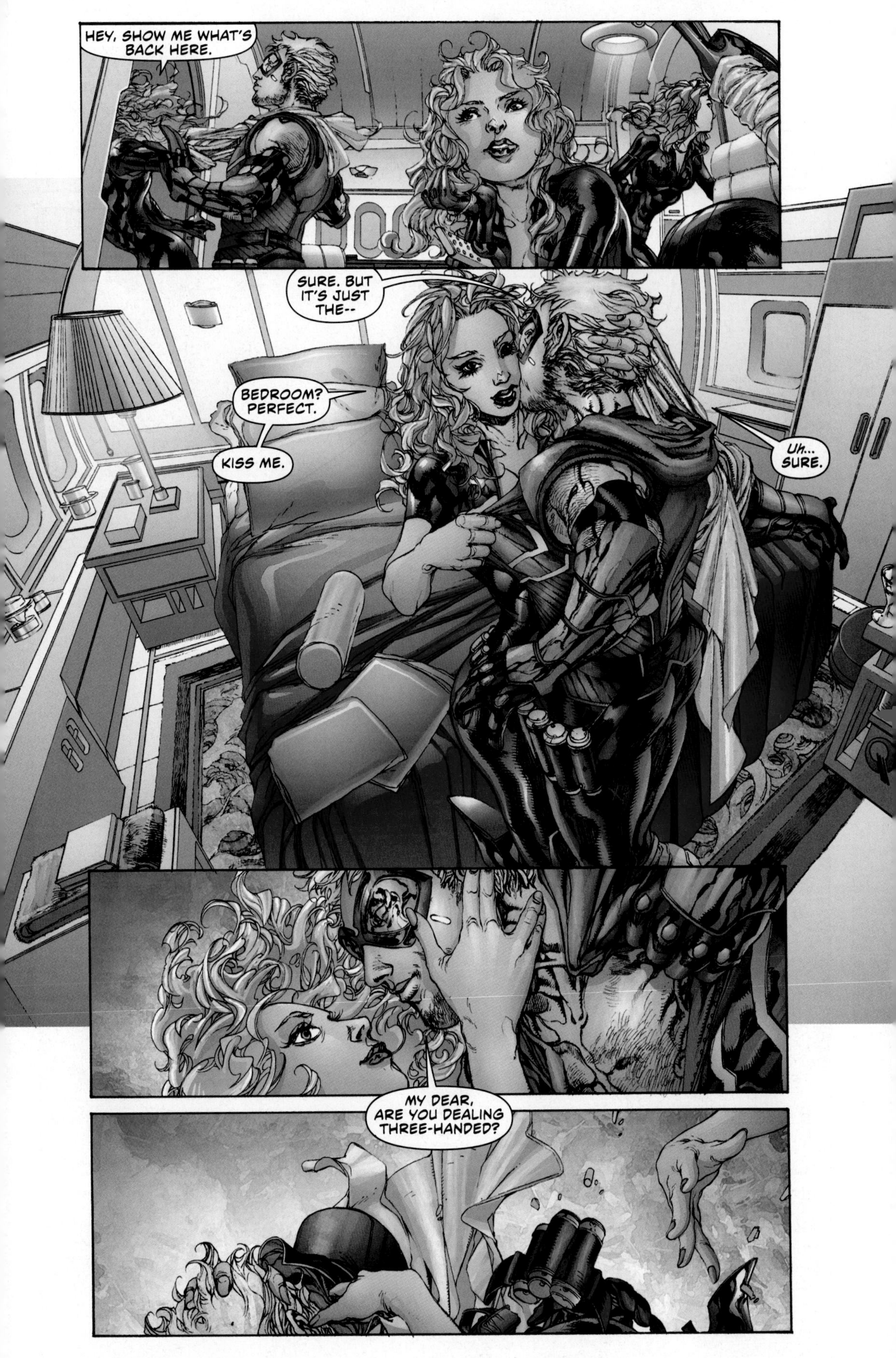
HEY, SHOW ME WHAT'S BACK HERE.
SURE. BUT IT'S JUST THE--
BEDROOM? PERFECT.
KISS ME.
Uh... SURE.
MY DEAR, ARE YOU DEALING THREE-HANDED?
!

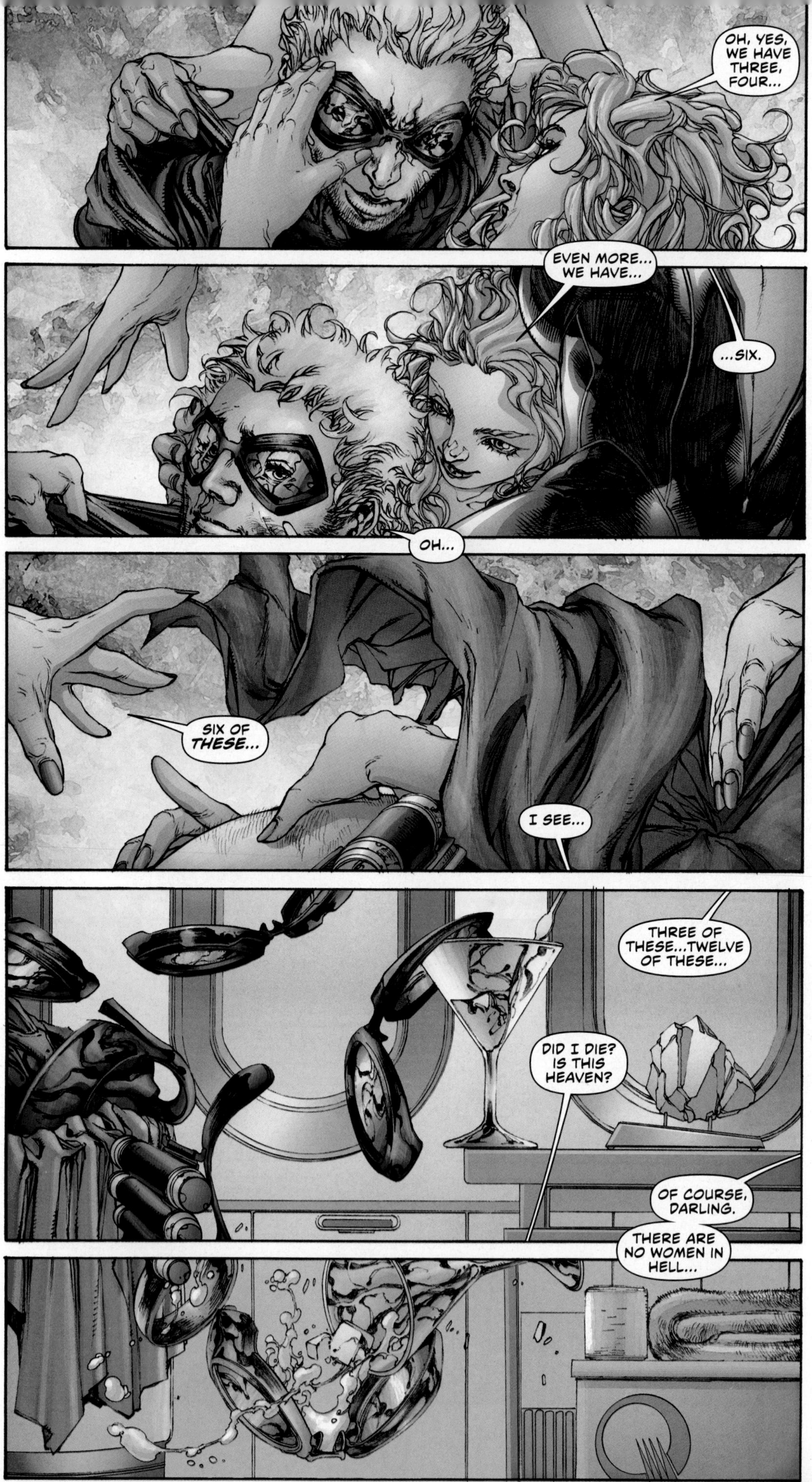
OH, YES, WE HAVE THREE, FOUR...
EVEN MORE... WE HAVE...
...SIX.
OH...
SIX OF THESE...
I SEE...
THREE OF THESE...TWELVE OF THESE...
DID I DIE? IS THIS HEAVEN?
OF COURSE, DARLING.
THERE ARE NO WOMEN IN HELL...

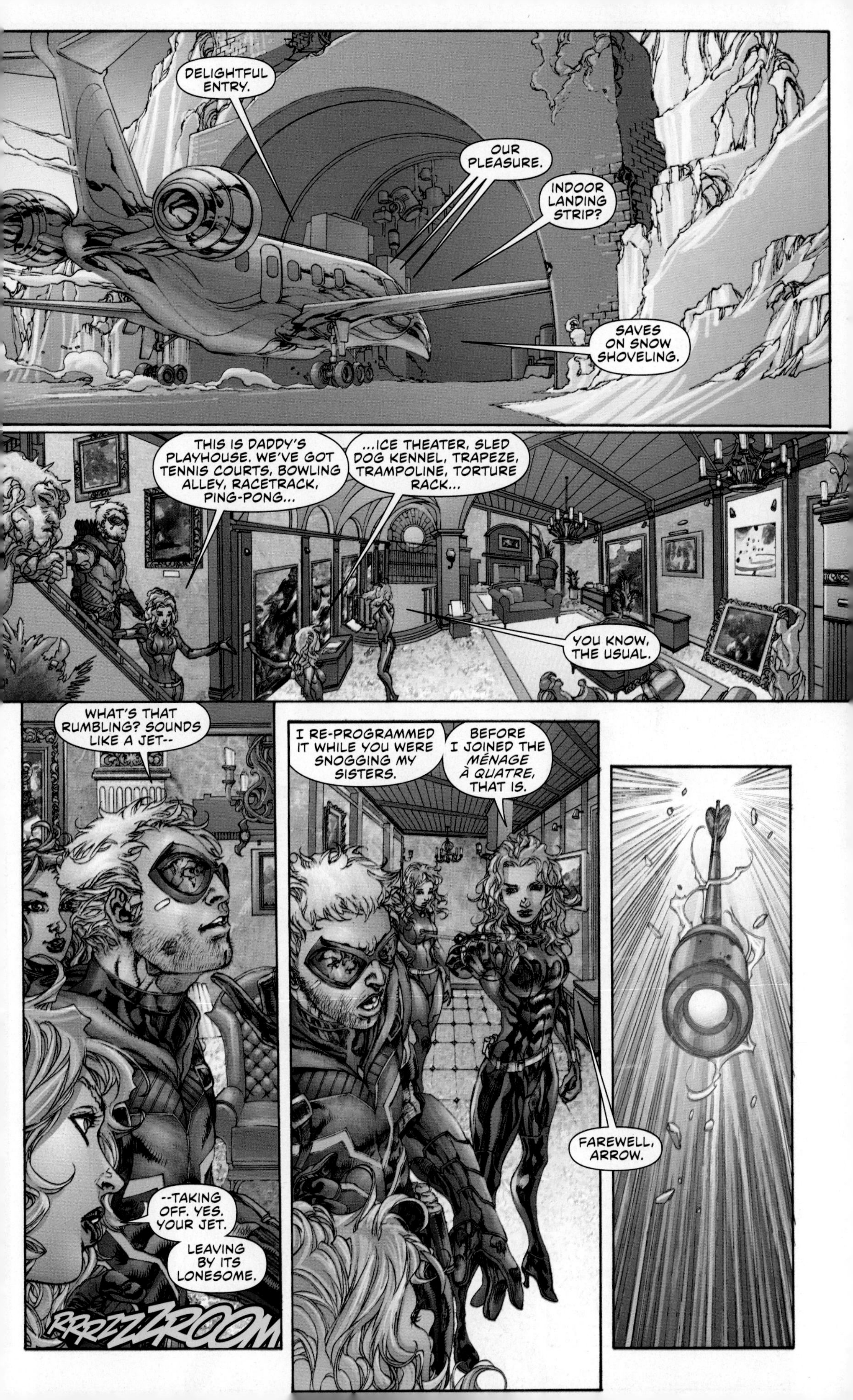
DELIGHTFUL ENTRY.
OUR PLEASURE.
INDOOR LANDING STRIP?
SAVES ON SNOW SHOVELING.
THIS IS DADDY'S PLAYHOUSE. WE'VE GOT TENNIS COURTS, BOWLING ALLEY, RACETRACK, PING-PONG...
...ICE THEATER, SLED DOG KENNEL, TRAPEZE, TRAMPOLINE, TORTURE RACK...
YOU KNOW, THE USUAL.
WHAT'S THAT RUMBLING? SOUNDS LIKE A JET--
--TAKING OFF. YES. YOUR JET.
LEAVING BY ITS LONESOME.
RRRZZZROOM
I RE-PROGRAMMED IT WHILE YOU WERE SNOGGING MY SISTERS.
BEFORE I JOINED THE *MÉNAGE À QUATRE*, THAT IS.
FAREWELL, ARROW.

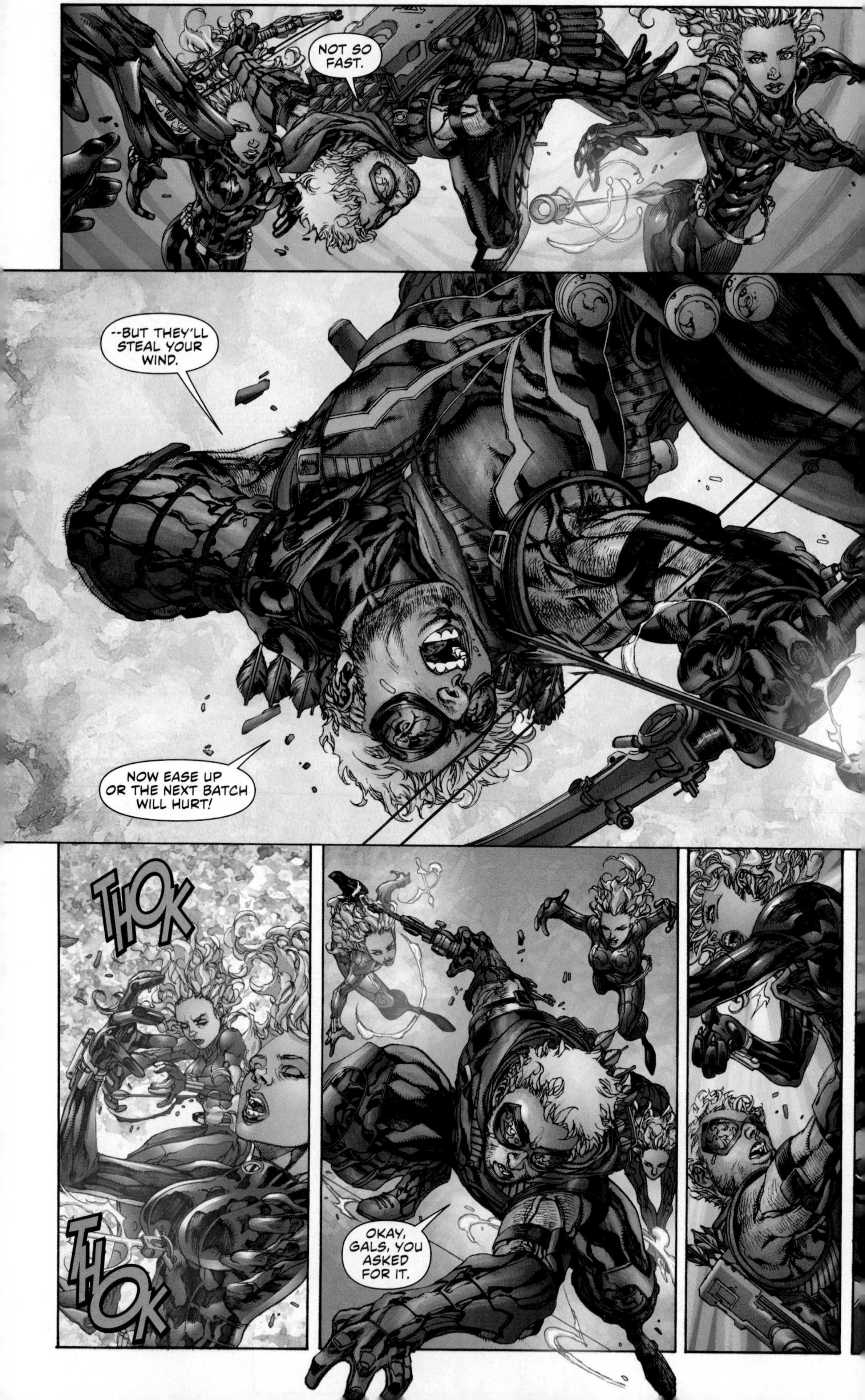
NOT SO FAST.
--BUT THEY'LL STEAL YOUR WIND.
NOW EASE UP OR THE NEXT BATCH WILL HURT!
THOK
THOK
OKAY, GALS, YOU ASKED FOR IT.

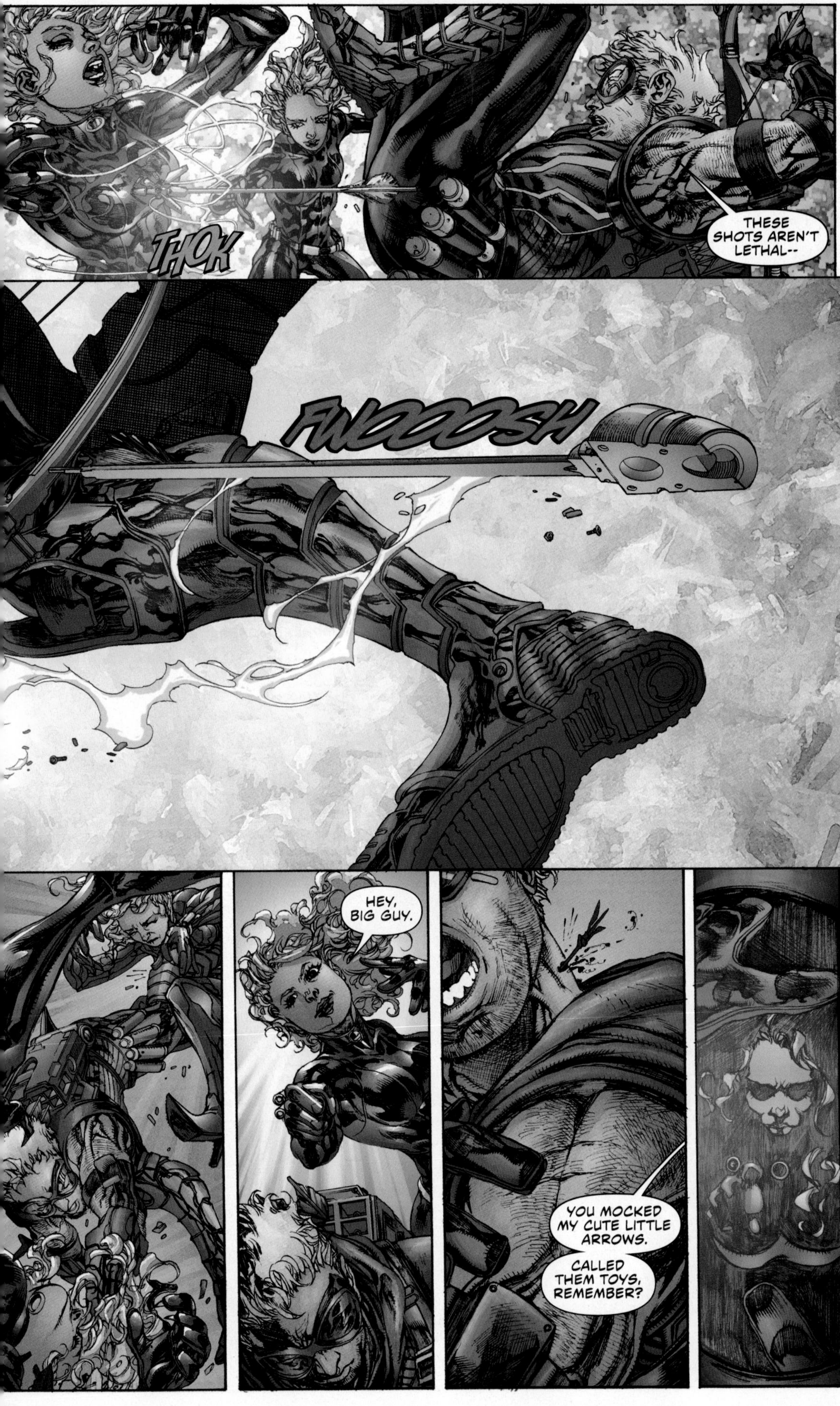
THOK
THESE SHOTS AREN'T LETHAL--
FWOOOOSH
HEY, BIG GUY.
YOU MOCKED MY CUTE LITTLE ARROWS.
CALLED THEM TOYS, REMEMBER?

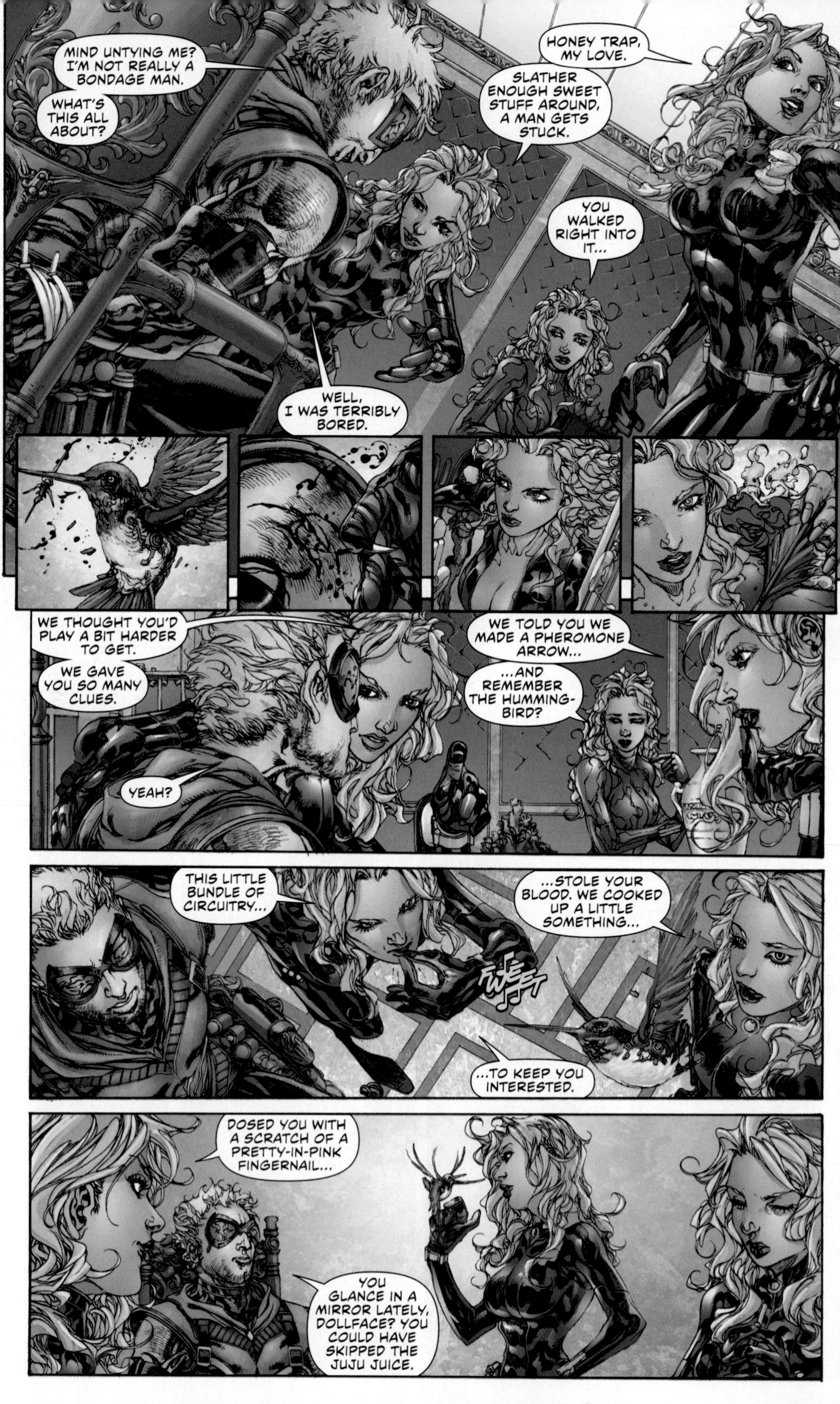
MIND UNTYING ME? I'M NOT REALLY A BONDAGE MAN.
WHAT'S THIS ALL ABOUT?
HONEY TRAP, MY LOVE.
SLATHER ENOUGH SWEET STUFF AROUND, A MAN GETS STUCK.
YOU WALKED RIGHT INTO IT...
WELL, I WAS TERRIBLY BORED.
WE THOUGHT YOU'D PLAY A BIT HARDER TO GET.
WE GAVE YOU SO MANY CLUES.
YEAH?
WE TOLD YOU WE MADE A PHEROMONE ARROW...
...AND REMEMBER THE HUMMING-BIRD?
THIS LITTLE BUNDLE OF CIRCUITRY...
...STOLE YOUR BLOOD. WE COOKED UP A LITTLE SOMETHING...
FWEET
...TO KEEP YOU INTERESTED.
DOSED YOU WITH A SCRATCH OF A PRETTY-IN-PINK FINGERNAIL...
YOU GLANCE IN A MIRROR LATELY, DOLLFACE? YOU COULD HAVE SKIPPED THE JUJU JUICE.

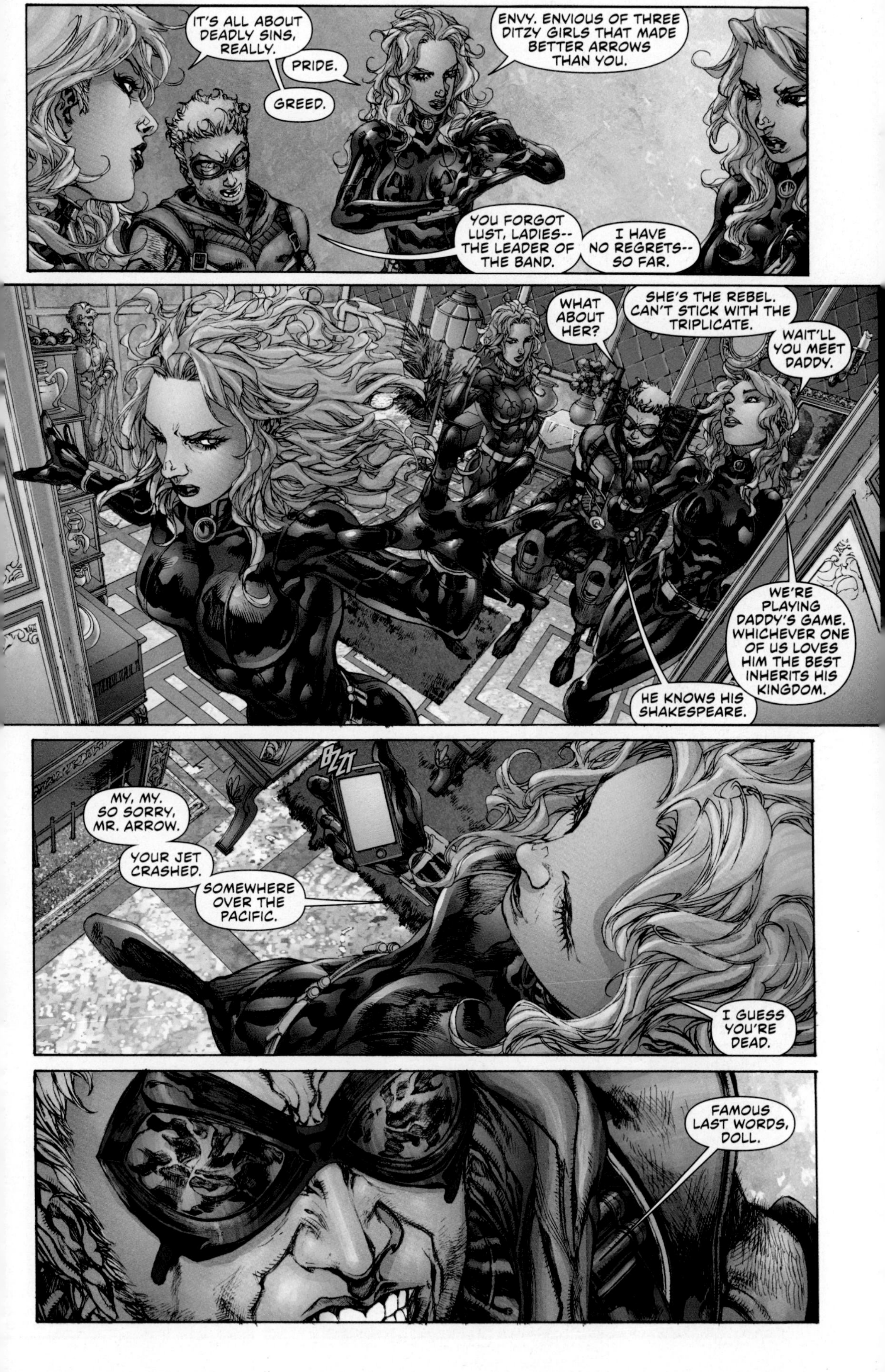
IT'S ALL ABOUT DEADLY SINS, REALLY.
PRIDE.
GREED.
ENVY. ENVIOUS OF THREE DITZY GIRLS THAT MADE BETTER ARROWS THAN YOU.
YOU FORGOT LUST, LADIES-- THE LEADER OF THE BAND.
I HAVE NO REGRETS-- SO FAR.
WHAT ABOUT HER?
SHE'S THE REBEL. CAN'T STICK WITH THE TRIPLICATE.
WAIT'LL YOU MEET DADDY.
WE'RE PLAYING DADDY'S GAME. WHICHEVER ONE OF US LOVES HIM THE BEST INHERITS HIS KINGDOM.
HE KNOWS HIS SHAKESPEARE.
BZZT
MY, MY. SO SORRY, MR. ARROW.
YOUR JET CRASHED.
SOMEWHERE OVER THE PACIFIC.
I GUESS YOU'RE DEAD.
FAMOUS LAST WORDS, DOLL.

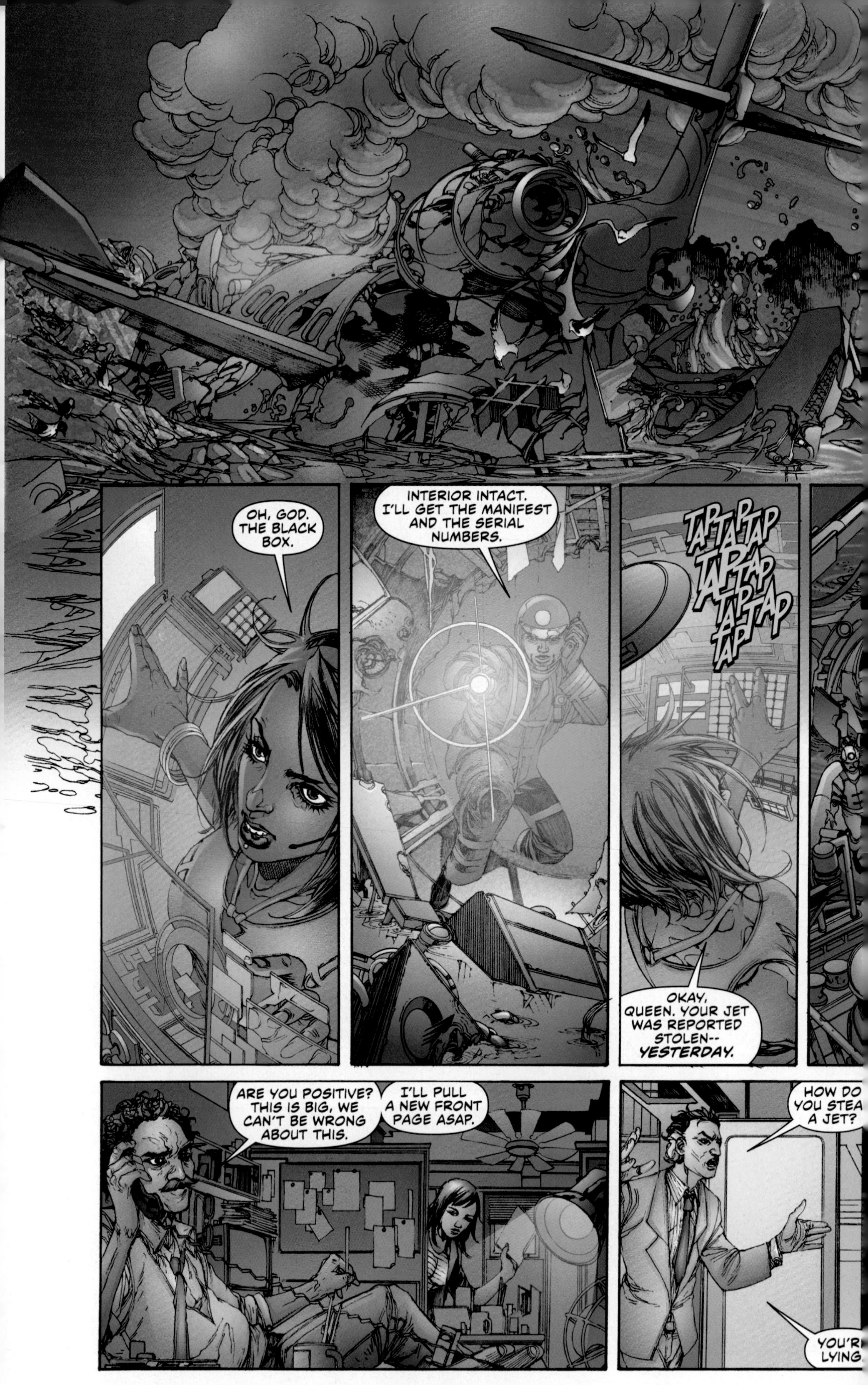
OH, GOD. THE BLACK BOX.
INTERIOR INTACT. I'LL GET THE MANIFEST AND THE SERIAL NUMBERS.
TAPTAPTAP TAPTAP TAPTAP TAPTAP
OKAY, QUEEN. YOUR JET WAS REPORTED STOLEN-- YESTERDAY.
ARE YOU POSITIVE? THIS IS BIG, WE CAN'T BE WRONG ABOUT THIS.
I'LL PULL A NEW FRONT PAGE ASAP.
HOW DO YOU STEA A JET?
YOU'R LYING

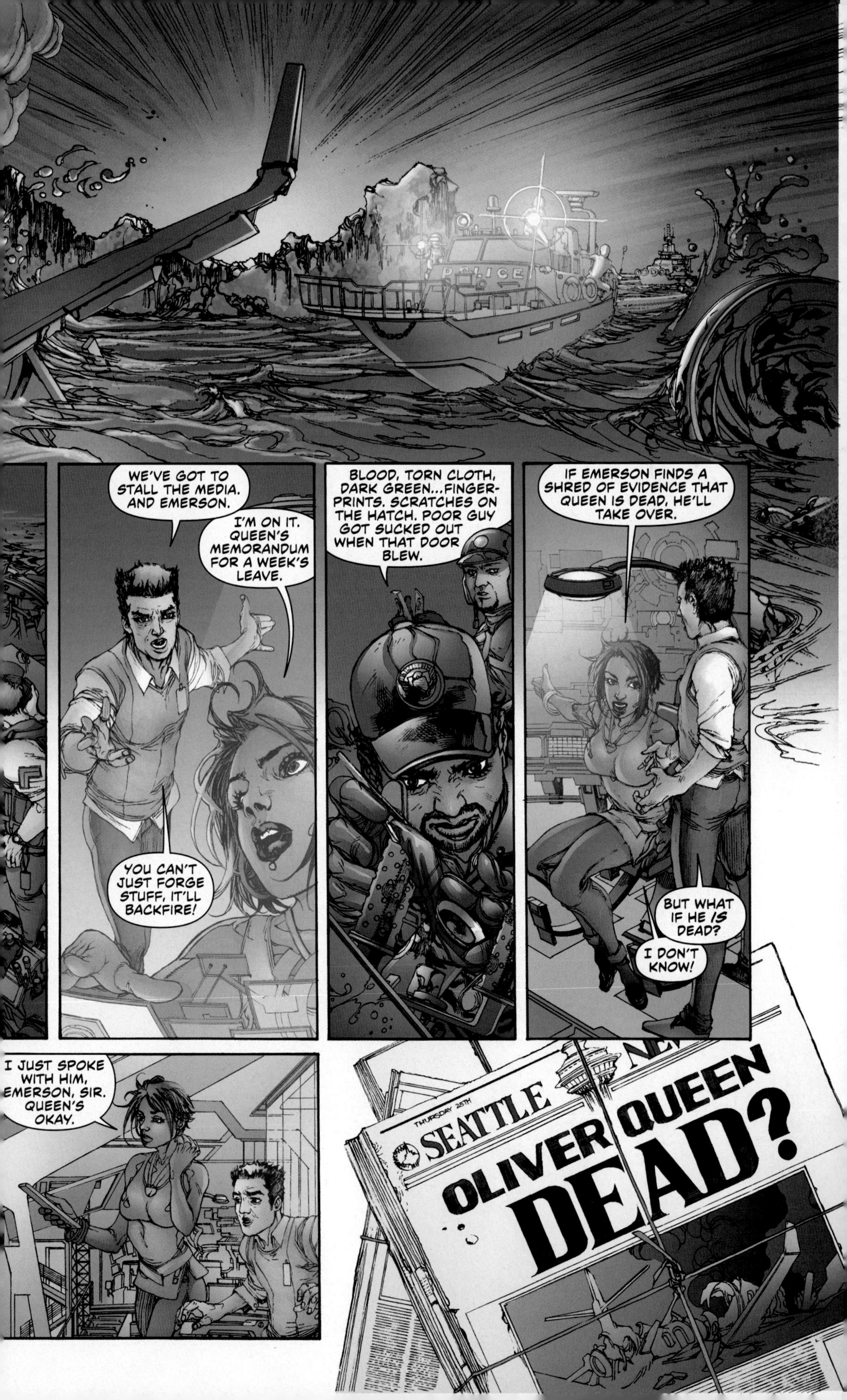
POLICE
WE'VE GOT TO STALL THE MEDIA. AND EMERSON.
I'M ON IT. QUEEN'S MEMORANDUM FOR A WEEK'S LEAVE.
YOU CAN'T JUST FORGE STUFF, IT'LL BACKFIRE!
BLOOD, TORN CLOTH, DARK GREEN...FINGER-PRINTS. SCRATCHES ON THE HATCH. POOR GUY GOT SUCKED OUT WHEN THAT DOOR BLEW.
IF EMERSON FINDS A SHRED OF EVIDENCE THAT QUEEN IS DEAD, HE'LL TAKE OVER.
BUT WHAT IF HE *IS* DEAD?
I DON'T KNOW!
I JUST SPOKE WITH HIM, EMERSON, SIR. QUEEN'S OKAY.
THURSDAY 25TH
SEATTLE NEW
OLIVER QUEEN DEAD?

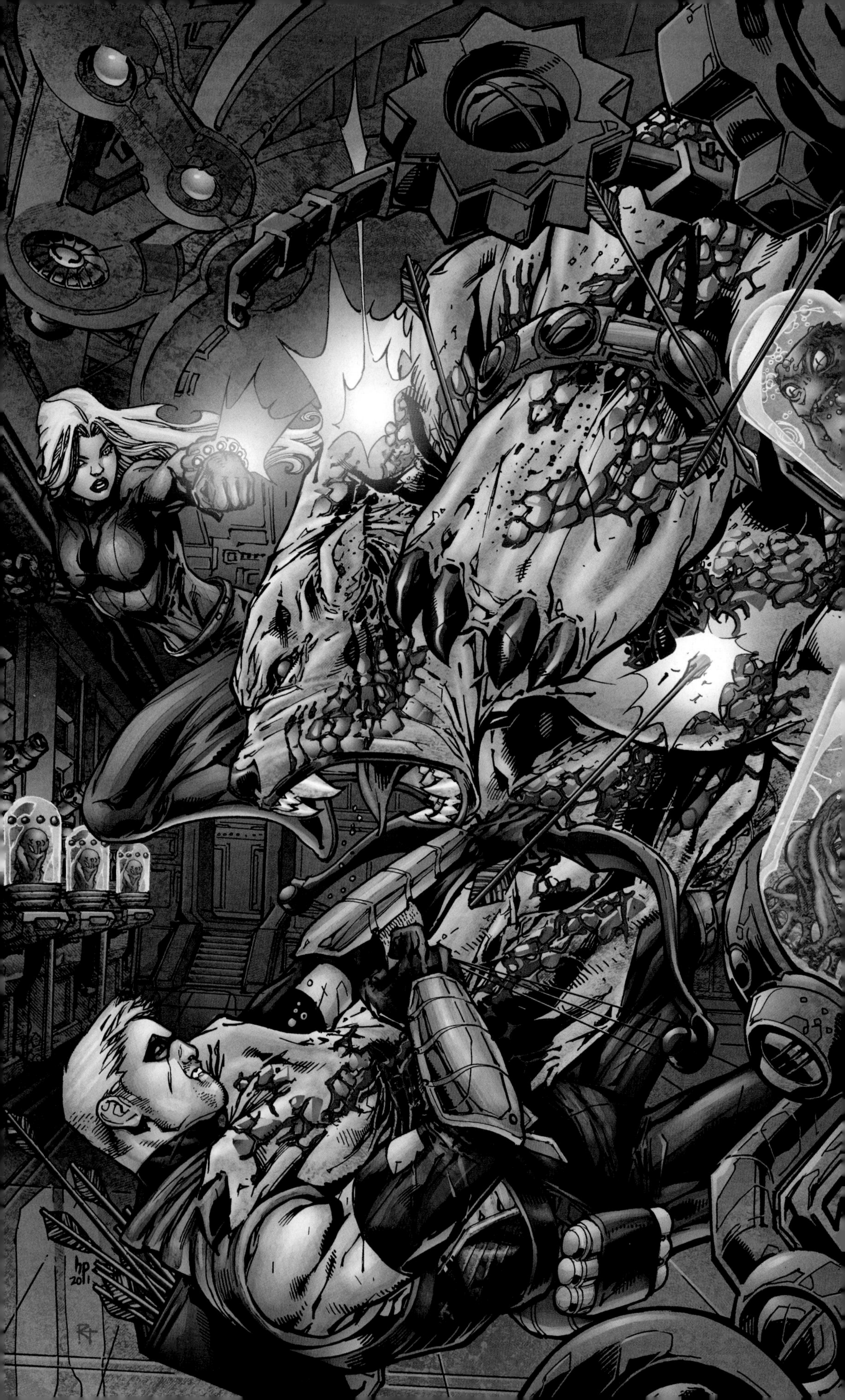
hp
2011

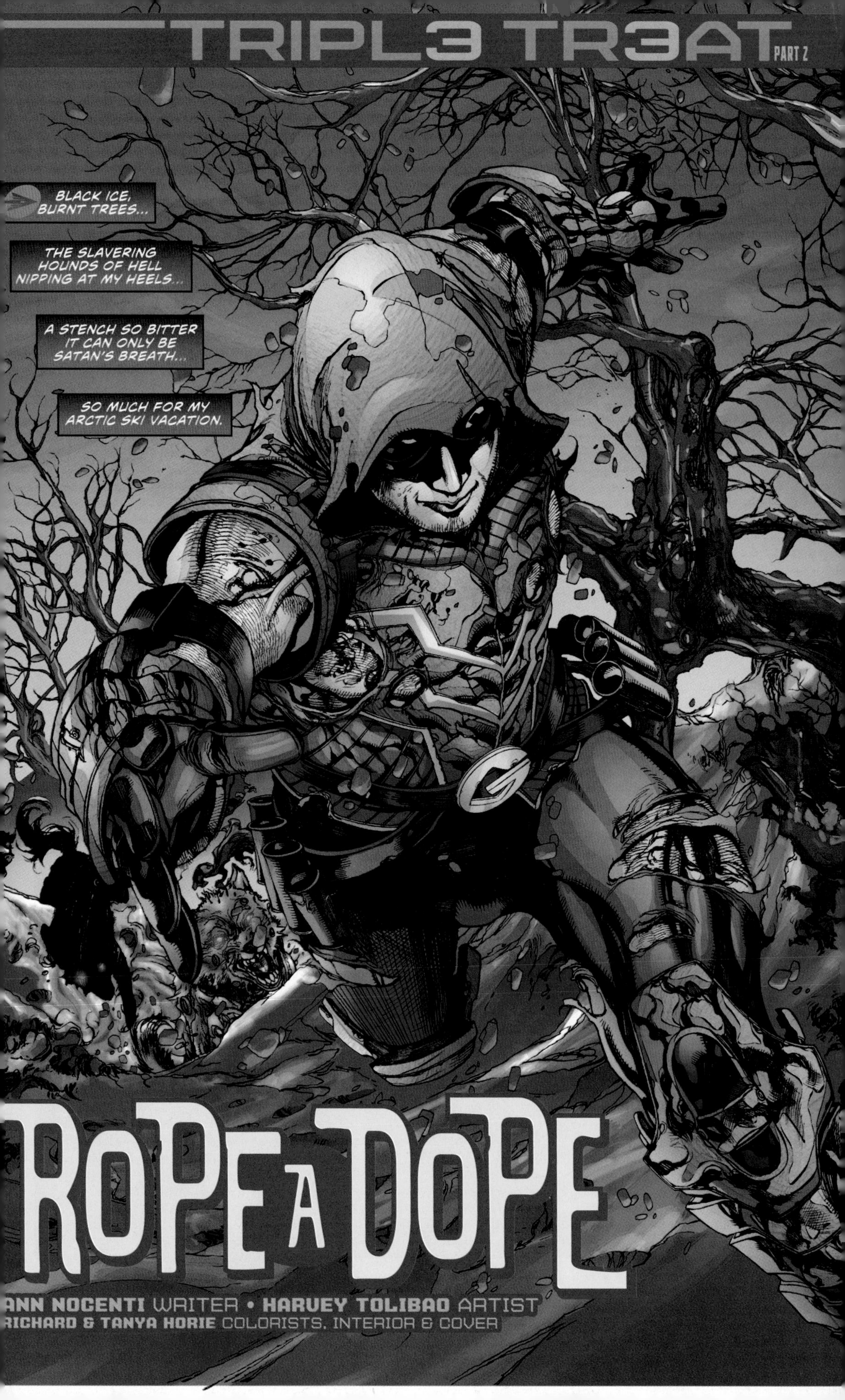
TRIPL3 TR3AT PART 2
BLACK ICE, BURNT TREES...
THE SLAVERING HOUNDS OF HELL NIPPING AT MY HEELS...
A STENCH SO BITTER IT CAN ONLY BE SATAN'S BREATH...
SO MUCH FOR MY ARCTIC SKI VACATION.
ROPE A DOPE
ANN NOCENTI WRITER • HARVEY TOLIBAO ARTIST
RICHARD & TANYA HORIE COLORISTS, INTERIOR & COVER

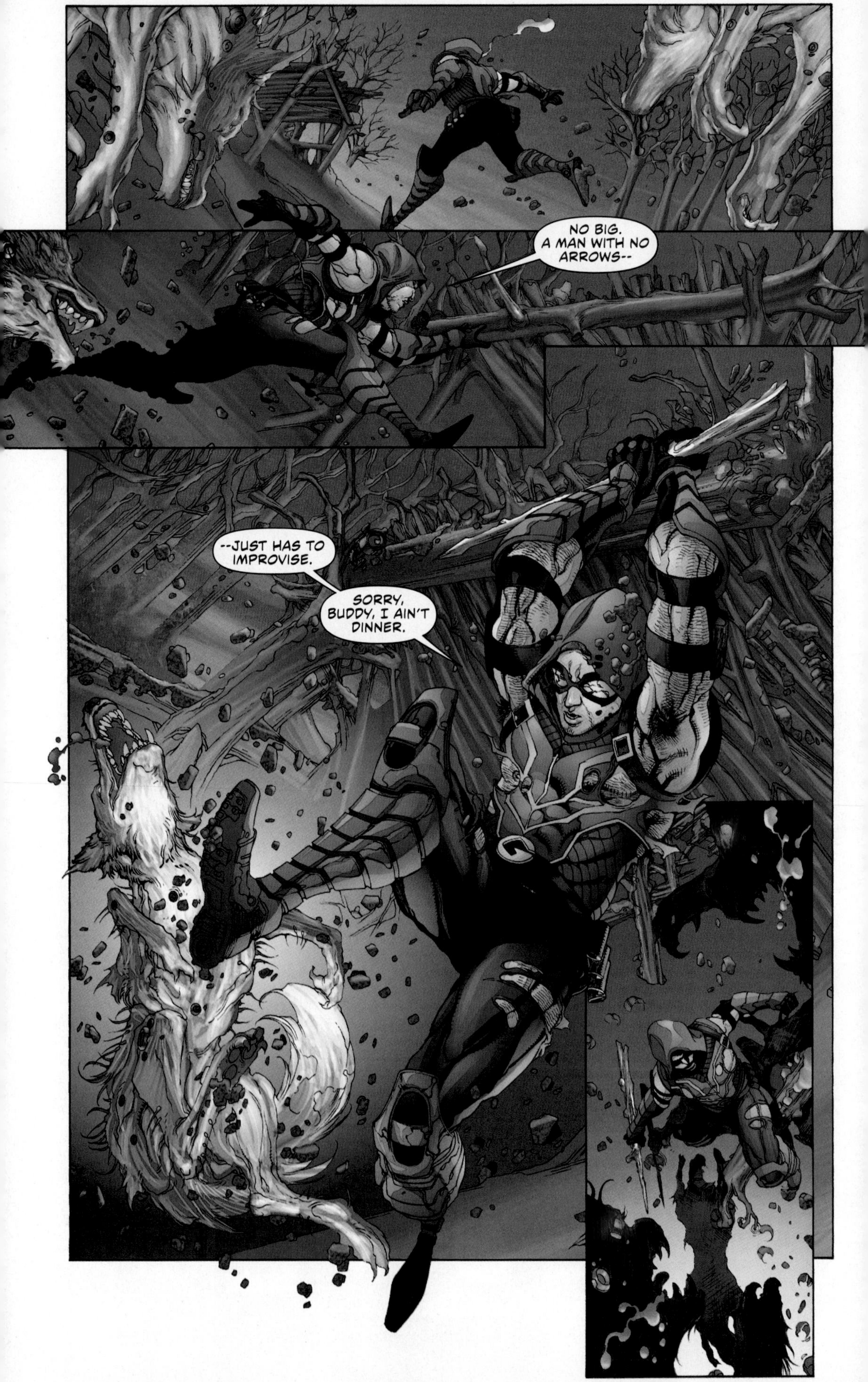
NO BIG. A MAN WITH NO ARROWS--
--JUST HAS TO IMPROVISE.
SORRY, BUDDY, I AIN'T DINNER.

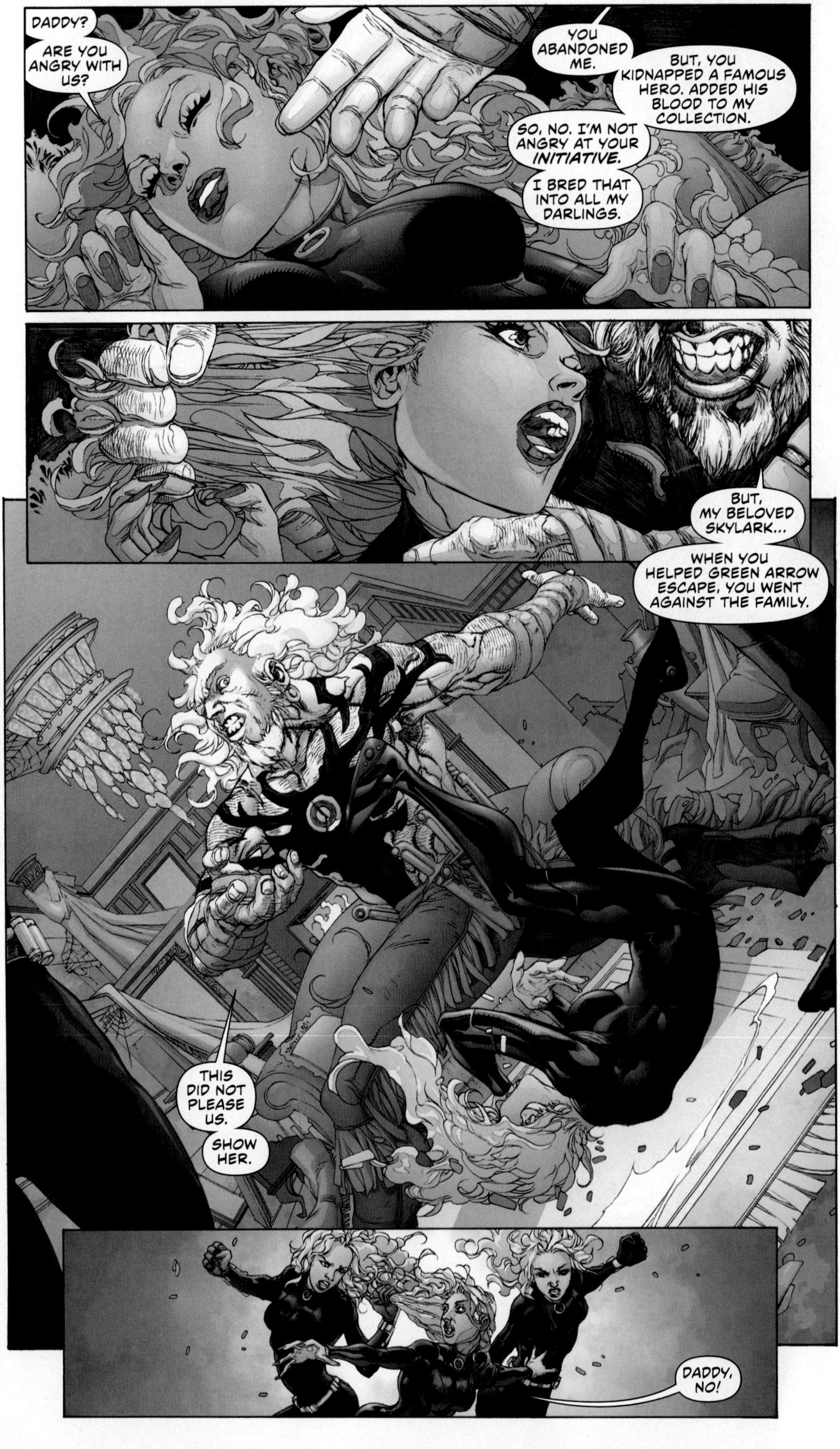
DADDY?
ARE YOU ANGRY WITH US?
YOU ABANDONED ME.
BUT, YOU KIDNAPPED A FAMOUS HERO. ADDED HIS BLOOD TO MY COLLECTION.
SO, NO. I'M NOT ANGRY AT YOUR *INITIATIVE.*
I BRED THAT INTO ALL MY DARLINGS.
BUT, MY BELOVED SKYLARK...
WHEN YOU HELPED GREEN ARROW ESCAPE, YOU WENT AGAINST THE FAMILY.
THIS DID NOT PLEASE US.
SHOW HER.
DADDY, NO!

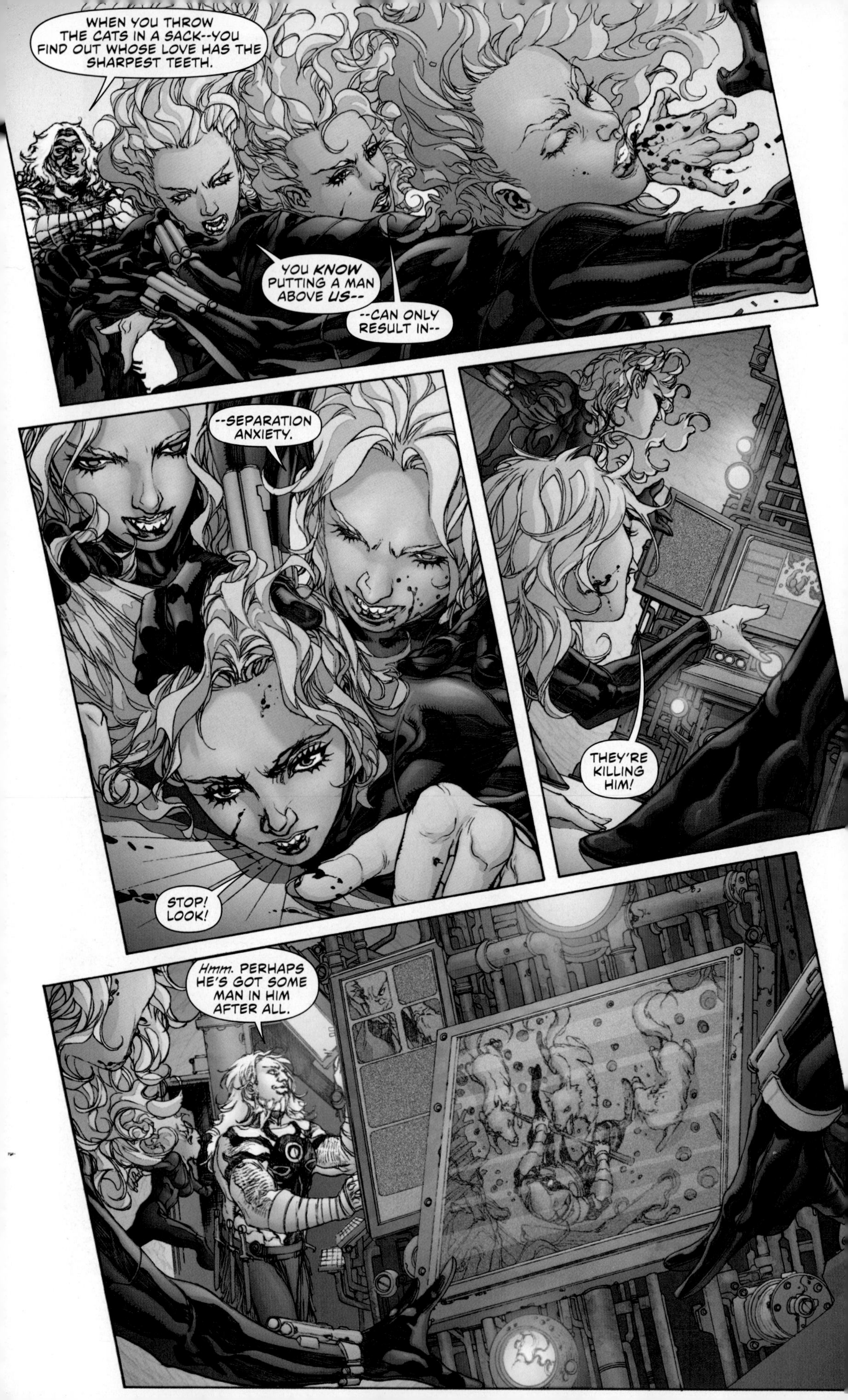
WHEN YOU THROW THE CATS IN A SACK--YOU FIND OUT WHOSE LOVE HAS THE SHARPEST TEETH.
YOU *KNOW* PUTTING A MAN ABOVE *US*--
--CAN ONLY RESULT IN--
--SEPARATION ANXIETY.
THEY'RE KILLING HIM!
STOP! LOOK!
Hmm. PERHAPS HE'S GOT SOME MAN IN HIM AFTER ALL.

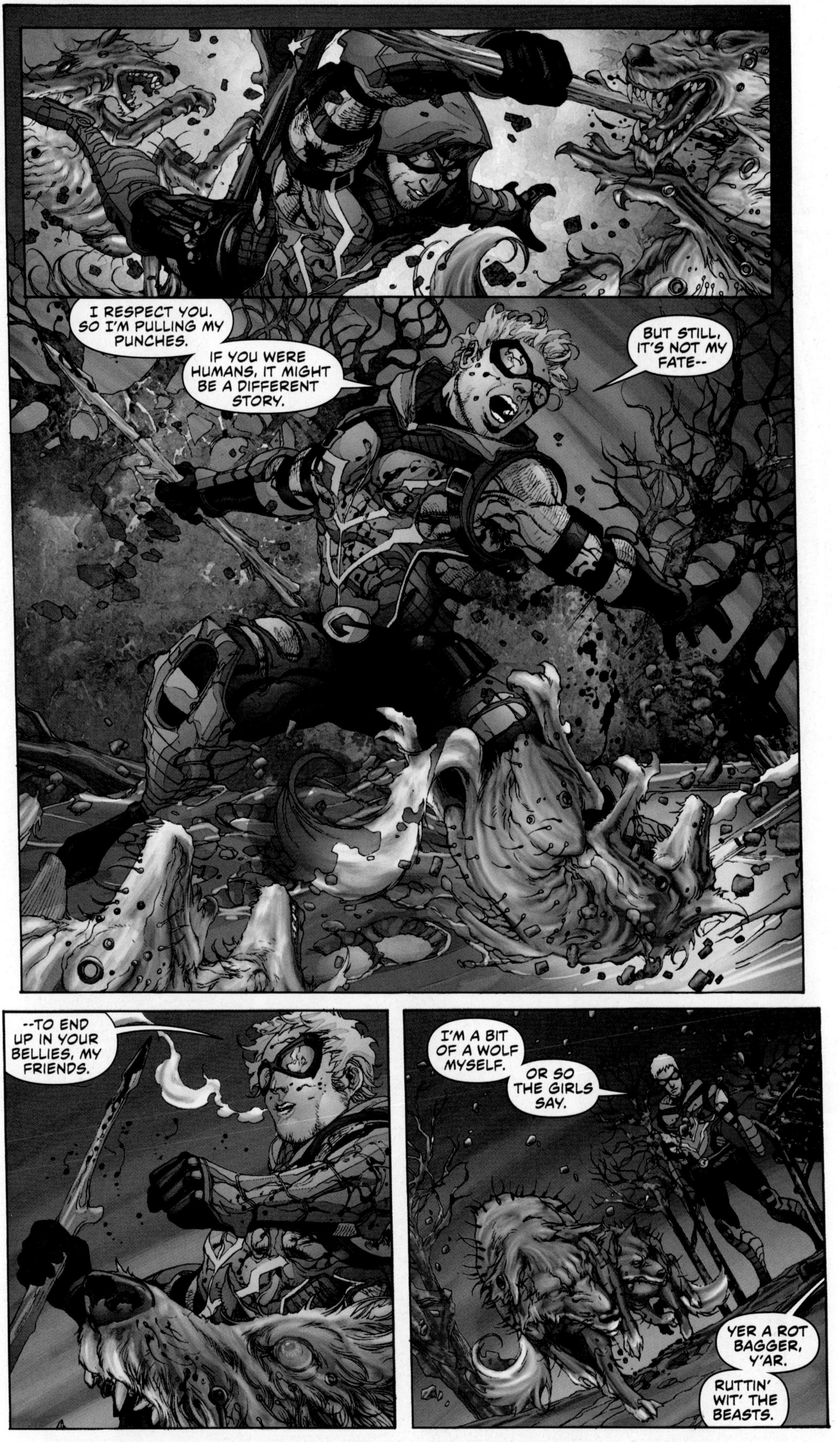
I RESPECT YOU. SO I'M PULLING MY PUNCHES.
IF YOU WERE HUMANS, IT MIGHT BE A DIFFERENT STORY.
BUT STILL, IT'S NOT MY FATE--
--TO END UP IN YOUR BELLIES, MY FRIENDS.
I'M A BIT OF A WOLF MYSELF.
OR SO THE GIRLS SAY.
YER A ROT BAGGER, Y'AR.
RUTTIN' WIT' THE BEASTS.

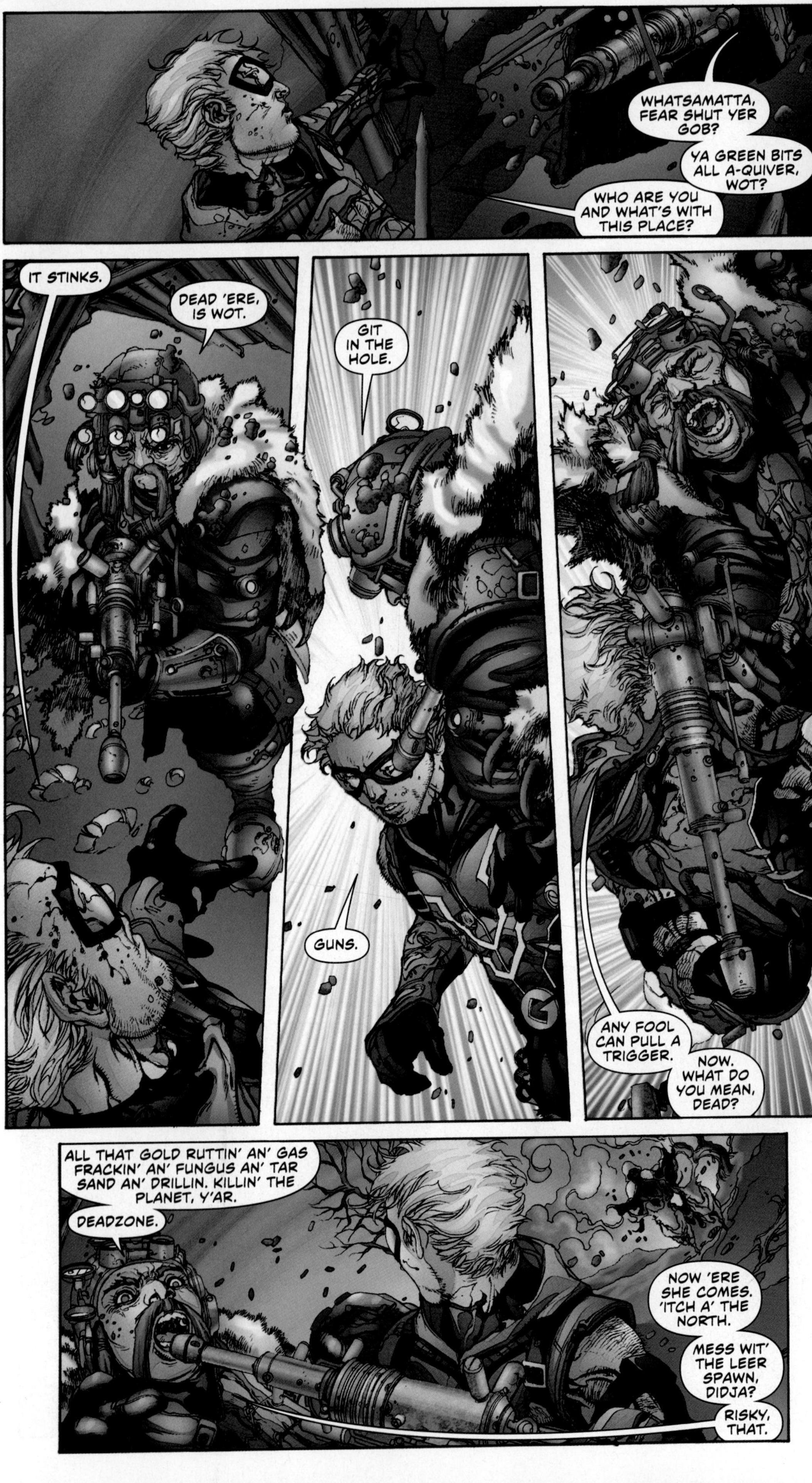

WHATSAMATTA, FEAR SHUT YER GOB?
YA GREEN BITS ALL A-QUIVER, WOT?
WHO ARE YOU AND WHAT'S WITH THIS PLACE?
IT STINKS.
DEAD 'ERE, IS WOT.
GIT IN THE HOLE.
GUNS.
ANY FOOL CAN PULL A TRIGGER.
NOW. WHAT DO YOU MEAN, DEAD?
ALL THAT GOLD RUTTIN' AN' GAS FRACKIN' AN' FUNGUS AN' TAR SAND AN' DRILLIN. KILLIN' THE PLANET, Y'AR.
DEADZONE.
NOW 'ERE SHE COMES. 'ITCH A' THE NORTH.
MESS WIT' THE LEER SPAWN, DIDJA?
RISKY, THAT.

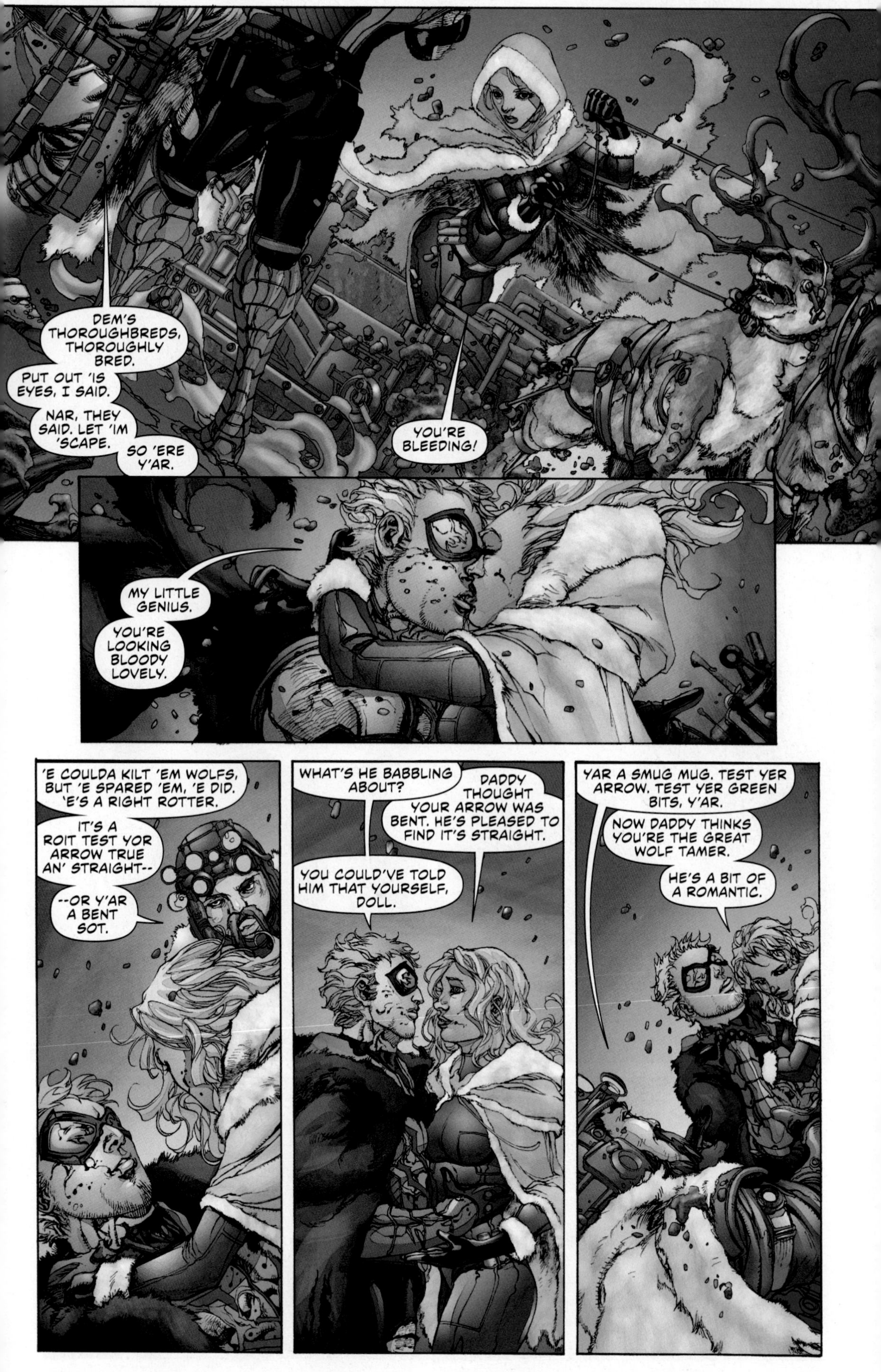
DEM'S THOROUGHBREDS, THOROUGHLY BRED.
PUT OUT 'IS EYES, I SAID.
NAR, THEY SAID. LET 'IM 'SCAPE.
SO 'ERE Y'AR.
YOU'RE BLEEDING!
MY LITTLE GENIUS.
YOU'RE LOOKING BLOODY LOVELY.
'E COULDA KILT 'EM WOLFS, BUT 'E SPARED 'EM, 'E DID. 'E'S A RIGHT ROTTER.
IT'S A ROIT TEST YOR ARROW TRUE AN' STRAIGHT--
--OR Y'AR A BENT SOT.
WHAT'S HE BABBLING ABOUT?
DADDY THOUGHT YOUR ARROW WAS BENT. HE'S PLEASED TO FIND IT'S STRAIGHT.
YOU COULD'VE TOLD HIM THAT YOURSELF, DOLL.
YAR A SMUG MUG. TEST YER ARROW. TEST YER GREEN BITS, Y'AR.
NOW DADDY THINKS YOU'RE THE GREAT WOLF TAMER.
HE'S A BIT OF A ROMANTIC.

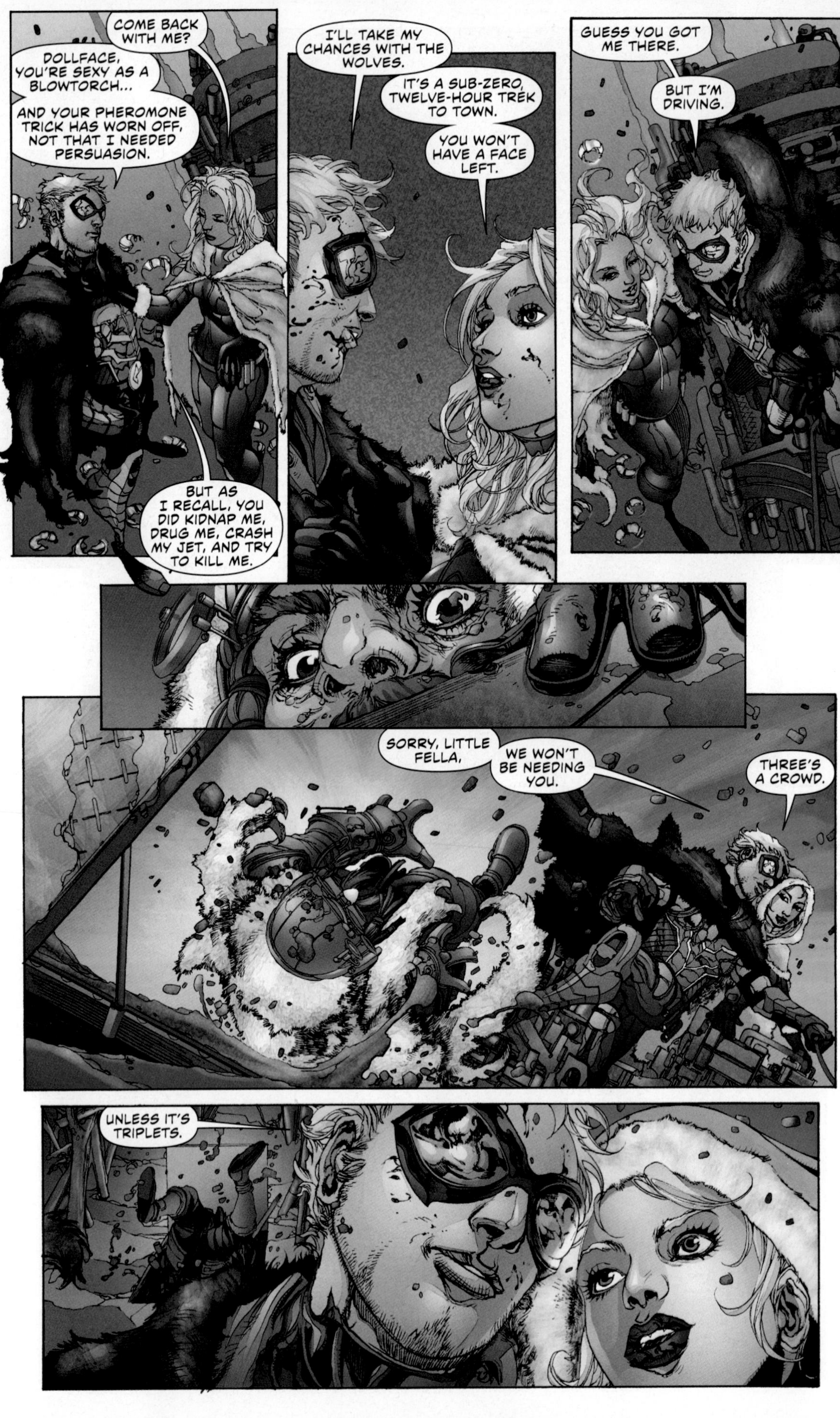
COME BACK WITH ME?
DOLLFACE, YOU'RE SEXY AS A BLOWTORCH...
AND YOUR PHEROMONE TRICK HAS WORN OFF, NOT THAT I NEEDED PERSUASION.
BUT AS I RECALL, YOU DID KIDNAP ME, DRUG ME, CRASH MY JET, AND TRY TO KILL ME.
I'LL TAKE MY CHANCES WITH THE WOLVES.
IT'S A SUB-ZERO, TWELVE-HOUR TREK TO TOWN.
YOU WON'T HAVE A FACE LEFT.
GUESS YOU GOT ME THERE.
BUT I'M DRIVING.
SORRY, LITTLE FELLA,
WE WON'T BE NEEDING YOU.
THREE'S A CROWD.
UNLESS IT'S TRIPLETS.

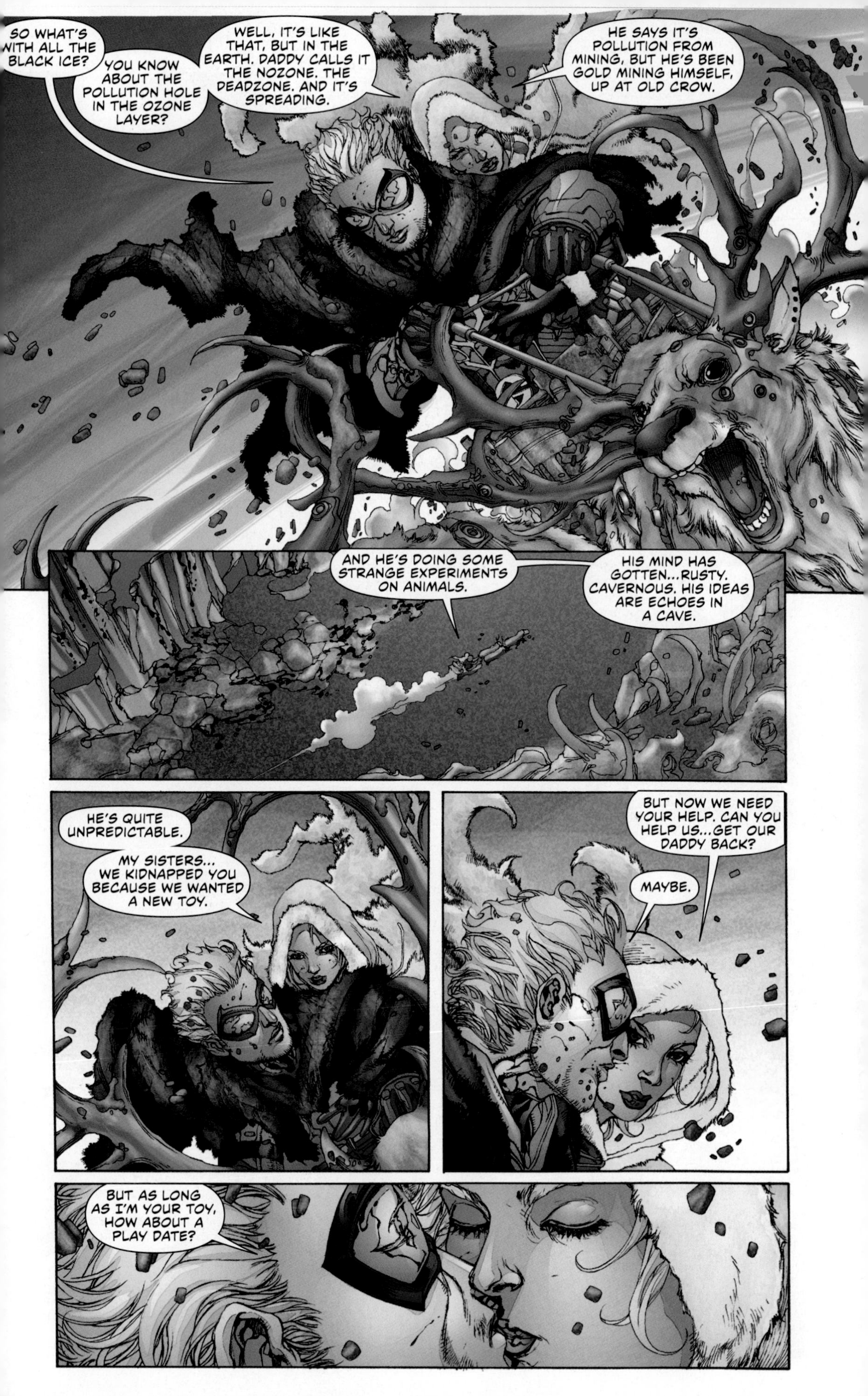
SO WHAT'S WITH ALL THE BLACK ICE?
YOU KNOW ABOUT THE POLLUTION HOLE IN THE OZONE LAYER?
WELL, IT'S LIKE THAT, BUT IN THE EARTH. DADDY CALLS IT THE NOZONE. THE DEADZONE. AND IT'S SPREADING.
HE SAYS IT'S POLLUTION FROM MINING, BUT HE'S BEEN GOLD MINING HIMSELF, UP AT OLD CROW.
AND HE'S DOING SOME STRANGE EXPERIMENTS ON ANIMALS.
HIS MIND HAS GOTTEN...RUSTY. CAVERNOUS. HIS IDEAS ARE ECHOES IN A CAVE.
HE'S QUITE UNPREDICTABLE.
MY SISTERS... WE KIDNAPPED YOU BECAUSE WE WANTED A NEW TOY.
BUT NOW WE NEED YOUR HELP. CAN YOU HELP US...GET OUR DADDY BACK?
MAYBE.
BUT AS LONG AS I'M YOUR TOY, HOW ABOUT A PLAY DATE?

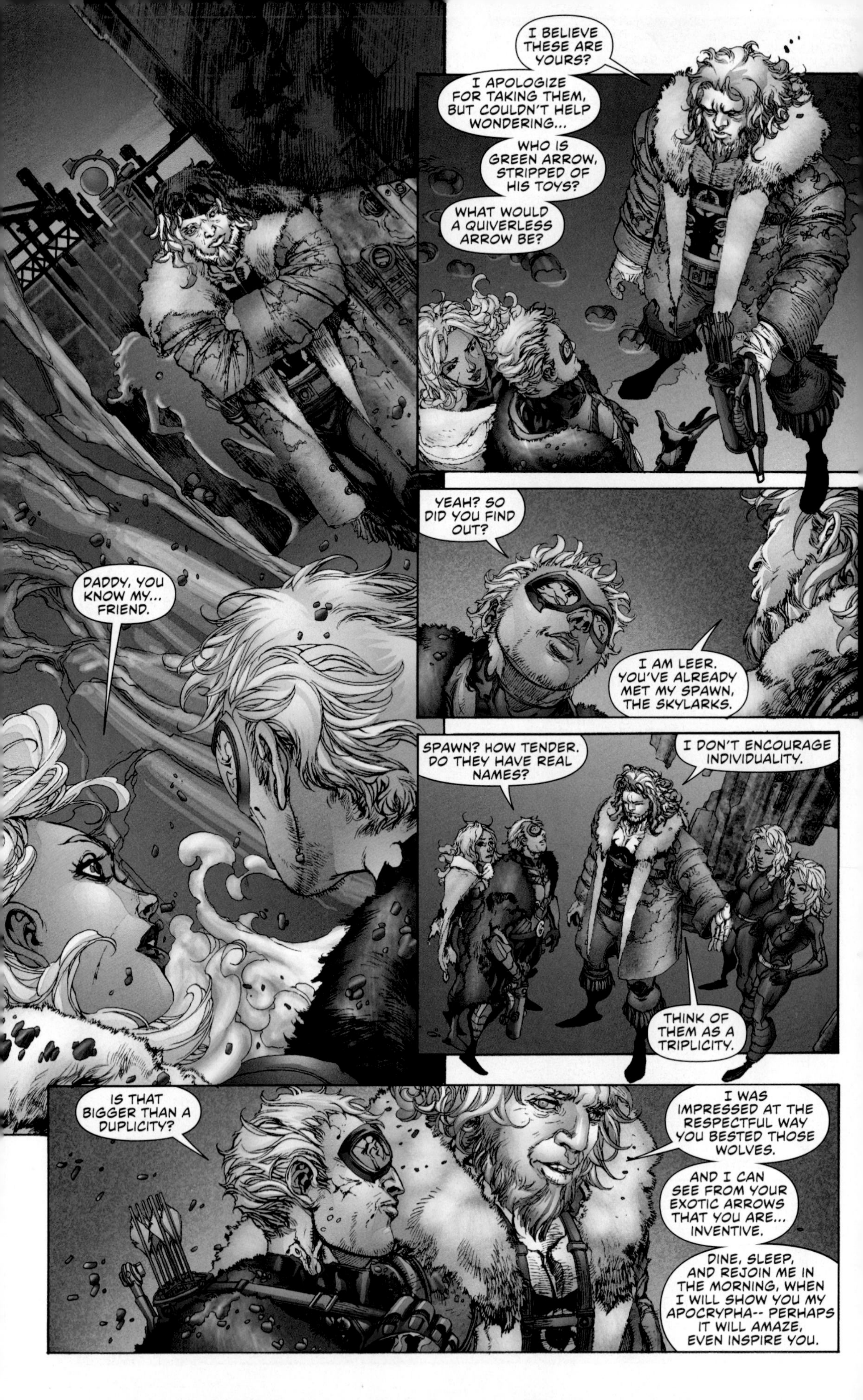
I BELIEVE THESE ARE YOURS?
I APOLOGIZE FOR TAKING THEM, BUT COULDN'T HELP WONDERING...
WHO IS GREEN ARROW, STRIPPED OF HIS TOYS?
WHAT WOULD A QUIVERLESS ARROW BE?
DADDY, YOU KNOW MY... FRIEND.
YEAH? SO DID YOU FIND OUT?
I AM LEER. YOU'VE ALREADY MET MY SPAWN, THE SKYLARKS.
SPAWN? HOW TENDER. DO THEY HAVE REAL NAMES?
I DON'T ENCOURAGE INDIVIDUALITY.
THINK OF THEM AS A TRIPLICITY.
IS THAT BIGGER THAN A DUPLICITY?
I WAS IMPRESSED AT THE RESPECTFUL WAY YOU BESTED THOSE WOLVES.
AND I CAN SEE FROM YOUR EXOTIC ARROWS THAT YOU ARE... INVENTIVE.
DINE, SLEEP, AND REJOIN ME IN THE MORNING, WHEN I WILL SHOW YOU MY APOCRYPHA-- PERHAPS IT WILL AMAZE, EVEN INSPIRE YOU.

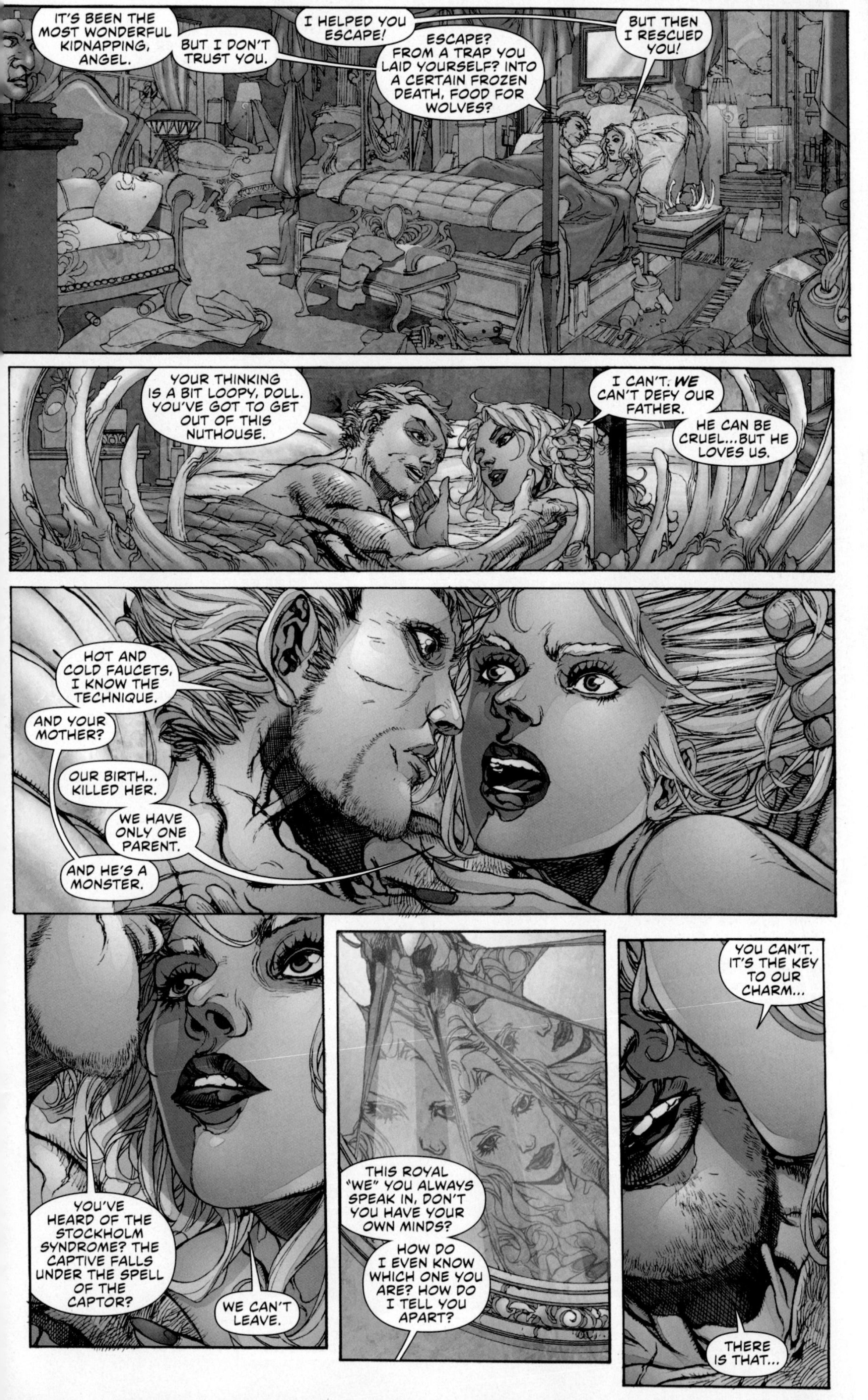

IT'S BEEN THE MOST WONDERFUL KIDNAPPING, ANGEL.
BUT I DON'T TRUST YOU.
I HELPED YOU ESCAPE!
ESCAPE? FROM A TRAP YOU LAID YOURSELF? INTO A CERTAIN FROZEN DEATH, FOOD FOR WOLVES?
BUT THEN I RESCUED YOU!
YOUR THINKING IS A BIT LOOPY, DOLL. YOU'VE GOT TO GET OUT OF THIS NUTHOUSE.
I CAN'T. ***WE*** CAN'T DEFY OUR FATHER.
HE CAN BE CRUEL...BUT HE LOVES US.
HOT AND COLD FAUCETS, I KNOW THE TECHNIQUE.
AND YOUR MOTHER?
OUR BIRTH... KILLED HER.
WE HAVE ONLY ONE PARENT.
AND HE'S A MONSTER.
YOU'VE HEARD OF THE STOCKHOLM SYNDROME? THE CAPTIVE FALLS UNDER THE SPELL OF THE CAPTOR?
WE CAN'T LEAVE.
THIS ROYAL "WE" YOU ALWAYS SPEAK IN, DON'T YOU HAVE YOUR OWN MINDS?
HOW DO I EVEN KNOW WHICH ONE YOU ARE? HOW DO I TELL YOU APART?
YOU CAN'T. IT'S THE KEY TO OUR CHARM...
THERE IS THAT...

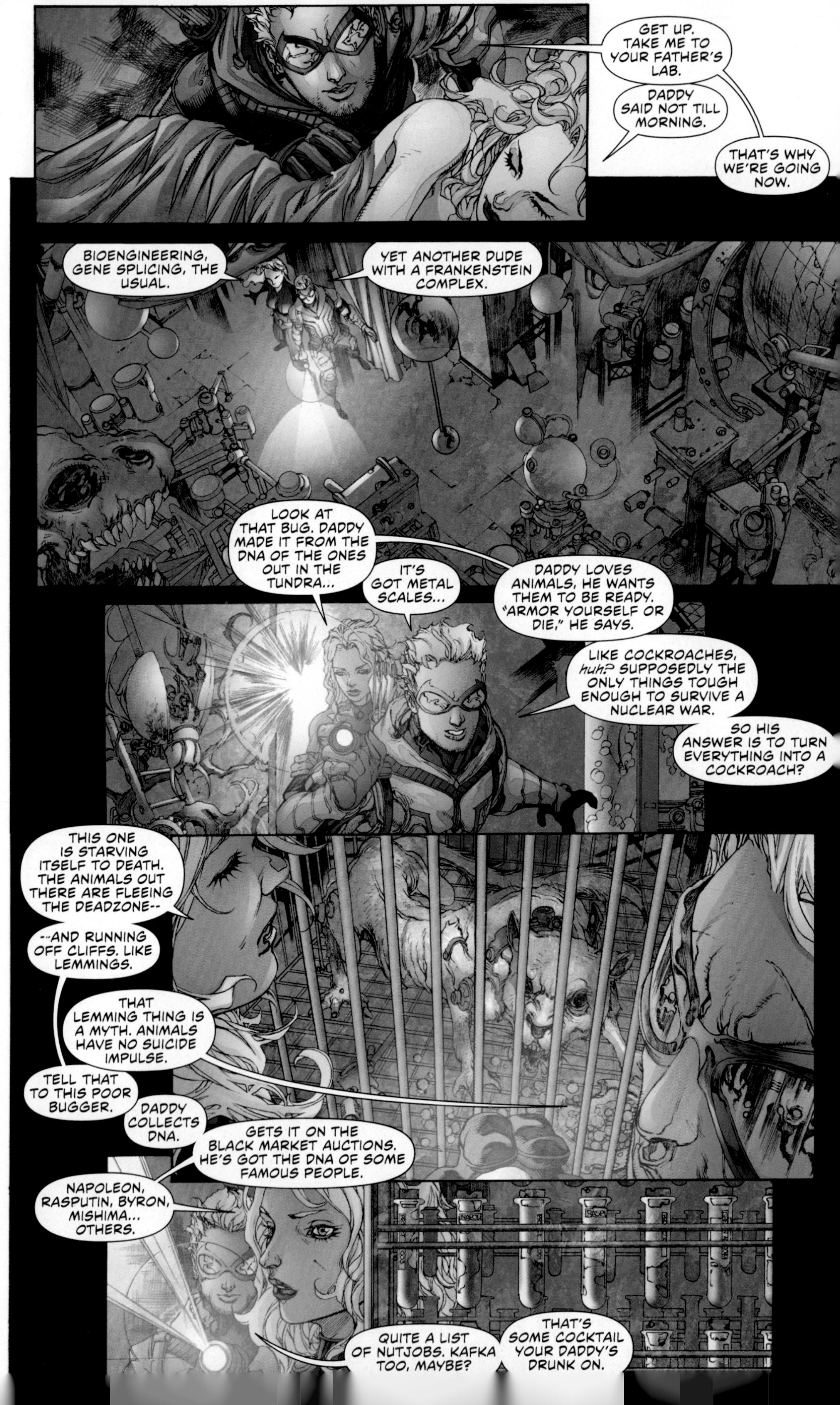
GET UP. TAKE ME TO YOUR FATHER'S LAB.
DADDY SAID NOT TILL MORNING.
THAT'S WHY WE'RE GOING NOW.
BIOENGINEERING, GENE SPLICING, THE USUAL.
YET ANOTHER DUDE WITH A FRANKENSTEIN COMPLEX.
LOOK AT THAT BUG. DADDY MADE IT FROM THE DNA OF THE ONES OUT IN THE TUNDRA...
IT'S GOT METAL SCALES...
DADDY LOVES ANIMALS, HE WANTS THEM TO BE READY. "ARMOR YOURSELF OR DIE," HE SAYS.
LIKE COCKROACHES, *huh?* SUPPOSEDLY THE ONLY THINGS TOUGH ENOUGH TO SURVIVE A NUCLEAR WAR.
SO HIS ANSWER IS TO TURN EVERYTHING INTO A COCKROACH?
THIS ONE IS STARVING ITSELF TO DEATH. THE ANIMALS OUT THERE ARE FLEEING THE DEADZONE--
--AND RUNNING OFF CLIFFS. LIKE LEMMINGS.
THAT LEMMING THING IS A MYTH. ANIMALS HAVE NO SUICIDE IMPULSE.
TELL THAT TO THIS POOR BUGGER.
DADDY COLLECTS DNA.
GETS IT ON THE BLACK MARKET AUCTIONS. HE'S GOT THE DNA OF SOME FAMOUS PEOPLE.
NAPOLEON, RASPUTIN, BYRON, MISHIMA... OTHERS.
QUITE A LIST OF NUTJOBS. KAFKA TOO, MAYBE?
THAT'S SOME COCKTAIL YOUR DADDY'S DRUNK ON.

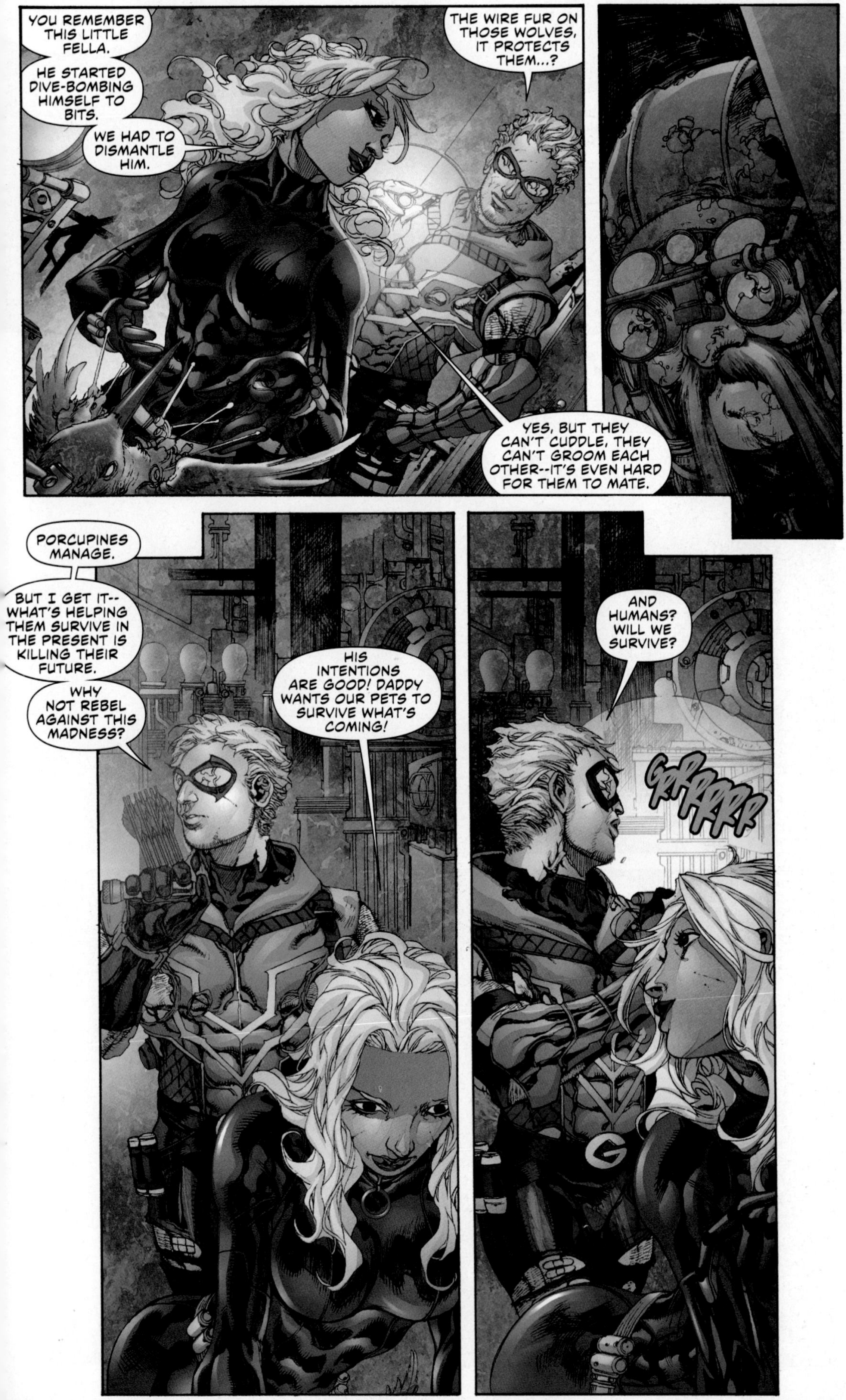
YOU REMEMBER THIS LITTLE FELLA.
HE STARTED DIVE-BOMBING HIMSELF TO BITS.
WE HAD TO DISMANTLE HIM.
THE WIRE FUR ON THOSE WOLVES, IT PROTECTS THEM...?
YES, BUT THEY CAN'T CUDDLE, THEY CAN'T GROOM EACH OTHER--IT'S EVEN HARD FOR THEM TO MATE.
PORCUPINES MANAGE.
BUT I GET IT--WHAT'S HELPING THEM SURVIVE IN THE PRESENT IS KILLING THEIR FUTURE.
WHY NOT REBEL AGAINST THIS MADNESS?
HIS INTENTIONS ARE GOOD! DADDY WANTS OUR PETS TO SURVIVE WHAT'S COMING!
AND HUMANS? WILL WE SURVIVE?
GRRRRRR

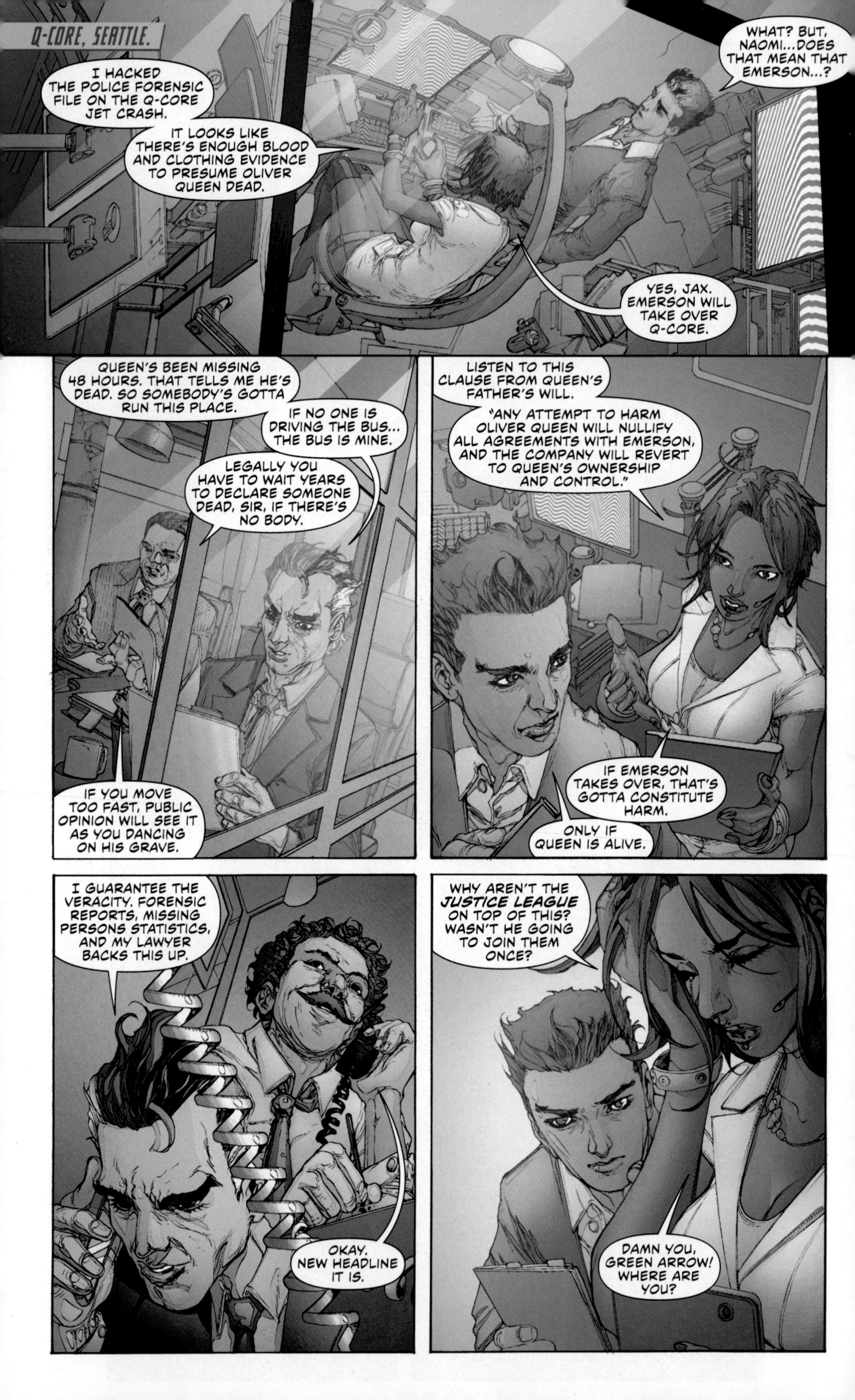
Q-CORE, SEATTLE.
I HACKED THE POLICE FORENSIC FILE ON THE Q-CORE JET CRASH.
IT LOOKS LIKE THERE'S ENOUGH BLOOD AND CLOTHING EVIDENCE TO PRESUME OLIVER QUEEN DEAD.
WHAT? BUT, NAOMI...DOES THAT MEAN THAT EMERSON...?
YES, JAX. EMERSON WILL TAKE OVER Q-CORE.
QUEEN'S BEEN MISSING 48 HOURS. THAT TELLS ME HE'S DEAD. SO SOMEBODY'S GOTTA RUN THIS PLACE.
IF NO ONE IS DRIVING THE BUS... THE BUS IS MINE.
LEGALLY YOU HAVE TO WAIT YEARS TO DECLARE SOMEONE DEAD, SIR, IF THERE'S NO BODY.
IF YOU MOVE TOO FAST, PUBLIC OPINION WILL SEE IT AS YOU DANCING ON HIS GRAVE.
LISTEN TO THIS CLAUSE FROM QUEEN'S FATHER'S WILL.
"ANY ATTEMPT TO HARM OLIVER QUEEN WILL NULLIFY ALL AGREEMENTS WITH EMERSON, AND THE COMPANY WILL REVERT TO QUEEN'S OWNERSHIP AND CONTROL."
IF EMERSON TAKES OVER, THAT'S GOTTA CONSTITUTE HARM.
ONLY IF QUEEN IS ALIVE.
I GUARANTEE THE VERACITY. FORENSIC REPORTS, MISSING PERSONS STATISTICS, AND MY LAWYER BACKS THIS UP.
OKAY. NEW HEADLINE IT IS.
WHY AREN'T THE JUSTICE LEAGUE ON TOP OF THIS? WASN'T HE GOING TO JOIN THEM ONCE?
DAMN YOU, GREEN ARROW! WHERE ARE YOU?

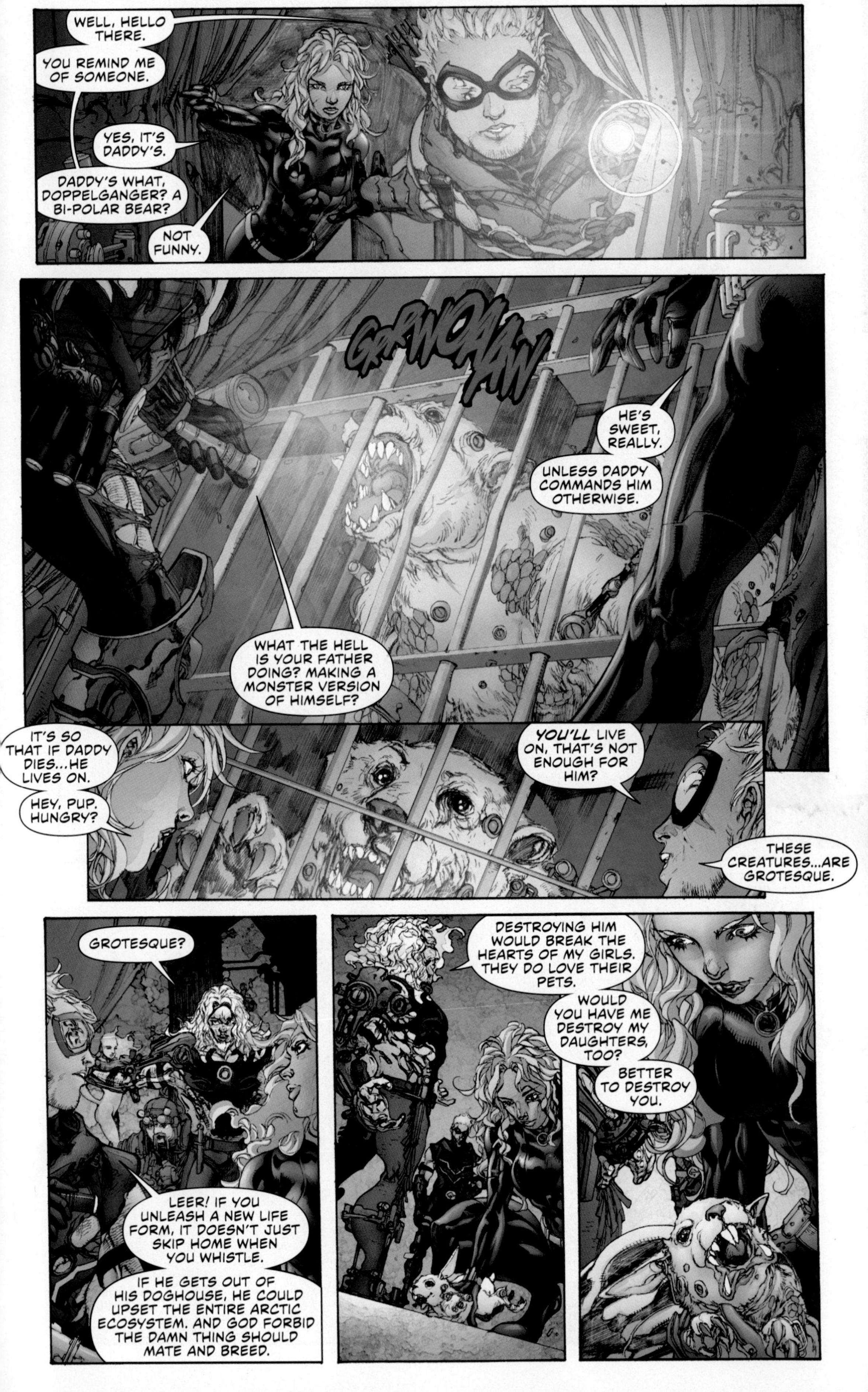
WELL, HELLO THERE.
YOU REMIND ME OF SOMEONE.
YES, IT'S DADDY'S.
DADDY'S WHAT, DOPPELGANGER? A BI-POLAR BEAR?
NOT FUNNY.
GRRWOAAAAAW
HE'S SWEET, REALLY.
UNLESS DADDY COMMANDS HIM OTHERWISE.
WHAT THE HELL IS YOUR FATHER DOING? MAKING A MONSTER VERSION OF HIMSELF?
IT'S SO THAT IF DADDY DIES...HE LIVES ON.
HEY, PUP. HUNGRY?
YOU'LL LIVE ON, THAT'S NOT ENOUGH FOR HIM?
THESE CREATURES...ARE GROTESQUE.
GROTESQUE?
LEER! IF YOU UNLEASH A NEW LIFE FORM, IT DOESN'T JUST SKIP HOME WHEN YOU WHISTLE.
IF HE GETS OUT OF HIS DOGHOUSE, HE COULD UPSET THE ENTIRE ARCTIC ECOSYSTEM. AND GOD FORBID THE DAMN THING SHOULD MATE AND BREED.
DESTROYING HIM WOULD BREAK THE HEARTS OF MY GIRLS. THEY DO LOVE THEIR PETS.
WOULD YOU HAVE ME DESTROY MY DAUGHTERS, TOO?
BETTER TO DESTROY YOU.

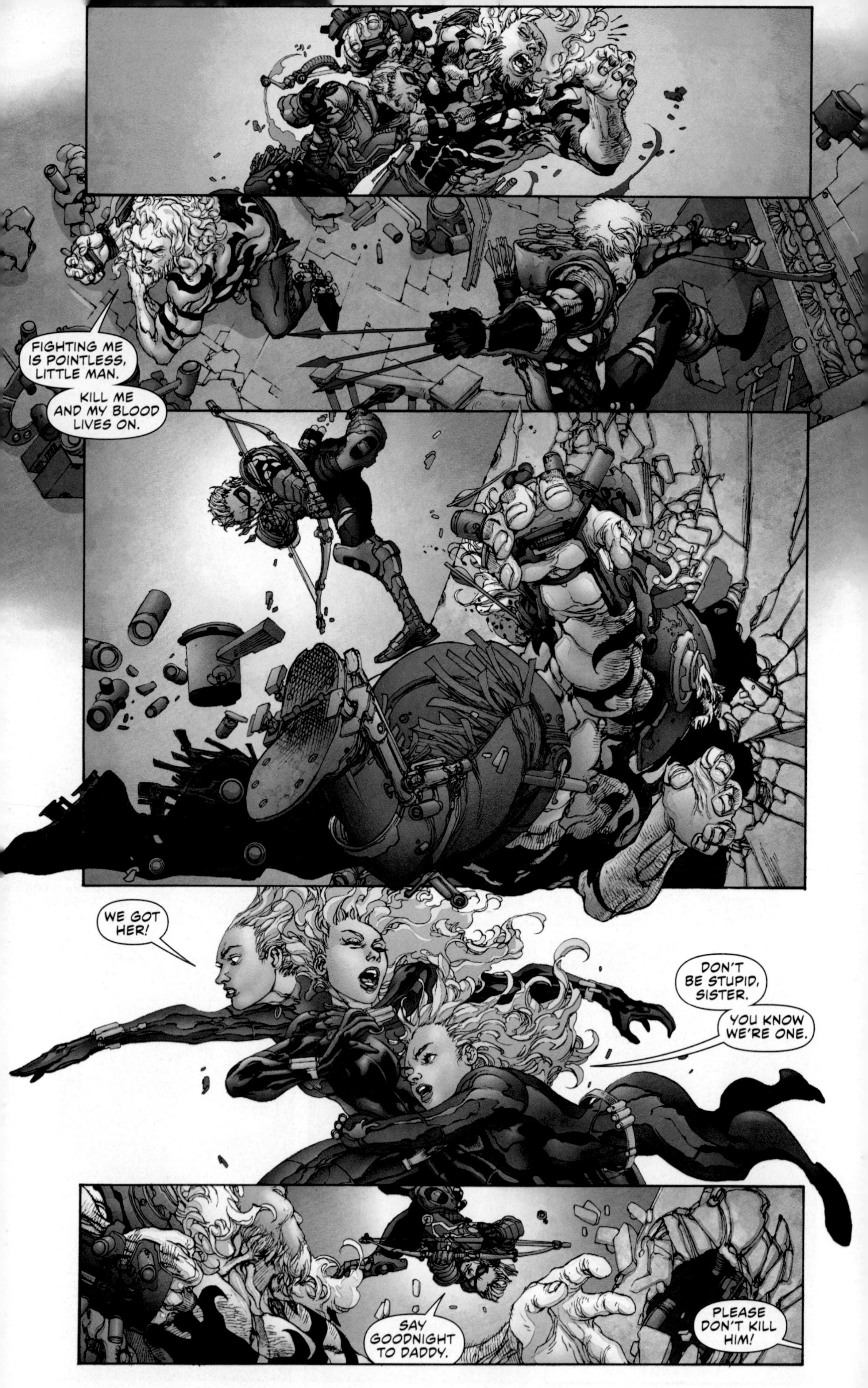
FIGHTING ME IS POINTLESS, LITTLE MAN.
KILL ME AND MY BLOOD LIVES ON.
WE GOT HER!
DON'T BE STUPID, SISTER.
YOU KNOW WE'RE ONE.
SAY GOODNIGHT TO DADDY.
PLEASE DON'T KILL HIM!

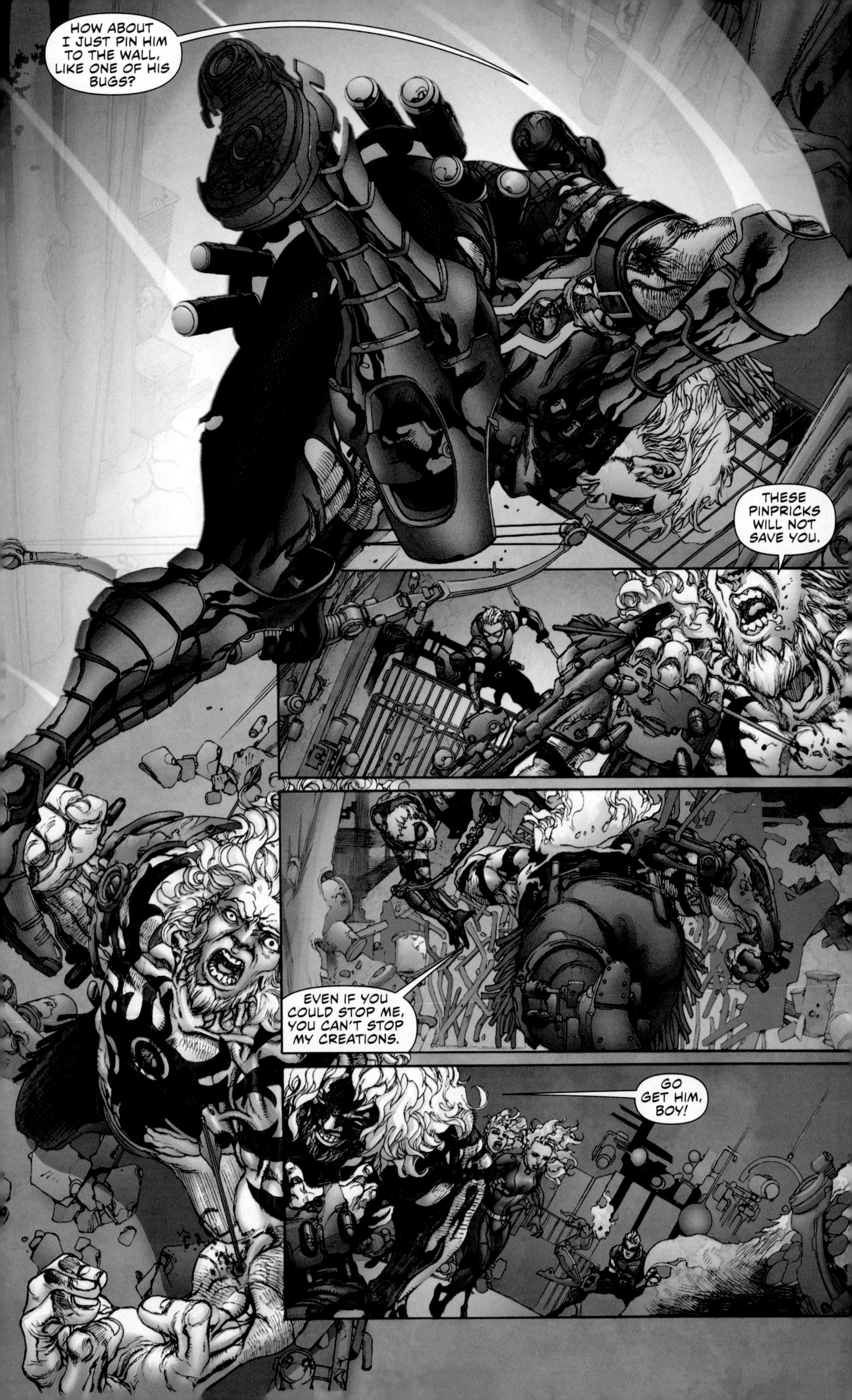
HOW ABOUT I JUST PIN HIM TO THE WALL, LIKE ONE OF HIS BUGS?
THESE PINPRICKS WILL NOT SAVE YOU.
EVEN IF YOU COULD STOP ME, YOU CAN'T STOP MY CREATIONS.
GO GET HIM, BOY!

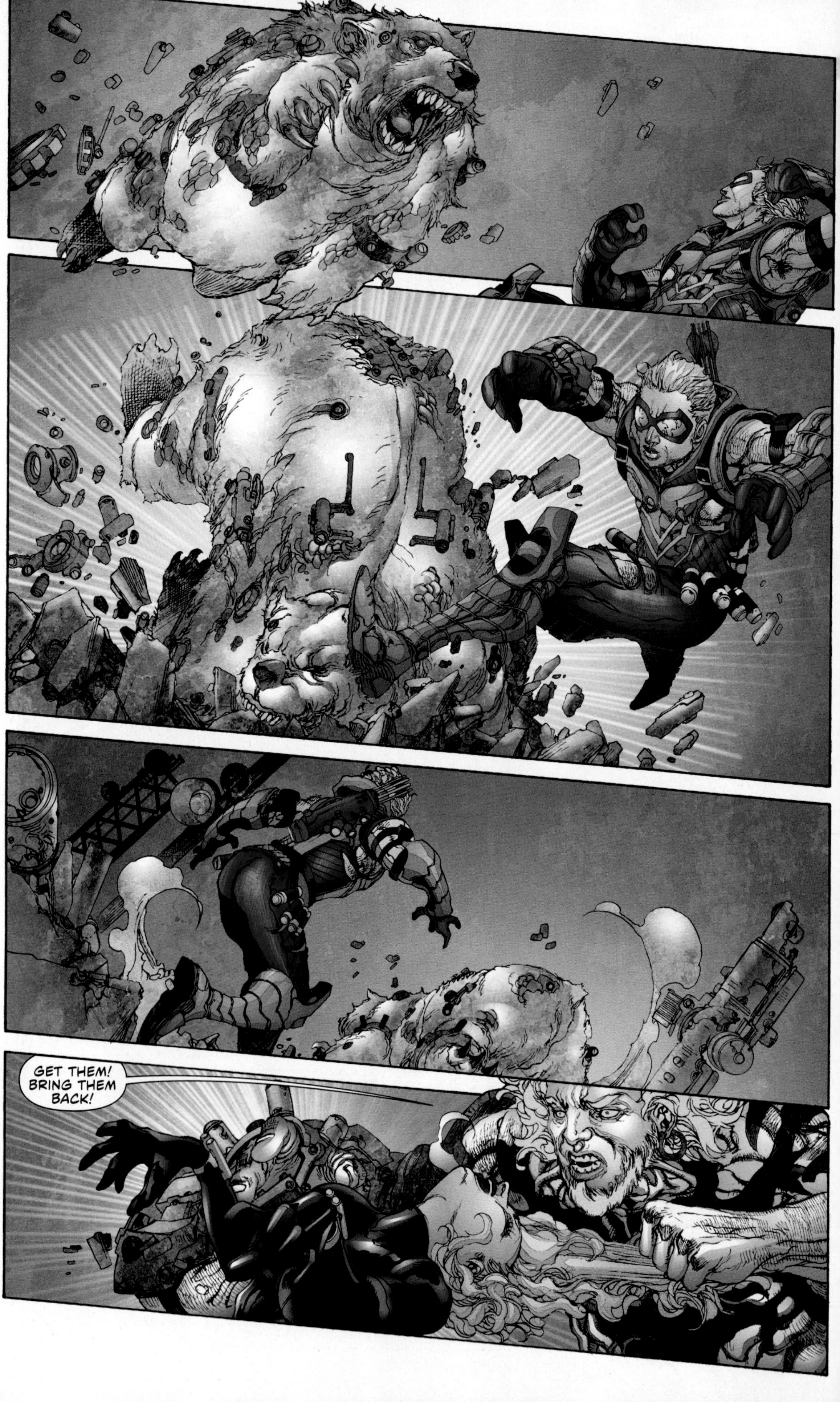
GET THEM! BRING THEM BACK!

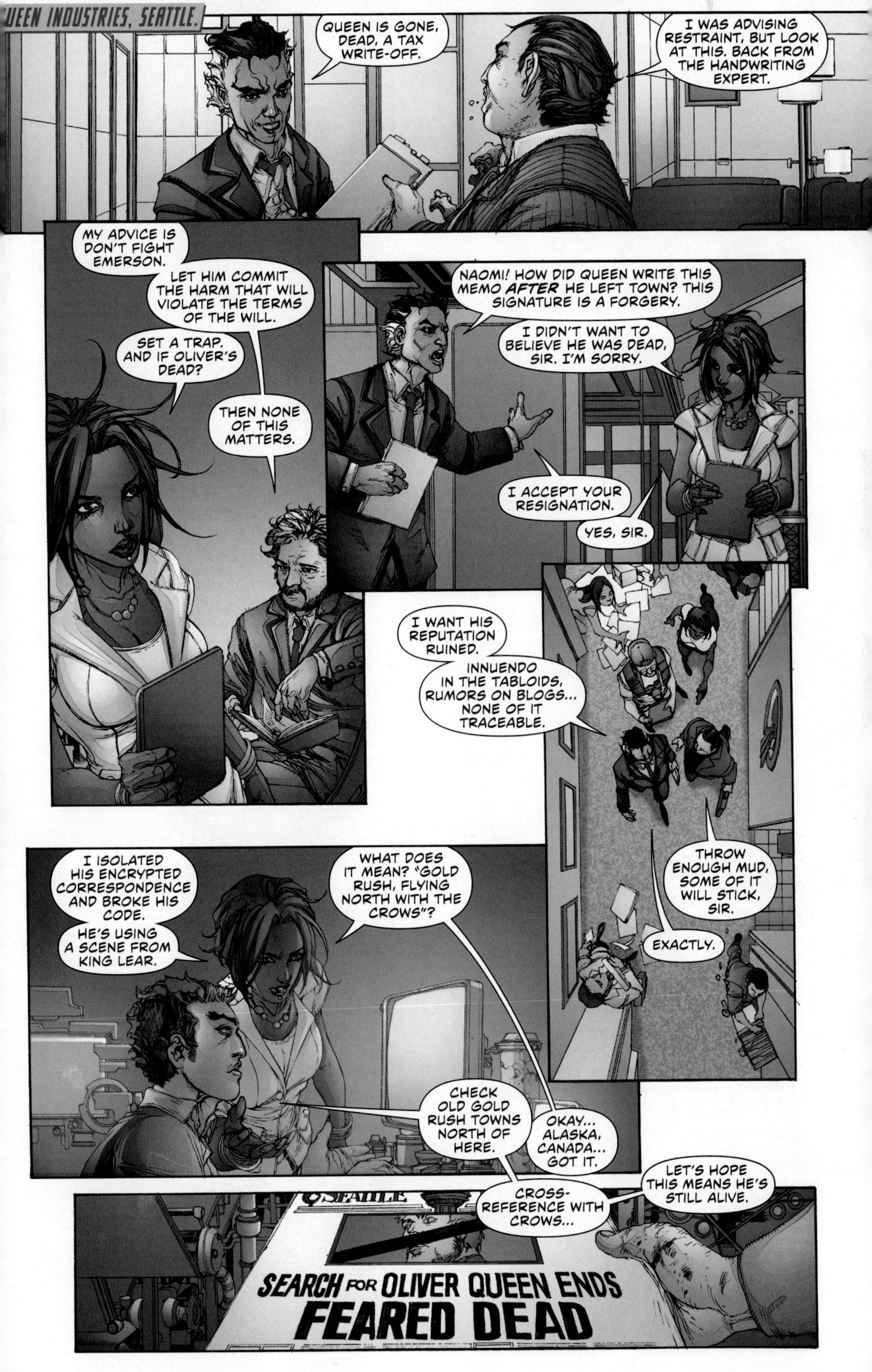

QUEEN INDUSTRIES, SEATTLE.
QUEEN IS GONE, DEAD, A TAX WRITE-OFF.
I WAS ADVISING RESTRAINT, BUT LOOK AT THIS. BACK FROM THE HANDWRITING EXPERT.
MY ADVICE IS DON'T FIGHT EMERSON.
LET HIM COMMIT THE HARM THAT WILL VIOLATE THE TERMS OF THE WILL.
SET A TRAP. AND IF OLIVER'S DEAD?
THEN NONE OF THIS MATTERS.
NAOMI! HOW DID QUEEN WRITE THIS MEMO AFTER HE LEFT TOWN? THIS SIGNATURE IS A FORGERY.
I DIDN'T WANT TO BELIEVE HE WAS DEAD, SIR. I'M SORRY.
I ACCEPT YOUR RESIGNATION.
YES, SIR.
I WANT HIS REPUTATION RUINED.
INNUENDO IN THE TABLOIDS, RUMORS ON BLOGS... NONE OF IT TRACEABLE.
THROW ENOUGH MUD, SOME OF IT WILL STICK, SIR.
EXACTLY.
I ISOLATED HIS ENCRYPTED CORRESPONDENCE AND BROKE HIS CODE.
HE'S USING A SCENE FROM KING LEAR.
WHAT DOES IT MEAN? "GOLD RUSH, FLYING NORTH WITH THE CROWS"?
CHECK OLD GOLD RUSH TOWNS NORTH OF HERE.
OKAY... ALASKA, CANADA... GOT IT.
CROSS-REFERENCE WITH CROWS...
LET'S HOPE THIS MEANS HE'S STILL ALIVE.
SEATTLE
SEARCH FOR OLIVER QUEEN ENDS
FEARED DEAD

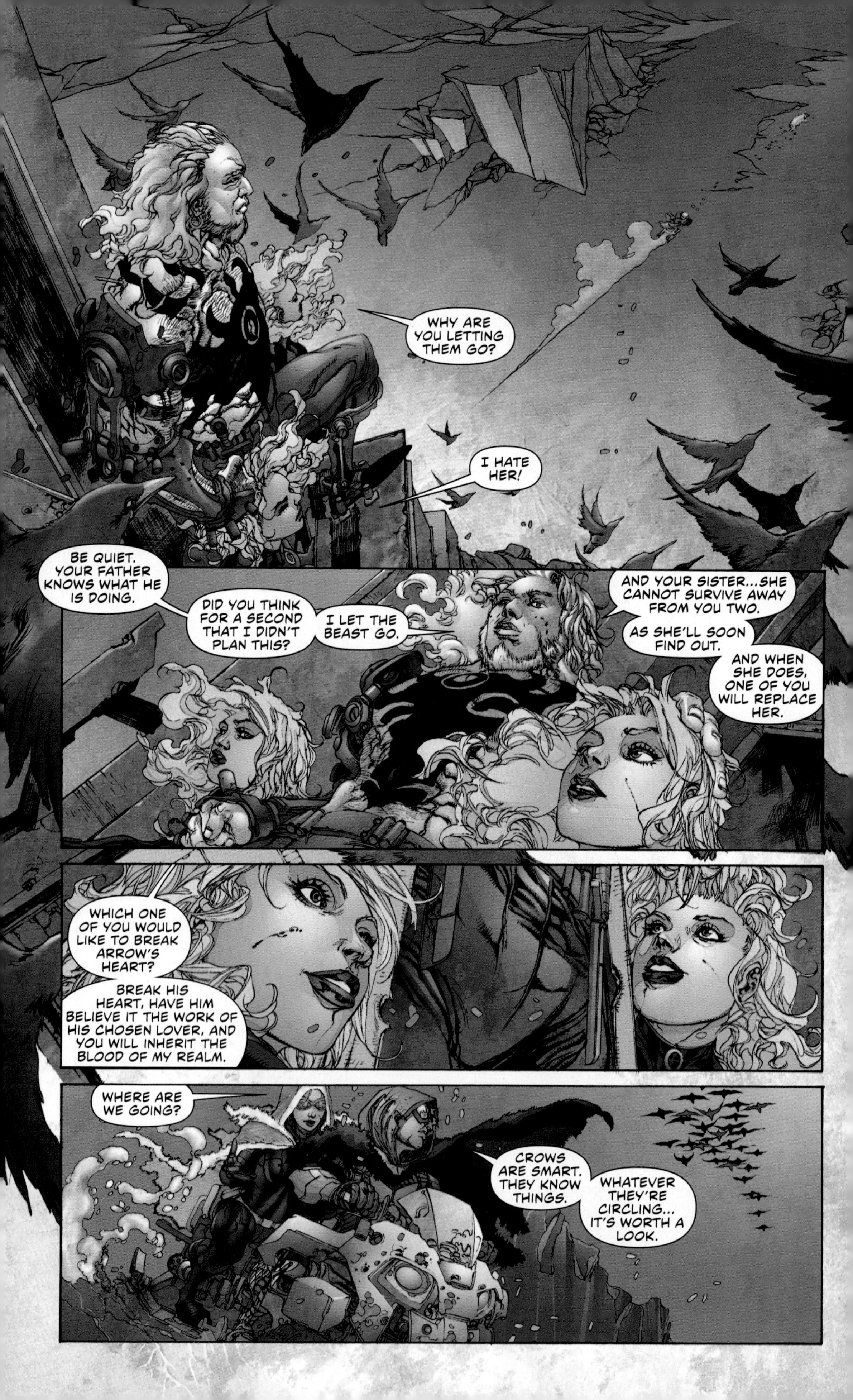
WHY ARE YOU LETTING THEM GO?
I HATE HER!
BE QUIET. YOUR FATHER KNOWS WHAT HE IS DOING.
DID YOU THINK FOR A SECOND THAT I DIDN'T PLAN THIS?
I LET THE BEAST GO.
AND YOUR SISTER...SHE CANNOT SURVIVE AWAY FROM YOU TWO.
AS SHE'LL SOON FIND OUT.
AND WHEN SHE DOES, ONE OF YOU WILL REPLACE HER.
WHICH ONE OF YOU WOULD LIKE TO BREAK ARROW'S HEART?
BREAK HIS HEART, HAVE HIM BELIEVE IT THE WORK OF HIS CHOSEN LOVER, AND YOU WILL INHERIT THE BLOOD OF MY REALM.
WHERE ARE WE GOING?
CROWS ARE SMART. THEY KNOW THINGS.
WHATEVER THEY'RE CIRCLING... IT'S WORTH A LOOK.

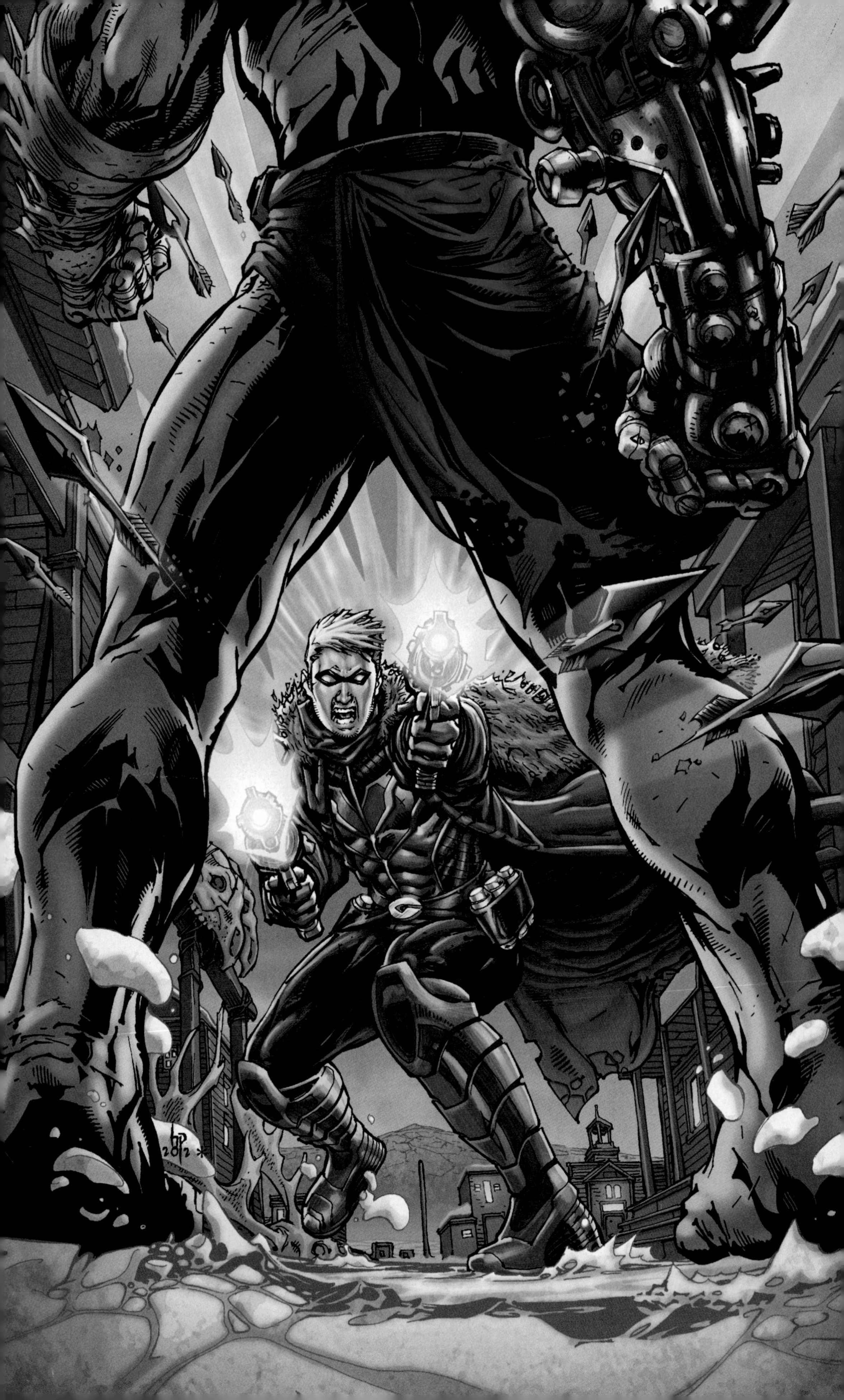

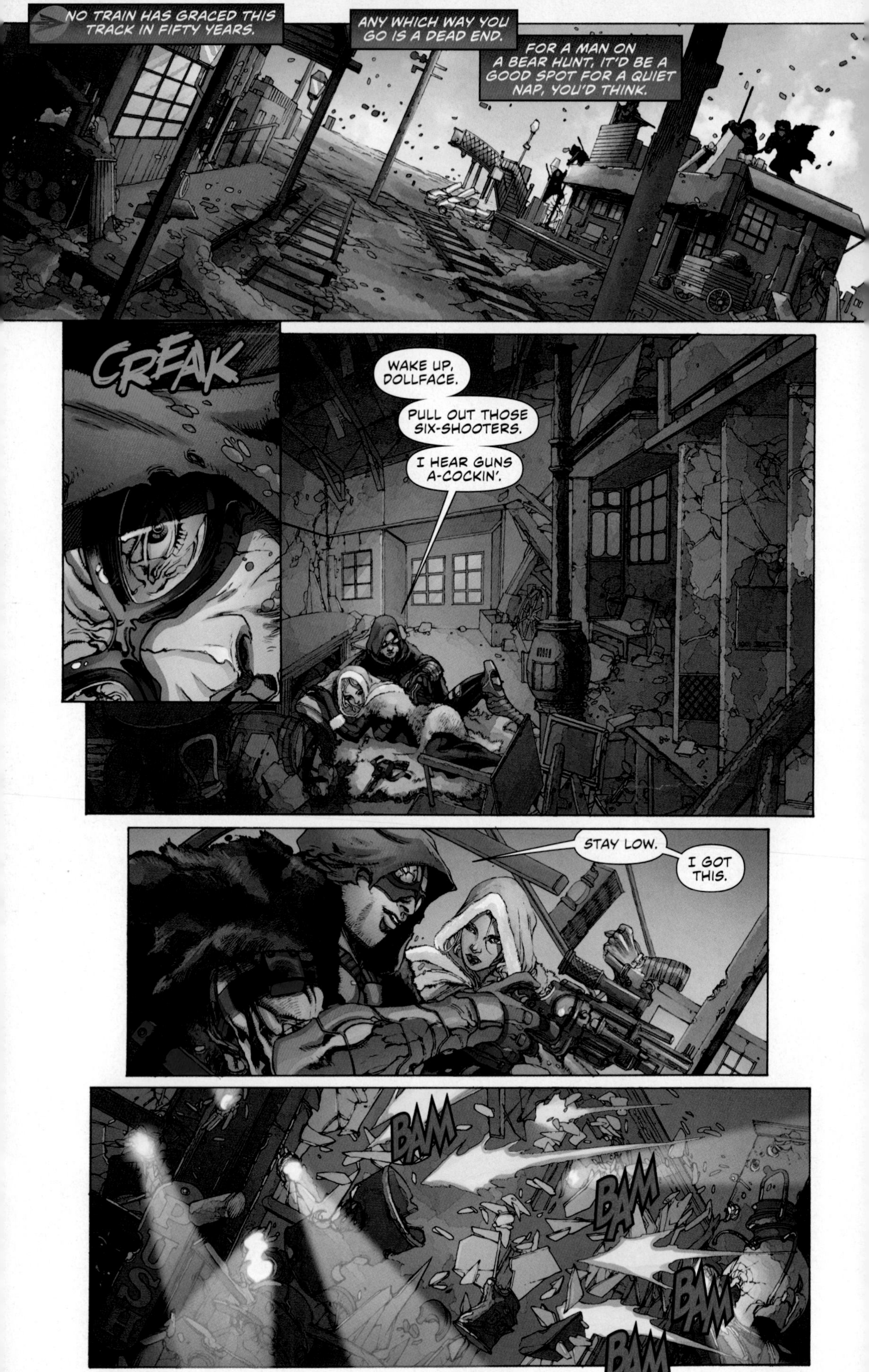
NO TRAIN HAS GRACED THIS TRACK IN FIFTY YEARS.
ANY WHICH WAY YOU GO IS A DEAD END.
FOR A MAN ON A BEAR HUNT, IT'D BE A GOOD SPOT FOR A QUIET NAP, YOU'D THINK.
CREAK
WAKE UP, DOLLFACE.
PULL OUT THOSE SIX-SHOOTERS.
I HEAR GUNS A-COCKIN'.
STAY LOW.
I GOT THIS.
BAM
BAM
BAM
BAM

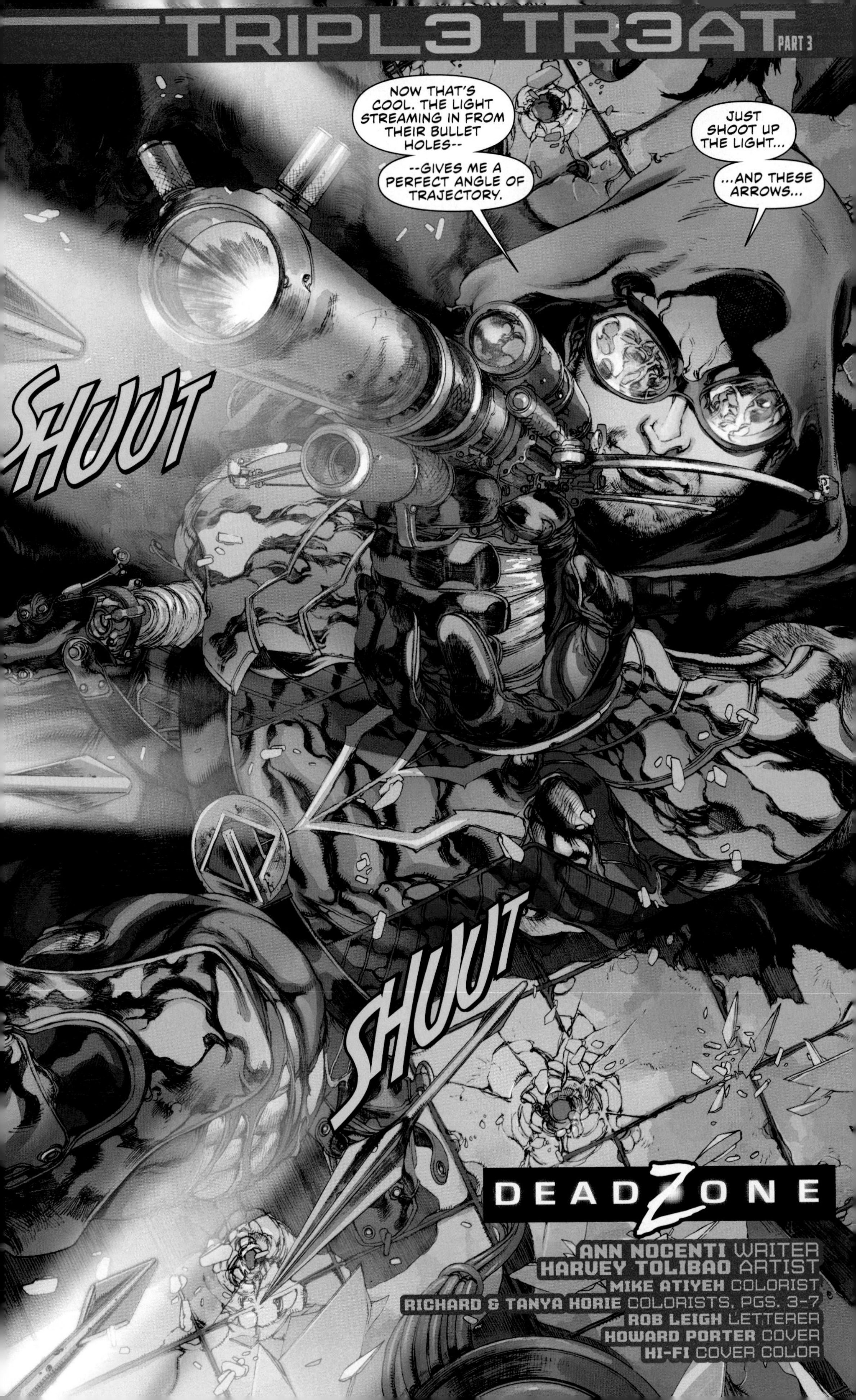

TRIPL3 TR3AT PART 3
NOW THAT'S COOL. THE LIGHT STREAMING IN FROM THEIR BULLET HOLES--
--GIVES ME A PERFECT ANGLE OF TRAJECTORY.
JUST SHOOT UP THE LIGHT...
...AND THESE ARROWS...
SHUUT
SHUUT
DEADZONE
ANN NOCENTI WRITER
HARVEY TOLIBAO ARTIST
MIKE ATIYEH COLORIST
RICHARD & TANYA HORIE COLORISTS, PGS. 3-7
ROB LEIGH LETTERER
HOWARD PORTER COVER
HI-FI COVER COLOR

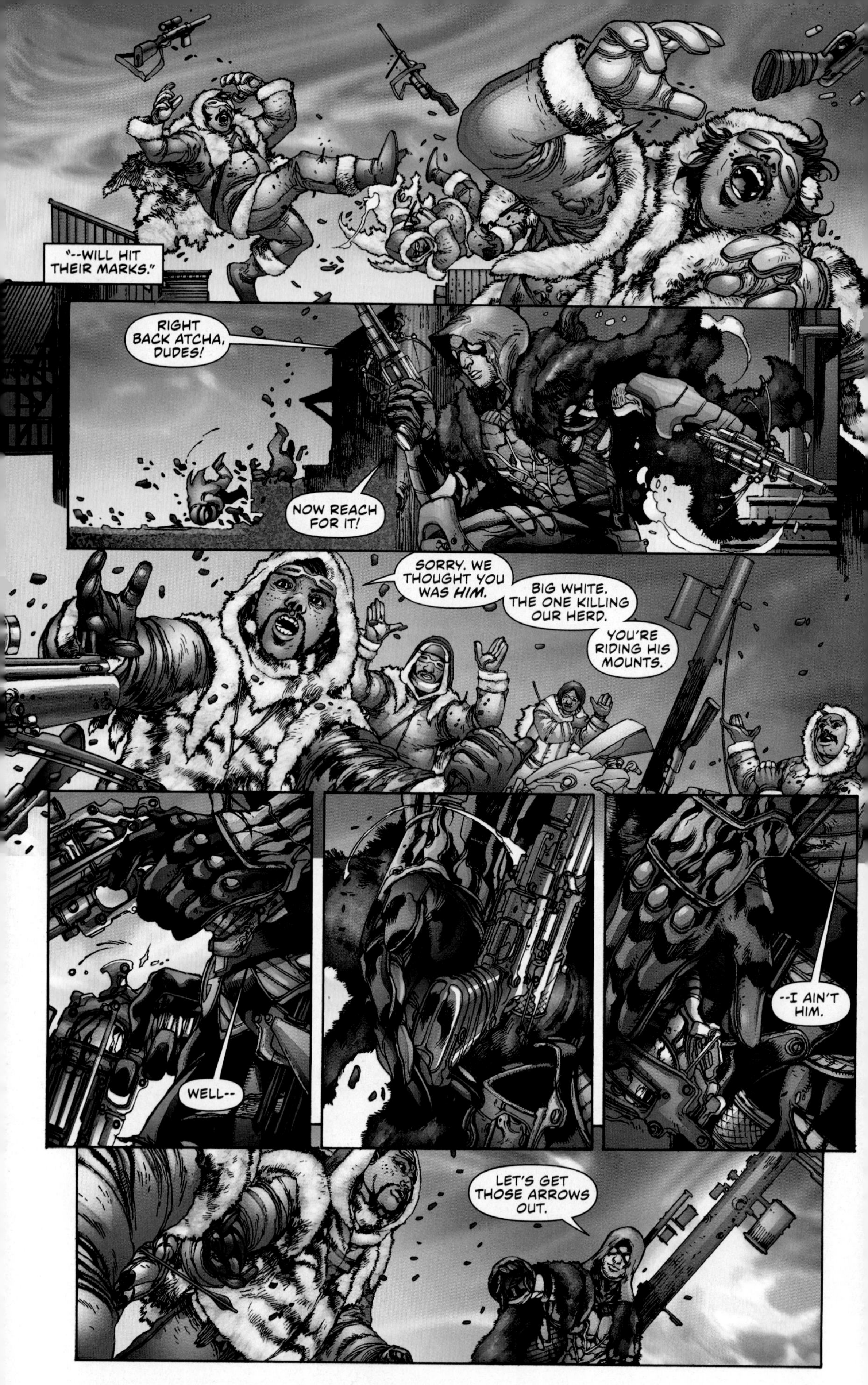
"--WILL HIT THEIR MARKS."
RIGHT BACK ATCHA, DUDES!
NOW REACH FOR IT!
SORRY. WE THOUGHT YOU WAS *HIM*.
BIG WHITE. THE ONE KILLING OUR HERD.
YOU'RE RIDING HIS MOUNTS.
WELL--
--I AIN'T HIM.
LET'S GET THOSE ARROWS OUT.

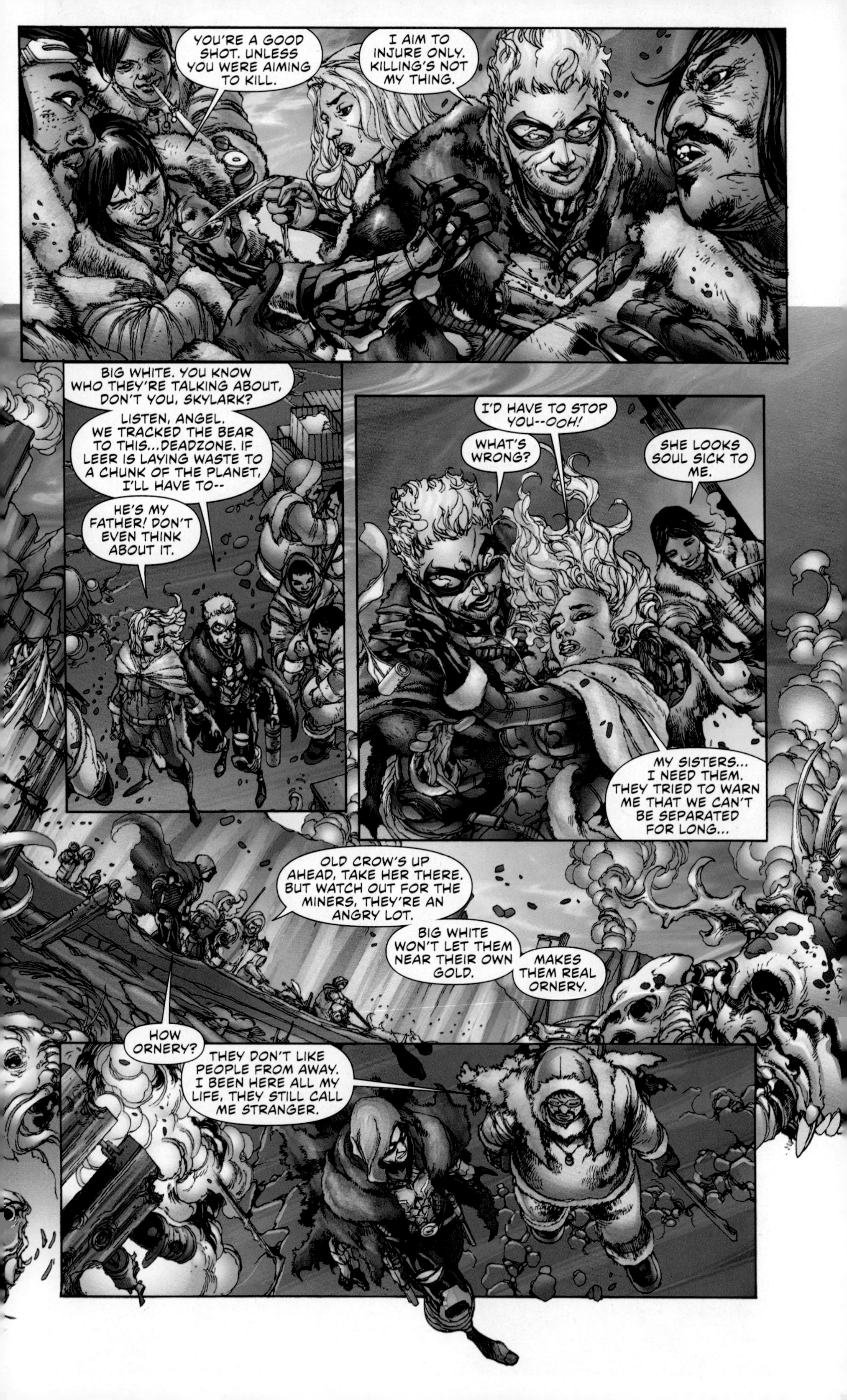
YOU'RE A GOOD SHOT. UNLESS YOU WERE AIMING TO KILL.
I AIM TO INJURE ONLY. KILLING'S NOT MY THING.
BIG WHITE. YOU KNOW WHO THEY'RE TALKING ABOUT, DON'T YOU, SKYLARK?
LISTEN, ANGEL. WE TRACKED THE BEAR TO THIS...DEADZONE. IF LEER IS LAYING WASTE TO A CHUNK OF THE PLANET, I'LL HAVE TO--
HE'S MY FATHER! DON'T EVEN THINK ABOUT IT.
I'D HAVE TO STOP YOU--OOH!
WHAT'S WRONG?
SHE LOOKS SOUL SICK TO ME.
MY SISTERS... I NEED THEM. THEY TRIED TO WARN ME THAT WE CAN'T BE SEPARATED FOR LONG...
OLD CROW'S UP AHEAD, TAKE HER THERE. BUT WATCH OUT FOR THE MINERS, THEY'RE AN ANGRY LOT.
BIG WHITE WON'T LET THEM NEAR THEIR OWN GOLD.
MAKES THEM REAL ORNERY.
HOW ORNERY?
THEY DON'T LIKE PEOPLE FROM AWAY. I BEEN HERE ALL MY LIFE, THEY STILL CALL ME STRANGER.

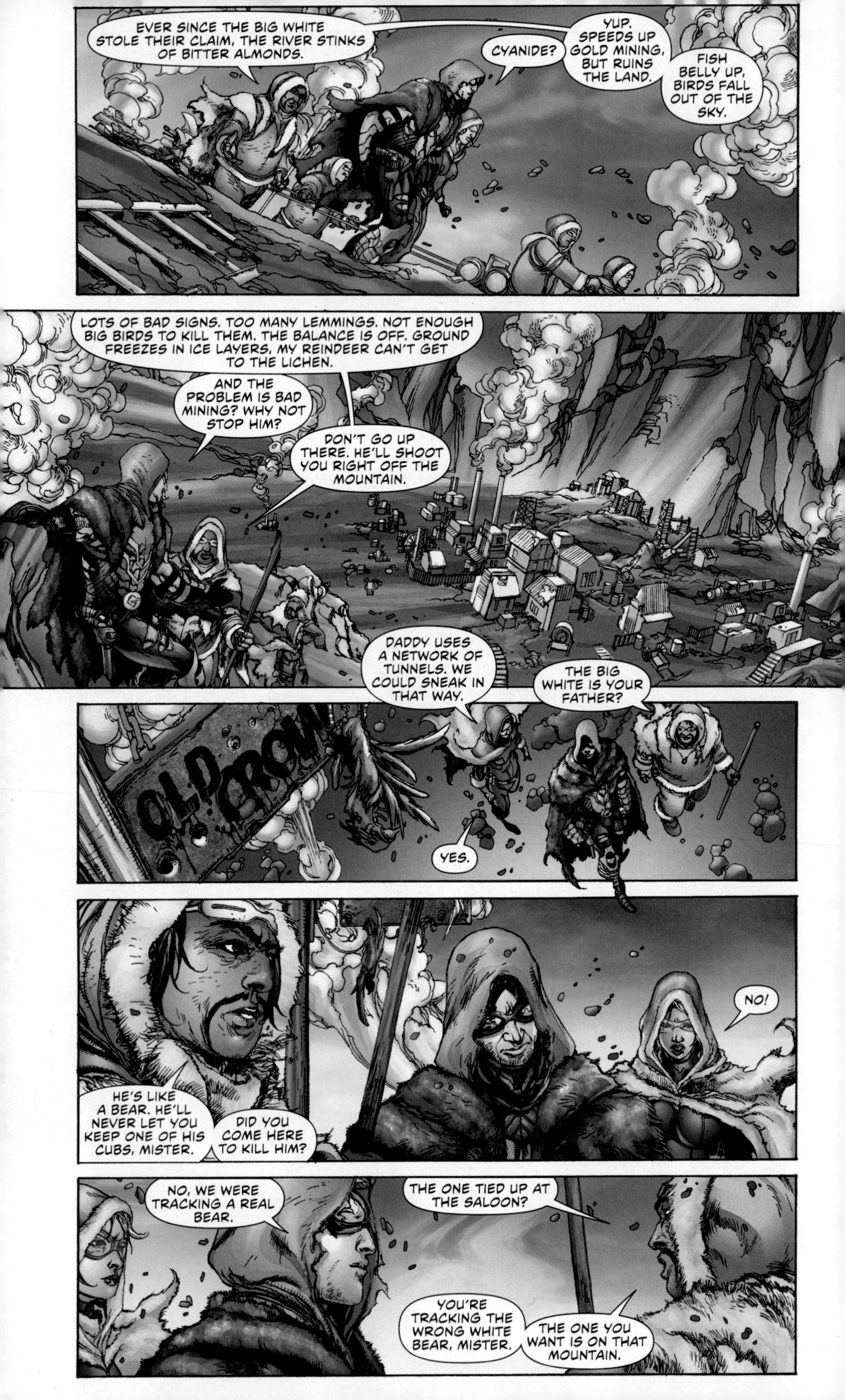
EVER SINCE THE BIG WHITE STOLE THEIR CLAIM, THE RIVER STINKS OF BITTER ALMONDS.
CYANIDE?
YUP. SPEEDS UP GOLD MINING, BUT RUINS THE LAND.
FISH BELLY UP, BIRDS FALL OUT OF THE SKY.
LOTS OF BAD SIGNS. TOO MANY LEMMINGS. NOT ENOUGH BIG BIRDS TO KILL THEM. THE BALANCE IS OFF. GROUND FREEZES IN ICE LAYERS, MY REINDEER CAN'T GET TO THE LICHEN.
AND THE PROBLEM IS BAD MINING? WHY NOT STOP HIM?
DON'T GO UP THERE. HE'LL SHOOT YOU RIGHT OFF THE MOUNTAIN.
DADDY USES A NETWORK OF TUNNELS. WE COULD SNEAK IN THAT WAY.
THE BIG WHITE IS YOUR FATHER?
OLD CROW
YES.
NO!
HE'S LIKE A BEAR. HE'LL NEVER LET YOU KEEP ONE OF HIS CUBS, MISTER.
DID YOU COME HERE TO KILL HIM?
NO, WE WERE TRACKING A REAL BEAR.
THE ONE TIED UP AT THE SALOON?
YOU'RE TRACKING THE WRONG WHITE BEAR, MISTER.
THE ONE YOU WANT IS ON THAT MOUNTAIN.

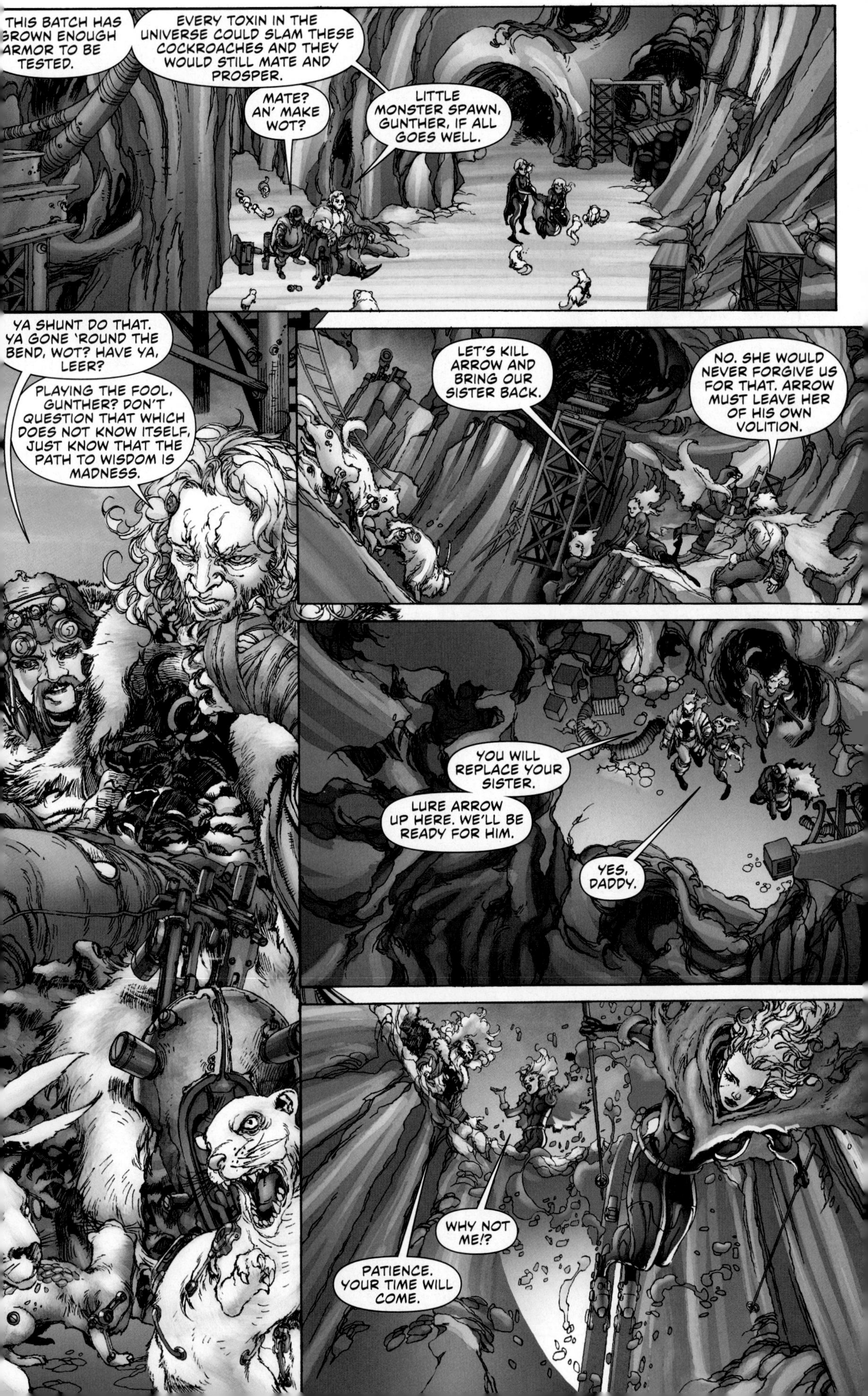
THIS BATCH HAS GROWN ENOUGH ARMOR TO BE TESTED.
EVERY TOXIN IN THE UNIVERSE COULD SLAM THESE COCKROACHES AND THEY WOULD STILL MATE AND PROSPER.
MATE? AN' MAKE WOT?
LITTLE MONSTER SPAWN, GUNTHER, IF ALL GOES WELL.
YA SHUNT DO THAT. YA GONE 'ROUND THE BEND, WOT? HAVE YA, LEER?
PLAYING THE FOOL, GUNTHER? DON'T QUESTION THAT WHICH DOES NOT KNOW ITSELF, JUST KNOW THAT THE PATH TO WISDOM IS MADNESS.
LET'S KILL ARROW AND BRING OUR SISTER BACK.
NO. SHE WOULD NEVER FORGIVE US FOR THAT. ARROW MUST LEAVE HER OF HIS OWN VOLITION.
YOU WILL REPLACE YOUR SISTER.
LURE ARROW UP HERE. WE'LL BE READY FOR HIM.
YES, DADDY.
WHY NOT ME!?
PATIENCE. YOUR TIME WILL COME.

THIS IS THEIR IDEA OF A BIG CITY?

LOOK AT THAT SIGN. WE COULD GET MARRIED, STAKE A CLAIM, GET DRUNK, LIVE ABOVE THE BAR.

ROOMS, HOMEBREW
JUSTICE OF THE PEACE
SHERIFF, TAX COLLECTOR,
MINING CLAIMS,
GOLD AND FURS BOUGHT & SOLD

ONE-STOP SHOPPING.

"BEER, BAIT, BEANS, BUCKSHOT, BULLETS, BEAVER..."

"BEAR"?

THAT AIN'T RIGHT.

NICE MOUNT, MISTER.

AND I DON'T MEAN THE SKI-DOO.

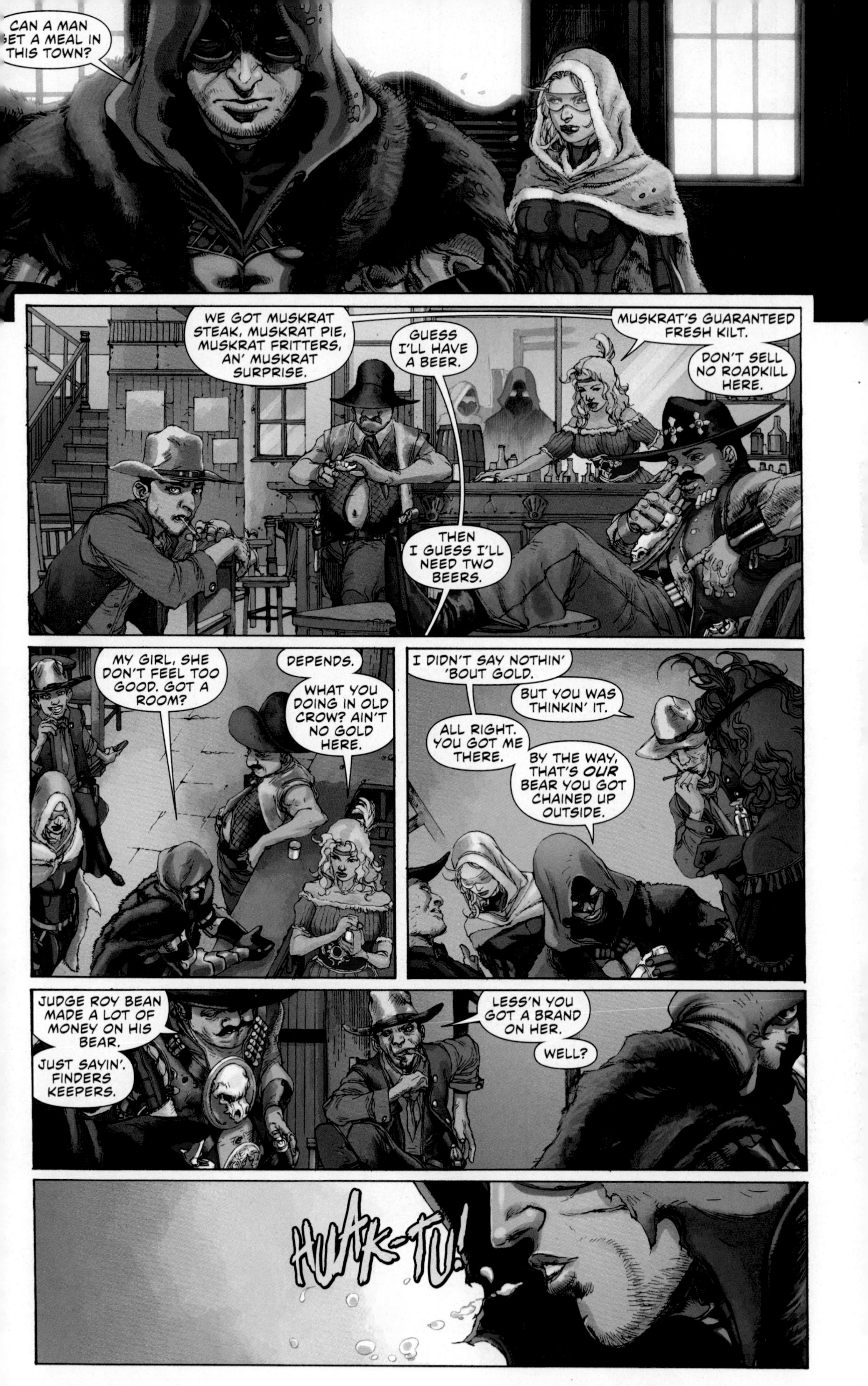
CAN A MAN GET A MEAL IN THIS TOWN?
WE GOT MUSKRAT STEAK, MUSKRAT PIE, MUSKRAT FRITTERS, AN' MUSKRAT SURPRISE.
GUESS I'LL HAVE A BEER.
MUSKRAT'S GUARANTEED FRESH KILT.
DON'T SELL NO ROADKILL HERE.
THEN I GUESS I'LL NEED TWO BEERS.
MY GIRL, SHE DON'T FEEL TOO GOOD. GOT A ROOM?
DEPENDS.
WHAT YOU DOING IN OLD CROW? AIN'T NO GOLD HERE.
I DIDN'T SAY NOTHIN' 'BOUT GOLD.
BUT YOU WAS THINKIN' IT.
ALL RIGHT. YOU GOT ME THERE.
BY THE WAY, THAT'S *OUR* BEAR YOU GOT CHAINED UP OUTSIDE.
JUDGE ROY BEAN MADE A LOT OF MONEY ON HIS BEAR.
JUST SAYIN'. FINDERS KEEPERS.
LESS'N YOU GOT A BRAND ON HER.
WELL?
HUAK-TU!

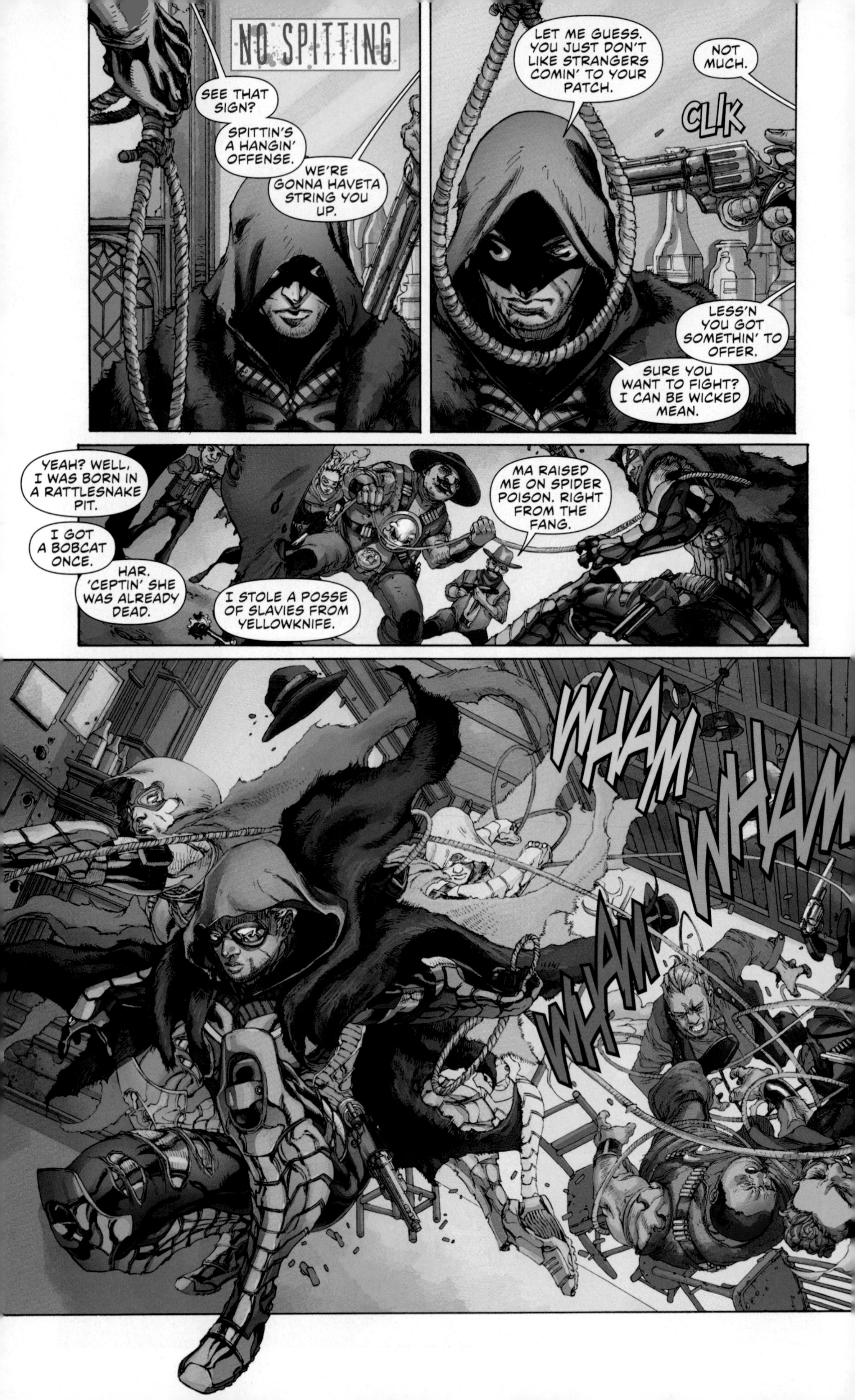

NO SPITTING
SEE THAT SIGN?
SPITTIN'S A HANGIN' OFFENSE.
WE'RE GONNA HAVETA STRING YOU UP.
LET ME GUESS. YOU JUST DON'T LIKE STRANGERS COMIN' TO YOUR PATCH.
NOT MUCH.
CLIK
LESS'N YOU GOT SOMETHIN' TO OFFER.
SURE YOU WANT TO FIGHT? I CAN BE WICKED MEAN.
YEAH? WELL, I WAS BORN IN A RATTLESNAKE PIT.
I GOT A BOBCAT ONCE.
HAR. 'CEPTIN' SHE WAS ALREADY DEAD.
I STOLE A POSSE OF SLAVIES FROM YELLOWKNIFE.
MA RAISED ME ON SPIDER POISON. RIGHT FROM THE FANG.
WHAM
WHAM
WHAM

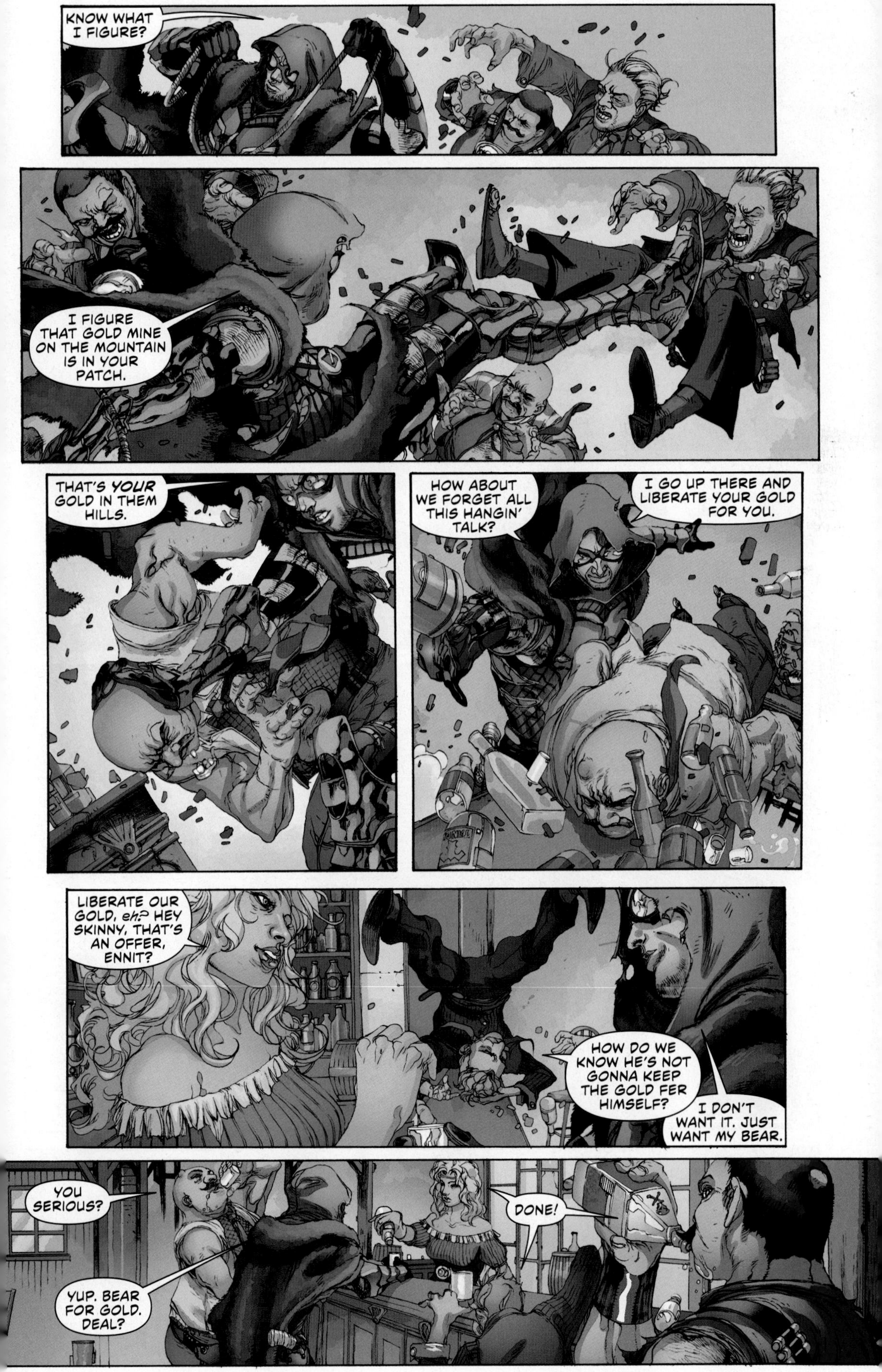
KNOW WHAT I FIGURE?
I FIGURE THAT GOLD MINE ON THE MOUNTAIN IS IN YOUR PATCH.
THAT'S *YOUR* GOLD IN THEM HILLS.
HOW ABOUT WE FORGET ALL THIS HANGIN' TALK?
I GO UP THERE AND LIBERATE YOUR GOLD FOR YOU.
LIBERATE OUR GOLD, *eh?* HEY SKINNY, THAT'S AN OFFER, ENNIT?
HOW DO WE KNOW HE'S NOT GONNA KEEP THE GOLD FER HIMSELF?
I DON'T WANT IT. JUST WANT MY BEAR.
YOU SERIOUS?
YUP. BEAR FOR GOLD. DEAL?
DONE!

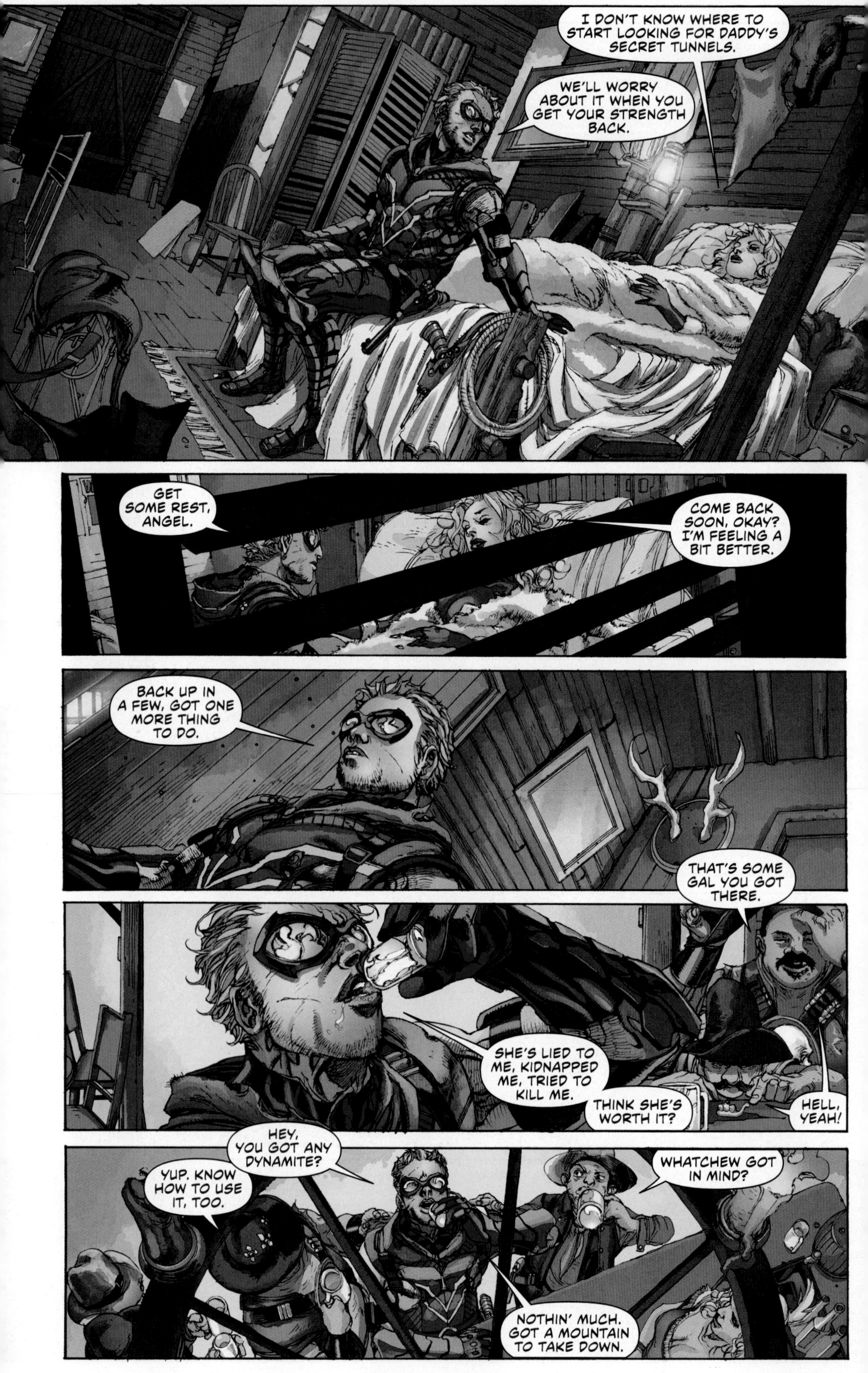
I DON'T KNOW WHERE TO START LOOKING FOR DADDY'S SECRET TUNNELS.
WE'LL WORRY ABOUT IT WHEN YOU GET YOUR STRENGTH BACK.
GET SOME REST, ANGEL.
COME BACK SOON, OKAY? I'M FEELING A BIT BETTER.
BACK UP IN A FEW, GOT ONE MORE THING TO DO.
THAT'S SOME GAL YOU GOT THERE.
SHE'S LIED TO ME, KIDNAPPED ME, TRIED TO KILL ME.
THINK SHE'S WORTH IT?
HELL, YEAH!
HEY, YOU GOT ANY DYNAMITE?
YUP. KNOW HOW TO USE IT, TOO.
WHATCHEW GOT IN MIND?
NOTHIN' MUCH. GOT A MOUNTAIN TO TAKE DOWN.

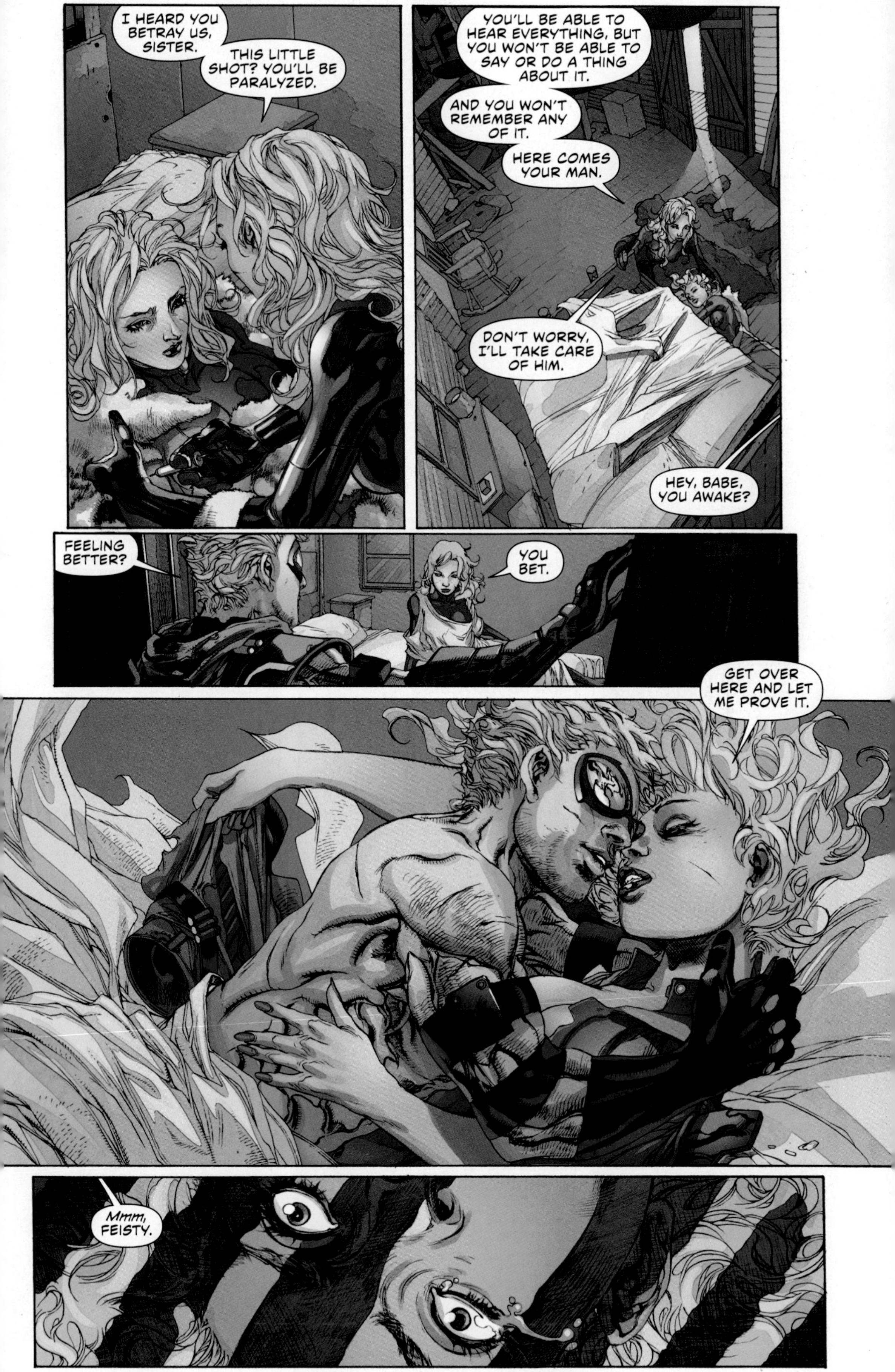
I HEARD YOU BETRAY US, SISTER.
THIS LITTLE SHOT? YOU'LL BE PARALYZED.
YOU'LL BE ABLE TO HEAR EVERYTHING, BUT YOU WON'T BE ABLE TO SAY OR DO A THING ABOUT IT.
AND YOU WON'T REMEMBER ANY OF IT.
HERE COMES YOUR MAN.
DON'T WORRY, I'LL TAKE CARE OF HIM.
HEY, BABE, YOU AWAKE?
FEELING BETTER?
YOU BET.
GET OVER HERE AND LET ME PROVE IT.
Mmm, FEISTY.

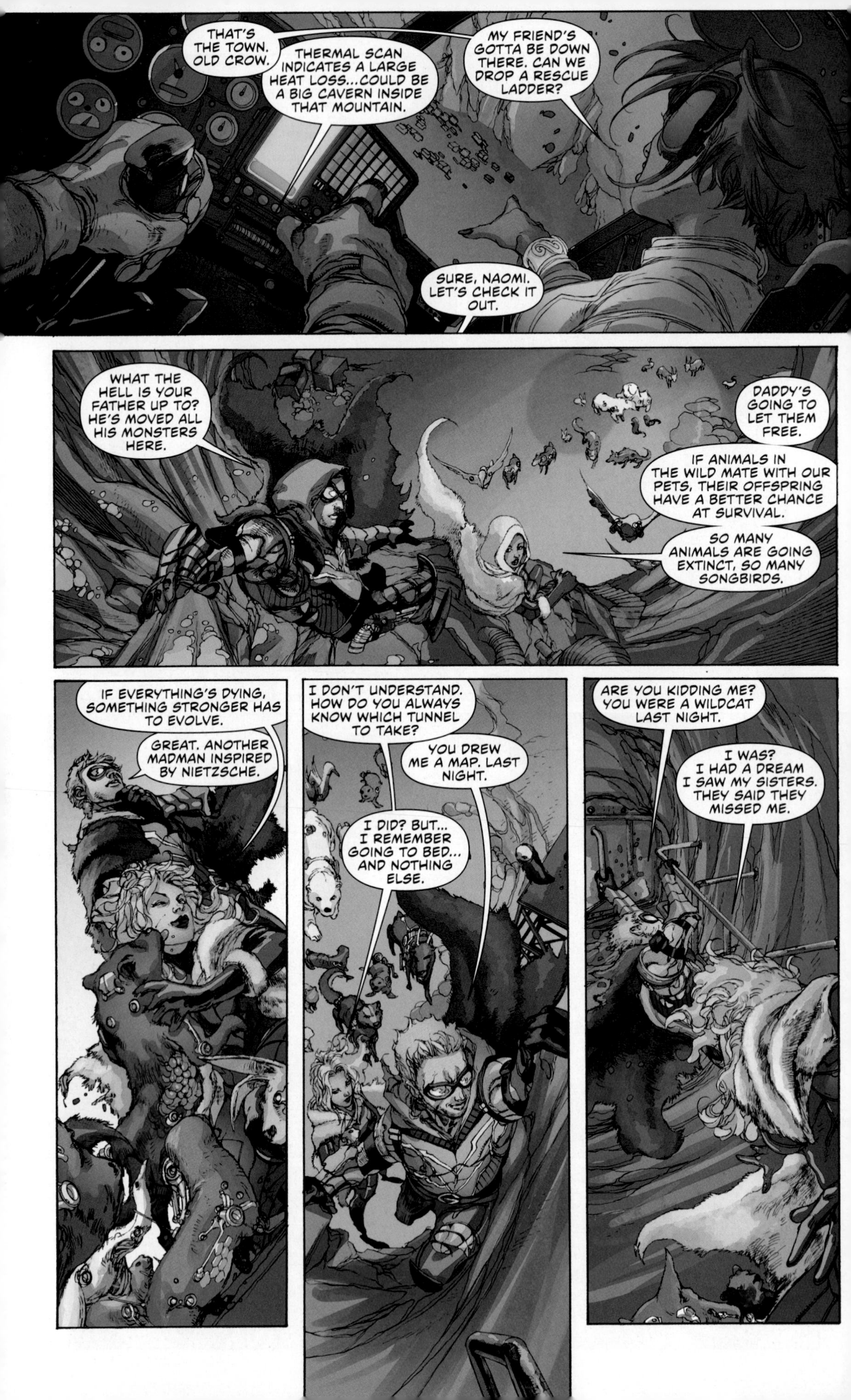
THAT'S THE TOWN. OLD CROW.
THERMAL SCAN INDICATES A LARGE HEAT LOSS...COULD BE A BIG CAVERN INSIDE THAT MOUNTAIN.
MY FRIEND'S GOTTA BE DOWN THERE. CAN WE DROP A RESCUE LADDER?
SURE, NAOMI. LET'S CHECK IT OUT.
WHAT THE HELL IS YOUR FATHER UP TO? HE'S MOVED ALL HIS MONSTERS HERE.
DADDY'S GOING TO LET THEM FREE.
IF ANIMALS IN THE WILD MATE WITH OUR PETS, THEIR OFFSPRING HAVE A BETTER CHANCE AT SURVIVAL.
SO MANY ANIMALS ARE GOING EXTINCT, SO MANY SONGBIRDS.
IF EVERYTHING'S DYING, SOMETHING STRONGER HAS TO EVOLVE.
GREAT. ANOTHER MADMAN INSPIRED BY NIETZSCHE.
I DON'T UNDERSTAND. HOW DO YOU ALWAYS KNOW WHICH TUNNEL TO TAKE?
YOU DREW ME A MAP. LAST NIGHT.
I DID? BUT... I REMEMBER GOING TO BED... AND NOTHING ELSE.
ARE YOU KIDDING ME? YOU WERE A WILDCAT LAST NIGHT.
I WAS? I HAD A DREAM I SAW MY SISTERS. THEY SAID THEY MISSED ME.

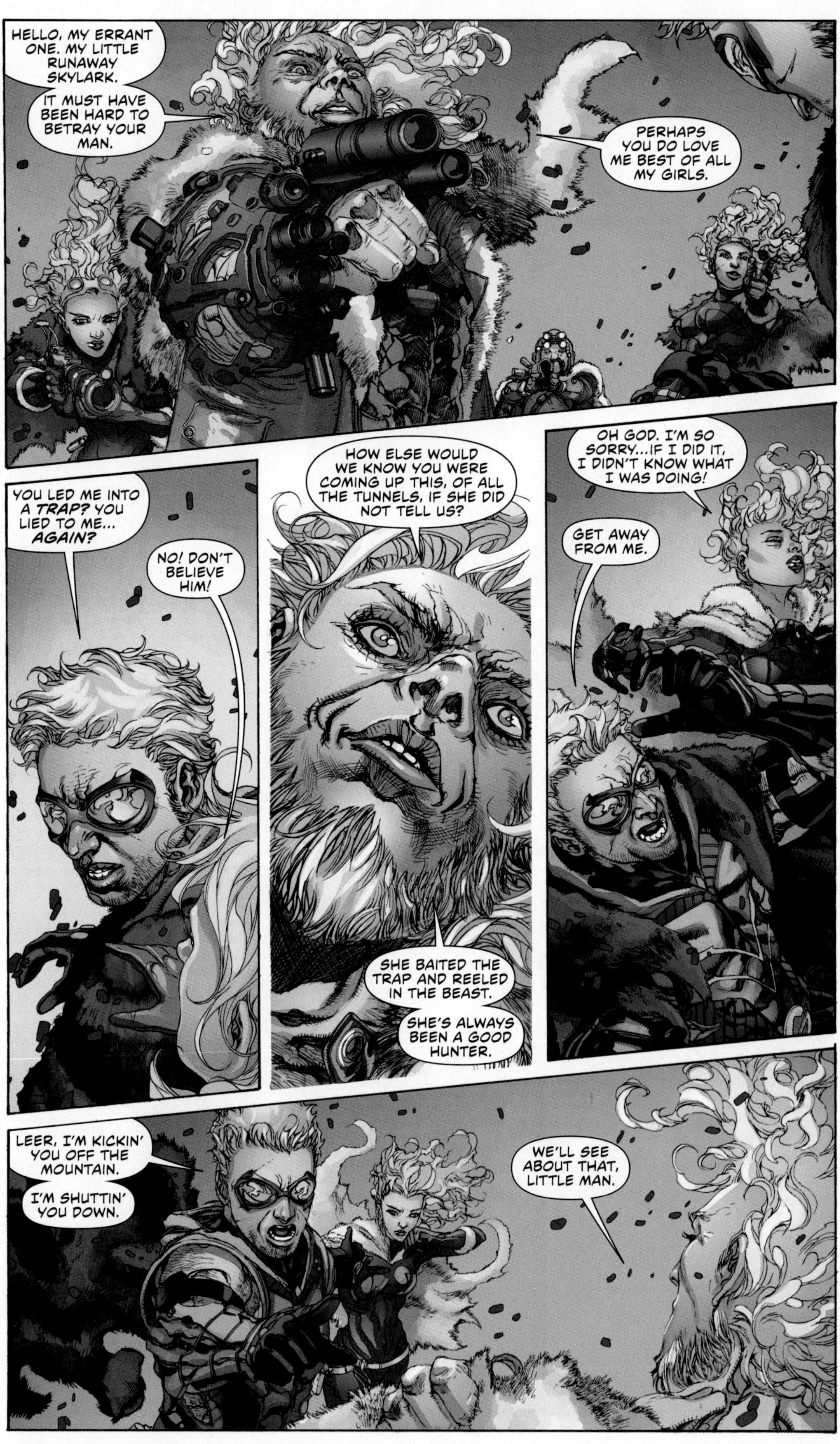
HELLO, MY ERRANT ONE. MY LITTLE RUNAWAY SKYLARK.
IT MUST HAVE BEEN HARD TO BETRAY YOUR MAN.
PERHAPS YOU DO LOVE ME BEST OF ALL MY GIRLS.
YOU LED ME INTO A *TRAP?* YOU LIED TO ME... *AGAIN?*
NO! DON'T BELIEVE HIM!
HOW ELSE WOULD WE KNOW YOU WERE COMING UP THIS, OF ALL THE TUNNELS, IF SHE DID NOT TELL US?
SHE BAITED THE TRAP AND REELED IN THE BEAST.
SHE'S ALWAYS BEEN A GOOD HUNTER.
OH GOD. I'M SO SORRY...IF I DID IT, I DIDN'T KNOW WHAT I WAS DOING!
GET AWAY FROM ME.
LEER, I'M KICKIN' YOU OFF THE MOUNTAIN.
I'M SHUTTIN' YOU DOWN.
WE'LL SEE ABOUT THAT, LITTLE MAN.

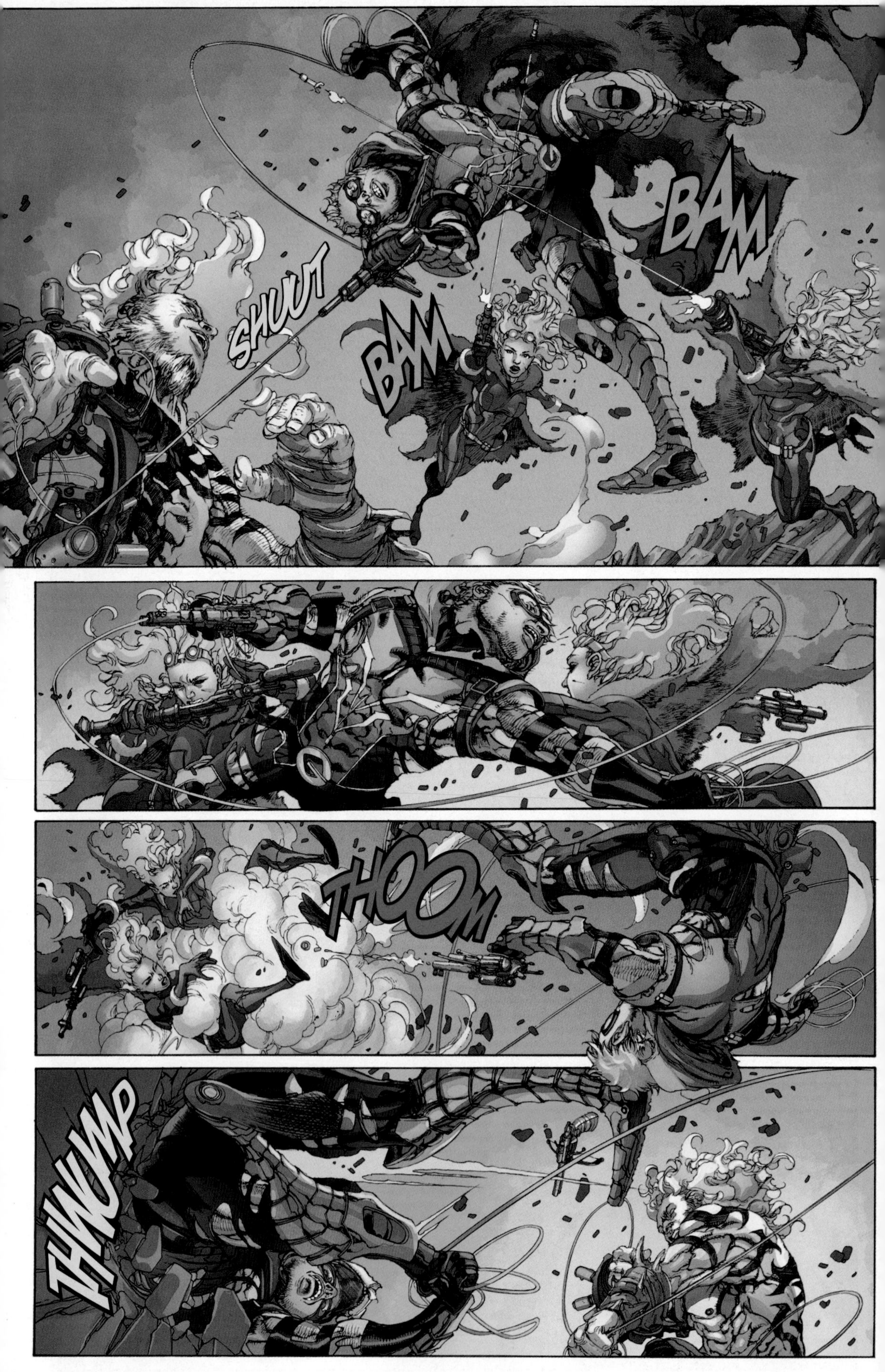
SHUUT
BAM
BAM
THOOM
THWUMP

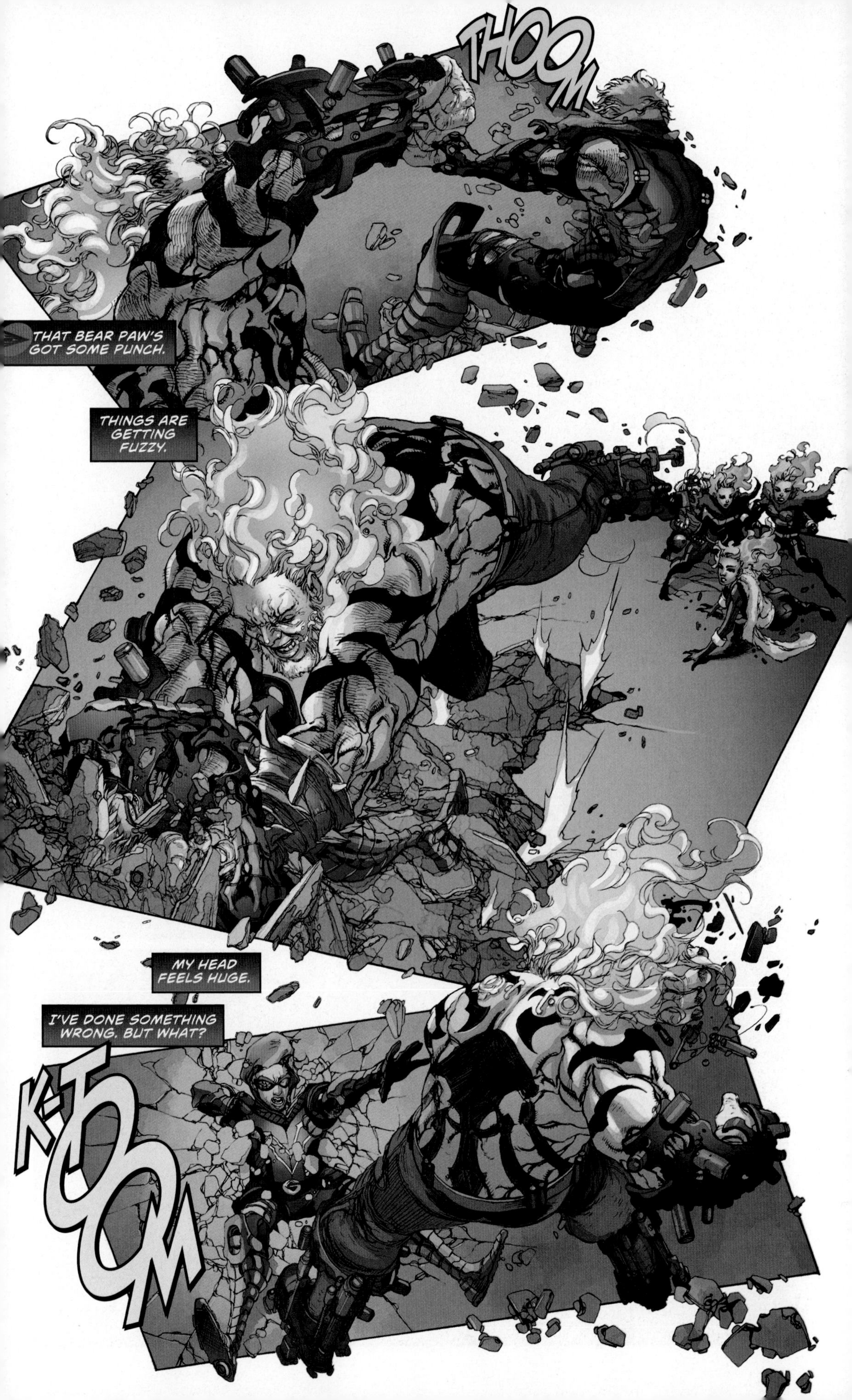
THOOM
THAT BEAR PAW'S GOT SOME PUNCH.
THINGS ARE GETTING FUZZY.
MY HEAD FEELS HUGE.
I'VE DONE SOMETHING WRONG. BUT WHAT?
K-TOOM

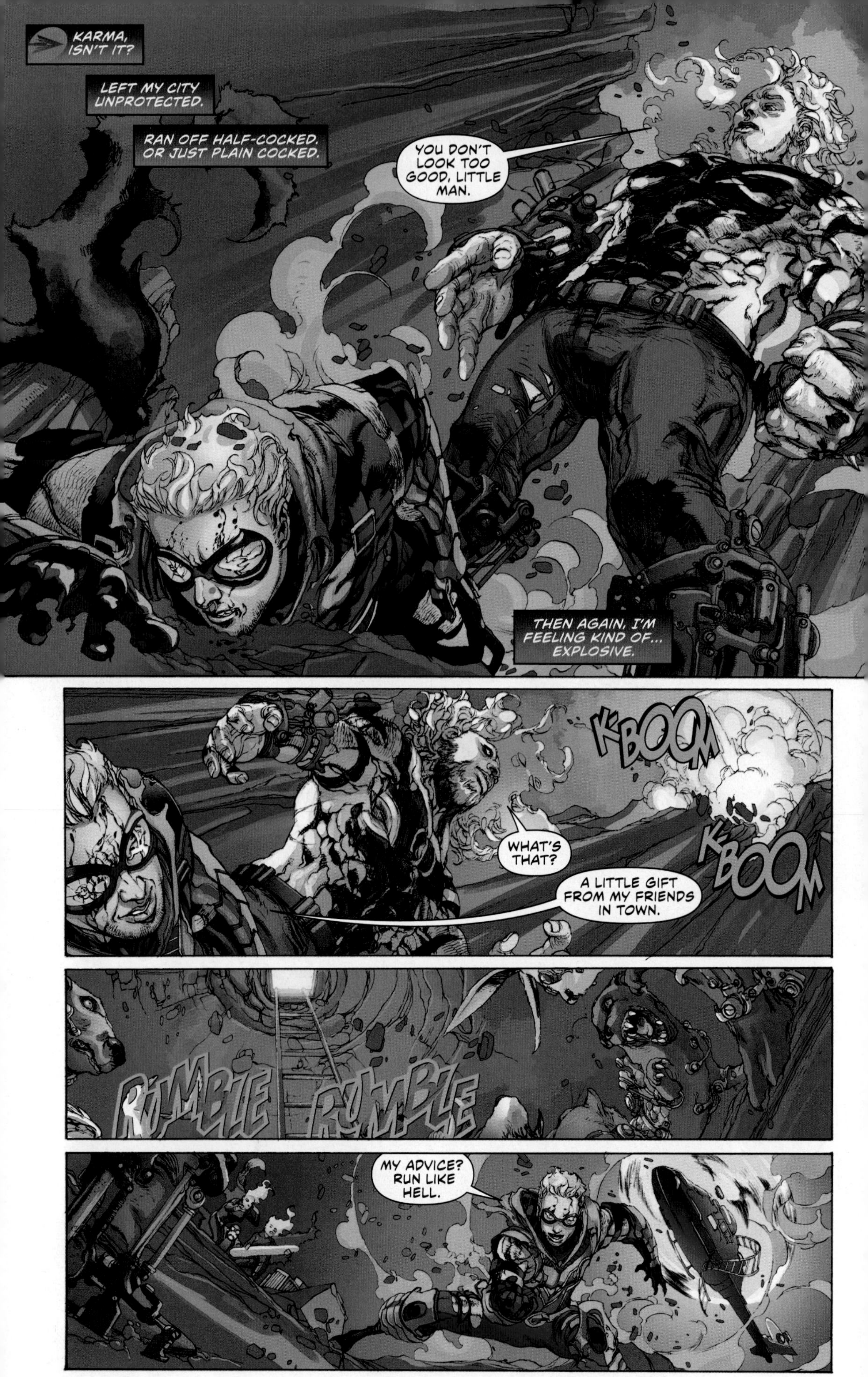
KARMA, ISN'T IT?
LEFT MY CITY UNPROTECTED.
RAN OFF HALF-COCKED. OR JUST PLAIN COCKED.
YOU DON'T LOOK TOO GOOD, LITTLE MAN.
THEN AGAIN, I'M FEELING KIND OF... EXPLOSIVE.
K'BOOM
K'BOOM
WHAT'S THAT?
A LITTLE GIFT FROM MY FRIENDS IN TOWN.
RUMBLE RUMBLE
MY ADVICE? RUN LIKE HELL.

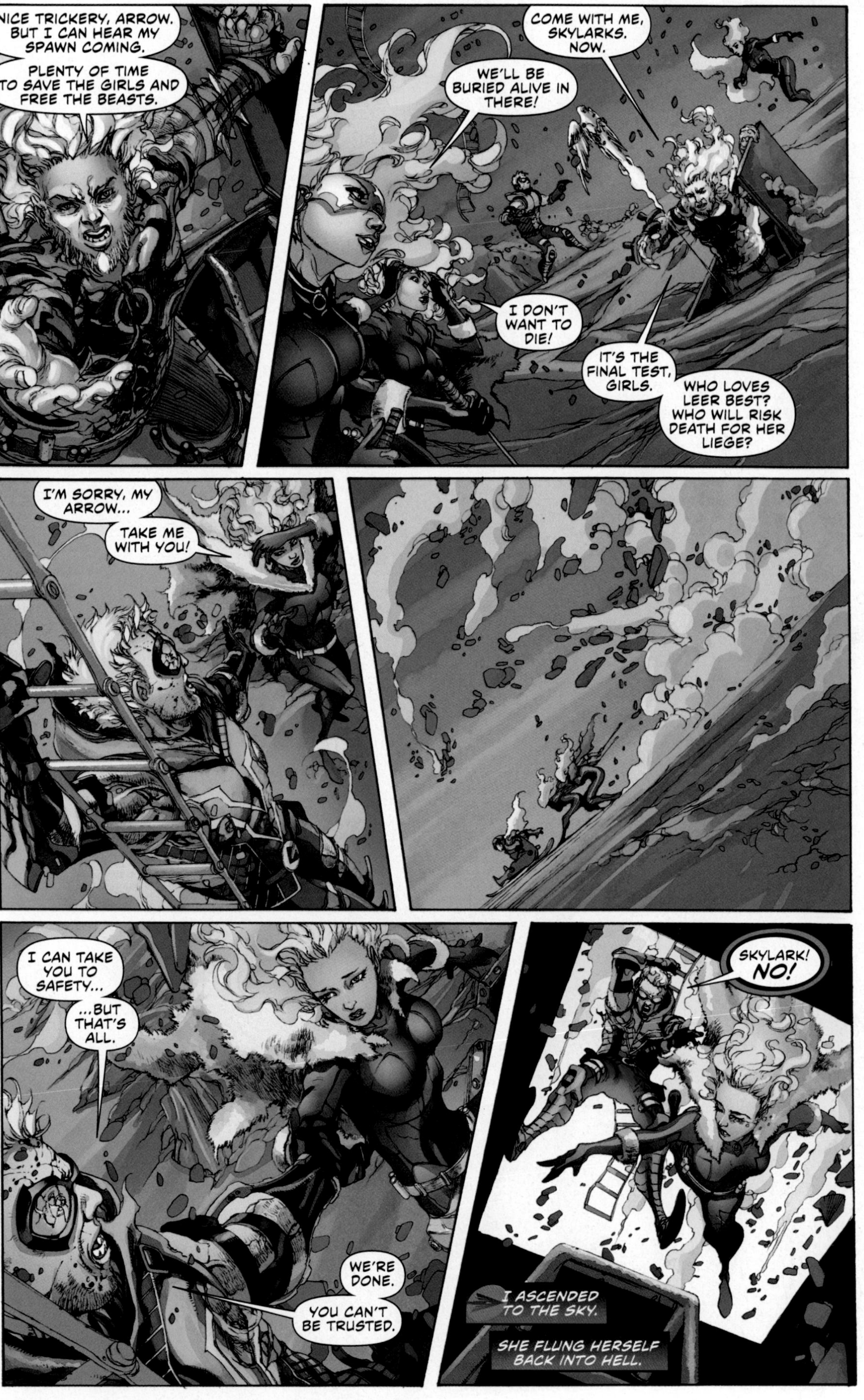
NICE TRICKERY, ARROW. BUT I CAN HEAR MY SPAWN COMING.
PLENTY OF TIME TO SAVE THE GIRLS AND FREE THE BEASTS.
COME WITH ME, SKYLARKS. NOW.
WE'LL BE BURIED ALIVE IN THERE!
I DON'T WANT TO DIE!
IT'S THE FINAL TEST, GIRLS.
WHO LOVES LEER BEST? WHO WILL RISK DEATH FOR HER LIEGE?
I'M SORRY, MY ARROW...
TAKE ME WITH YOU!
I CAN TAKE YOU TO SAFETY...
...BUT THAT'S ALL.
WE'RE DONE.
YOU CAN'T BE TRUSTED.
SKYLARK! NO!
I ASCENDED TO THE SKY.
SHE FLUNG HERSELF BACK INTO HELL.

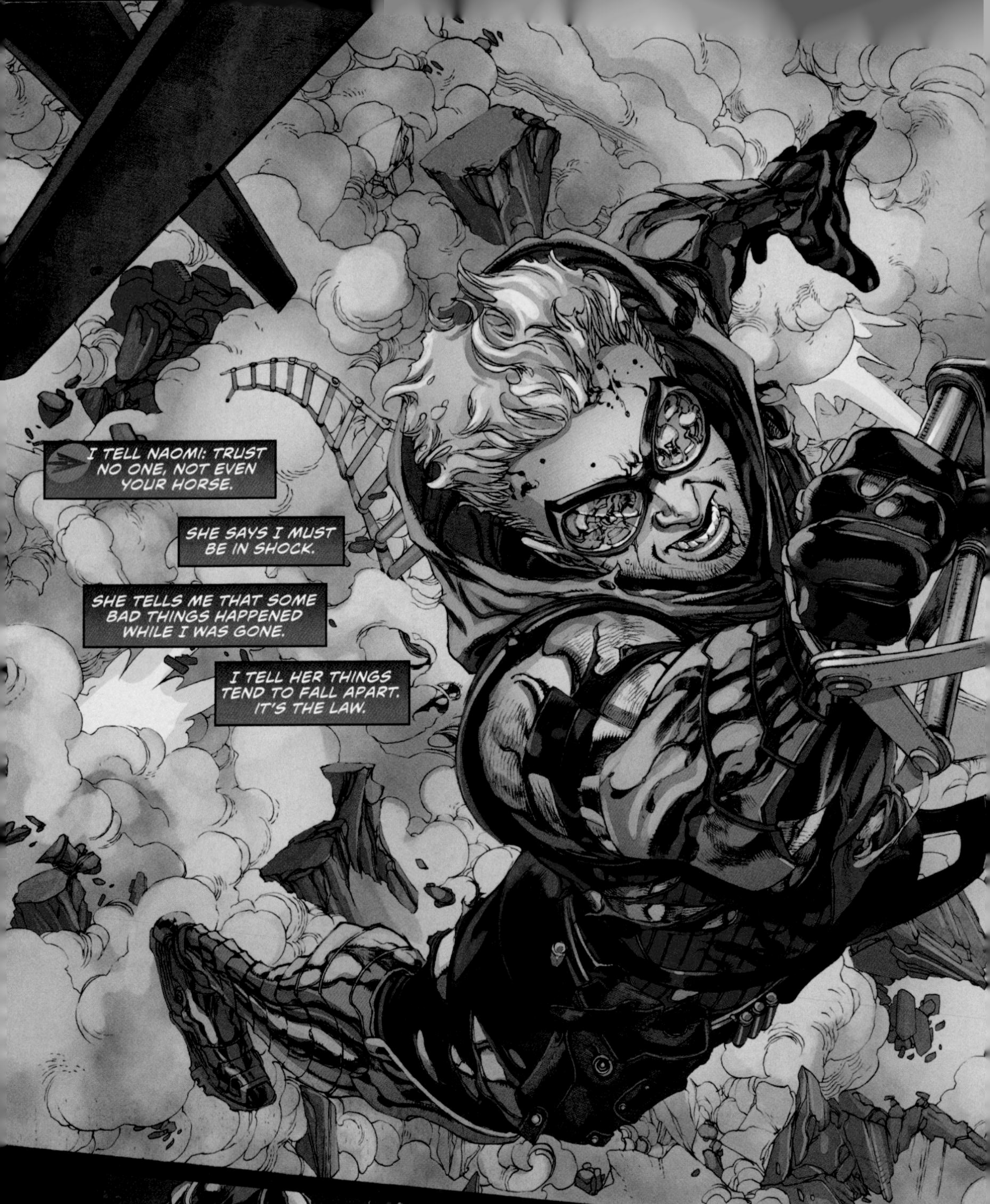
I TELL NAOMI: TRUST NO ONE, NOT EVEN YOUR HORSE.
SHE SAYS I MUST BE IN SHOCK.
SHE TELLS ME THAT SOME BAD THINGS HAPPENED WHILE I WAS GONE.
I TELL HER THINGS TEND TO FALL APART. IT'S THE LAW.

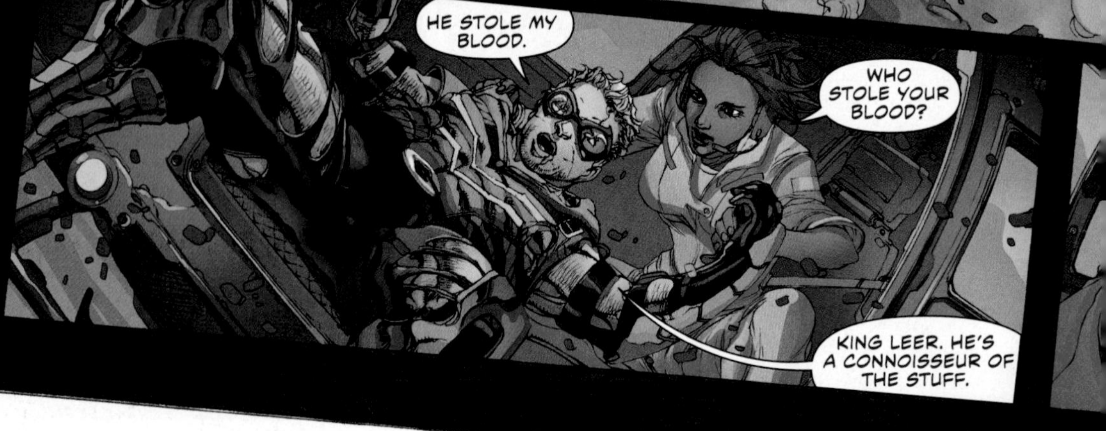
HE STOLE MY BLOOD.
WHO STOLE YOUR BLOOD?
KING LEER. HE'S A CONNOISSEUR OF THE STUFF.

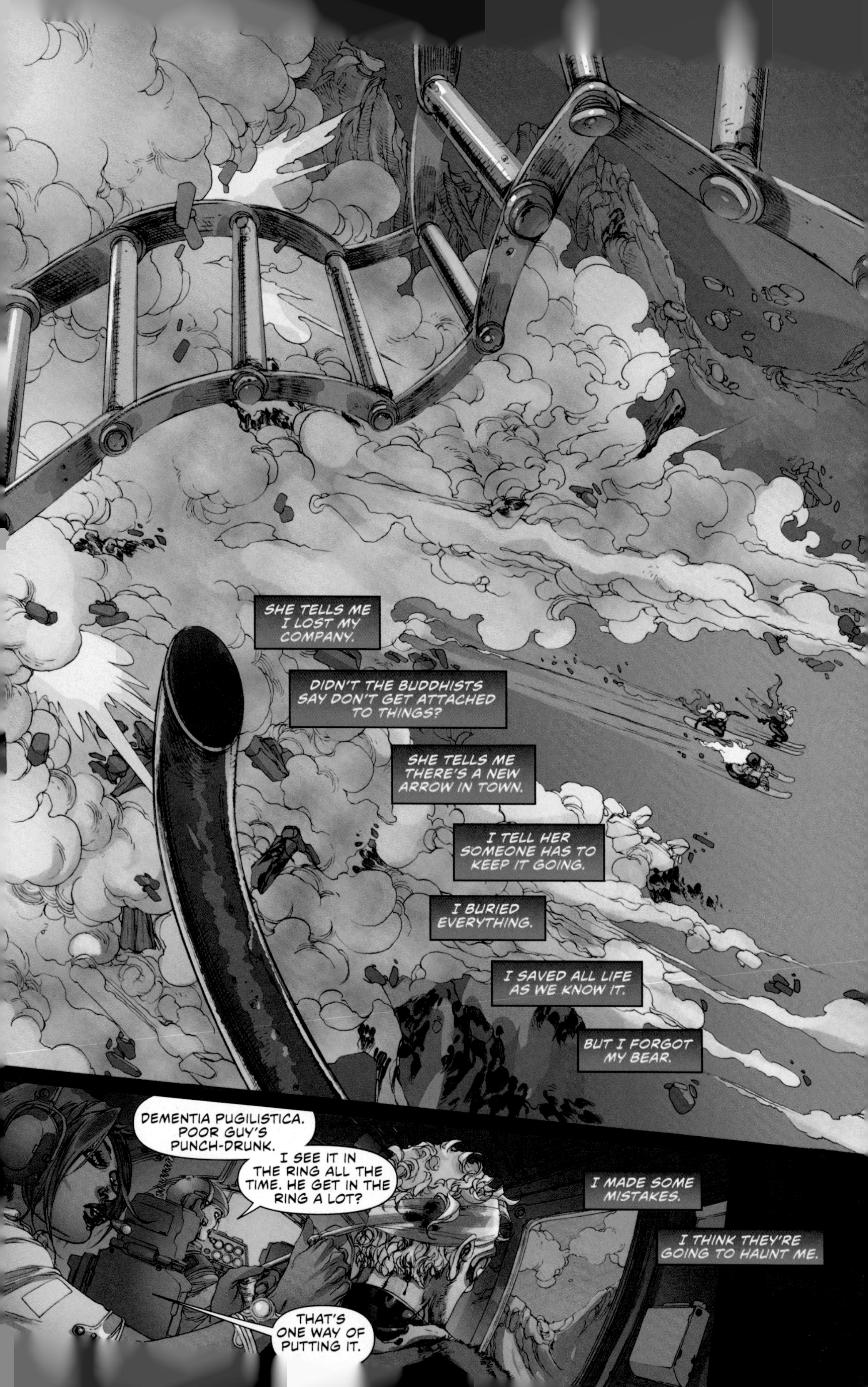
SHE TELLS ME I LOST MY COMPANY.
DIDN'T THE BUDDHISTS SAY DON'T GET ATTACHED TO THINGS?
SHE TELLS ME THERE'S A NEW ARROW IN TOWN.
I TELL HER SOMEONE HAS TO KEEP IT GOING.
I BURIED EVERYTHING.
I SAVED ALL LIFE AS WE KNOW IT.
BUT I FORGOT MY BEAR.
DEMENTIA PUGILISTICA. POOR GUY'S PUNCH-DRUNK.
I SEE IT IN THE RING ALL THE TIME. HE GET IN THE RING A LOT?
I MADE SOME MISTAKES.
I THINK THEY'RE GOING TO HAUNT ME.
THAT'S ONE WAY OF PUTTING IT.

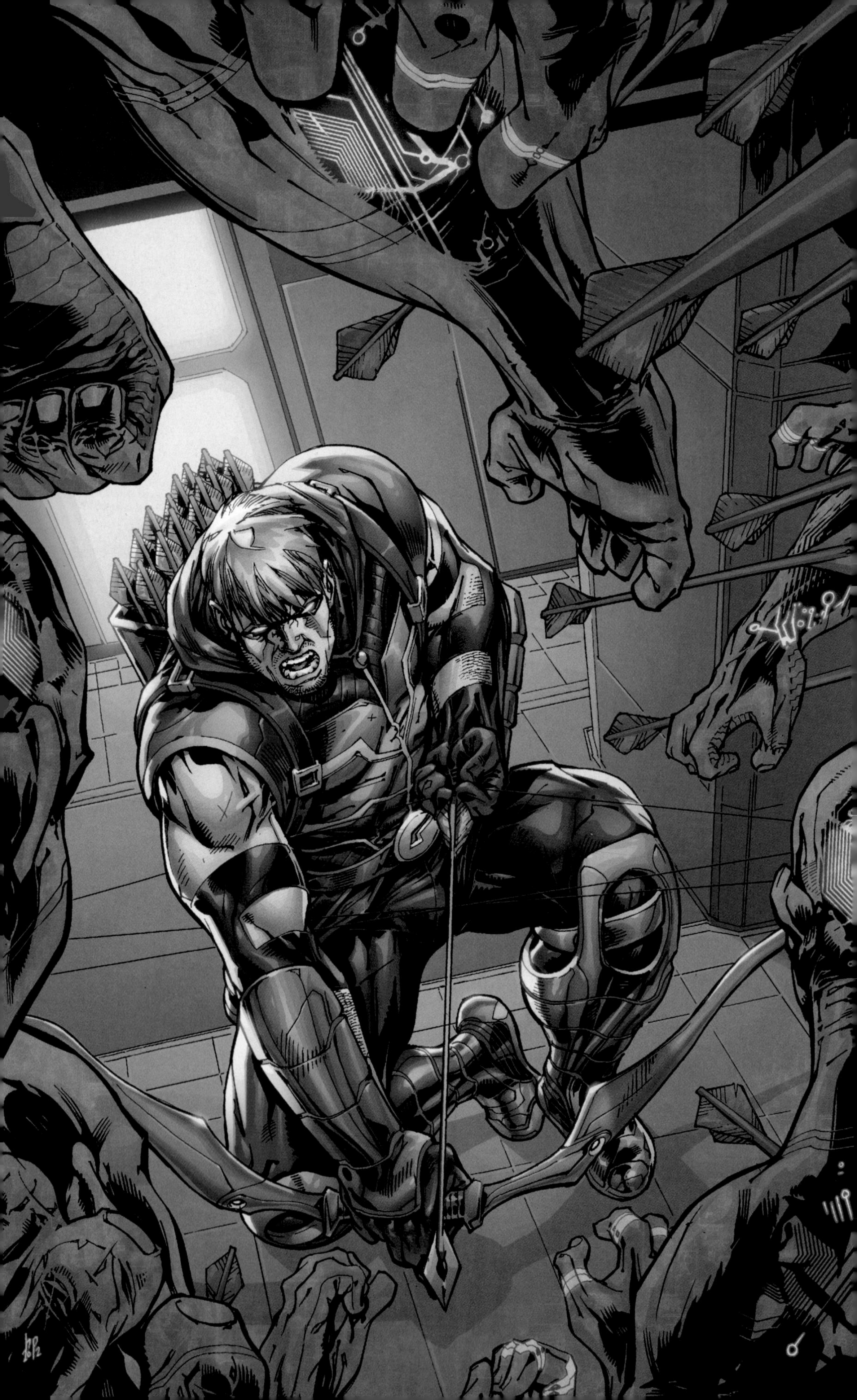

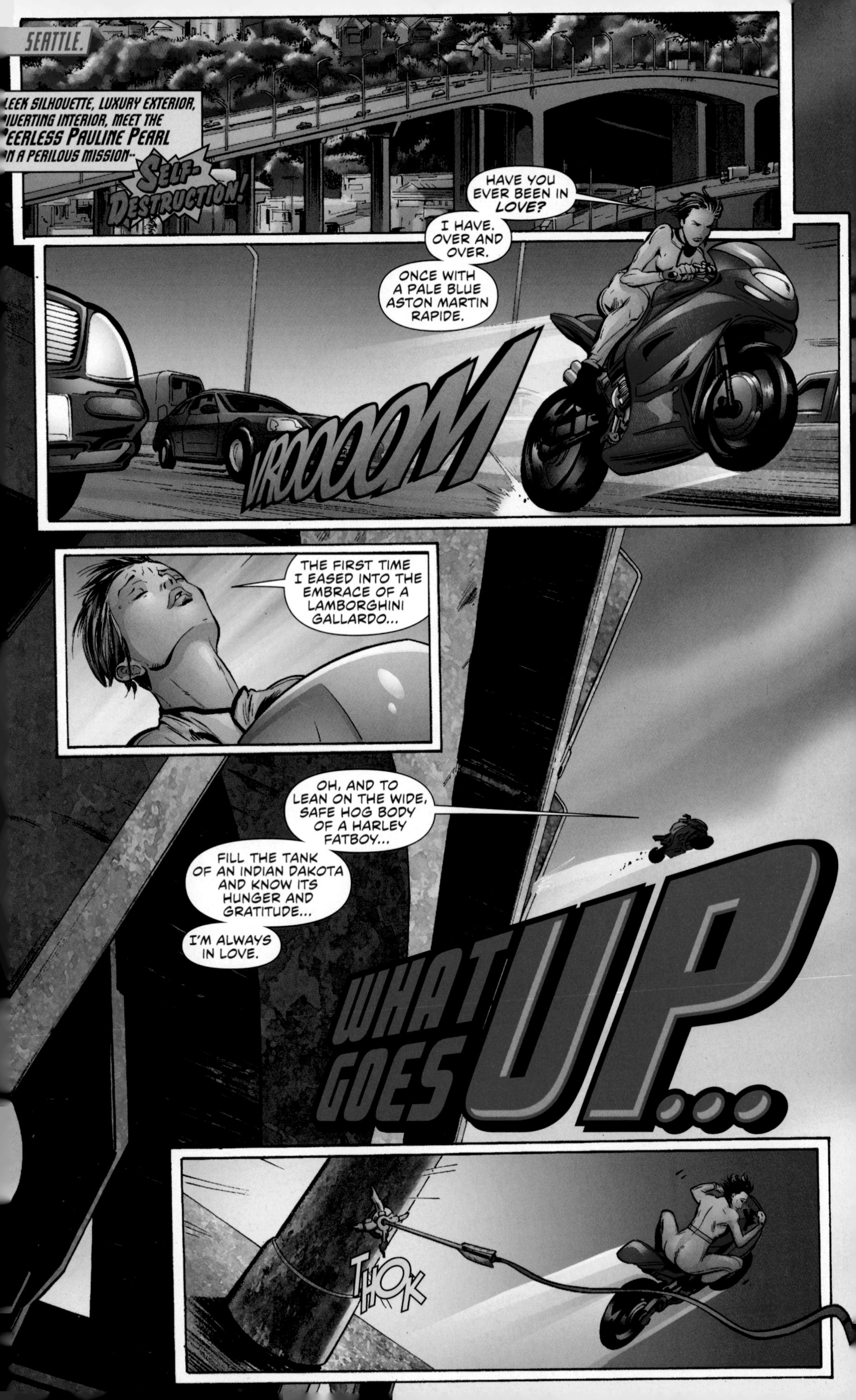

SEATTLE.
LEEK SILHOUETTE, LUXURY EXTERIOR, IVERTING INTERIOR, MEET THE EERLESS PAULINE PEARL IN A PERILOUS MISSION--
SELF-DESTRUCTION!
HAVE YOU EVER BEEN IN LOVE?
I HAVE. OVER AND OVER.
ONCE WITH A PALE BLUE ASTON MARTIN RAPIDE.
VROOOOM
THE FIRST TIME I EASED INTO THE EMBRACE OF A LAMBORGHINI GALLARDO...
OH, AND TO LEAN ON THE WIDE, SAFE HOG BODY OF A HARLEY FATBOY...
FILL THE TANK OF AN INDIAN DAKOTA AND KNOW ITS HUNGER AND GRATITUDE...
I'M ALWAYS IN LOVE.
WHAT GOES UP...
THOK

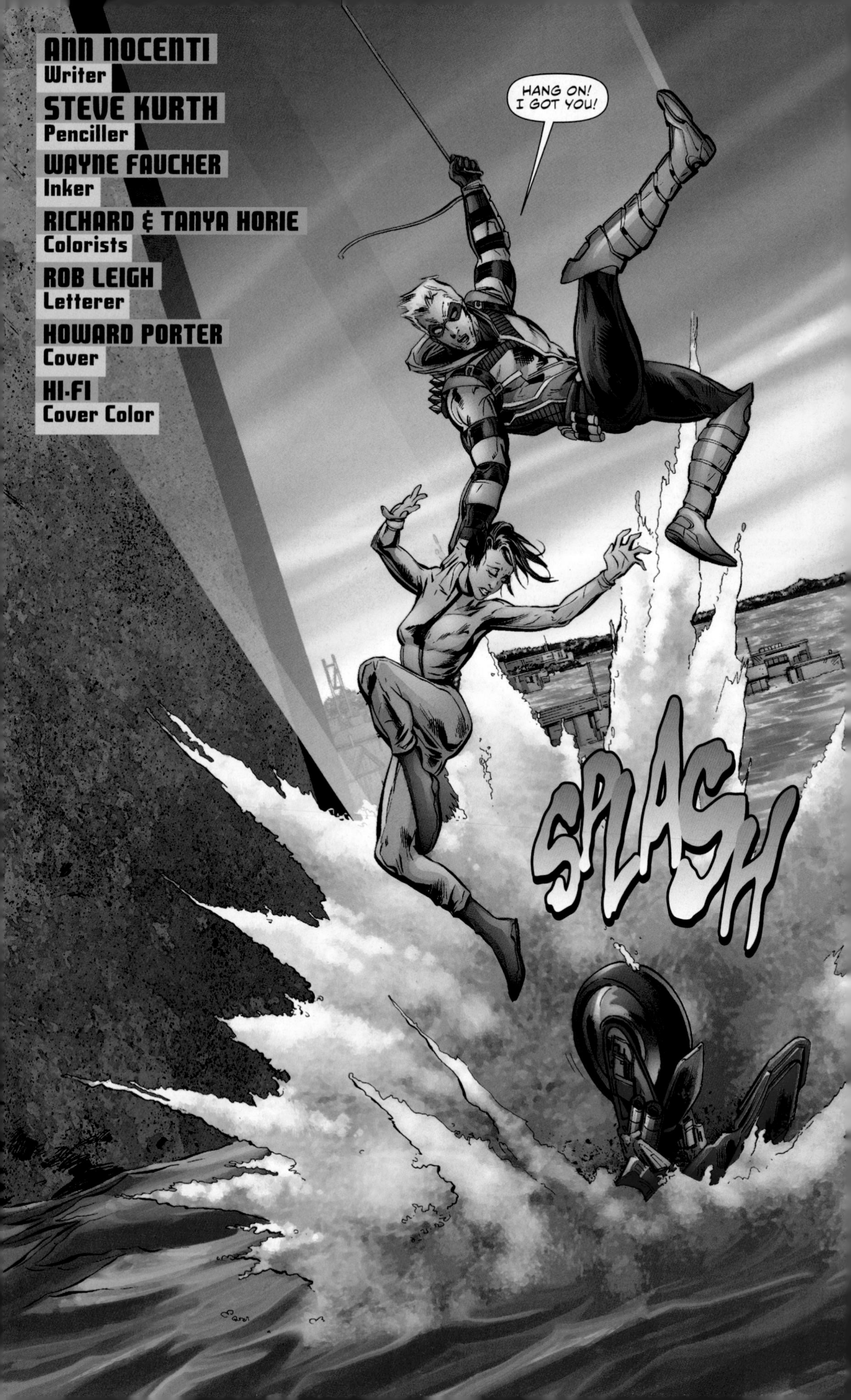
ANN NOCENTI
Writer
STEVE KURTH
Penciller
WAYNE FAUCHER
Inker
RICHARD & TANYA HORIE
Colorists
ROB LEIGH
Letterer
HOWARD PORTER
Cover
HI-FI
Cover Color
HANG ON! I GOT YOU!
SPLASH

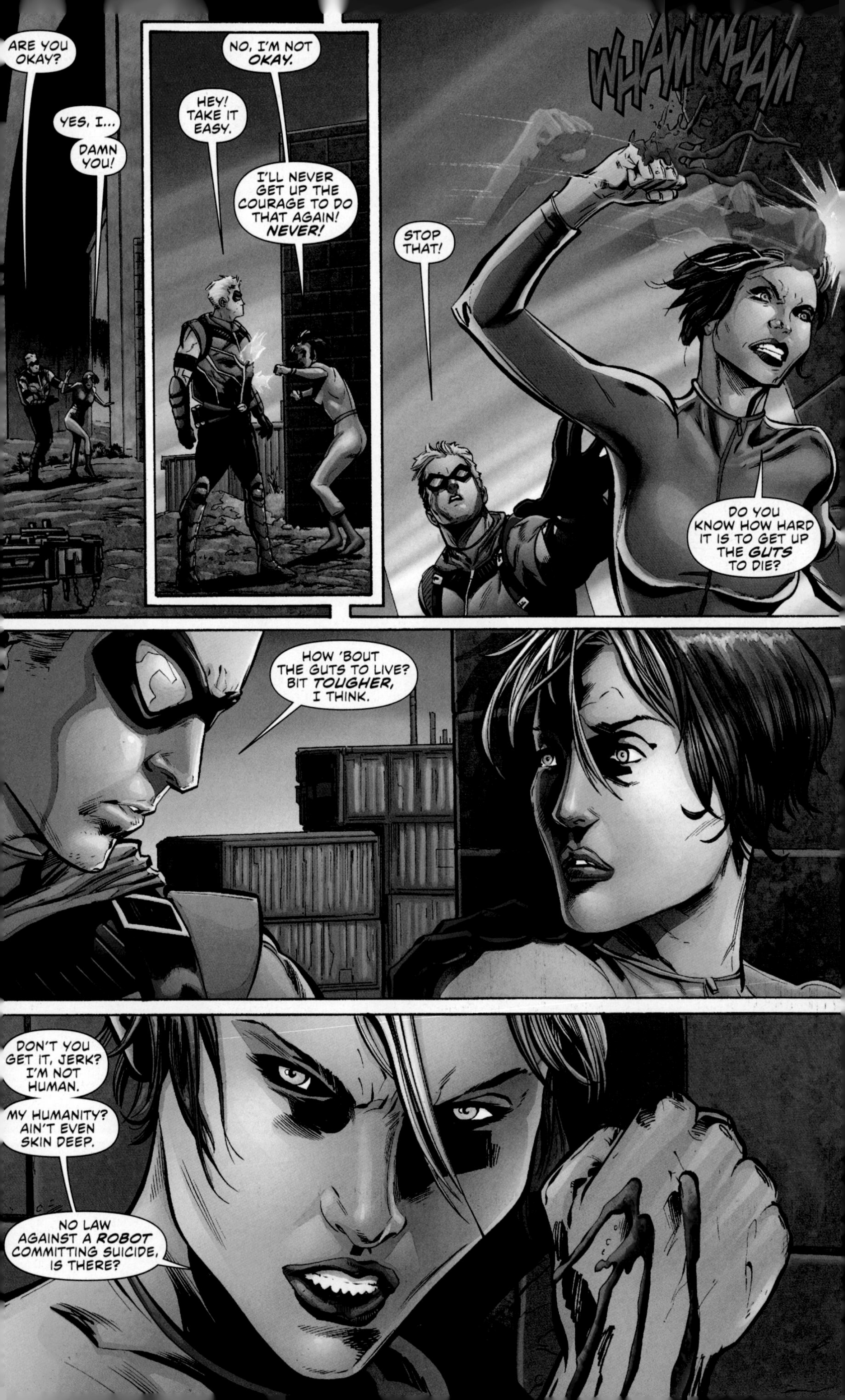
ARE YOU OKAY?
YES, I...
DAMN YOU!
NO, I'M NOT OKAY.
HEY! TAKE IT EASY.
I'LL NEVER GET UP THE COURAGE TO DO THAT AGAIN! NEVER!
WHAM WHAM
STOP THAT!
DO YOU KNOW HOW HARD IT IS TO GET UP THE GUTS TO DIE?
HOW 'BOUT THE GUTS TO LIVE? BIT TOUGHER, I THINK.
DON'T YOU GET IT, JERK? I'M NOT HUMAN.
MY HUMANITY? AIN'T EVEN SKIN DEEP.
NO LAW AGAINST A ROBOT COMMITTING SUICIDE, IS THERE?

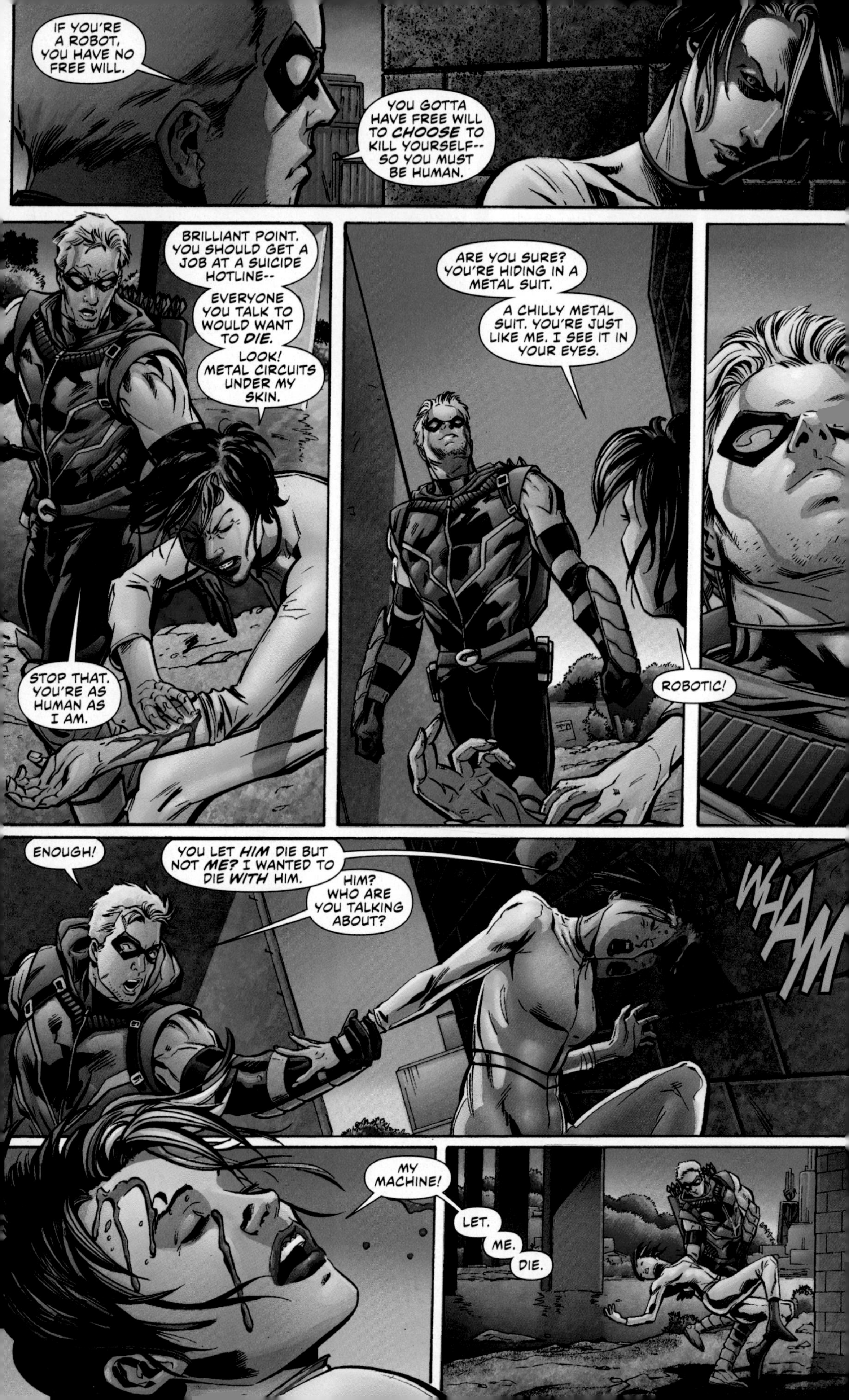
IF YOU'RE A ROBOT, YOU HAVE NO FREE WILL.
YOU GOTTA HAVE FREE WILL TO CHOOSE TO KILL YOURSELF-- SO YOU MUST BE HUMAN.
BRILLIANT POINT. YOU SHOULD GET A JOB AT A SUICIDE HOTLINE--
EVERYONE YOU TALK TO WOULD WANT TO DIE.
LOOK! METAL CIRCUITS UNDER MY SKIN.
STOP THAT. YOU'RE AS HUMAN AS I AM.
ARE YOU SURE? YOU'RE HIDING IN A METAL SUIT.
A CHILLY METAL SUIT. YOU'RE JUST LIKE ME. I SEE IT IN YOUR EYES.
ROBOTIC!
ENOUGH!
YOU LET HIM DIE BUT NOT ME? I WANTED TO DIE WITH HIM.
HIM? WHO ARE YOU TALKING ABOUT?
WHAM
MY MACHINE!
LET.
ME.
DIE.

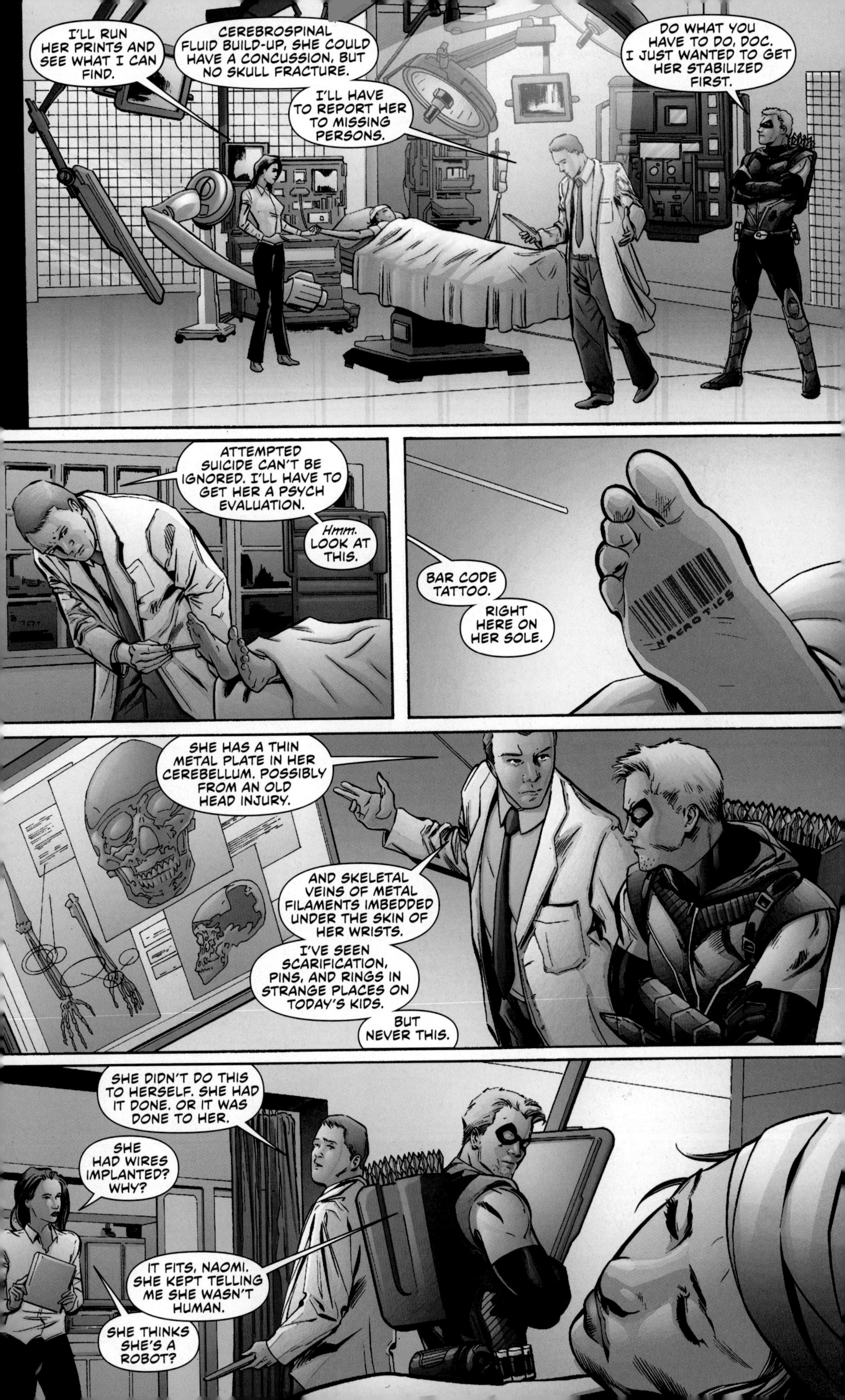
I'LL RUN HER PRINTS AND SEE WHAT I CAN FIND.
CEREBROSPINAL FLUID BUILD-UP, SHE COULD HAVE A CONCUSSION, BUT NO SKULL FRACTURE.
I'LL HAVE TO REPORT HER TO MISSING PERSONS.
DO WHAT YOU HAVE TO DO, DOC. I JUST WANTED TO GET HER STABILIZED FIRST.
ATTEMPTED SUICIDE CAN'T BE IGNORED. I'LL HAVE TO GET HER A PSYCH EVALUATION.
Hmm. LOOK AT THIS.
BAR CODE TATTOO.
RIGHT HERE ON HER SOLE.
NACROTICS
SHE HAS A THIN METAL PLATE IN HER CEREBELLUM. POSSIBLY FROM AN OLD HEAD INJURY.
AND SKELETAL VEINS OF METAL FILAMENTS IMBEDDED UNDER THE SKIN OF HER WRISTS.
I'VE SEEN SCARIFICATION, PINS, AND RINGS IN STRANGE PLACES ON TODAY'S KIDS.
BUT NEVER THIS.
SHE DIDN'T DO THIS TO HERSELF. SHE HAD IT DONE. OR IT WAS DONE TO HER.
SHE HAD WIRES IMPLANTED? WHY?
IT FITS, NAOMI. SHE KEPT TELLING ME SHE WASN'T HUMAN.
SHE THINKS SHE'S A ROBOT?

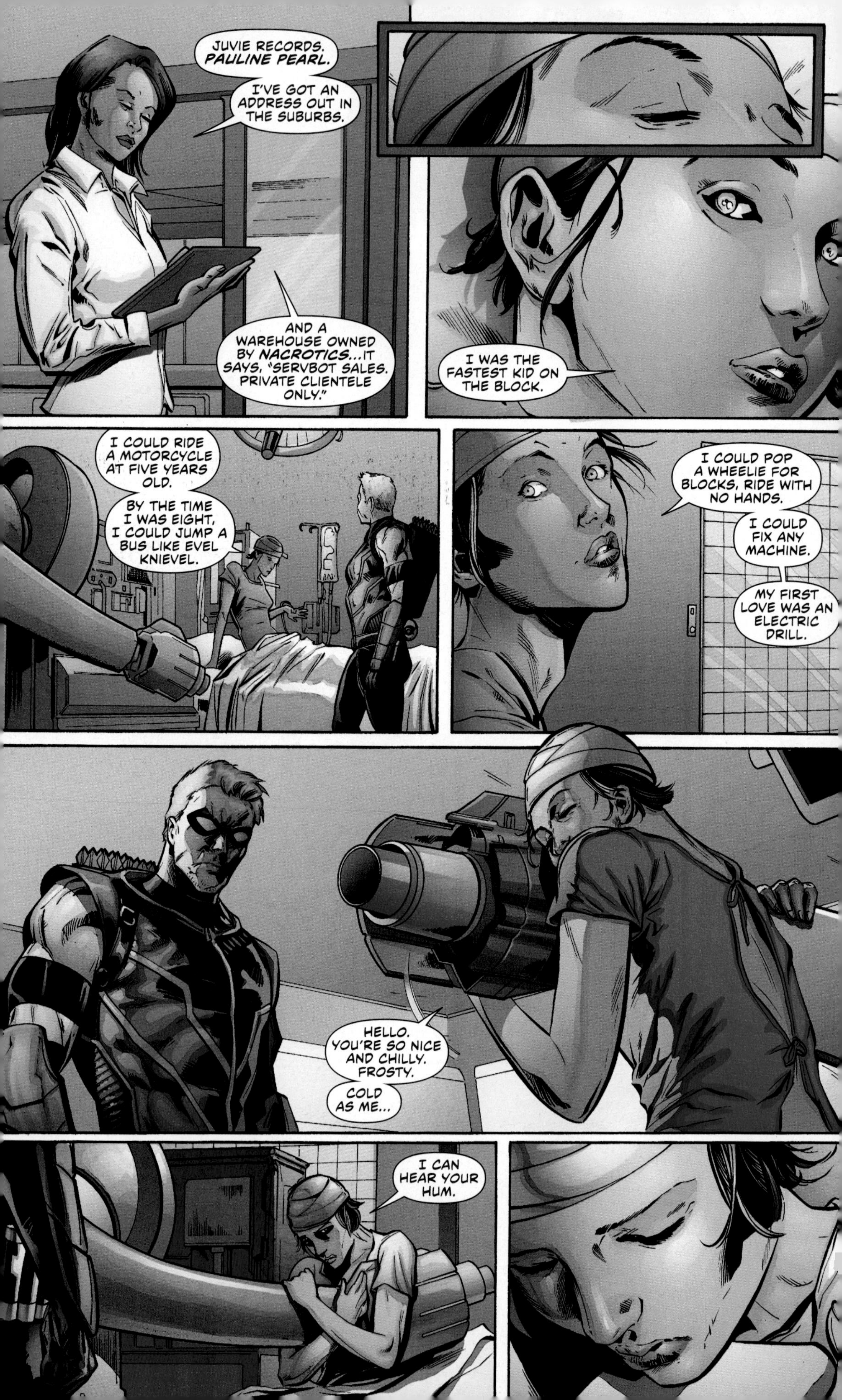
JUVIE RECORDS. PAULINE PEARL.
I'VE GOT AN ADDRESS OUT IN THE SUBURBS.
AND A WAREHOUSE OWNED BY NACROTICS...IT SAYS, "SERVBOT SALES. PRIVATE CLIENTELE ONLY."
I WAS THE FASTEST KID ON THE BLOCK.
I COULD RIDE A MOTORCYCLE AT FIVE YEARS OLD.
BY THE TIME I WAS EIGHT, I COULD JUMP A BUS LIKE EVEL KNIEVEL.
I COULD POP A WHEELIE FOR BLOCKS, RIDE WITH NO HANDS.
I COULD FIX ANY MACHINE.
MY FIRST LOVE WAS AN ELECTRIC DRILL.
HELLO. YOU'RE SO NICE AND CHILLY. FROSTY.
COLD AS ME...
I CAN HEAR YOUR HUM.

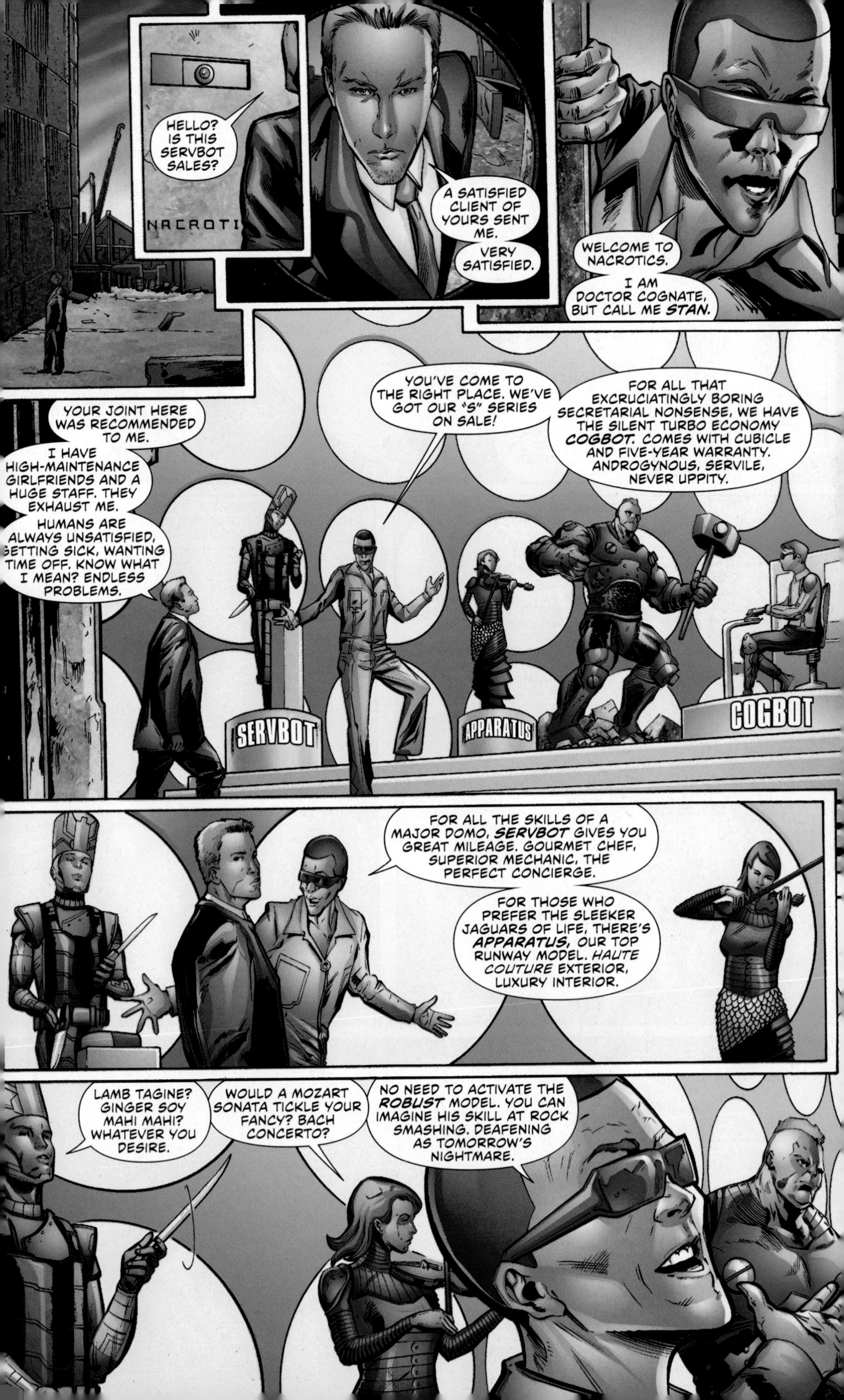

HELLO? IS THIS SERVBOT SALES?
NACROTI
A SATISFIED CLIENT OF YOURS SENT ME.
VERY SATISFIED.
WELCOME TO NACROTICS.
I AM DOCTOR COGNATE, BUT CALL ME STAN.
YOUR JOINT HERE WAS RECOMMENDED TO ME.
I HAVE HIGH-MAINTENANCE GIRLFRIENDS AND A HUGE STAFF. THEY EXHAUST ME.
HUMANS ARE ALWAYS UNSATISFIED, GETTING SICK, WANTING TIME OFF. KNOW WHAT I MEAN? ENDLESS PROBLEMS.
YOU'VE COME TO THE RIGHT PLACE. WE'VE GOT OUR "S" SERIES ON SALE!
FOR ALL THAT EXCRUCIATINGLY BORING SECRETARIAL NONSENSE, WE HAVE THE SILENT TURBO ECONOMY COGBOT. COMES WITH CUBICLE AND FIVE-YEAR WARRANTY. ANDROGYNOUS, SERVILE, NEVER UPPITY.
SERVBOT
APPARATUS
COGBOT
FOR ALL THE SKILLS OF A MAJOR DOMO, SERVBOT GIVES YOU GREAT MILEAGE. GOURMET CHEF, SUPERIOR MECHANIC, THE PERFECT CONCIERGE.
FOR THOSE WHO PREFER THE SLEEKER JAGUARS OF LIFE, THERE'S APPARATUS, OUR TOP RUNWAY MODEL. HAUTE COUTURE EXTERIOR, LUXURY INTERIOR.
LAMB TAGINE? GINGER SOY MAHI MAHI? WHATEVER YOU DESIRE.
WOULD A MOZART SONATA TICKLE YOUR FANCY? BACH CONCERTO?
NO NEED TO ACTIVATE THE ROBUST MODEL. YOU CAN IMAGINE HIS SKILL AT ROCK SMASHING. DEAFENING AS TOMORROW'S NIGHTMARE.

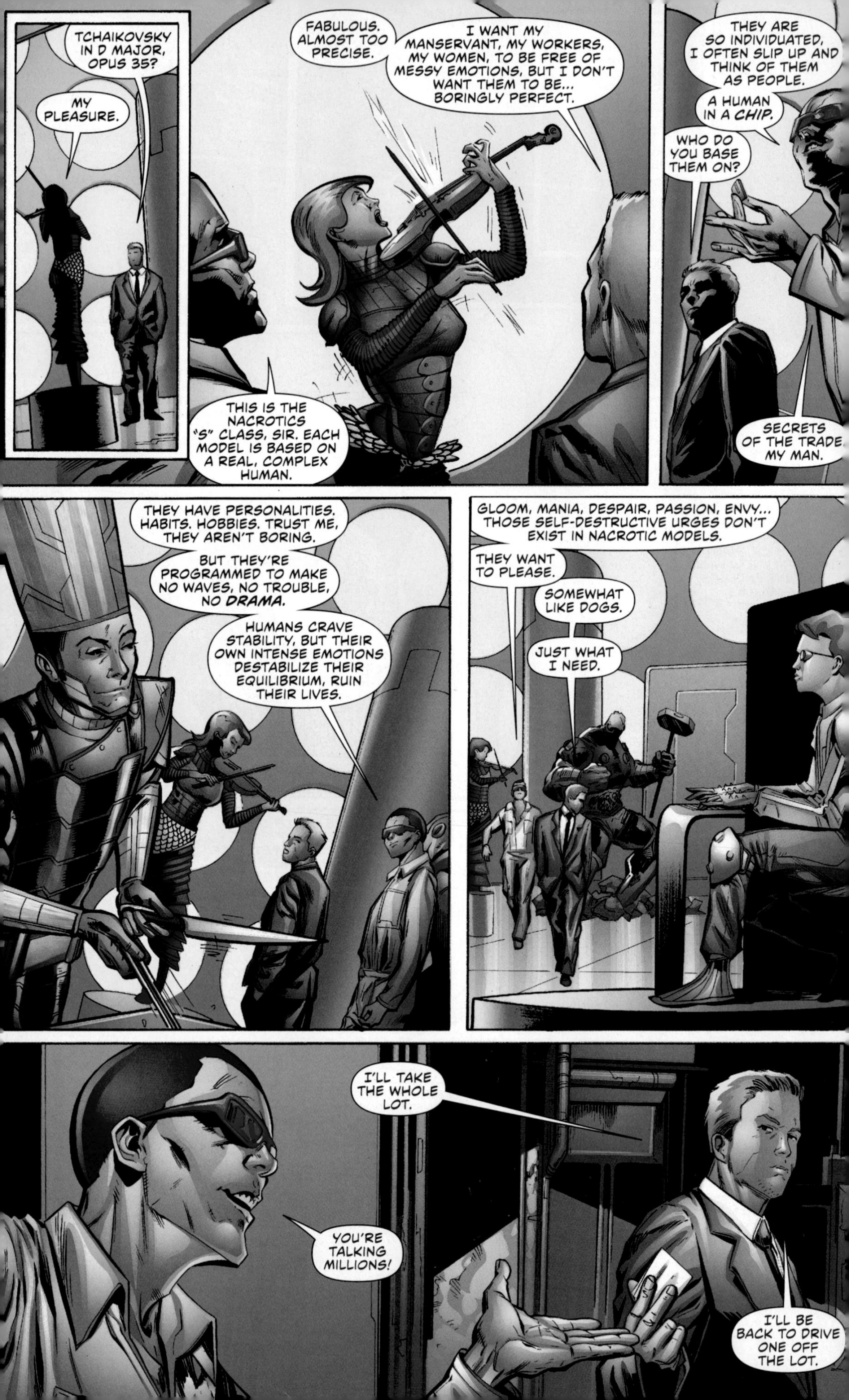
TCHAIKOVSKY IN D MAJOR, OPUS 35?
MY PLEASURE.
FABULOUS. ALMOST TOO PRECISE.
I WANT MY MANSERVANT, MY WORKERS, MY WOMEN, TO BE FREE OF MESSY EMOTIONS, BUT I DON'T WANT THEM TO BE... BORINGLY PERFECT.
THIS IS THE NACROTICS "S" CLASS, SIR. EACH MODEL IS BASED ON A REAL, COMPLEX HUMAN.
THEY ARE SO INDIVIDUATED, I OFTEN SLIP UP AND THINK OF THEM AS PEOPLE.
A HUMAN IN A CHIP.
WHO DO YOU BASE THEM ON?
SECRETS OF THE TRADE MY MAN.
THEY HAVE PERSONALITIES. HABITS. HOBBIES. TRUST ME, THEY AREN'T BORING.
BUT THEY'RE PROGRAMMED TO MAKE NO WAVES, NO TROUBLE, NO DRAMA.
HUMANS CRAVE STABILITY, BUT THEIR OWN INTENSE EMOTIONS DESTABILIZE THEIR EQUILIBRIUM, RUIN THEIR LIVES.
GLOOM, MANIA, DESPAIR, PASSION, ENVY... THOSE SELF-DESTRUCTIVE URGES DON'T EXIST IN NACROTIC MODELS.
THEY WANT TO PLEASE.
SOMEWHAT LIKE DOGS.
JUST WHAT I NEED.
I'LL TAKE THE WHOLE LOT.
YOU'RE TALKING MILLIONS!
I'LL BE BACK TO DRIVE ONE OFF THE LOT.

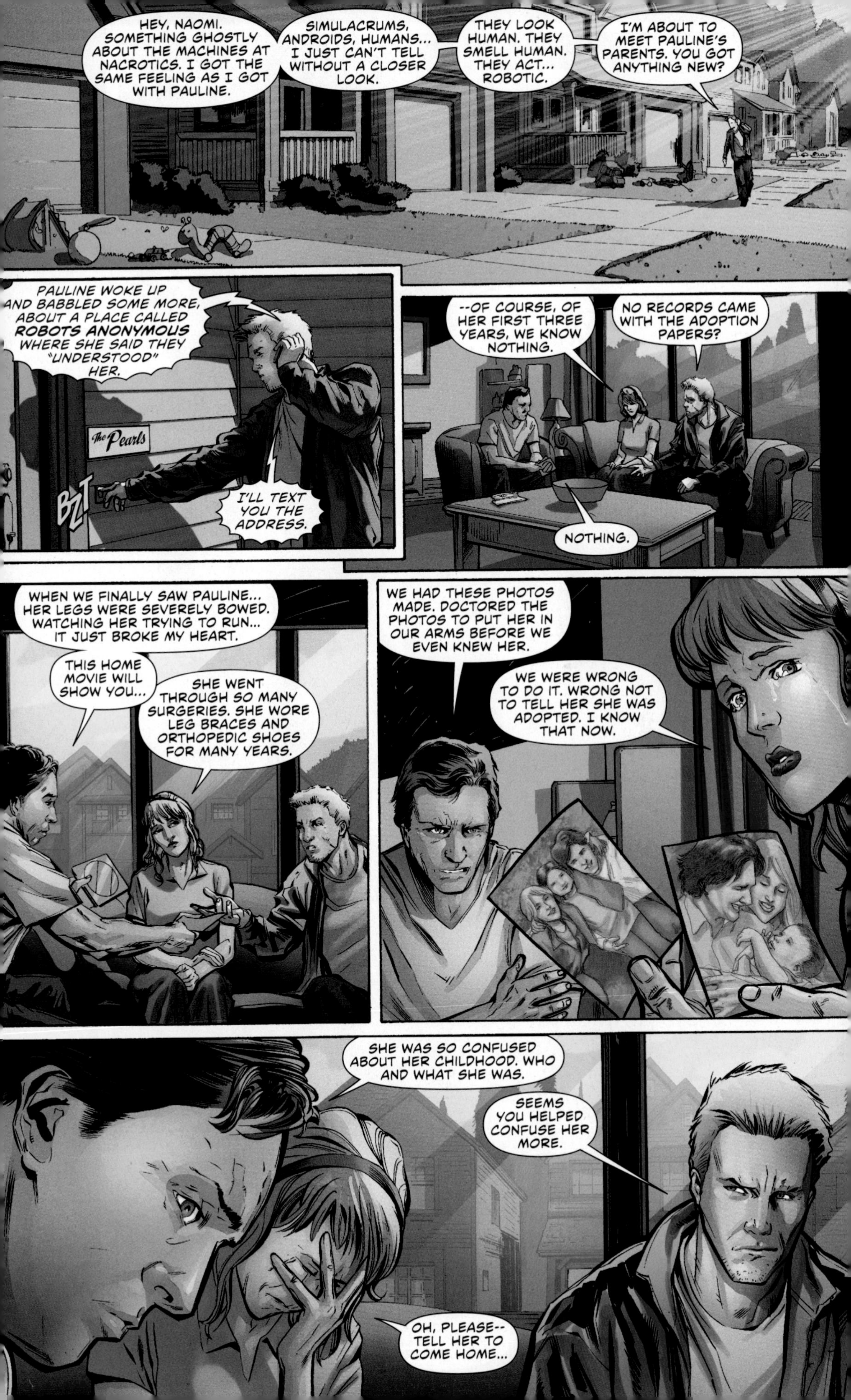
HEY, NAOMI. SOMETHING GHOSTLY ABOUT THE MACHINES AT NACROTICS. I GOT THE SAME FEELING AS I GOT WITH PAULINE.
SIMULACRUMS, ANDROIDS, HUMANS... I JUST CAN'T TELL WITHOUT A CLOSER LOOK.
THEY LOOK HUMAN. THEY SMELL HUMAN. THEY ACT... ROBOTIC.
I'M ABOUT TO MEET PAULINE'S PARENTS. YOU GOT ANYTHING NEW?
PAULINE WOKE UP AND BABBLED SOME MORE, ABOUT A PLACE CALLED ROBOTS ANONYMOUS WHERE SHE SAID THEY "UNDERSTOOD" HER.
The Pearls
BZZT
I'LL TEXT YOU THE ADDRESS.
--OF COURSE, OF HER FIRST THREE YEARS, WE KNOW NOTHING.
NO RECORDS CAME WITH THE ADOPTION PAPERS?
NOTHING.
WHEN WE FINALLY SAW PAULINE... HER LEGS WERE SEVERELY BOWED. WATCHING HER TRYING TO RUN... IT JUST BROKE MY HEART.
THIS HOME MOVIE WILL SHOW YOU...
SHE WENT THROUGH SO MANY SURGERIES. SHE WORE LEG BRACES AND ORTHOPEDIC SHOES FOR MANY YEARS.
WE HAD THESE PHOTOS MADE. DOCTORED THE PHOTOS TO PUT HER IN OUR ARMS BEFORE WE EVEN KNEW HER.
WE WERE WRONG TO DO IT. WRONG NOT TO TELL HER SHE WAS ADOPTED. I KNOW THAT NOW.
SHE WAS SO CONFUSED ABOUT HER CHILDHOOD. WHO AND WHAT SHE WAS.
SEEMS YOU HELPED CONFUSE HER MORE.
OH, PLEASE-- TELL HER TO COME HOME...

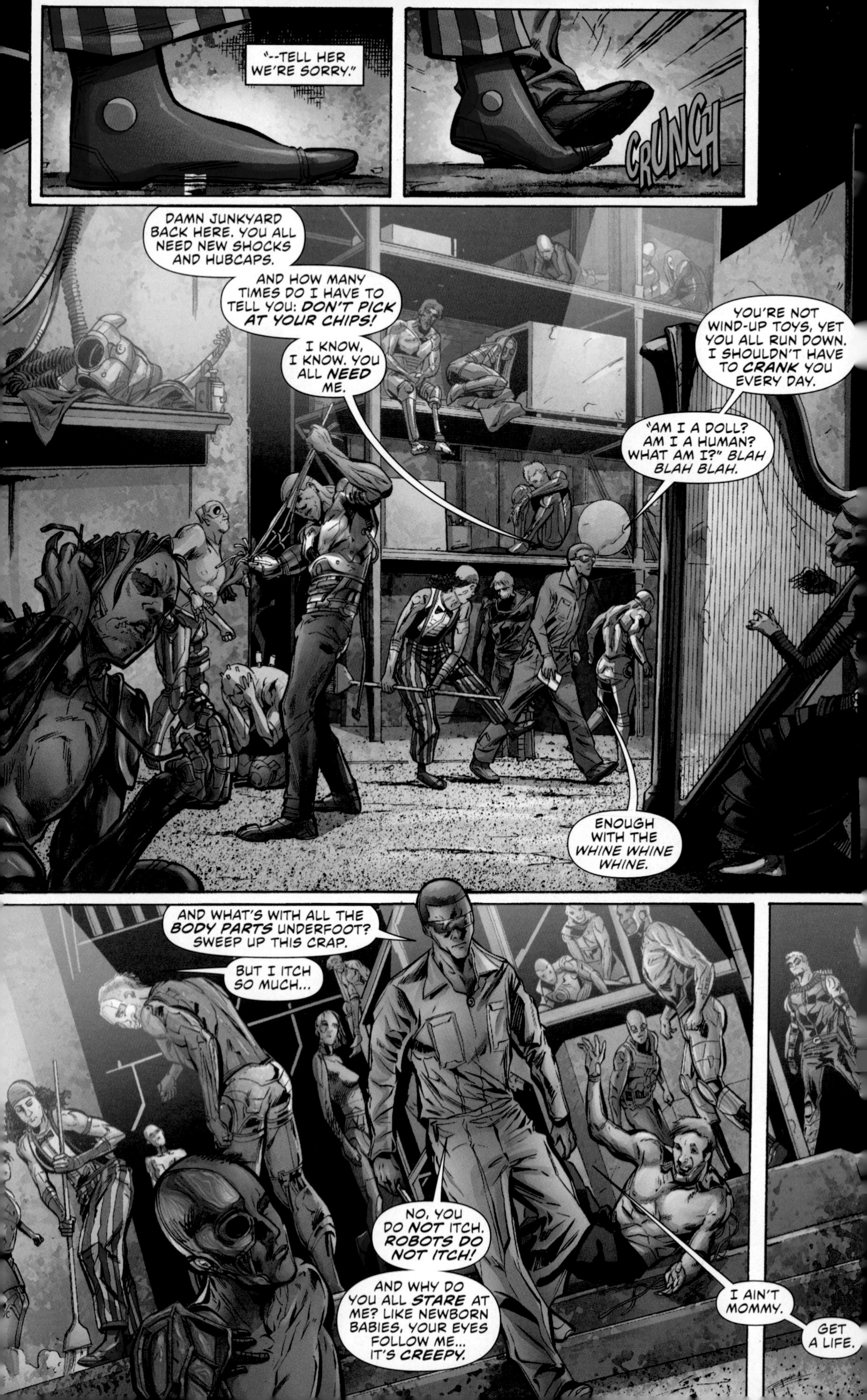
"--TELL HER WE'RE SORRY."
CRUNCH
DAMN JUNKYARD BACK HERE. YOU ALL NEED NEW SHOCKS AND HUBCAPS.
AND HOW MANY TIMES DO I HAVE TO TELL YOU: DON'T PICK AT YOUR CHIPS!
I KNOW, I KNOW. YOU ALL NEED ME.
YOU'RE NOT WIND-UP TOYS, YET YOU ALL RUN DOWN. I SHOULDN'T HAVE TO CRANK YOU EVERY DAY.
"AM I A DOLL? AM I A HUMAN? WHAT AM I?" BLAH BLAH BLAH.
ENOUGH WITH THE WHINE WHINE WHINE.
AND WHAT'S WITH ALL THE BODY PARTS UNDERFOOT? SWEEP UP THIS CRAP.
BUT I ITCH SO MUCH...
NO, YOU DO NOT ITCH. ROBOTS DO NOT ITCH!
AND WHY DO YOU ALL STARE AT ME? LIKE NEWBORN BABIES, YOUR EYES FOLLOW ME... IT'S CREEPY.
I AIN'T MOMMY.
GET A LIFE.

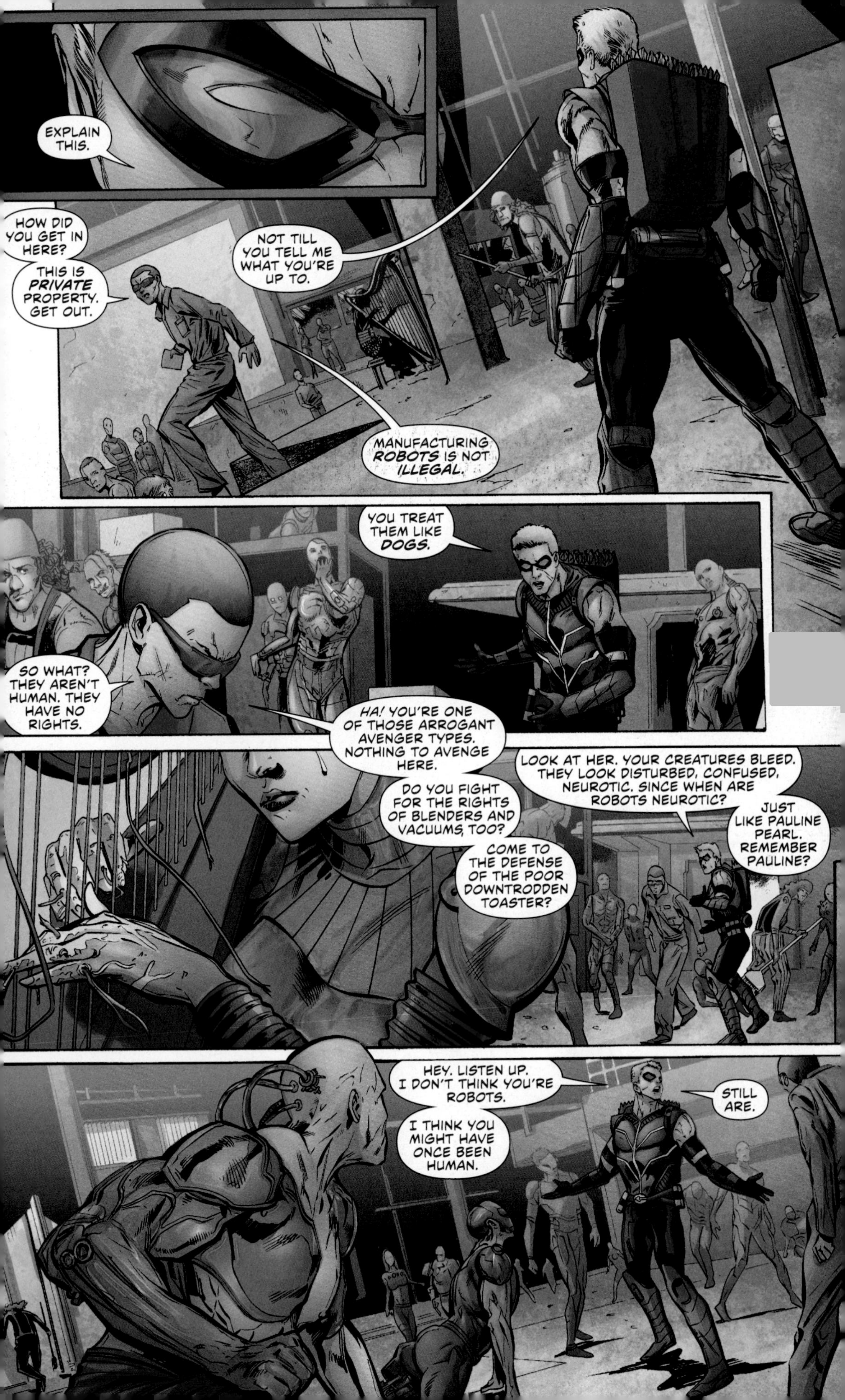
EXPLAIN THIS.
HOW DID YOU GET IN HERE?
THIS IS *PRIVATE* PROPERTY. GET OUT.
NOT TILL YOU TELL ME WHAT YOU'RE UP TO.
MANUFACTURING *ROBOTS* IS NOT *ILLEGAL.*
YOU TREAT THEM LIKE *DOGS.*
SO WHAT? THEY AREN'T HUMAN. THEY HAVE NO RIGHTS.
HA! YOU'RE ONE OF THOSE ARROGANT AVENGER TYPES. NOTHING TO AVENGE HERE.
DO YOU FIGHT FOR THE RIGHTS OF BLENDERS AND VACUUMS, TOO?
COME TO THE DEFENSE OF THE POOR DOWNTRODDEN TOASTER?
LOOK AT HER. YOUR CREATURES BLEED. THEY LOOK DISTURBED, CONFUSED, NEUROTIC. SINCE WHEN ARE ROBOTS NEUROTIC?
JUST LIKE PAULINE PEARL. REMEMBER PAULINE?
HEY. LISTEN UP. I DON'T THINK YOU'RE ROBOTS.
I THINK YOU MIGHT HAVE ONCE BEEN HUMAN.
STILL ARE.

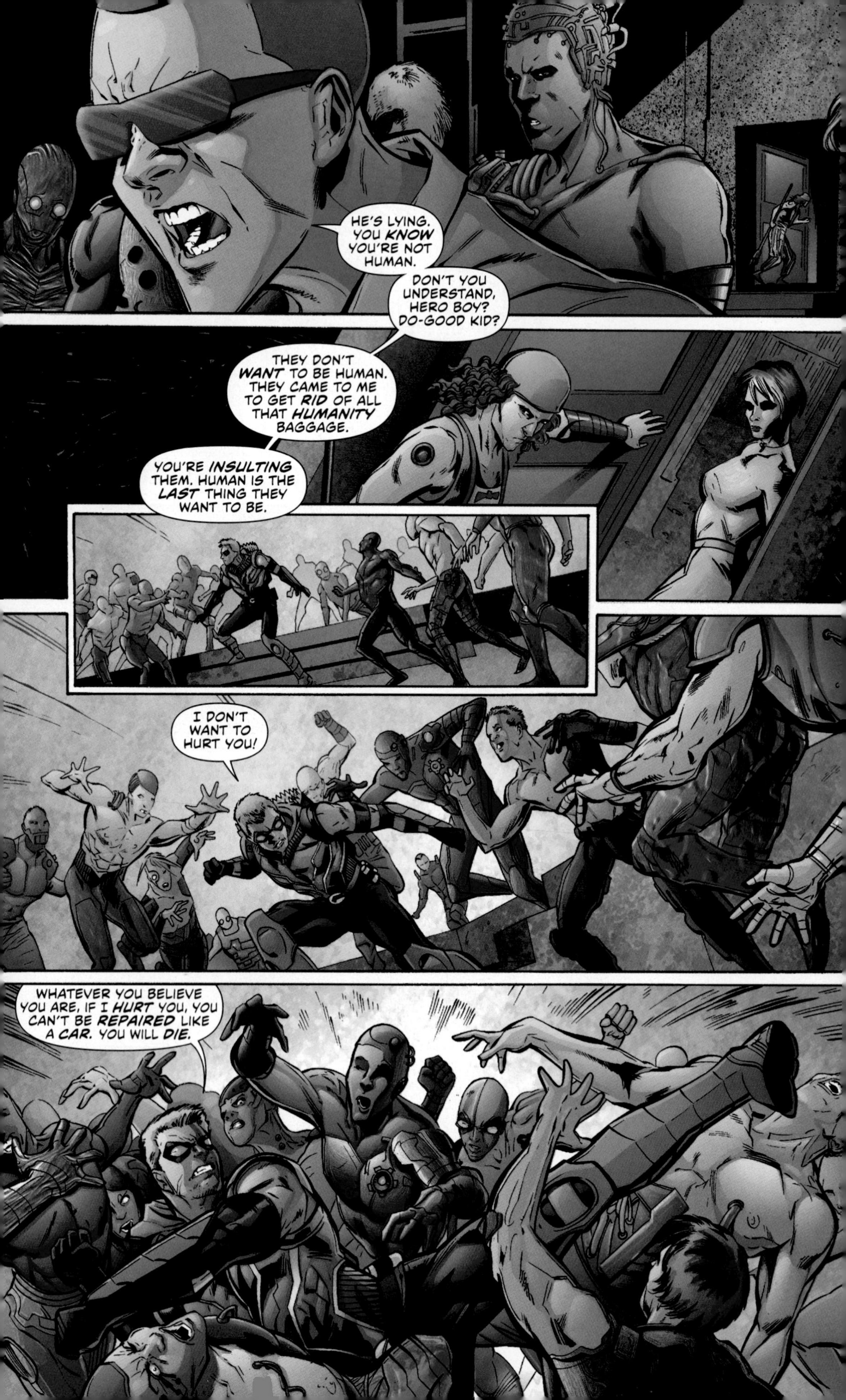
HE'S LYING. YOU KNOW YOU'RE NOT HUMAN.
DON'T YOU UNDERSTAND, HERO BOY? DO-GOOD KID?
THEY DON'T WANT TO BE HUMAN. THEY CAME TO ME TO GET RID OF ALL THAT HUMANITY BAGGAGE.
YOU'RE INSULTING THEM. HUMAN IS THE LAST THING THEY WANT TO BE.
I DON'T WANT TO HURT YOU!
WHATEVER YOU BELIEVE YOU ARE, IF I HURT YOU, YOU CAN'T BE REPAIRED LIKE A CAR. YOU WILL DIE.

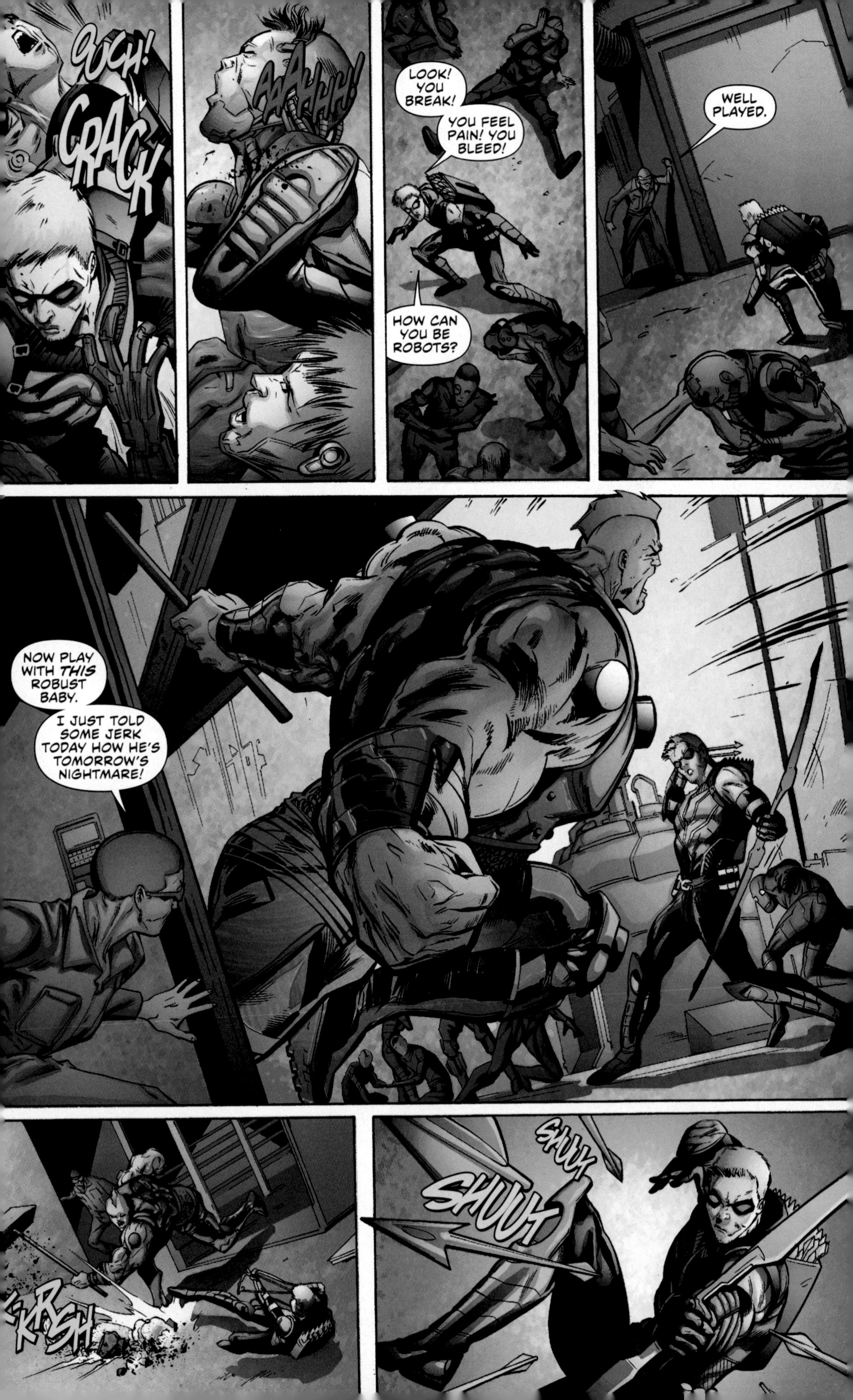
OUCH!
CRACK
AAAHHH!
LOOK! YOU BREAK!
YOU FEEL PAIN! YOU BLEED!
HOW CAN YOU BE ROBOTS?
WELL PLAYED.
NOW PLAY WITH THIS ROBUST BABY.
I JUST TOLD SOME JERK TODAY HOW HE'S TOMORROW'S NIGHTMARE!
KRRSH
SHUUK
SHUUK

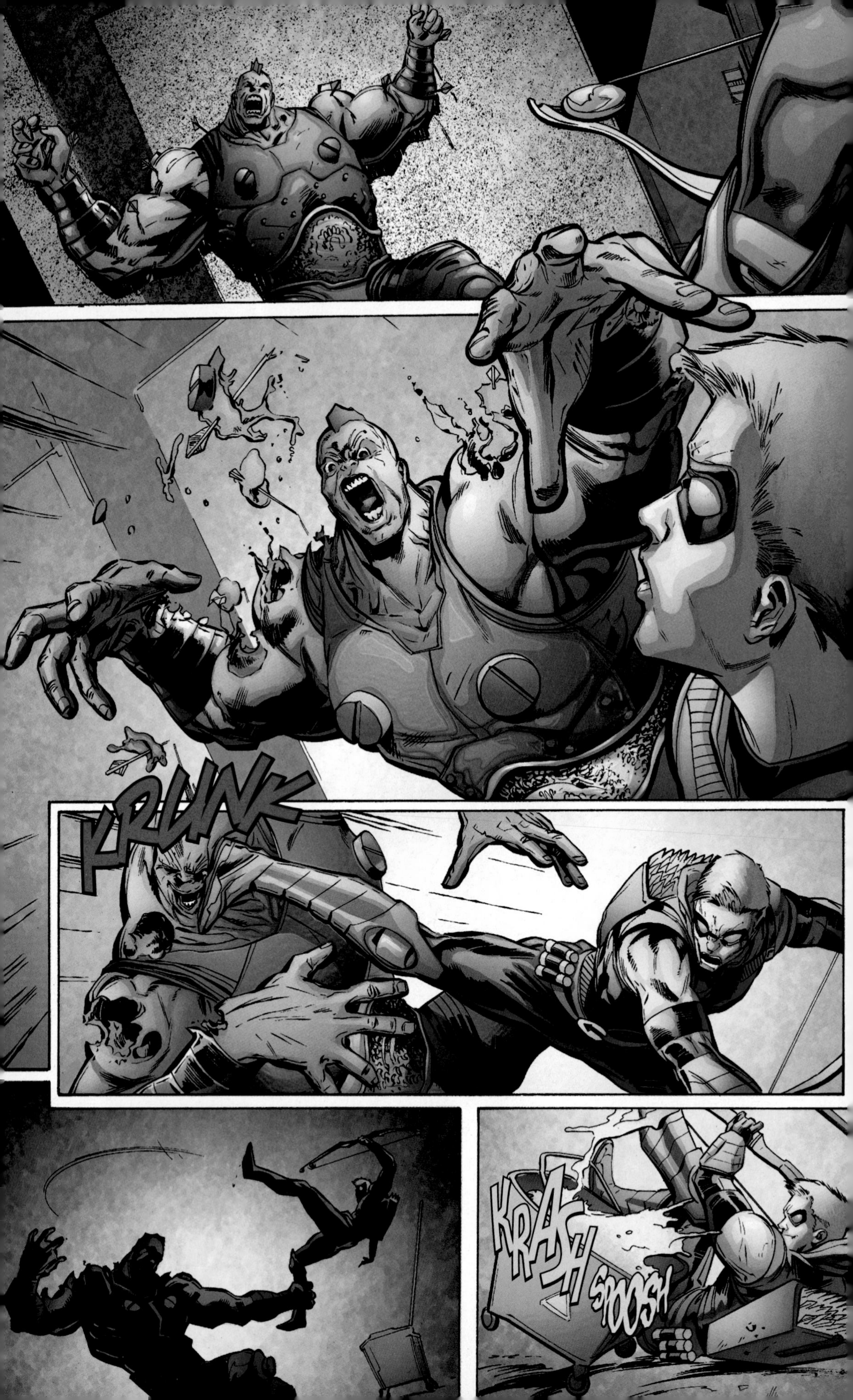
KRUNK
KRASH
SPOOSH

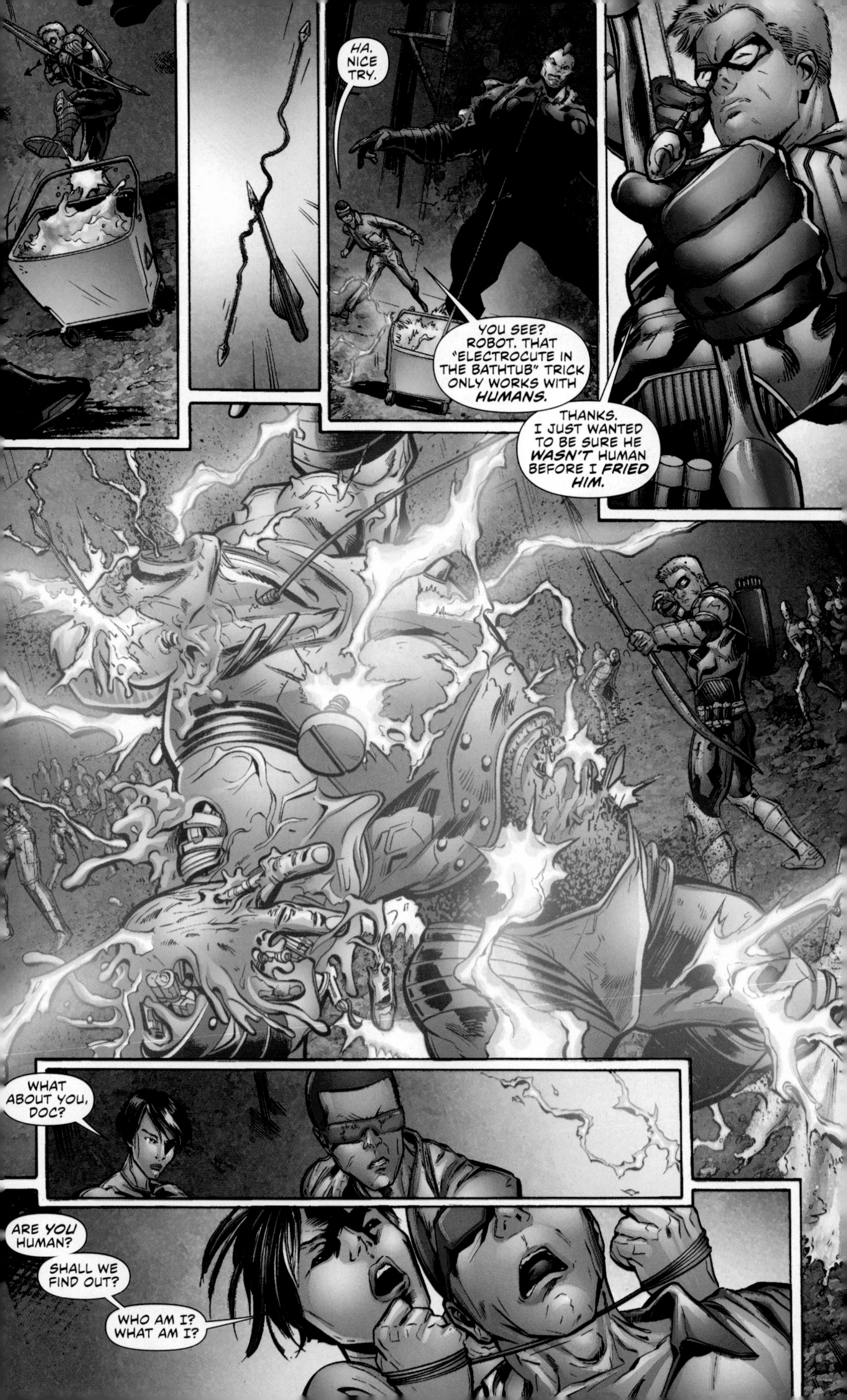
HA. NICE TRY.
YOU SEE? ROBOT. THAT "ELECTROCUTE IN THE BATHTUB" TRICK ONLY WORKS WITH HUMANS.
THANKS. I JUST WANTED TO BE SURE HE WASN'T HUMAN BEFORE I FRIED HIM.
WHAT ABOUT YOU, DOC?
ARE YOU HUMAN?
SHALL WE FIND OUT?
WHO AM I? WHAT AM I?

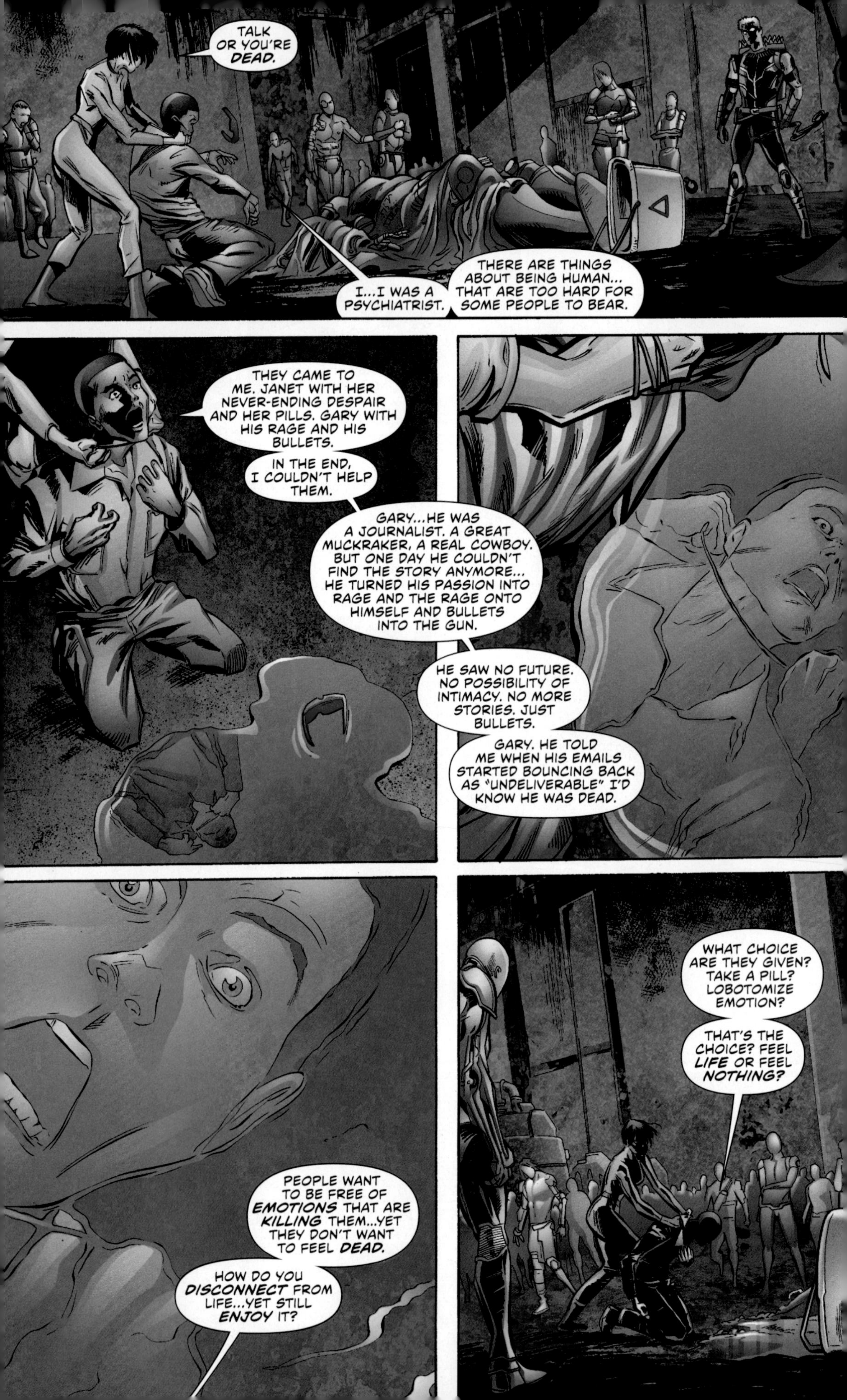
TALK OR YOU'RE DEAD.
I...I WAS A PSYCHIATRIST.
THERE ARE THINGS ABOUT BEING HUMAN... THAT ARE TOO HARD FOR SOME PEOPLE TO BEAR.
THEY CAME TO ME. JANET WITH HER NEVER-ENDING DESPAIR AND HER PILLS. GARY WITH HIS RAGE AND HIS BULLETS.
IN THE END, I COULDN'T HELP THEM.
GARY...HE WAS A JOURNALIST. A GREAT MUCKRAKER, A REAL COWBOY. BUT ONE DAY HE COULDN'T FIND THE STORY ANYMORE... HE TURNED HIS PASSION INTO RAGE AND THE RAGE ONTO HIMSELF AND BULLETS INTO THE GUN.
HE SAW NO FUTURE. NO POSSIBILITY OF INTIMACY. NO MORE STORIES. JUST BULLETS.
GARY. HE TOLD ME WHEN HIS EMAILS STARTED BOUNCING BACK AS "UNDELIVERABLE" I'D KNOW HE WAS DEAD.
PEOPLE WANT TO BE FREE OF EMOTIONS THAT ARE KILLING THEM...YET THEY DON'T WANT TO FEEL DEAD.
HOW DO YOU DISCONNECT FROM LIFE...YET STILL ENJOY IT?
WHAT CHOICE ARE THEY GIVEN? TAKE A PILL? LOBOTOMIZE EMOTION?
THAT'S THE CHOICE? FEEL LIFE OR FEEL NOTHING?

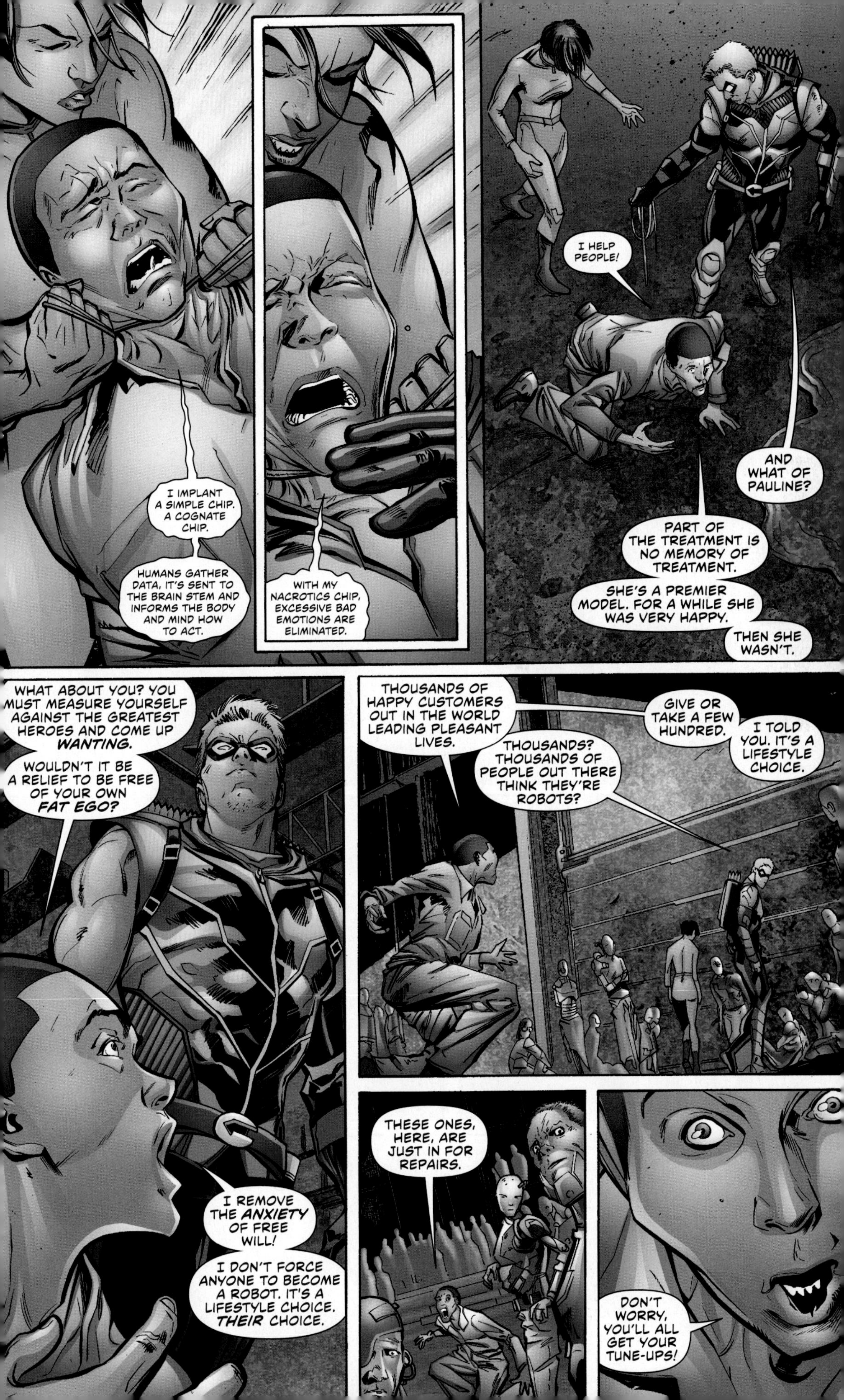
I IMPLANT A SIMPLE CHIP. A COGNATE CHIP.
HUMANS GATHER DATA, IT'S SENT TO THE BRAIN STEM AND INFORMS THE BODY AND MIND HOW TO ACT.
WITH MY NACROTICS CHIP, EXCESSIVE BAD EMOTIONS ARE ELIMINATED.
I HELP PEOPLE!
AND WHAT OF PAULINE?
PART OF THE TREATMENT IS NO MEMORY OF TREATMENT.
SHE'S A PREMIER MODEL. FOR A WHILE SHE WAS VERY HAPPY.
THEN SHE WASN'T.
WHAT ABOUT YOU? YOU MUST MEASURE YOURSELF AGAINST THE GREATEST HEROES AND COME UP *WANTING.*
WOULDN'T IT BE A RELIEF TO BE FREE OF YOUR OWN *FAT EGO?*
I REMOVE THE *ANXIETY* OF FREE WILL!
I DON'T FORCE ANYONE TO BECOME A ROBOT. IT'S A LIFESTYLE CHOICE. *THEIR* CHOICE.
THOUSANDS OF HAPPY CUSTOMERS OUT IN THE WORLD LEADING PLEASANT LIVES.
THOUSANDS? THOUSANDS OF PEOPLE OUT THERE THINK THEY'RE ROBOTS?
GIVE OR TAKE A FEW HUNDRED.
I TOLD YOU. IT'S A LIFESTYLE CHOICE.
THESE ONES, HERE, ARE JUST IN FOR REPAIRS.
DON'T WORRY, YOU'LL ALL GET YOUR TUNE-UPS!

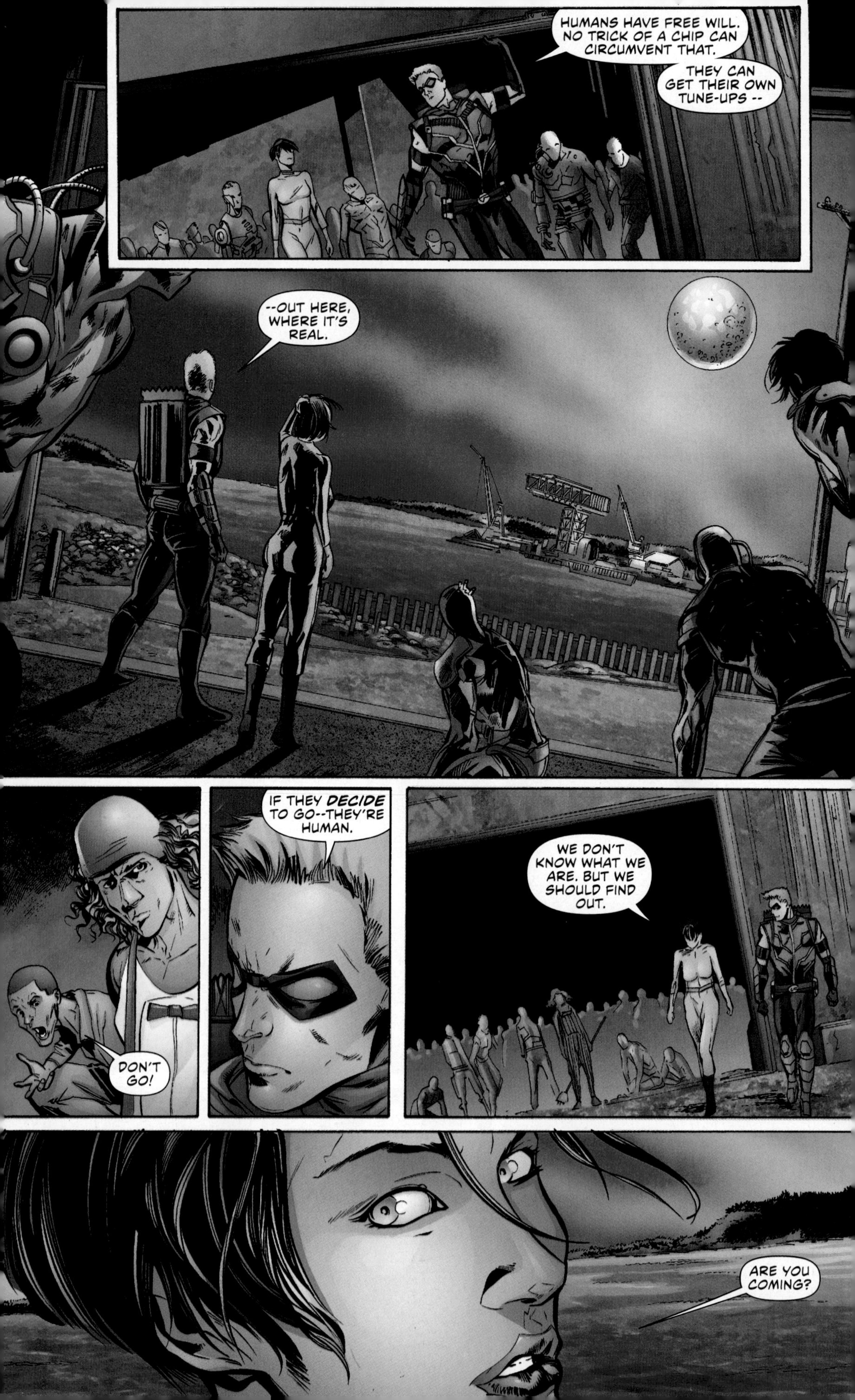
HUMANS HAVE FREE WILL. NO TRICK OF A CHIP CAN CIRCUMVENT THAT.
THEY CAN GET THEIR OWN TUNE-UPS --
--OUT HERE, WHERE IT'S REAL.
DON'T GO!
IF THEY *DECIDE* TO GO--THEY'RE HUMAN.
WE DON'T KNOW WHAT WE ARE. BUT WE SHOULD FIND OUT.
ARE YOU COMING?

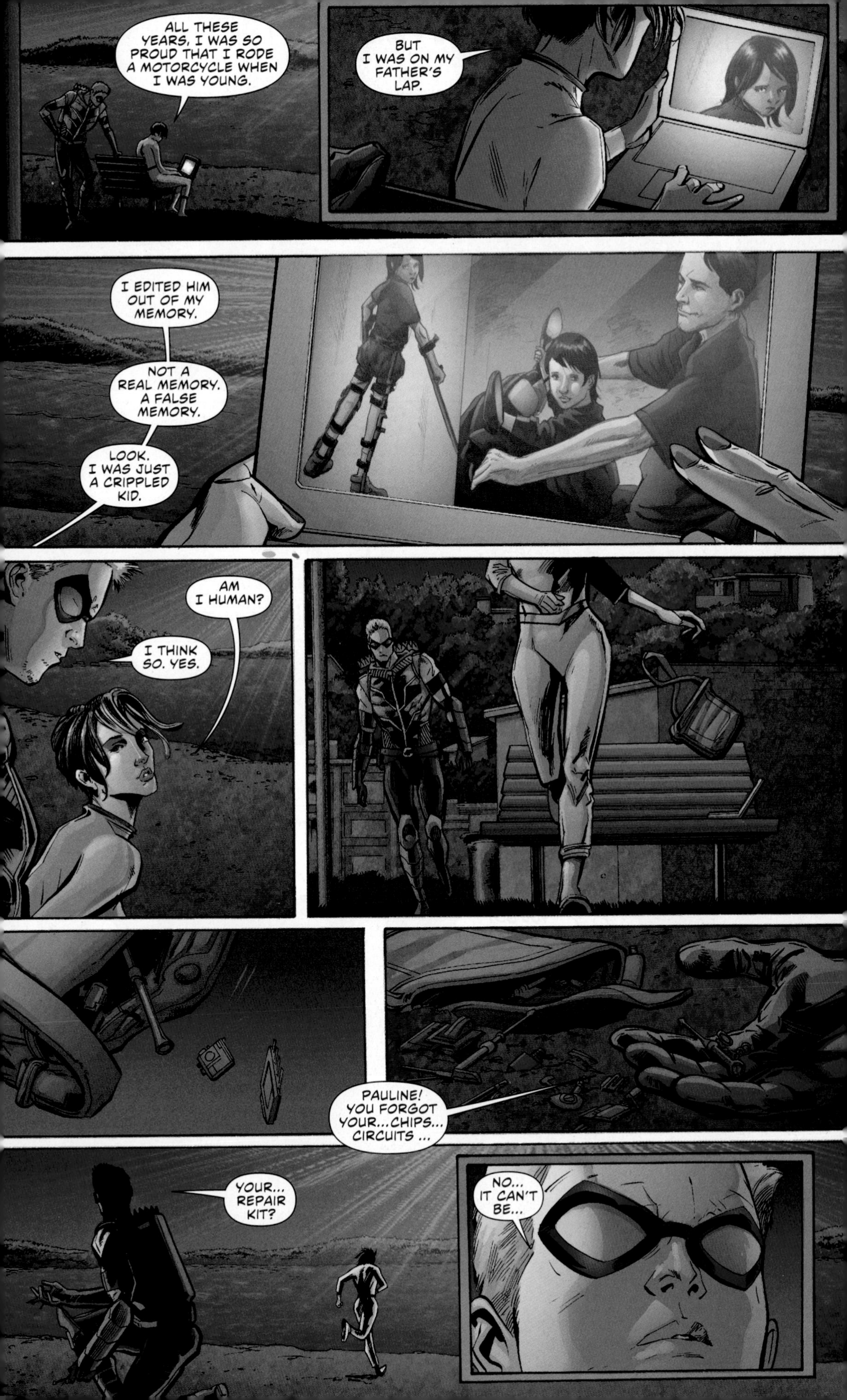
ALL THESE YEARS, I WAS SO PROUD THAT I RODE A MOTORCYCLE WHEN I WAS YOUNG.
BUT I WAS ON MY FATHER'S LAP.
I EDITED HIM OUT OF MY MEMORY.
NOT A REAL MEMORY. A FALSE MEMORY.
LOOK. I WAS JUST A CRIPPLED KID.
AM I HUMAN?
I THINK SO. YES.
PAULINE! YOU FORGOT YOUR...CHIPS... CIRCUITS ...
YOUR... REPAIR KIT?
NO... IT CAN'T BE...

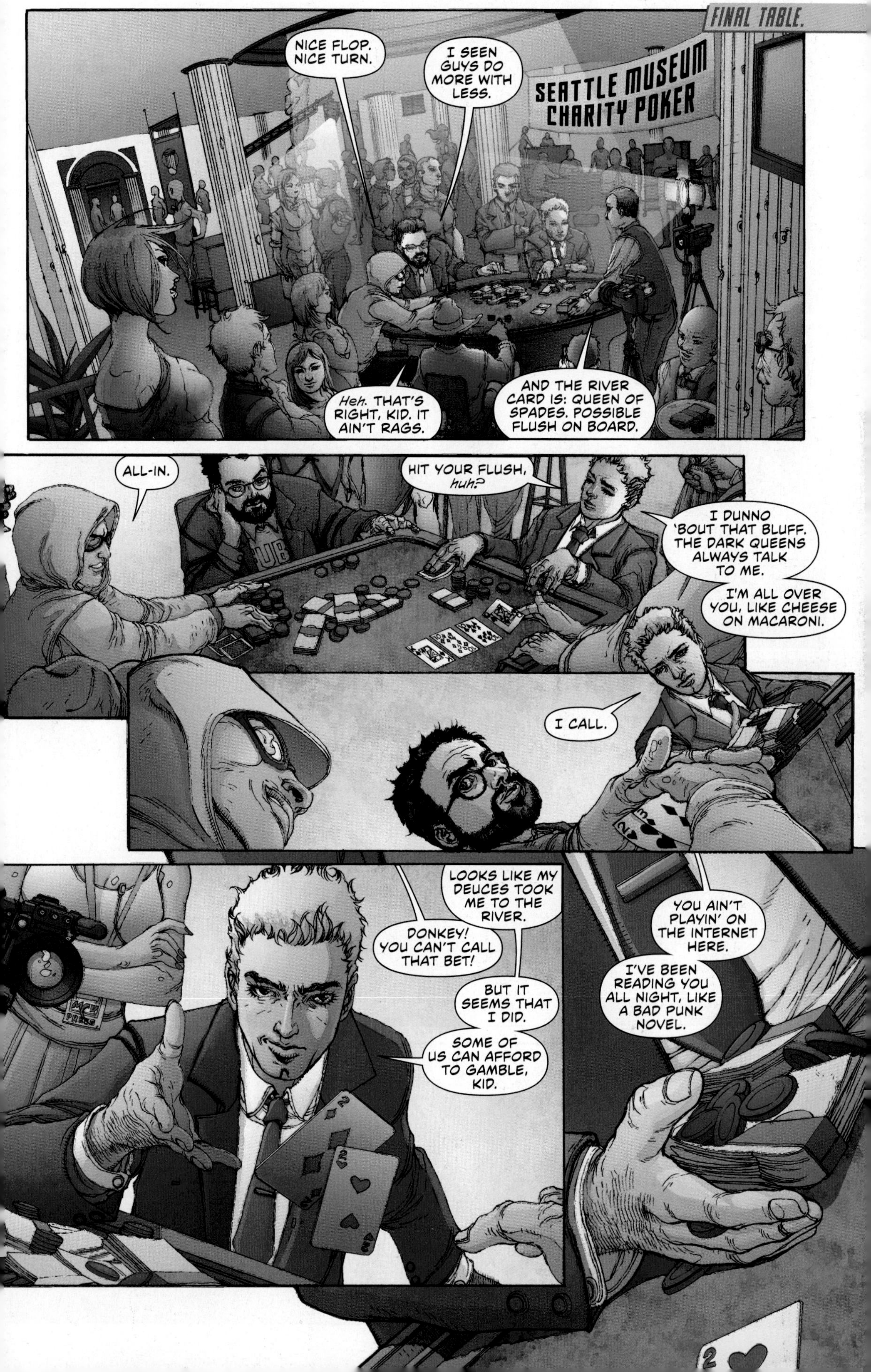
FINAL TABLE.
NICE FLOP. NICE TURN.
I SEEN GUYS DO MORE WITH LESS.
SEATTLE MUSEUM CHARITY POKER
Heh. THAT'S RIGHT, KID. IT AIN'T RAGS.
AND THE RIVER CARD IS: QUEEN OF SPADES. POSSIBLE FLUSH ON BOARD.
ALL-IN.
HIT YOUR FLUSH, huh?
I DUNNO 'BOUT THAT BLUFF. THE DARK QUEENS ALWAYS TALK TO ME.
I'M ALL OVER YOU, LIKE CHEESE ON MACARONI.
I CALL.
DONKEY! YOU CAN'T CALL THAT BET!
LOOKS LIKE MY DEUCES TOOK ME TO THE RIVER.
BUT IT SEEMS THAT I DID.
SOME OF US CAN AFFORD TO GAMBLE, KID.
YOU AIN'T PLAYIN' ON THE INTERNET HERE.
I'VE BEEN READING YOU ALL NIGHT, LIKE A BAD PUNK NOVEL.

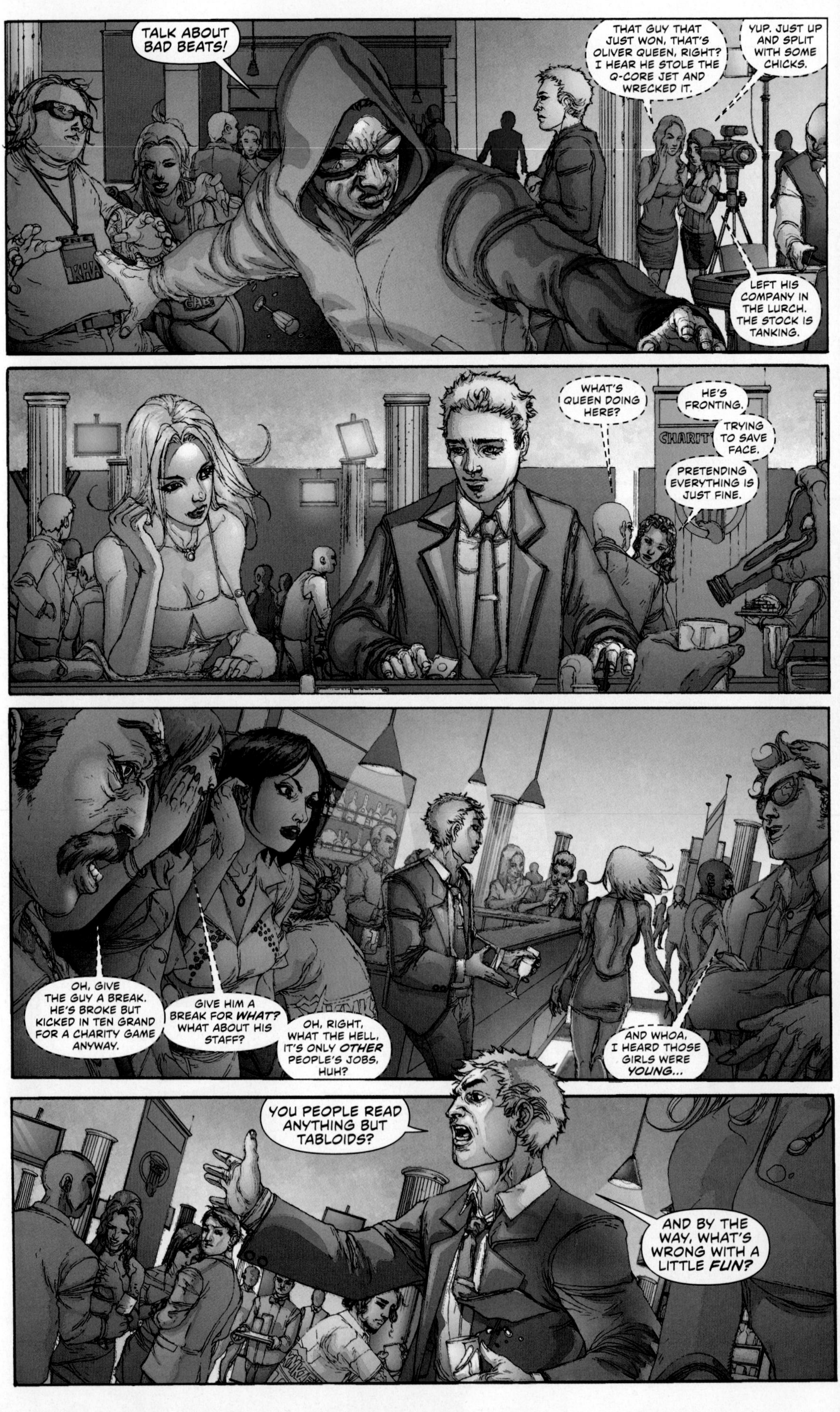
TALK ABOUT BAD BEATS!
THAT GUY THAT JUST WON, THAT'S OLIVER QUEEN, RIGHT? I HEAR HE STOLE THE Q-CORE JET AND WRECKED IT.
YUP. JUST UP AND SPLIT WITH SOME CHICKS.
LEFT HIS COMPANY IN THE LURCH. THE STOCK IS TANKING.
WHAT'S QUEEN DOING HERE?
HE'S FRONTING.
TRYING TO SAVE FACE.
PRETENDING EVERYTHING IS JUST FINE.
CHARIT
OH, GIVE THE GUY A BREAK. HE'S BROKE BUT KICKED IN TEN GRAND FOR A CHARITY GAME ANYWAY.
GIVE HIM A BREAK FOR *WHAT?* WHAT ABOUT HIS STAFF?
OH, RIGHT, WHAT THE HELL, IT'S ONLY *OTHER* PEOPLE'S JOBS, HUH?
AND WHOA, I HEARD THOSE GIRLS WERE *YOUNG...*
YOU PEOPLE READ ANYTHING BUT TABLOIDS?
AND BY THE WAY, WHAT'S WRONG WITH A LITTLE *FUN?*

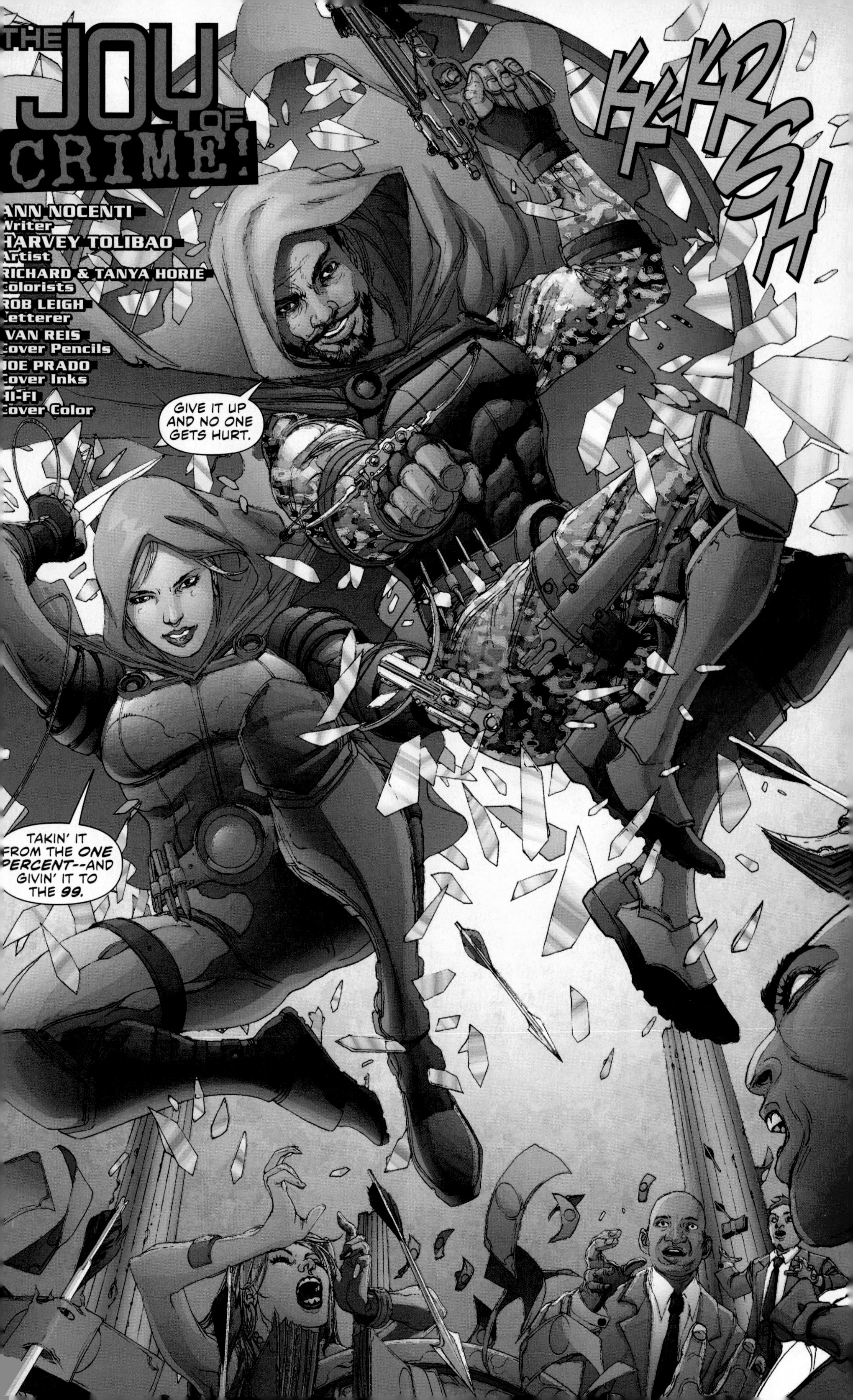
THE JOY OF CRIME!
ANN NOCENTI
Writer
HARVEY TOLIBAO
Artist
RICHARD & TANYA HORIE
Colorists
ROB LEIGH
Letterer
VAN REIS
Cover Pencils
JOE PRADO
Cover Inks
HI-FI
Cover Color
KKKRSH
GIVE IT UP AND NO ONE GETS HURT.
TAKIN' IT FROM THE ONE PERCENT--AND GIVIN' IT TO THE 99.

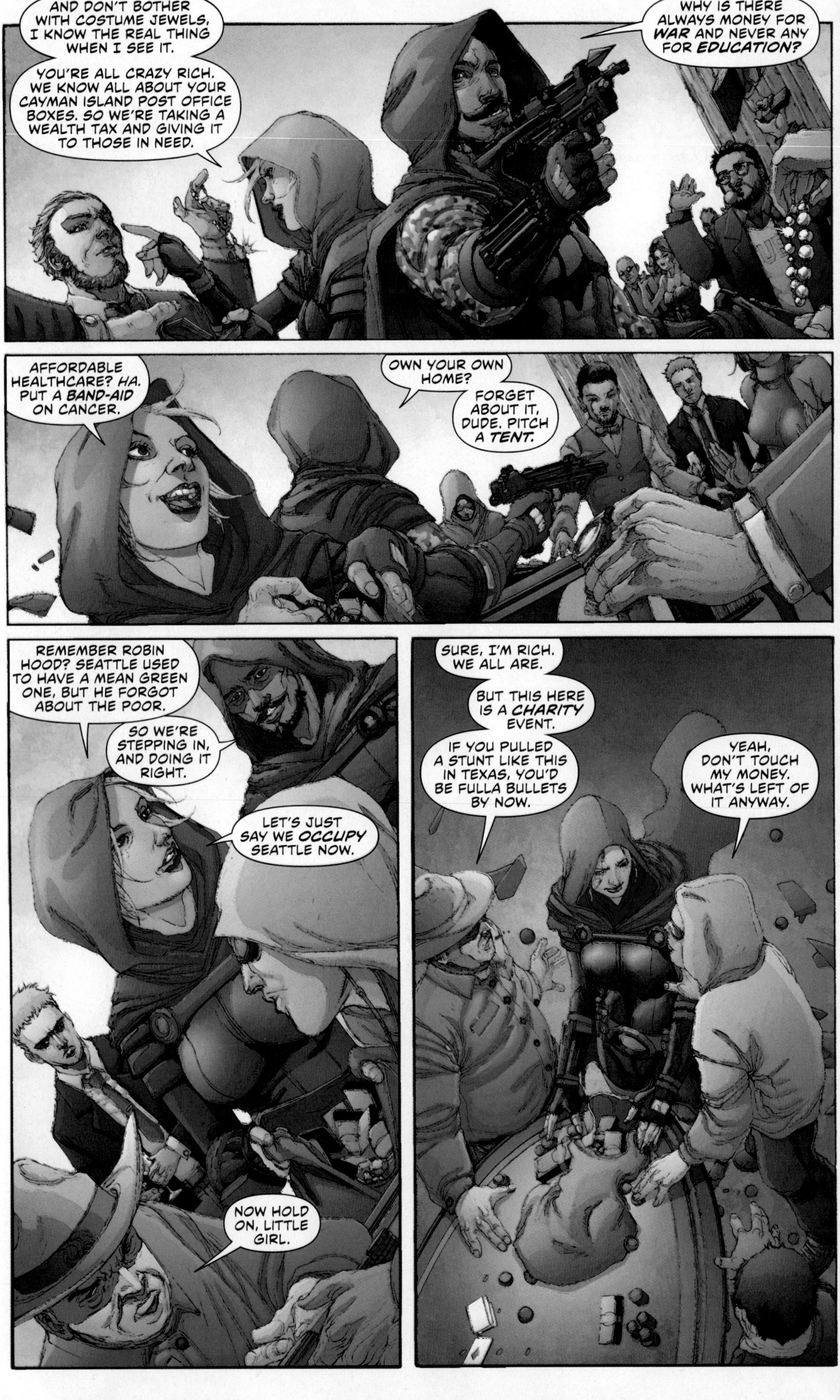
AND DON'T BOTHER WITH COSTUME JEWELS, I KNOW THE REAL THING WHEN I SEE IT.
YOU'RE ALL CRAZY RICH. WE KNOW ALL ABOUT YOUR CAYMAN ISLAND POST OFFICE BOXES. SO WE'RE TAKING A WEALTH TAX AND GIVING IT TO THOSE IN NEED.
WHY IS THERE ALWAYS MONEY FOR *WAR* AND NEVER ANY FOR *EDUCATION?*
AFFORDABLE HEALTHCARE? *HA.* PUT A *BAND-AID* ON CANCER.
OWN YOUR OWN HOME?
FORGET ABOUT IT, DUDE. PITCH A *TENT.*
REMEMBER ROBIN HOOD? SEATTLE USED TO HAVE A MEAN GREEN ONE, BUT HE FORGOT ABOUT THE POOR.
SO WE'RE STEPPING IN, AND DOING IT RIGHT.
LET'S JUST SAY WE *OCCUPY* SEATTLE NOW.
NOW HOLD ON, LITTLE GIRL.
SURE, I'M RICH. WE ALL ARE.
BUT THIS HERE IS A *CHARITY* EVENT.
IF YOU PULLED A STUNT LIKE THIS IN TEXAS, YOU'D BE FULLA BULLETS BY NOW.
YEAH, DON'T TOUCH MY MONEY. WHAT'S LEFT OF IT ANYWAY.

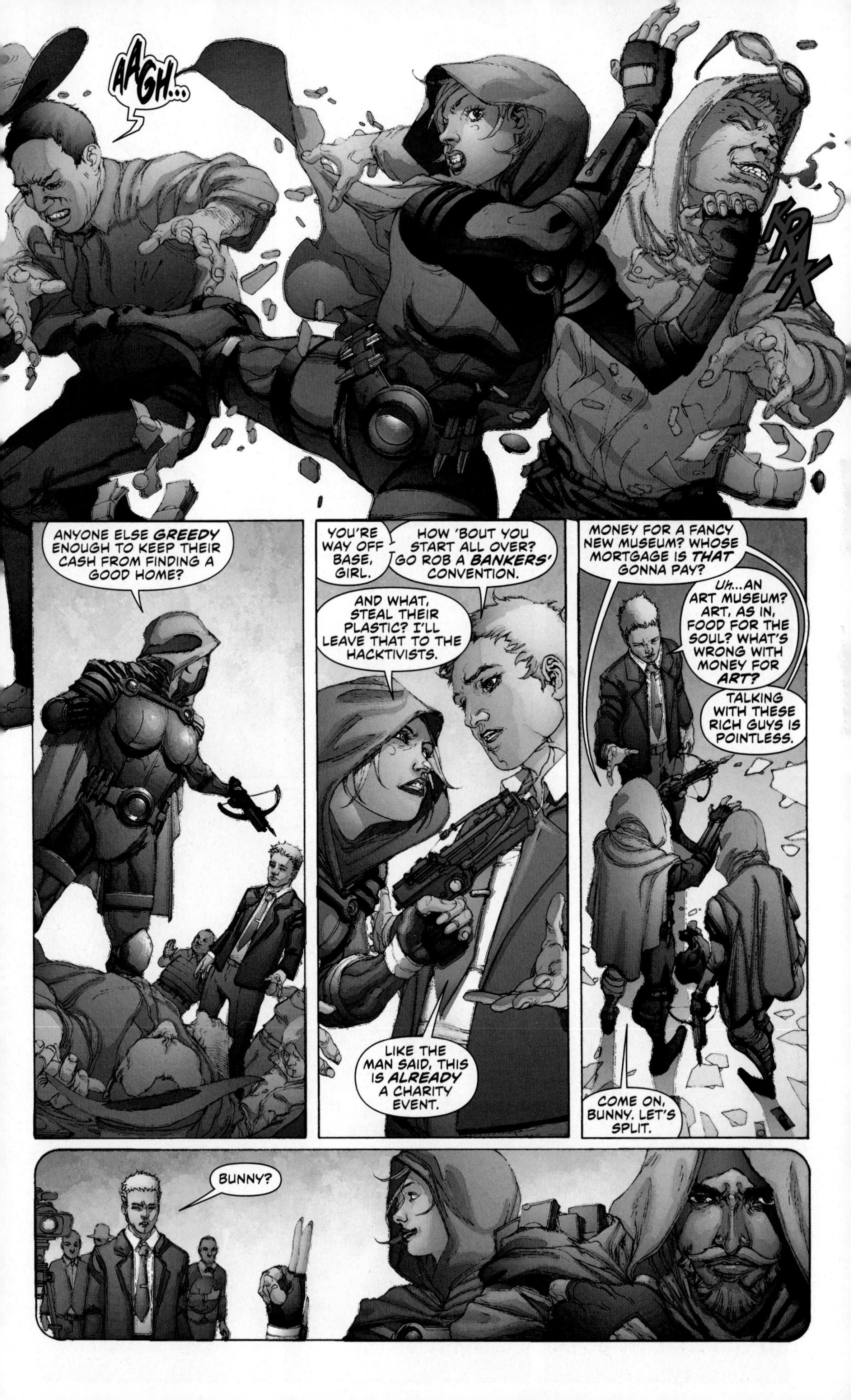
AAGH...
KRAK
ANYONE ELSE GREEDY ENOUGH TO KEEP THEIR CASH FROM FINDING A GOOD HOME?
YOU'RE WAY OFF BASE, GIRL.
HOW 'BOUT YOU START ALL OVER? GO ROB A BANKERS' CONVENTION.
AND WHAT, STEAL THEIR PLASTIC? I'LL LEAVE THAT TO THE HACKTIVISTS.
LIKE THE MAN SAID, THIS IS ALREADY A CHARITY EVENT.
MONEY FOR A FANCY NEW MUSEUM? WHOSE MORTGAGE IS THAT GONNA PAY?
Uh...AN ART MUSEUM? ART, AS IN, FOOD FOR THE SOUL? WHAT'S WRONG WITH MONEY FOR ART?
TALKING WITH THESE RICH GUYS IS POINTLESS.
COME ON, BUNNY. LET'S SPLIT.
BUNNY?

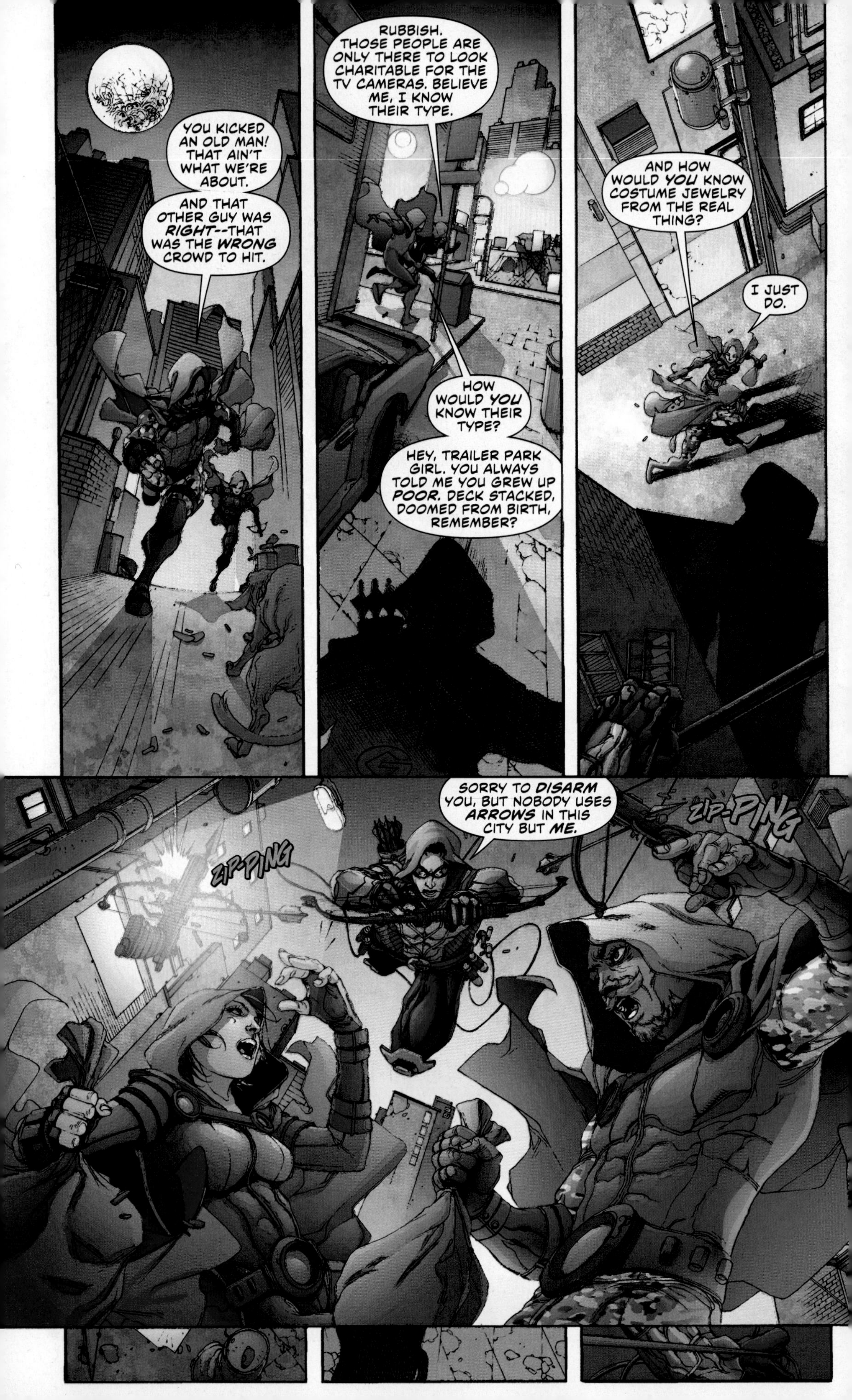
YOU KICKED AN OLD MAN! THAT AIN'T WHAT WE'RE ABOUT.
AND THAT OTHER GUY WAS RIGHT--THAT WAS THE WRONG CROWD TO HIT.
RUBBISH. THOSE PEOPLE ARE ONLY THERE TO LOOK CHARITABLE FOR THE TV CAMERAS. BELIEVE ME, I KNOW THEIR TYPE.
HOW WOULD YOU KNOW THEIR TYPE?
HEY, TRAILER PARK GIRL. YOU ALWAYS TOLD ME YOU GREW UP POOR. DECK STACKED, DOOMED FROM BIRTH, REMEMBER?
AND HOW WOULD YOU KNOW COSTUME JEWELRY FROM THE REAL THING?
I JUST DO.
ZIP-PING
SORRY TO DISARM YOU, BUT NOBODY USES ARROWS IN THIS CITY BUT ME.
ZIP-PING

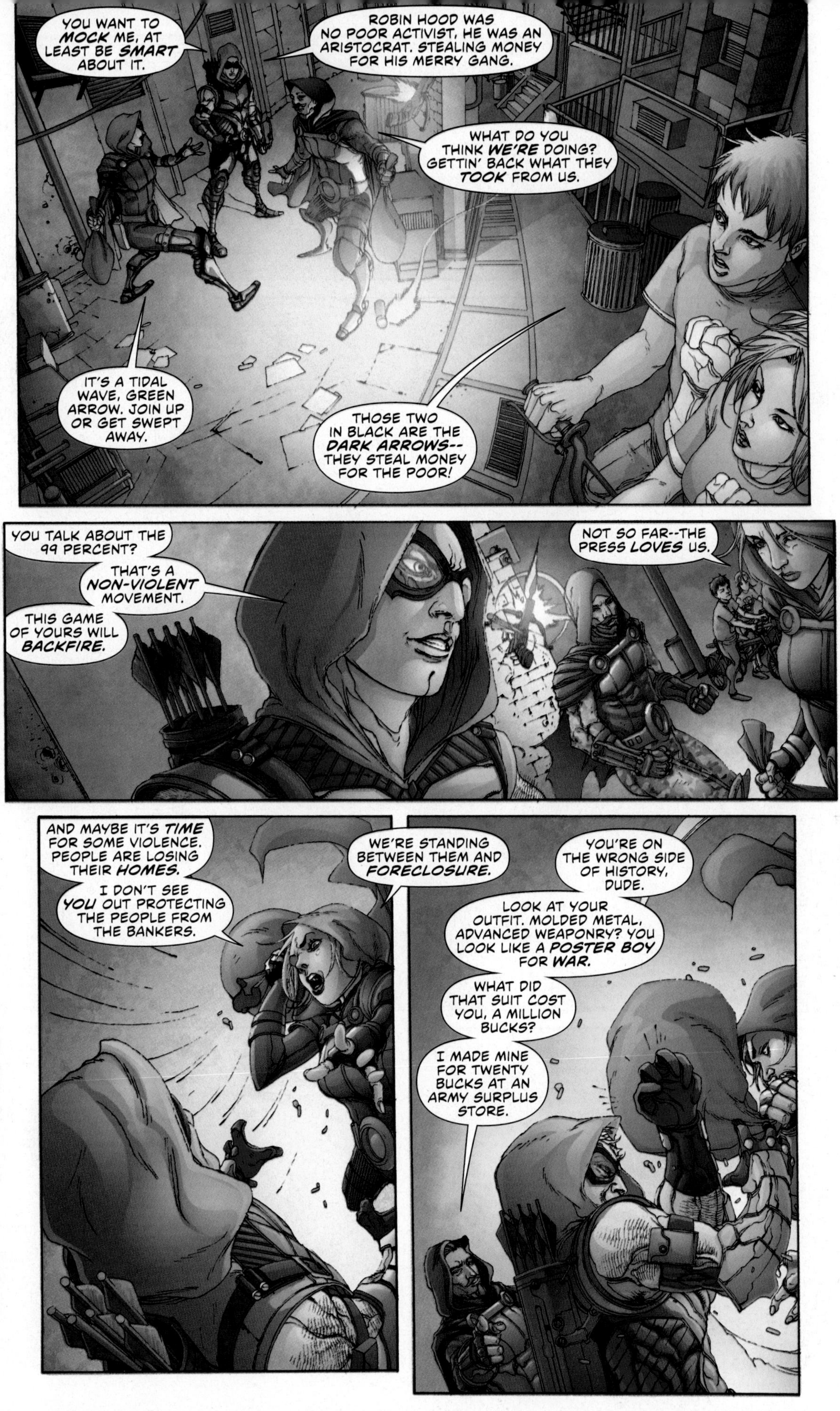

YOU WANT TO MOCK ME, AT LEAST BE SMART ABOUT IT.
ROBIN HOOD WAS NO POOR ACTIVIST, HE WAS AN ARISTOCRAT. STEALING MONEY FOR HIS MERRY GANG.
WHAT DO YOU THINK WE'RE DOING? GETTIN' BACK WHAT THEY TOOK FROM US.
IT'S A TIDAL WAVE, GREEN ARROW. JOIN UP OR GET SWEPT AWAY.
THOSE TWO IN BLACK ARE THE DARK ARROWS-- THEY STEAL MONEY FOR THE POOR!
YOU TALK ABOUT THE 99 PERCENT?
THAT'S A NON-VIOLENT MOVEMENT.
THIS GAME OF YOURS WILL BACKFIRE.
NOT SO FAR--THE PRESS LOVES US.
AND MAYBE IT'S TIME FOR SOME VIOLENCE. PEOPLE ARE LOSING THEIR HOMES.
I DON'T SEE YOU OUT PROTECTING THE PEOPLE FROM THE BANKERS.
WE'RE STANDING BETWEEN THEM AND FORECLOSURE.
YOU'RE ON THE WRONG SIDE OF HISTORY, DUDE.
LOOK AT YOUR OUTFIT. MOLDED METAL, ADVANCED WEAPONRY? YOU LOOK LIKE A POSTER BOY FOR WAR.
WHAT DID THAT SUIT COST YOU, A MILLION BUCKS?
I MADE MINE FOR TWENTY BUCKS AT AN ARMY SURPLUS STORE.

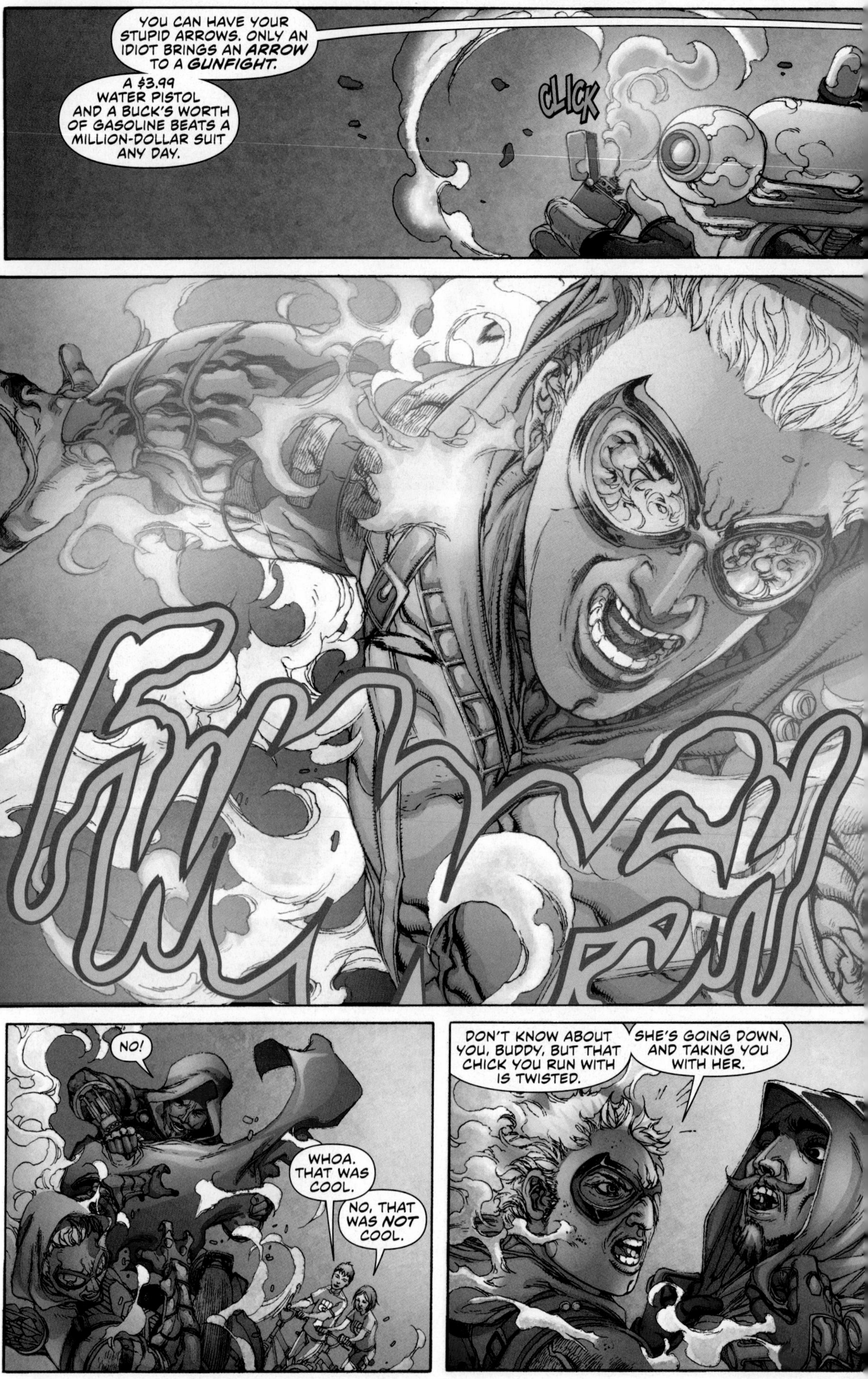
YOU CAN HAVE YOUR STUPID ARROWS. ONLY AN IDIOT BRINGS AN *ARROW* TO A *GUNFIGHT*.
A $3.99 WATER PISTOL AND A BUCK'S WORTH OF GASOLINE BEATS A MILLION-DOLLAR SUIT ANY DAY.
CLICK
NO!
WHOA. THAT WAS COOL.
NO, THAT WAS *NOT* COOL.
DON'T KNOW ABOUT YOU, BUDDY, BUT THAT CHICK YOU RUN WITH IS TWISTED.
SHE'S GOING DOWN, AND TAKING YOU WITH HER.

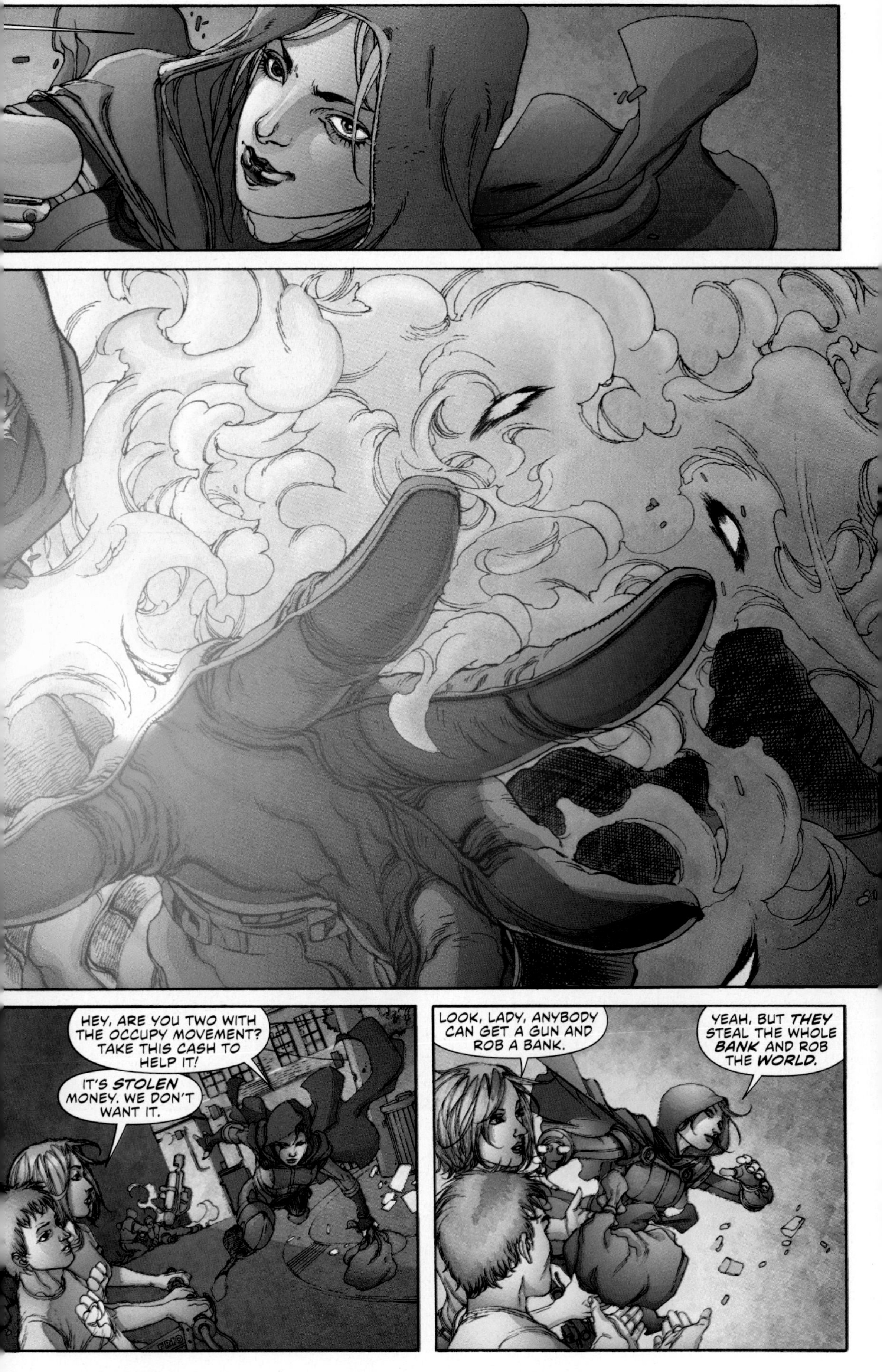
HEY, ARE YOU TWO WITH THE OCCUPY MOVEMENT? TAKE THIS CASH TO HELP IT!
IT'S STOLEN MONEY. WE DON'T WANT IT.
LOOK, LADY, ANYBODY CAN GET A GUN AND ROB A BANK.
YEAH, BUT THEY STEAL THE WHOLE BANK AND ROB THE WORLD.

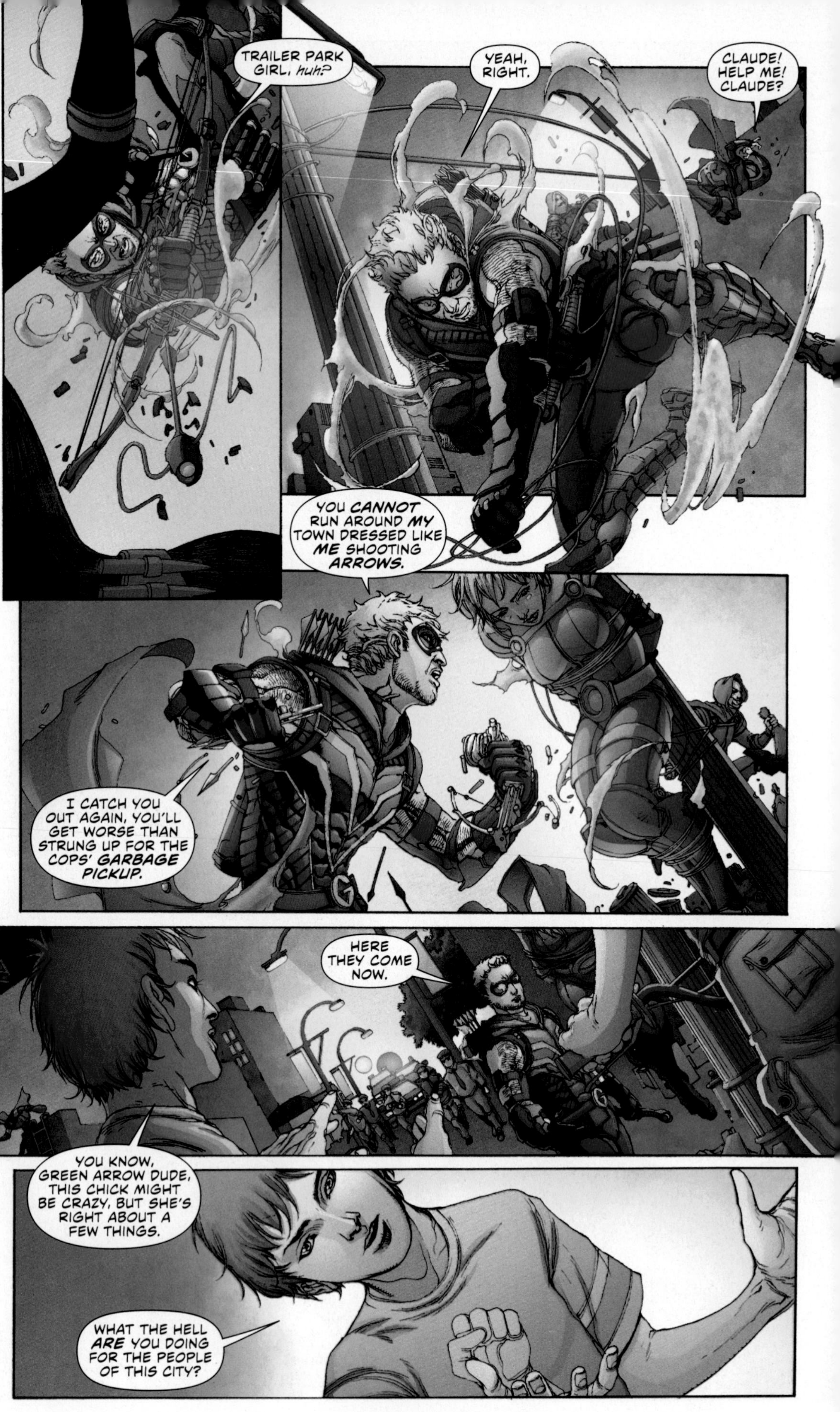
TRAILER PARK GIRL, *huh?*
YEAH, RIGHT.
CLAUDE! HELP ME! CLAUDE?
YOU **CANNOT** RUN AROUND **MY** TOWN DRESSED LIKE **ME** SHOOTING **ARROWS.**
I CATCH YOU OUT AGAIN, YOU'LL GET WORSE THAN STRUNG UP FOR THE COPS' **GARBAGE PICKUP.**
HERE THEY COME NOW.
YOU KNOW, GREEN ARROW DUDE, THIS CHICK MIGHT BE CRAZY, BUT SHE'S RIGHT ABOUT A FEW THINGS.
WHAT THE HELL **ARE** YOU DOING FOR THE PEOPLE OF THIS CITY?

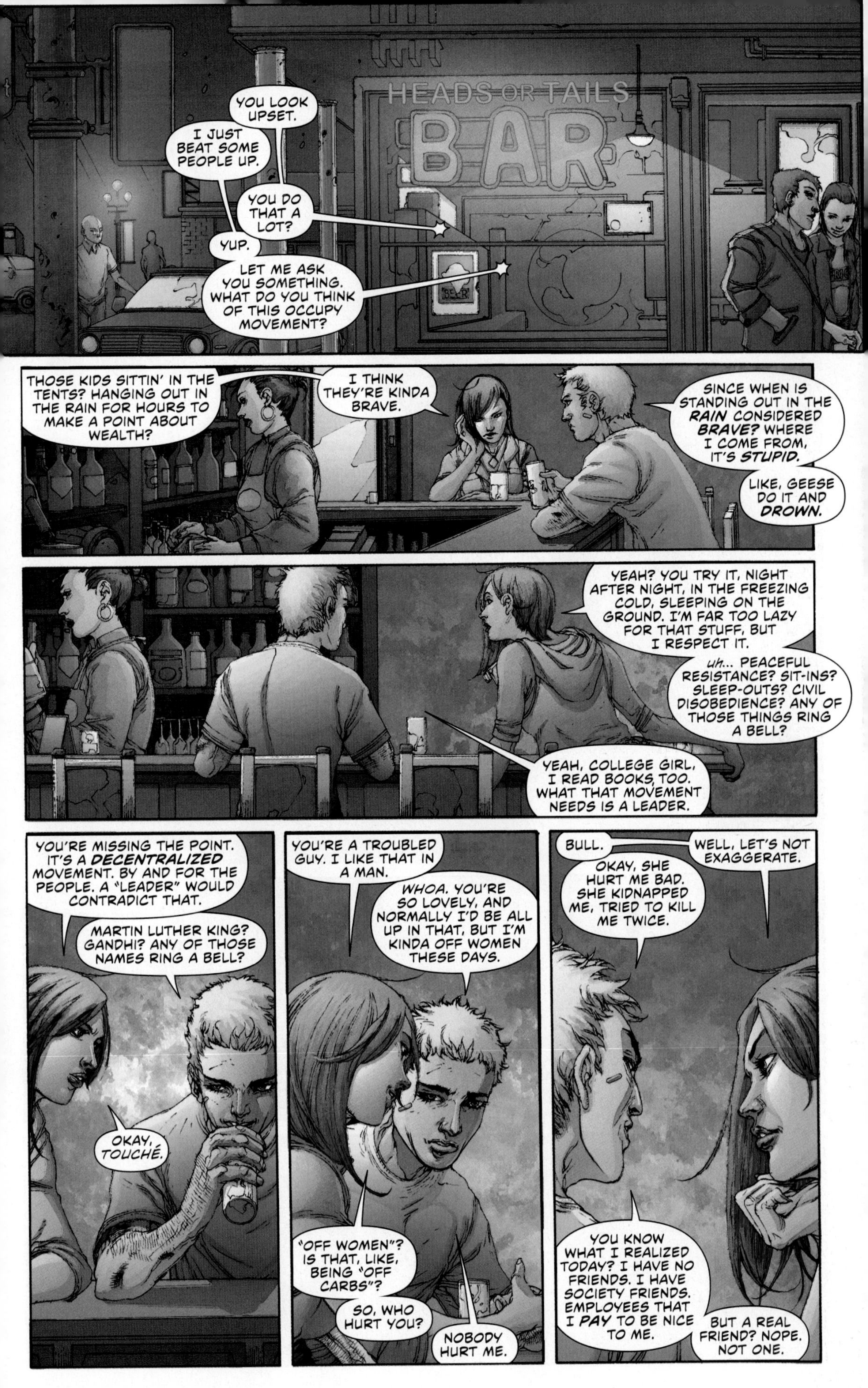
HEADS OR TAILS
BAR
YOU LOOK UPSET.
I JUST BEAT SOME PEOPLE UP.
YOU DO THAT A LOT?
YUP.
LET ME ASK YOU SOMETHING. WHAT DO YOU THINK OF THIS OCCUPY MOVEMENT?
THOSE KIDS SITTIN' IN THE TENTS? HANGING OUT IN THE RAIN FOR HOURS TO MAKE A POINT ABOUT WEALTH?
I THINK THEY'RE KINDA BRAVE.
SINCE WHEN IS STANDING OUT IN THE RAIN CONSIDERED BRAVE? WHERE I COME FROM, IT'S STUPID.
LIKE, GEESE DO IT AND DROWN.
YEAH? YOU TRY IT, NIGHT AFTER NIGHT, IN THE FREEZING COLD, SLEEPING ON THE GROUND. I'M FAR TOO LAZY FOR THAT STUFF, BUT I RESPECT IT.
uh... PEACEFUL RESISTANCE? SIT-INS? SLEEP-OUTS? CIVIL DISOBEDIENCE? ANY OF THOSE THINGS RING A BELL?
YEAH, COLLEGE GIRL, I READ BOOKS, TOO. WHAT THAT MOVEMENT NEEDS IS A LEADER.
YOU'RE MISSING THE POINT. IT'S A DECENTRALIZED MOVEMENT. BY AND FOR THE PEOPLE. A "LEADER" WOULD CONTRADICT THAT.
MARTIN LUTHER KING? GANDHI? ANY OF THOSE NAMES RING A BELL?
OKAY, TOUCHÉ.
YOU'RE A TROUBLED GUY. I LIKE THAT IN A MAN.
WHOA. YOU'RE SO LOVELY, AND NORMALLY I'D BE ALL UP IN THAT, BUT I'M KINDA OFF WOMEN THESE DAYS.
"OFF WOMEN"? IS THAT, LIKE, BEING "OFF CARBS"?
SO, WHO HURT YOU?
NOBODY HURT ME.
BULL.
WELL, LET'S NOT EXAGGERATE.
OKAY, SHE HURT ME BAD. SHE KIDNAPPED ME, TRIED TO KILL ME TWICE.
YOU KNOW WHAT I REALIZED TODAY? I HAVE NO FRIENDS. I HAVE SOCIETY FRIENDS. EMPLOYEES THAT I PAY TO BE NICE TO ME.
BUT A REAL FRIEND? NOPE. NOT ONE.

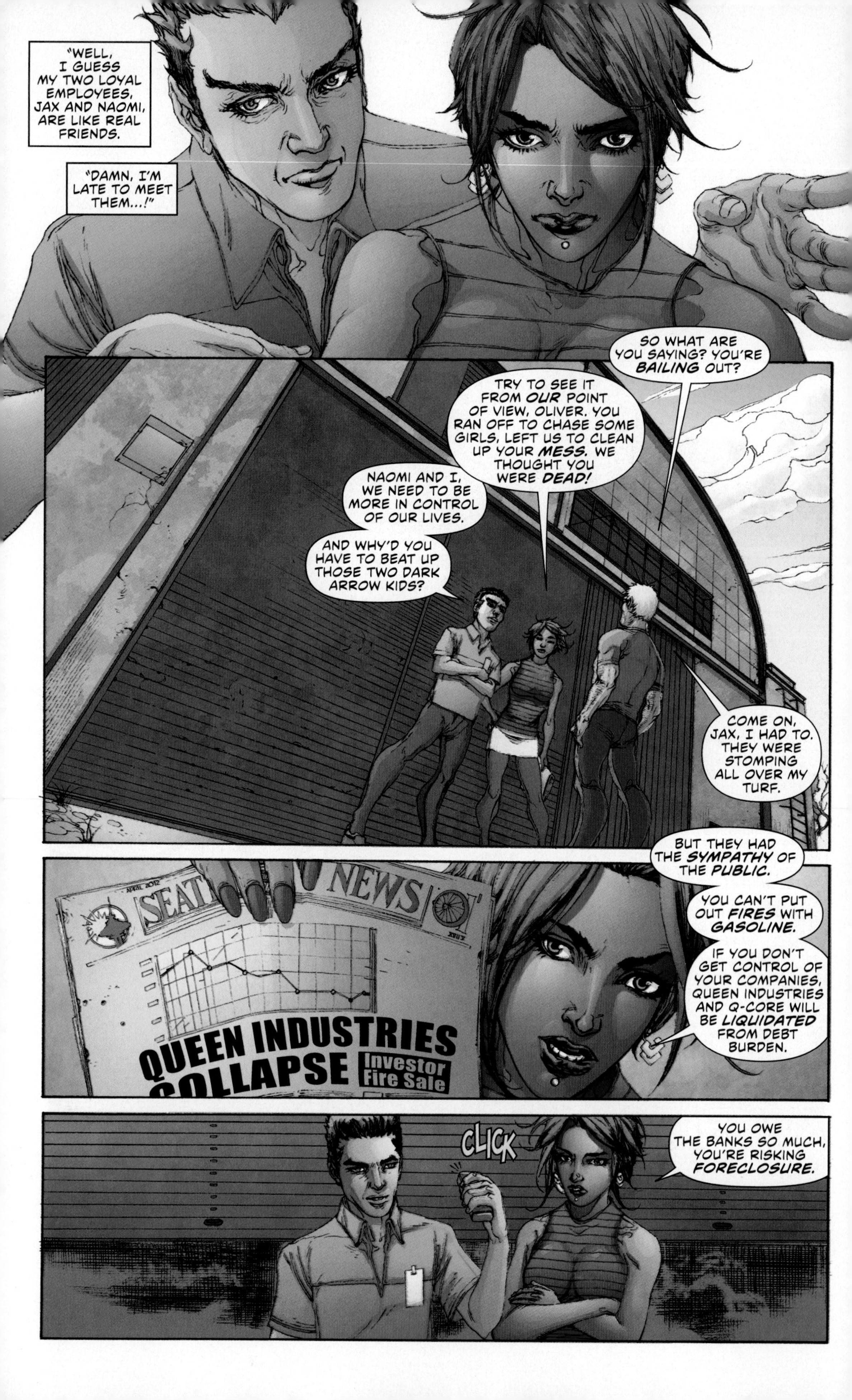
"WELL, I GUESS MY TWO LOYAL EMPLOYEES, JAX AND NAOMI, ARE LIKE REAL FRIENDS.
"DAMN, I'M LATE TO MEET THEM...!"
SO WHAT ARE YOU SAYING? YOU'RE BAILING OUT?
TRY TO SEE IT FROM OUR POINT OF VIEW, OLIVER. YOU RAN OFF TO CHASE SOME GIRLS, LEFT US TO CLEAN UP YOUR MESS. WE THOUGHT YOU WERE DEAD!
NAOMI AND I, WE NEED TO BE MORE IN CONTROL OF OUR LIVES.
AND WHY'D YOU HAVE TO BEAT UP THOSE TWO DARK ARROW KIDS?
COME ON, JAX, I HAD TO. THEY WERE STOMPING ALL OVER MY TURF.
BUT THEY HAD THE SYMPATHY OF THE PUBLIC.
YOU CAN'T PUT OUT FIRES WITH GASOLINE.
IF YOU DON'T GET CONTROL OF YOUR COMPANIES, QUEEN INDUSTRIES AND Q-CORE WILL BE LIQUIDATED FROM DEBT BURDEN.
APRIL 2012
NEWS
QUEEN INDUSTRIES COLLAPSE
Investor Fire Sale
CLICK
YOU OWE THE BANKS SO MUCH, YOU'RE RISKING FORECLOSURE.

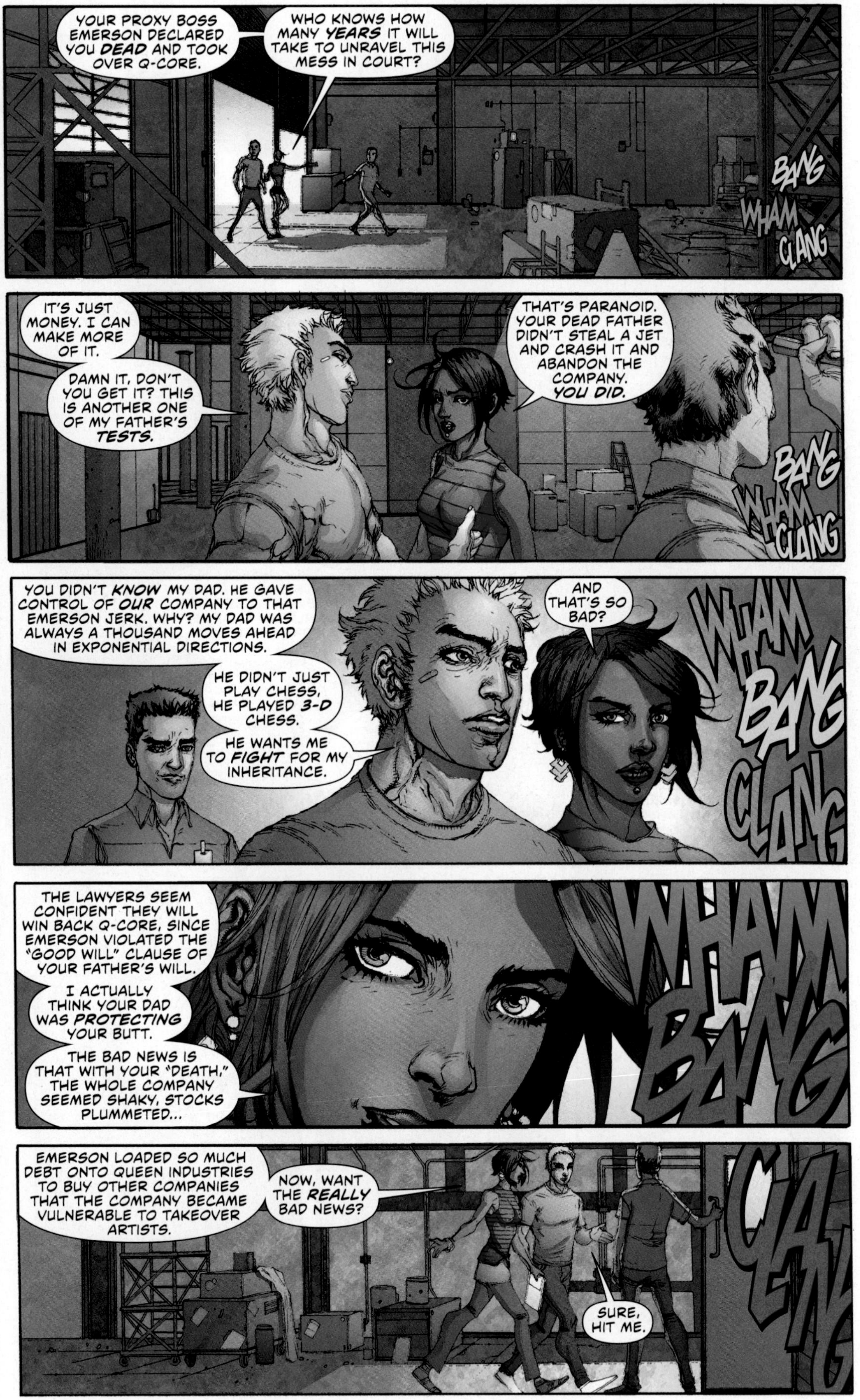
YOUR PROXY BOSS EMERSON DECLARED YOU DEAD AND TOOK OVER Q-CORE.
WHO KNOWS HOW MANY YEARS IT WILL TAKE TO UNRAVEL THIS MESS IN COURT?
BANG
WHAM
CLANG
IT'S JUST MONEY. I CAN MAKE MORE OF IT.
DAMN IT, DON'T YOU GET IT? THIS IS ANOTHER ONE OF MY FATHER'S TESTS.
THAT'S PARANOID. YOUR DEAD FATHER DIDN'T STEAL A JET AND CRASH IT AND ABANDON THE COMPANY. YOU DID.
BANG
WHAM
CLANG
YOU DIDN'T KNOW MY DAD. HE GAVE CONTROL OF OUR COMPANY TO THAT EMERSON JERK. WHY? MY DAD WAS ALWAYS A THOUSAND MOVES AHEAD IN EXPONENTIAL DIRECTIONS.
AND THAT'S SO BAD?
HE DIDN'T JUST PLAY CHESS, HE PLAYED 3-D CHESS.
HE WANTS ME TO FIGHT FOR MY INHERITANCE.
WHAM
BANG
CLANG
THE LAWYERS SEEM CONFIDENT THEY WILL WIN BACK Q-CORE, SINCE EMERSON VIOLATED THE "GOOD WILL" CLAUSE OF YOUR FATHER'S WILL.
I ACTUALLY THINK YOUR DAD WAS PROTECTING YOUR BUTT.
THE BAD NEWS IS THAT WITH YOUR "DEATH," THE WHOLE COMPANY SEEMED SHAKY, STOCKS PLUMMETED...
WHAM
BANG
EMERSON LOADED SO MUCH DEBT ONTO QUEEN INDUSTRIES TO BUY OTHER COMPANIES THAT THE COMPANY BECAME VULNERABLE TO TAKEOVER ARTISTS.
NOW, WANT THE REALLY BAD NEWS?
SURE, HIT ME.
CLANG

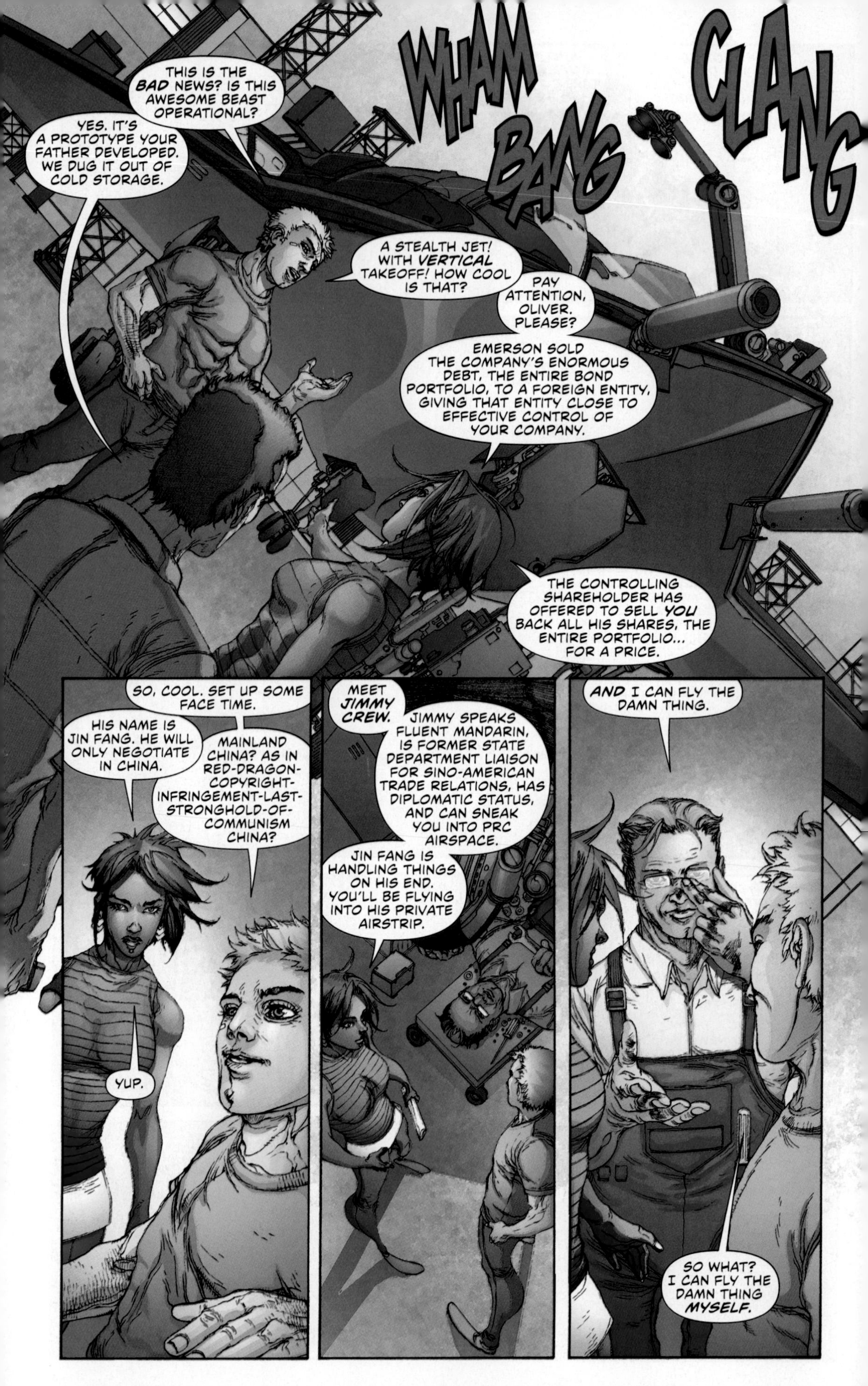
WHAM
BANG
CLANG
THIS IS THE BAD NEWS? IS THIS AWESOME BEAST OPERATIONAL?
YES. IT'S A PROTOTYPE YOUR FATHER DEVELOPED. WE DUG IT OUT OF COLD STORAGE.
A STEALTH JET! WITH VERTICAL TAKEOFF! HOW COOL IS THAT?
PAY ATTENTION, OLIVER. PLEASE?
EMERSON SOLD THE COMPANY'S ENORMOUS DEBT, THE ENTIRE BOND PORTFOLIO, TO A FOREIGN ENTITY, GIVING THAT ENTITY CLOSE TO EFFECTIVE CONTROL OF YOUR COMPANY.
THE CONTROLLING SHAREHOLDER HAS OFFERED TO SELL YOU BACK ALL HIS SHARES, THE ENTIRE PORTFOLIO... FOR A PRICE.
SO, COOL. SET UP SOME FACE TIME.
HIS NAME IS JIN FANG. HE WILL ONLY NEGOTIATE IN CHINA.
MAINLAND CHINA? AS IN RED-DRAGON-COPYRIGHT-INFRINGEMENT-LAST-STRONGHOLD-OF-COMMUNISM CHINA?
YUP.
MEET JIMMY CREW.
JIMMY SPEAKS FLUENT MANDARIN, IS FORMER STATE DEPARTMENT LIAISON FOR SINO-AMERICAN TRADE RELATIONS, HAS DIPLOMATIC STATUS, AND CAN SNEAK YOU INTO PRC AIRSPACE.
JIN FANG IS HANDLING THINGS ON HIS END. YOU'LL BE FLYING INTO HIS PRIVATE AIRSTRIP.
AND I CAN FLY THE DAMN THING.
SO WHAT? I CAN FLY THE DAMN THING MYSELF.

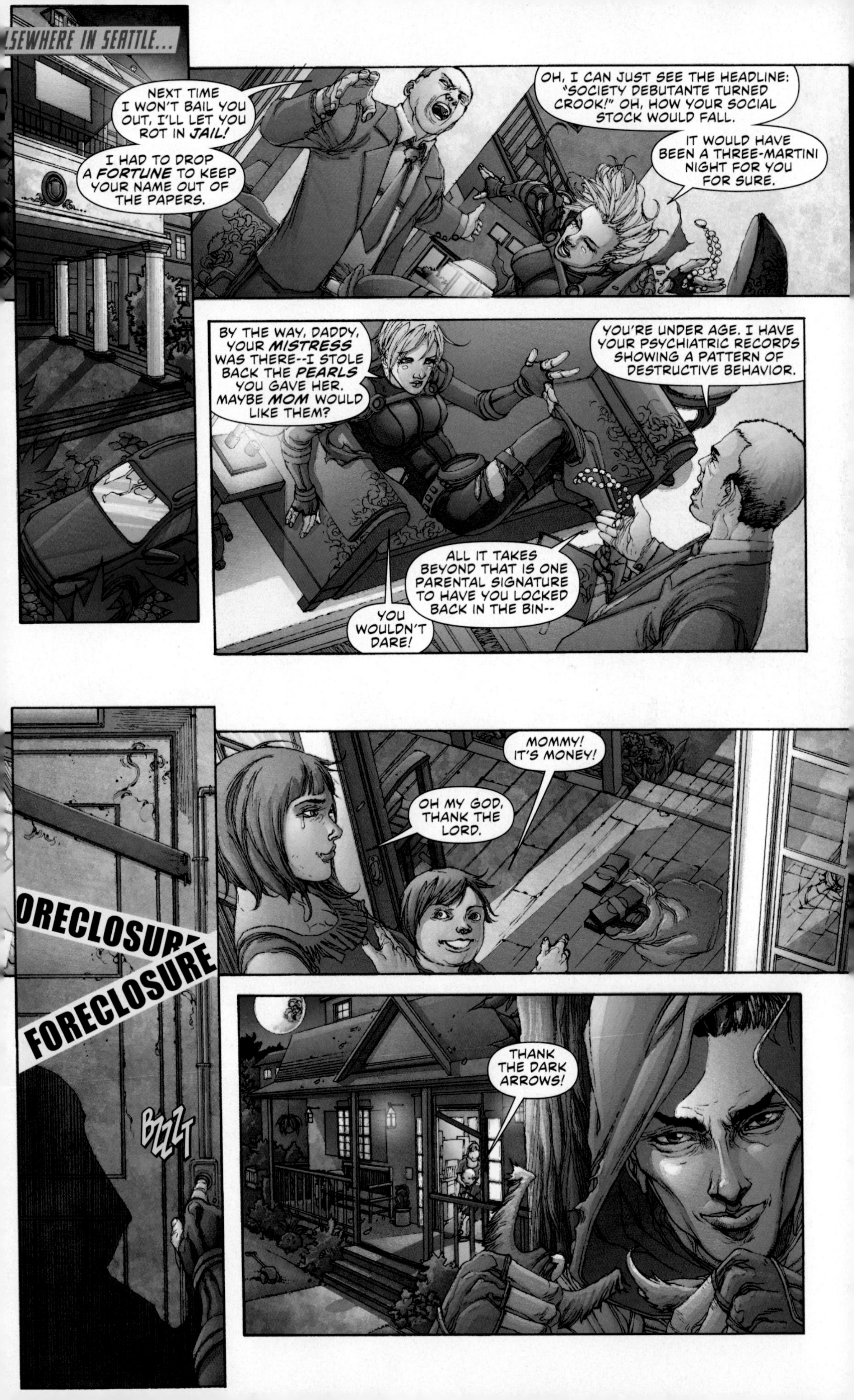
SEWHERE IN SEATTLE...
NEXT TIME I WON'T BAIL YOU OUT, I'LL LET YOU ROT IN JAIL!
I HAD TO DROP A FORTUNE TO KEEP YOUR NAME OUT OF THE PAPERS.
OH, I CAN JUST SEE THE HEADLINE: "SOCIETY DEBUTANTE TURNED CROOK!" OH, HOW YOUR SOCIAL STOCK WOULD FALL.
IT WOULD HAVE BEEN A THREE-MARTINI NIGHT FOR YOU FOR SURE.
BY THE WAY, DADDY, YOUR MISTRESS WAS THERE--I STOLE BACK THE PEARLS YOU GAVE HER. MAYBE MOM WOULD LIKE THEM?
YOU'RE UNDER AGE. I HAVE YOUR PSYCHIATRIC RECORDS SHOWING A PATTERN OF DESTRUCTIVE BEHAVIOR.
ALL IT TAKES BEYOND THAT IS ONE PARENTAL SIGNATURE TO HAVE YOU LOCKED BACK IN THE BIN--
YOU WOULDN'T DARE!
OreCLOSURE
FORECLOSURE
FORECLOSURE
BZZZT
MOMMY! IT'S MONEY!
OH MY GOD, THANK THE LORD.
THANK THE DARK ARROWS!

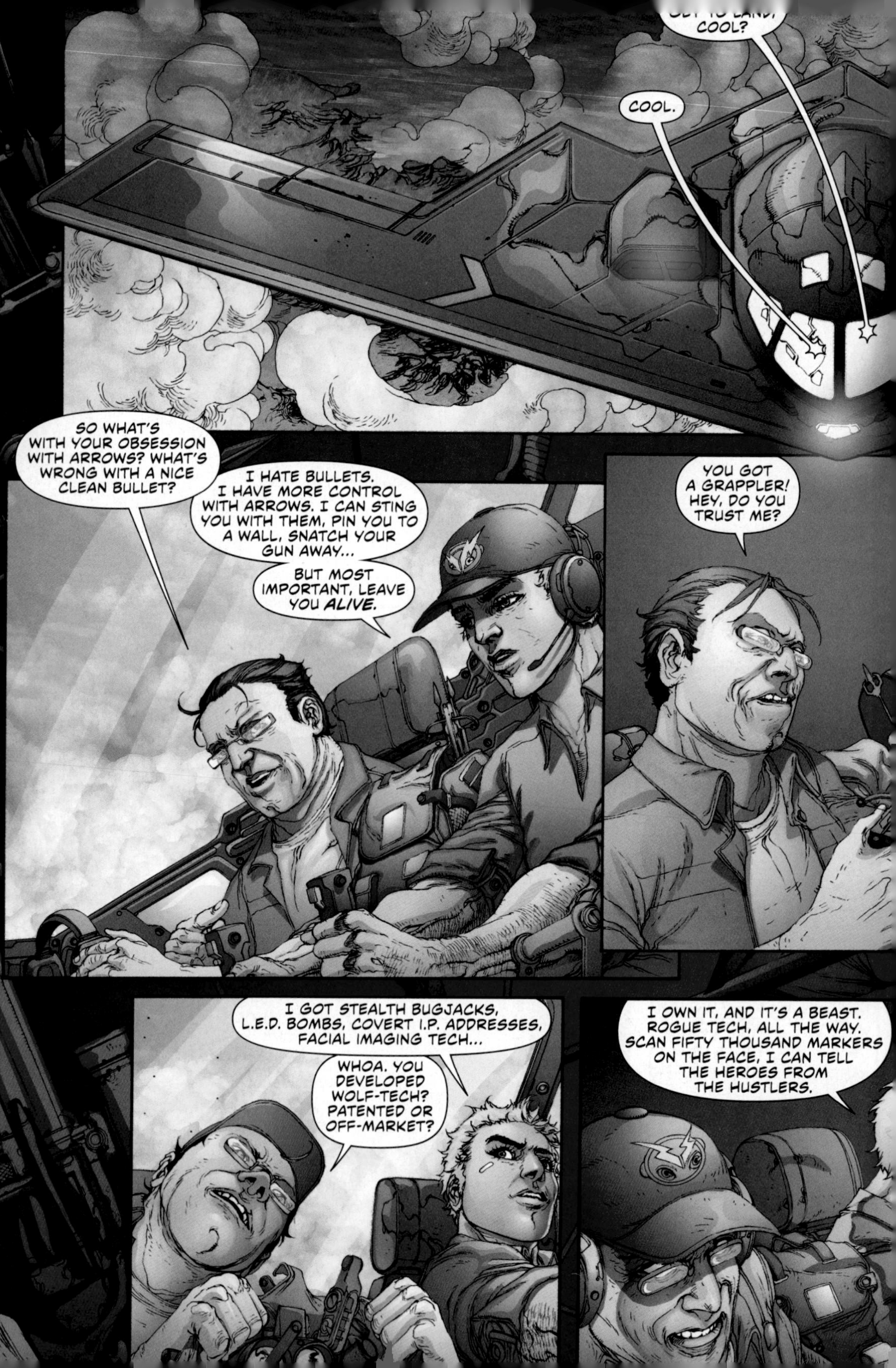
COOL?
COOL.
SO WHAT'S WITH YOUR OBSESSION WITH ARROWS? WHAT'S WRONG WITH A NICE CLEAN BULLET?
I HATE BULLETS. I HAVE MORE CONTROL WITH ARROWS. I CAN STING YOU WITH THEM, PIN YOU TO A WALL, SNATCH YOUR GUN AWAY...
BUT MOST IMPORTANT, LEAVE YOU *ALIVE*.
YOU GOT A GRAPPLER! HEY, DO YOU TRUST ME?
I GOT STEALTH BUGJACKS, L.E.D. BOMBS, COVERT I.P. ADDRESSES, FACIAL IMAGING TECH...
WHOA. YOU DEVELOPED WOLF-TECH? PATENTED OR OFF-MARKET?
I OWN IT, AND IT'S A BEAST. ROGUE TECH, ALL THE WAY. SCAN FIFTY THOUSAND MARKERS ON THE FACE, I CAN TELL THE HEROES FROM THE HUSTLERS.

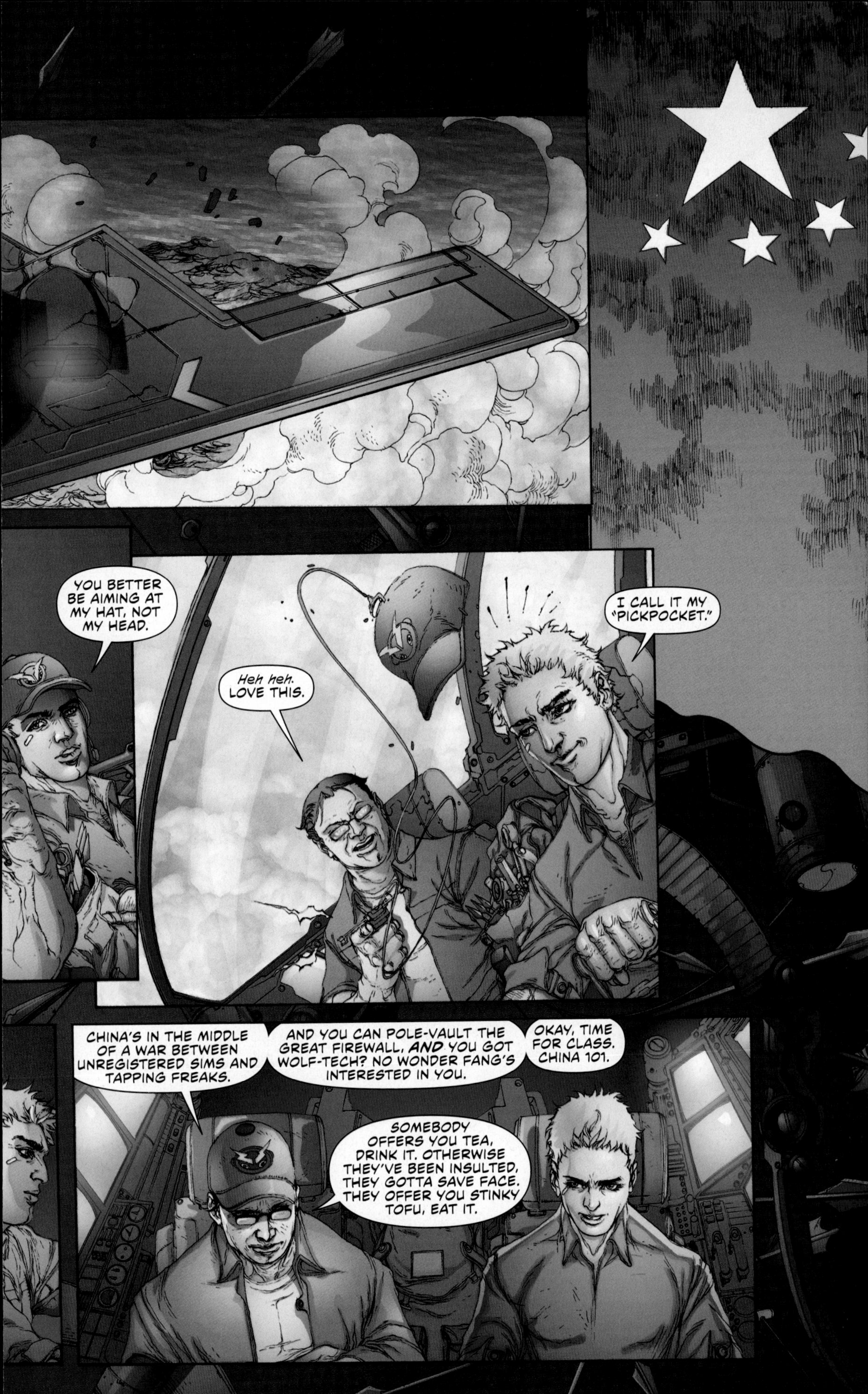
YOU BETTER BE AIMING AT MY HAT, NOT MY HEAD.
Heh heh. LOVE THIS.
I CALL IT MY "PICKPOCKET."
CHINA'S IN THE MIDDLE OF A WAR BETWEEN UNREGISTERED SIMS AND TAPPING FREAKS.
AND YOU CAN POLE-VAULT THE GREAT FIREWALL, AND YOU GOT WOLF-TECH? NO WONDER FANG'S INTERESTED IN YOU.
OKAY, TIME FOR CLASS. CHINA 101.
SOMEBODY OFFERS YOU TEA, DRINK IT. OTHERWISE THEY'VE BEEN INSULTED, THEY GOTTA SAVE FACE. THEY OFFER YOU STINKY TOFU, EAT IT.

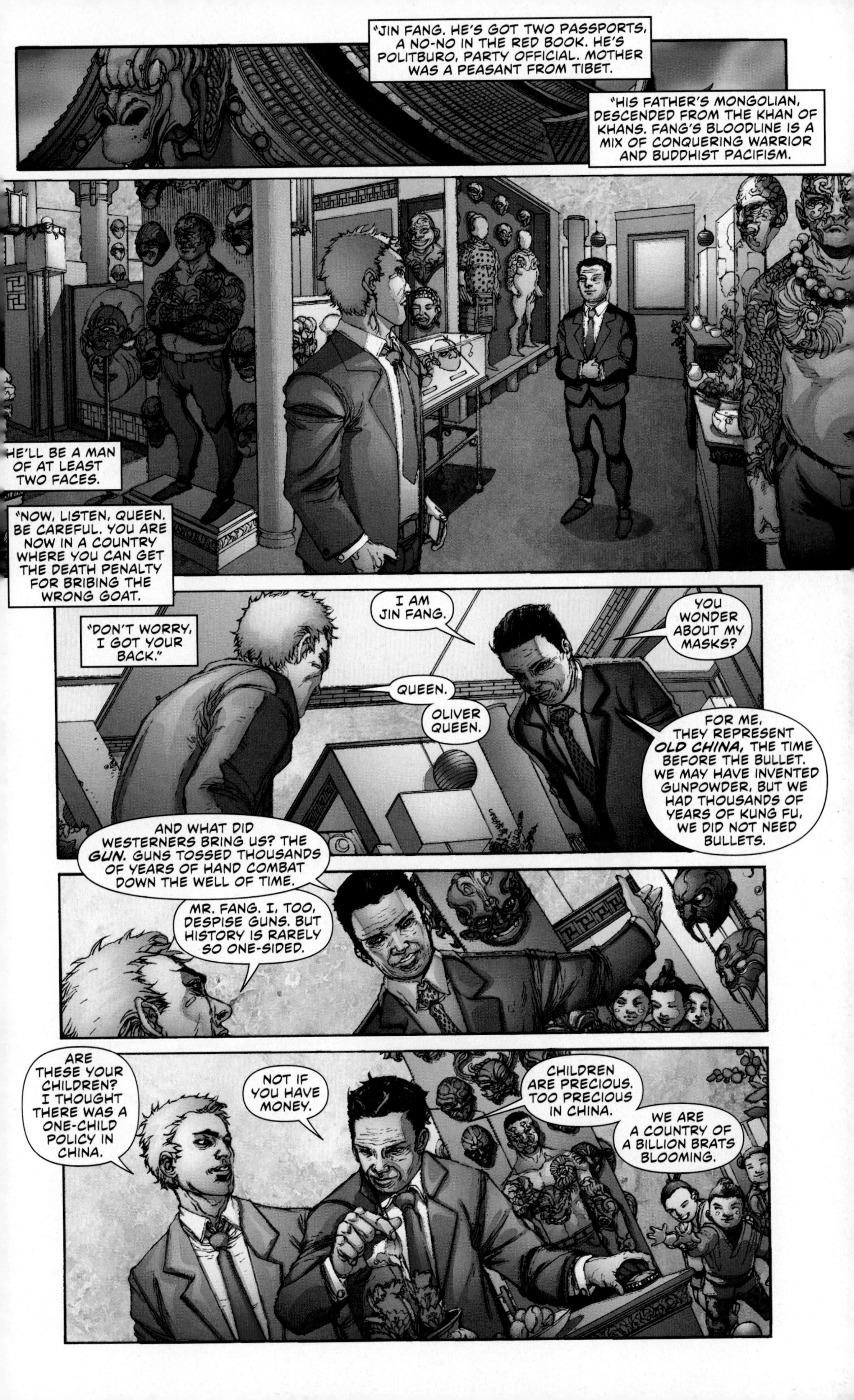
"JIN FANG. HE'S GOT TWO PASSPORTS, A NO-NO IN THE RED BOOK. HE'S POLITBURO, PARTY OFFICIAL. MOTHER WAS A PEASANT FROM TIBET.
"HIS FATHER'S MONGOLIAN, DESCENDED FROM THE KHAN OF KHANS. FANG'S BLOODLINE IS A MIX OF CONQUERING WARRIOR AND BUDDHIST PACIFISM.
HE'LL BE A MAN OF AT LEAST TWO FACES.
"NOW, LISTEN, QUEEN. BE CAREFUL. YOU ARE NOW IN A COUNTRY WHERE YOU CAN GET THE DEATH PENALTY FOR BRIBING THE WRONG GOAT.
"DON'T WORRY, I GOT YOUR BACK."
I AM JIN FANG.
QUEEN.
OLIVER QUEEN.
YOU WONDER ABOUT MY MASKS?
FOR ME, THEY REPRESENT *OLD CHINA,* THE TIME BEFORE THE BULLET. WE MAY HAVE INVENTED GUNPOWDER, BUT WE HAD THOUSANDS OF YEARS OF KUNG FU, WE DID NOT NEED BULLETS.
AND WHAT DID WESTERNERS BRING US? THE *GUN.* GUNS TOSSED THOUSANDS OF YEARS OF HAND COMBAT DOWN THE WELL OF TIME.
MR. FANG. I, TOO, DESPISE GUNS. BUT HISTORY IS RARELY SO ONE-SIDED.
ARE THESE YOUR CHILDREN? I THOUGHT THERE WAS A ONE-CHILD POLICY IN CHINA.
NOT IF YOU HAVE MONEY.
CHILDREN ARE PRECIOUS. TOO PRECIOUS IN CHINA.
WE ARE A COUNTRY OF A BILLION BRATS BLOOMING.

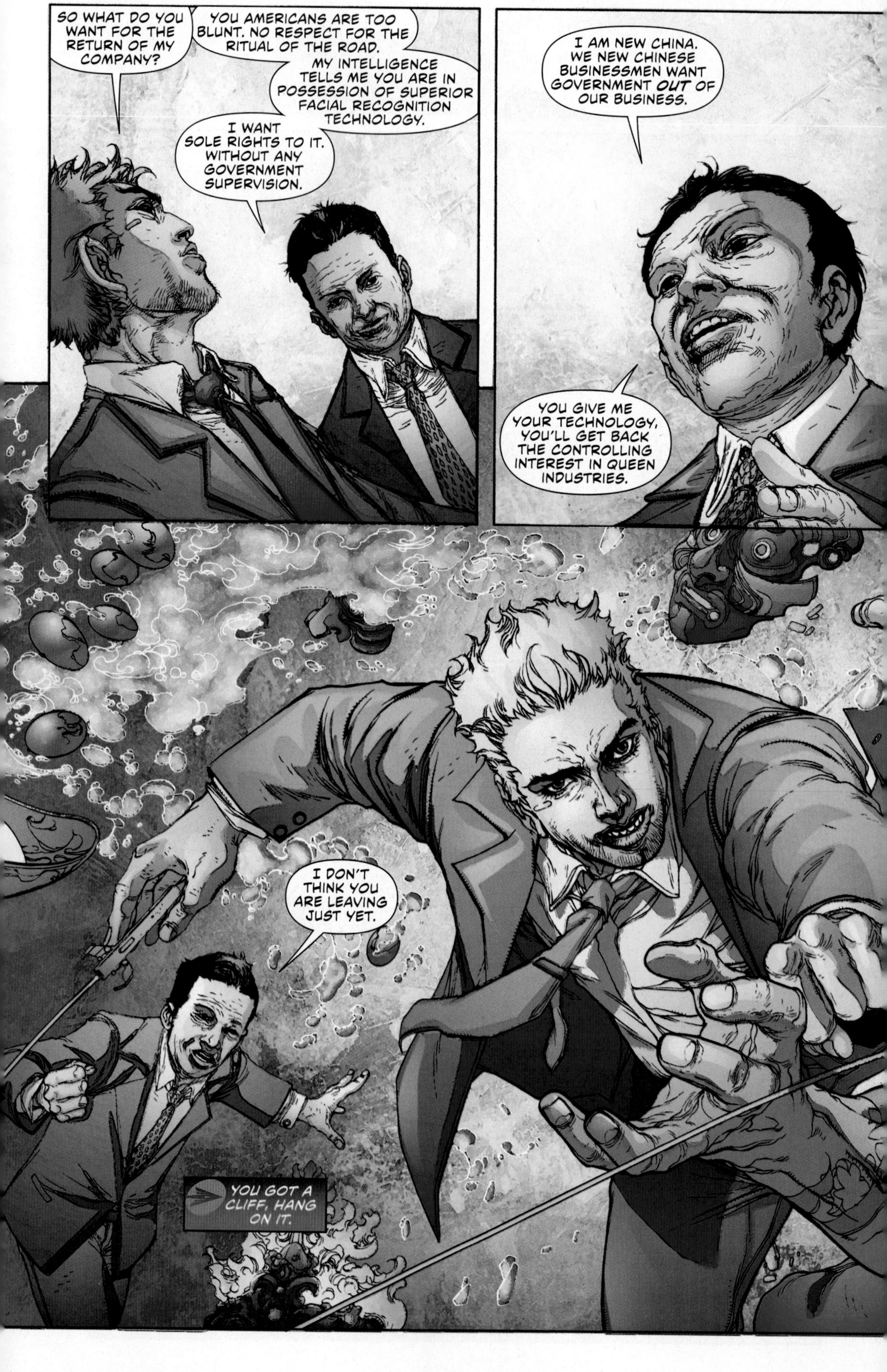
SO WHAT DO YOU WANT FOR THE RETURN OF MY COMPANY?
YOU AMERICANS ARE TOO BLUNT. NO RESPECT FOR THE RITUAL OF THE ROAD.
MY INTELLIGENCE TELLS ME YOU ARE IN POSSESSION OF SUPERIOR FACIAL RECOGNITION TECHNOLOGY.
I WANT SOLE RIGHTS TO IT. WITHOUT ANY GOVERNMENT SUPERVISION.
I AM NEW CHINA. WE NEW CHINESE BUSINESSMEN WANT GOVERNMENT OUT OF OUR BUSINESS.
YOU GIVE ME YOUR TECHNOLOGY, YOU'LL GET BACK THE CONTROLLING INTEREST IN QUEEN INDUSTRIES.
I DON'T THINK YOU ARE LEAVING JUST YET.
YOU GOT A CLIFF, HANG ON IT.

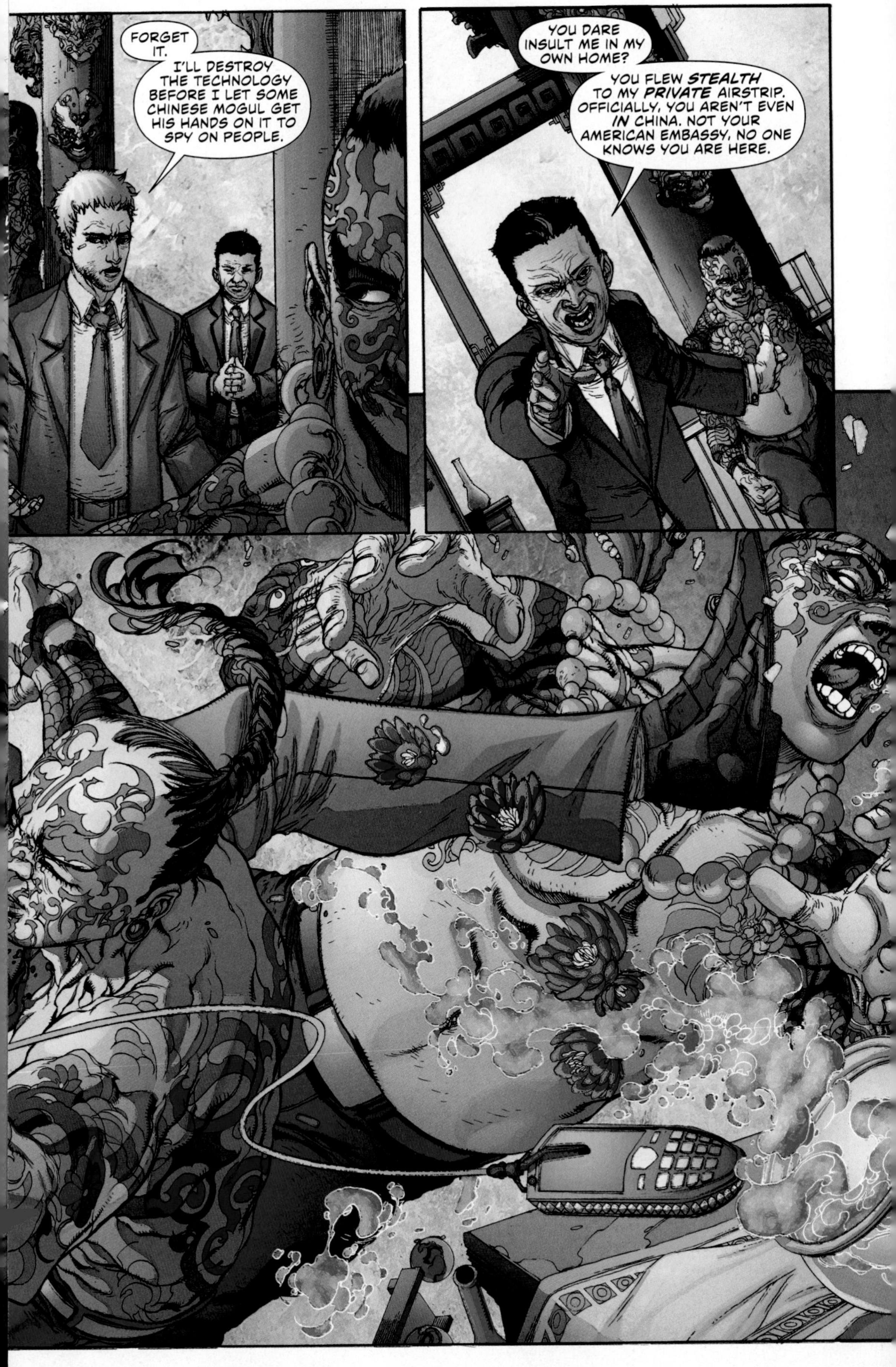
FORGET IT.
I'LL DESTROY THE TECHNOLOGY BEFORE I LET SOME CHINESE MOGUL GET HIS HANDS ON IT TO SPY ON PEOPLE.
YOU DARE INSULT ME IN MY OWN HOME?
YOU FLEW STEALTH TO MY PRIVATE AIRSTRIP. OFFICIALLY, YOU AREN'T EVEN IN CHINA. NOT YOUR AMERICAN EMBASSY, NO ONE KNOWS YOU ARE HERE.

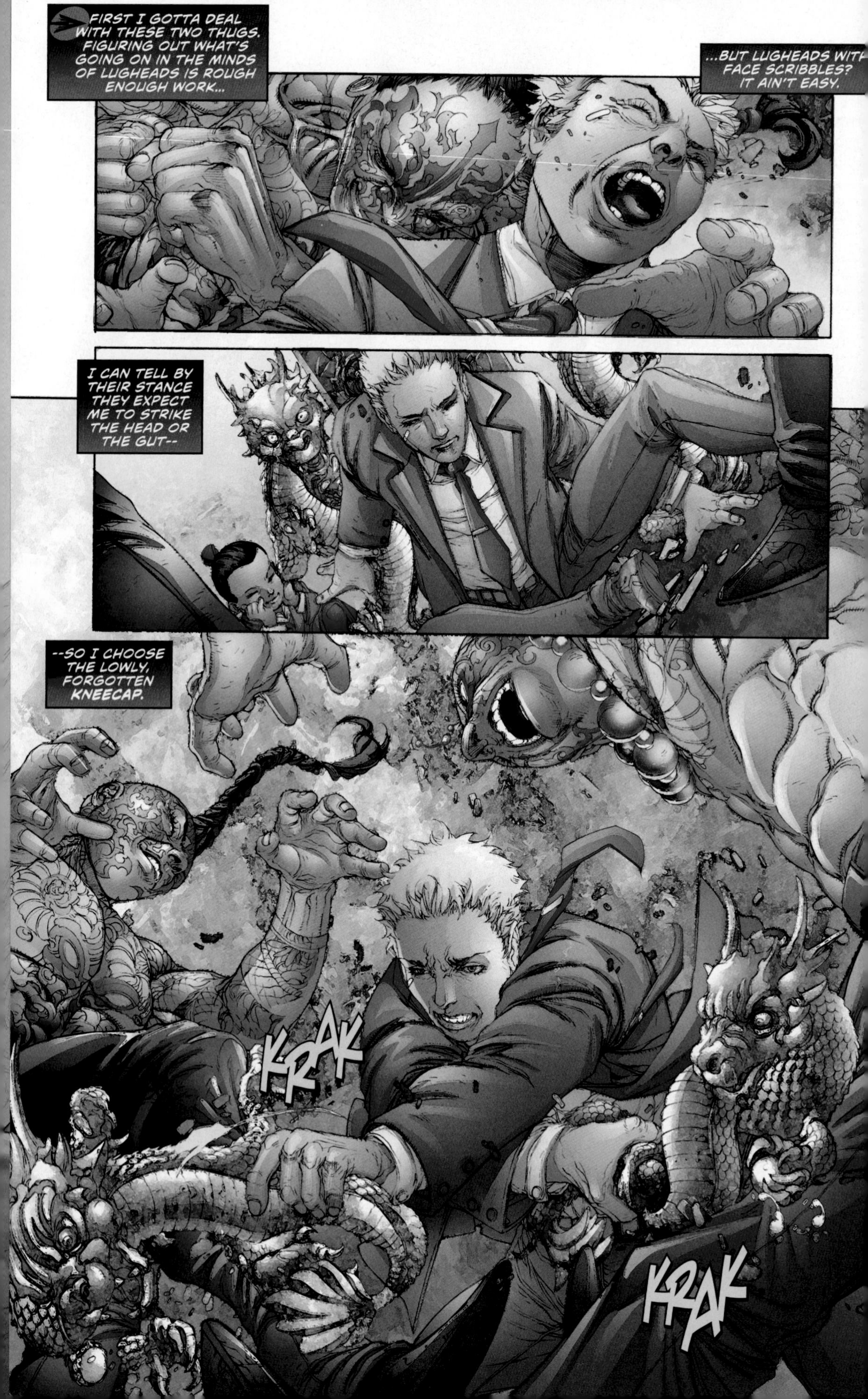
FIRST I GOTTA DEAL WITH THESE TWO THUGS. FIGURING OUT WHAT'S GOING ON IN THE MINDS OF LUGHEADS IS ROUGH ENOUGH WORK...
...BUT LUGHEADS WITH FACE SCRIBBLES? IT AIN'T EASY.
I CAN TELL BY THEIR STANCE THEY EXPECT ME TO STRIKE THE HEAD OR THE GUT--
--SO I CHOOSE THE LOWLY, FORGOTTEN KNEECAP.
KRAK
KRAK

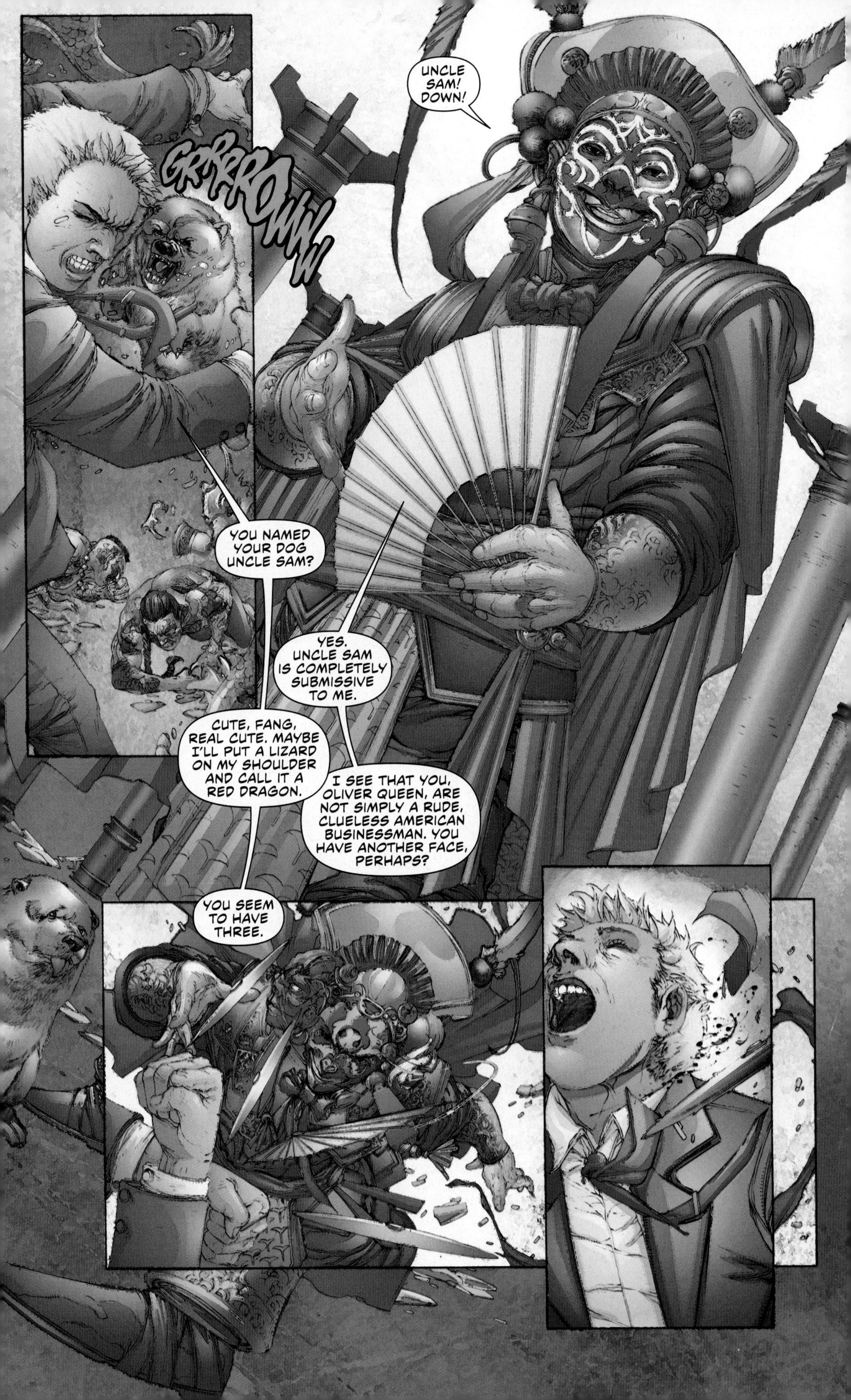

UNCLE SAM! DOWN!
GRRRROWW!
YOU NAMED YOUR DOG UNCLE SAM?
YES. UNCLE SAM IS COMPLETELY SUBMISSIVE TO ME.
CUTE, FANG, REAL CUTE. MAYBE I'LL PUT A LIZARD ON MY SHOULDER AND CALL IT A RED DRAGON.
I SEE THAT YOU, OLIVER QUEEN, ARE NOT SIMPLY A RUDE, CLUELESS AMERICAN BUSINESSMAN. YOU HAVE ANOTHER FACE, PERHAPS?
YOU SEEM TO HAVE THREE.

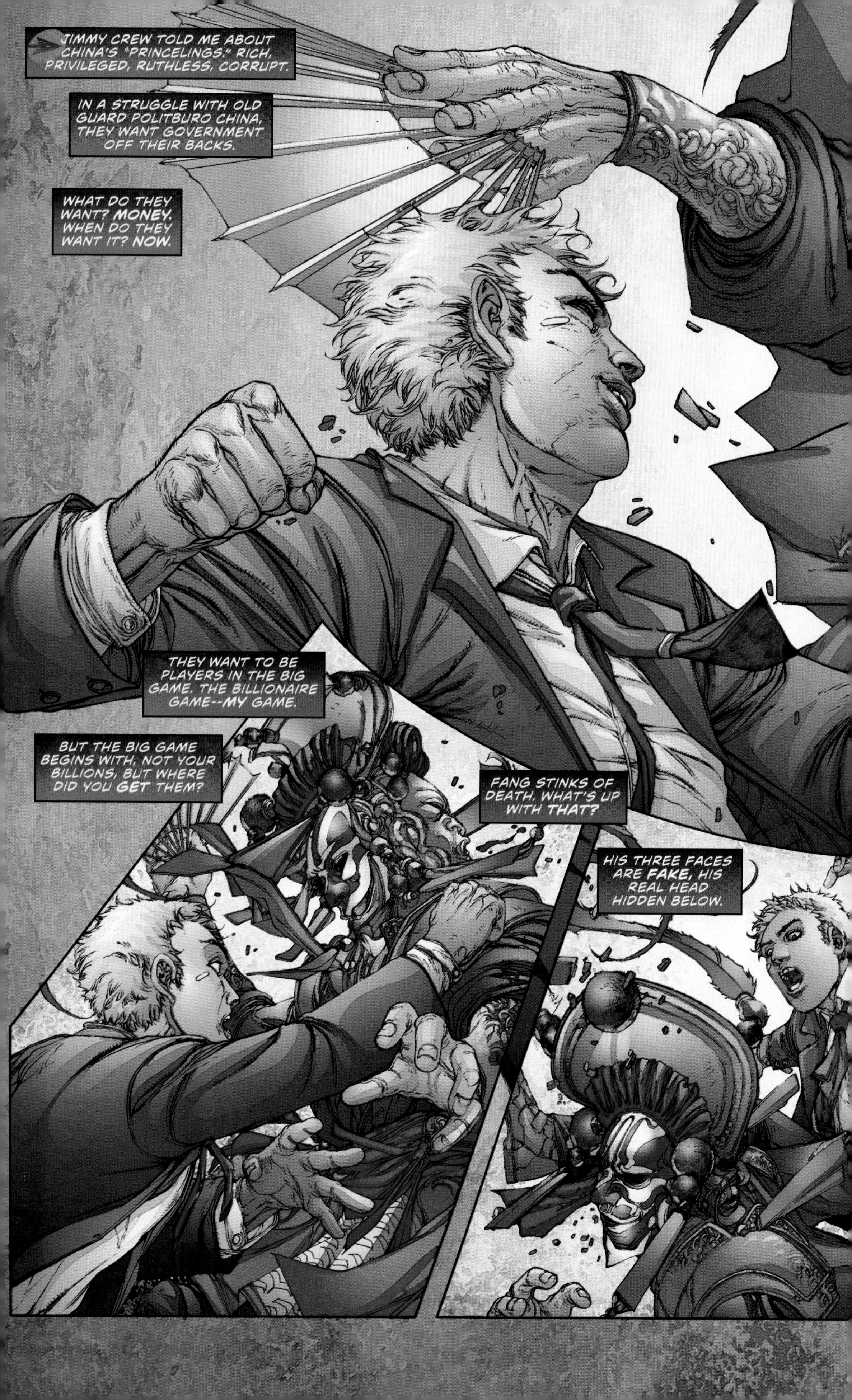
JIMMY CREW TOLD ME ABOUT CHINA'S "PRINCELINGS." RICH, PRIVILEGED, RUTHLESS, CORRUPT.
IN A STRUGGLE WITH OLD GUARD POLITBURO CHINA, THEY WANT GOVERNMENT OFF THEIR BACKS.
WHAT DO THEY WANT? MONEY. WHEN DO THEY WANT IT? NOW.
THEY WANT TO BE PLAYERS IN THE BIG GAME. THE BILLIONAIRE GAME--MY GAME.
BUT THE BIG GAME BEGINS WITH, NOT YOUR BILLIONS, BUT WHERE DID YOU GET THEM?
FANG STINKS OF DEATH. WHAT'S UP WITH THAT?
HIS THREE FACES ARE FAKE, HIS REAL HEAD HIDDEN BELOW.

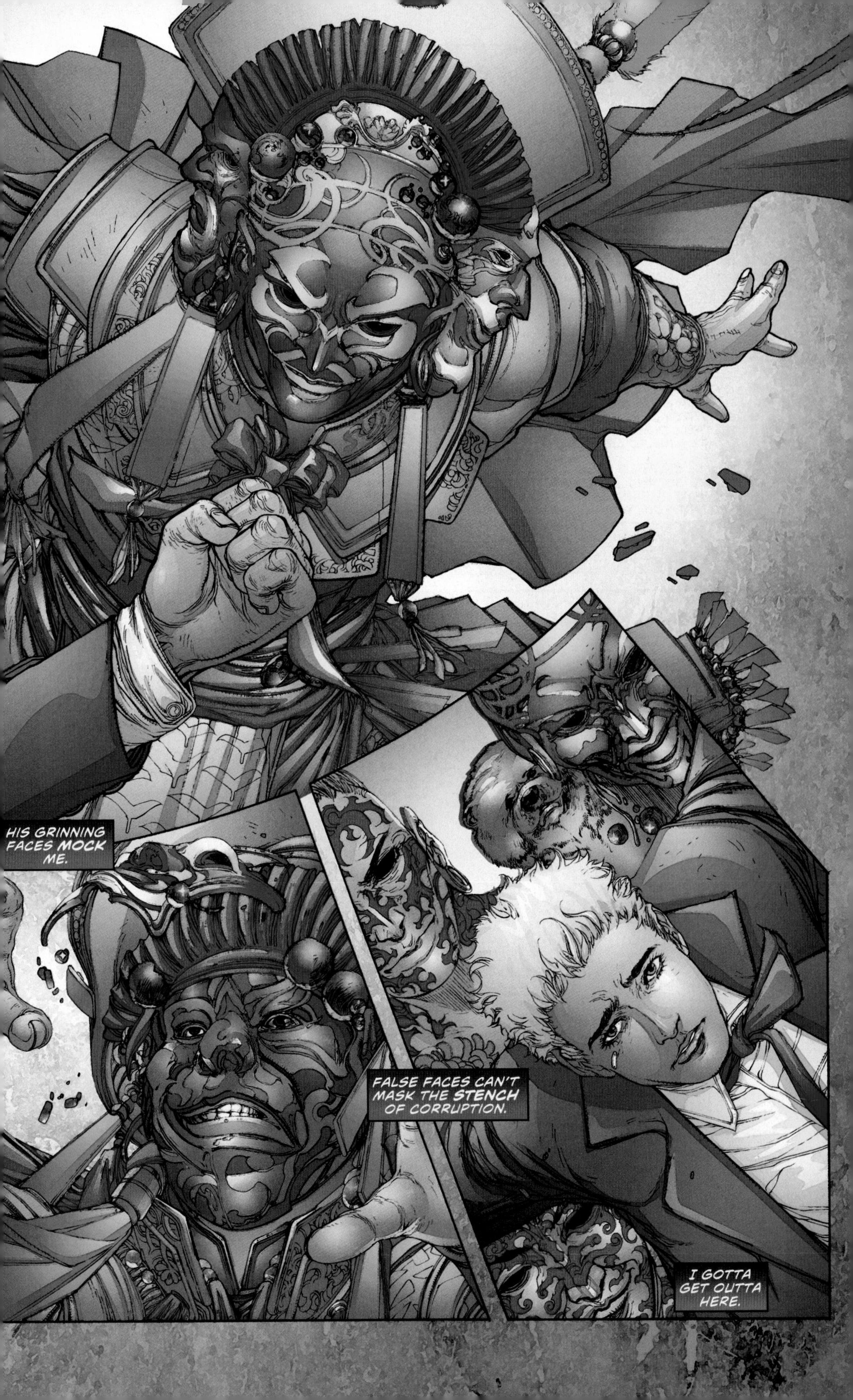
HIS GRINNING FACES MOCK ME.
FALSE FACES CAN'T MASK THE STENCH OF CORRUPTION.
I GOTTA GET OUTTA HERE.

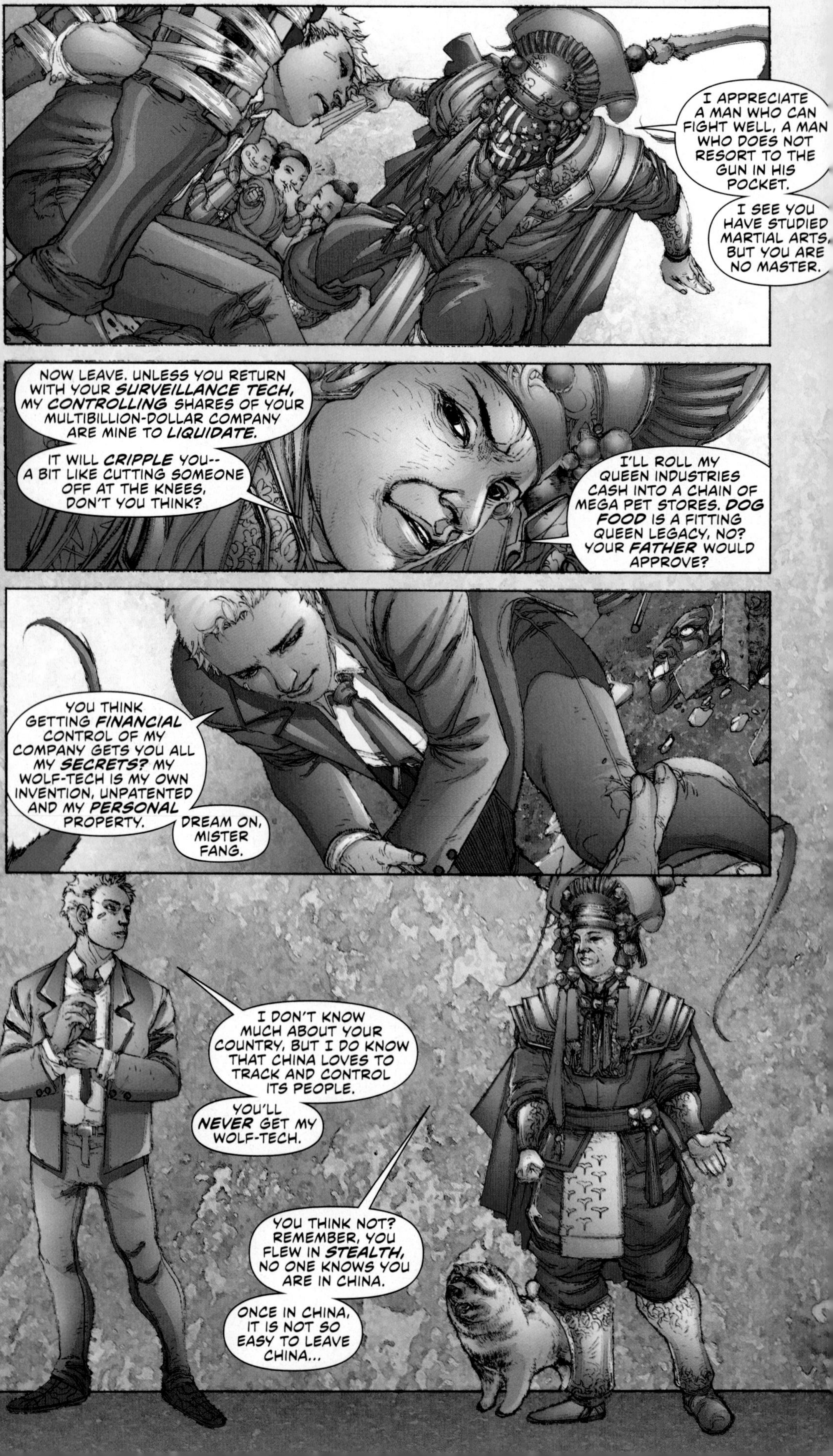
I APPRECIATE A MAN WHO CAN FIGHT WELL, A MAN WHO DOES NOT RESORT TO THE GUN IN HIS POCKET.
I SEE YOU HAVE STUDIED MARTIAL ARTS, BUT YOU ARE NO MASTER.
NOW LEAVE. UNLESS YOU RETURN WITH YOUR SURVEILLANCE TECH, MY CONTROLLING SHARES OF YOUR MULTIBILLION-DOLLAR COMPANY ARE MINE TO LIQUIDATE.
IT WILL CRIPPLE YOU-- A BIT LIKE CUTTING SOMEONE OFF AT THE KNEES, DON'T YOU THINK?
I'LL ROLL MY QUEEN INDUSTRIES CASH INTO A CHAIN OF MEGA PET STORES. DOG FOOD IS A FITTING QUEEN LEGACY, NO? YOUR FATHER WOULD APPROVE?
YOU THINK GETTING FINANCIAL CONTROL OF MY COMPANY GETS YOU ALL MY SECRETS? MY WOLF-TECH IS MY OWN INVENTION, UNPATENTED AND MY PERSONAL PROPERTY.
DREAM ON, MISTER FANG.
I DON'T KNOW MUCH ABOUT YOUR COUNTRY, BUT I DO KNOW THAT CHINA LOVES TO TRACK AND CONTROL ITS PEOPLE.
YOU'LL NEVER GET MY WOLF-TECH.
YOU THINK NOT? REMEMBER, YOU FLEW IN STEALTH, NO ONE KNOWS YOU ARE IN CHINA.
ONCE IN CHINA, IT IS NOT SO EASY TO LEAVE CHINA...

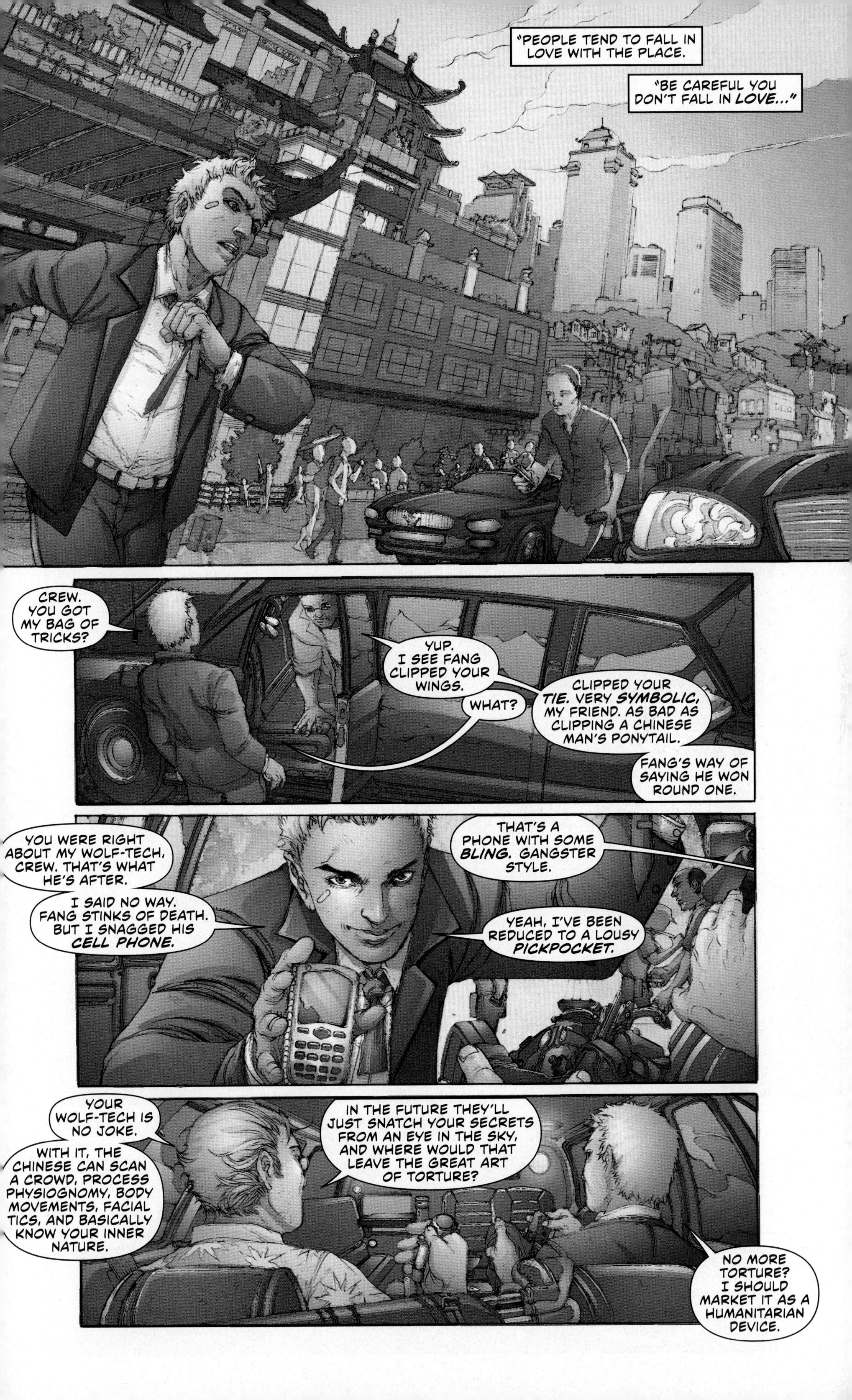
"PEOPLE TEND TO FALL IN LOVE WITH THE PLACE.
"BE CAREFUL YOU DON'T FALL IN *LOVE...*"
CREW. YOU GOT MY BAG OF TRICKS?
YUP. I SEE FANG CLIPPED YOUR WINGS.
WHAT?
CLIPPED YOUR *TIE*. VERY *SYMBOLIC*, MY FRIEND. AS BAD AS CLIPPING A CHINESE MAN'S PONYTAIL.
FANG'S WAY OF SAYING HE WON ROUND ONE.
YOU WERE RIGHT ABOUT MY WOLF-TECH, CREW. THAT'S WHAT HE'S AFTER.
I SAID NO WAY. FANG STINKS OF DEATH. BUT I SNAGGED HIS *CELL PHONE.*
THAT'S A PHONE WITH SOME *BLING.* GANGSTER STYLE.
YEAH, I'VE BEEN REDUCED TO A LOUSY *PICKPOCKET.*
YOUR WOLF-TECH IS NO JOKE.
WITH IT, THE CHINESE CAN SCAN A CROWD, PROCESS PHYSIOGNOMY, BODY MOVEMENTS, FACIAL TICS, AND BASICALLY KNOW YOUR INNER NATURE.
IN THE FUTURE THEY'LL JUST SNATCH YOUR SECRETS FROM AN EYE IN THE SKY, AND WHERE WOULD THAT LEAVE THE GREAT ART OF TORTURE?
NO MORE TORTURE? I SHOULD MARKET IT AS A HUMANITARIAN DEVICE.

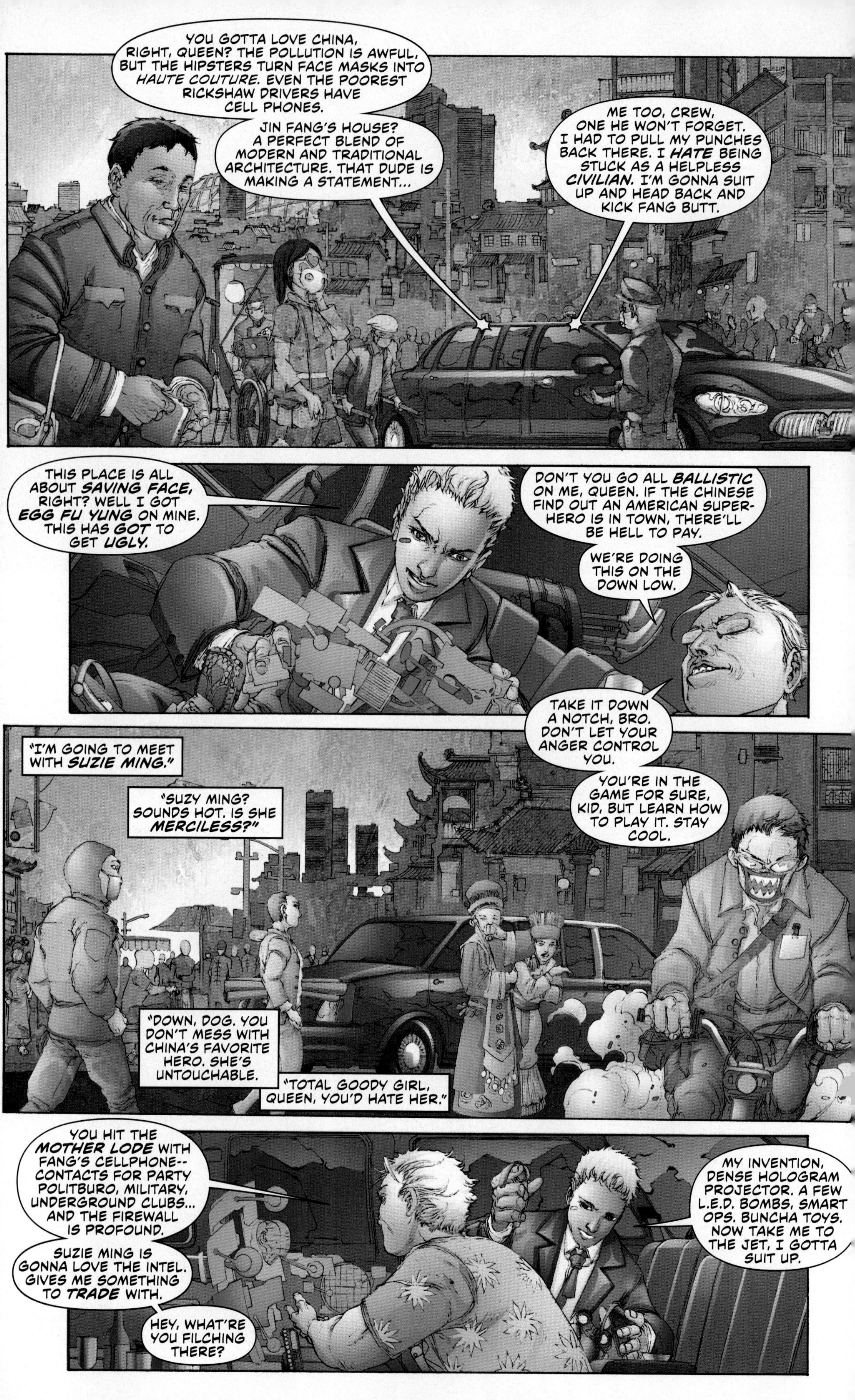
YOU GOTTA LOVE CHINA, RIGHT, QUEEN? THE POLLUTION IS AWFUL, BUT THE HIPSTERS TURN FACE MASKS INTO HAUTE COUTURE. EVEN THE POOREST RICKSHAW DRIVERS HAVE CELL PHONES.
JIN FANG'S HOUSE? A PERFECT BLEND OF MODERN AND TRADITIONAL ARCHITECTURE. THAT DUDE IS MAKING A STATEMENT...
ME TOO, CREW, ONE HE WON'T FORGET. I HAD TO PULL MY PUNCHES BACK THERE. I HATE BEING STUCK AS A HELPLESS CIVILIAN. I'M GONNA SUIT UP AND HEAD BACK AND KICK FANG BUTT.
THIS PLACE IS ALL ABOUT SAVING FACE, RIGHT? WELL I GOT EGG FU YUNG ON MINE. THIS HAS GOT TO GET UGLY.
DON'T YOU GO ALL BALLISTIC ON ME, QUEEN. IF THE CHINESE FIND OUT AN AMERICAN SUPER-HERO IS IN TOWN, THERE'LL BE HELL TO PAY.
WE'RE DOING THIS ON THE DOWN LOW.
TAKE IT DOWN A NOTCH, BRO. DON'T LET YOUR ANGER CONTROL YOU.
YOU'RE IN THE GAME FOR SURE, KID, BUT LEARN HOW TO PLAY IT. STAY COOL.
"I'M GOING TO MEET WITH SUZIE MING."
"SUZY MING? SOUNDS HOT. IS SHE MERCILESS?"
"DOWN, DOG. YOU DON'T MESS WITH CHINA'S FAVORITE HERO. SHE'S UNTOUCHABLE.
"TOTAL GOODY GIRL, QUEEN, YOU'D HATE HER."
YOU HIT THE MOTHER LODE WITH FANG'S CELLPHONE-- CONTACTS FOR PARTY POLITBURO, MILITARY, UNDERGROUND CLUBS... AND THE FIREWALL IS PROFOUND.
SUZIE MING IS GONNA LOVE THE INTEL. GIVES ME SOMETHING TO TRADE WITH.
HEY, WHAT'RE YOU FILCHING THERE?
MY INVENTION, DENSE HOLOGRAM PROJECTOR. A FEW L.E.D. BOMBS, SMART OPS. BUNCHA TOYS. NOW TAKE ME TO THE JET, I GOTTA SUIT UP.

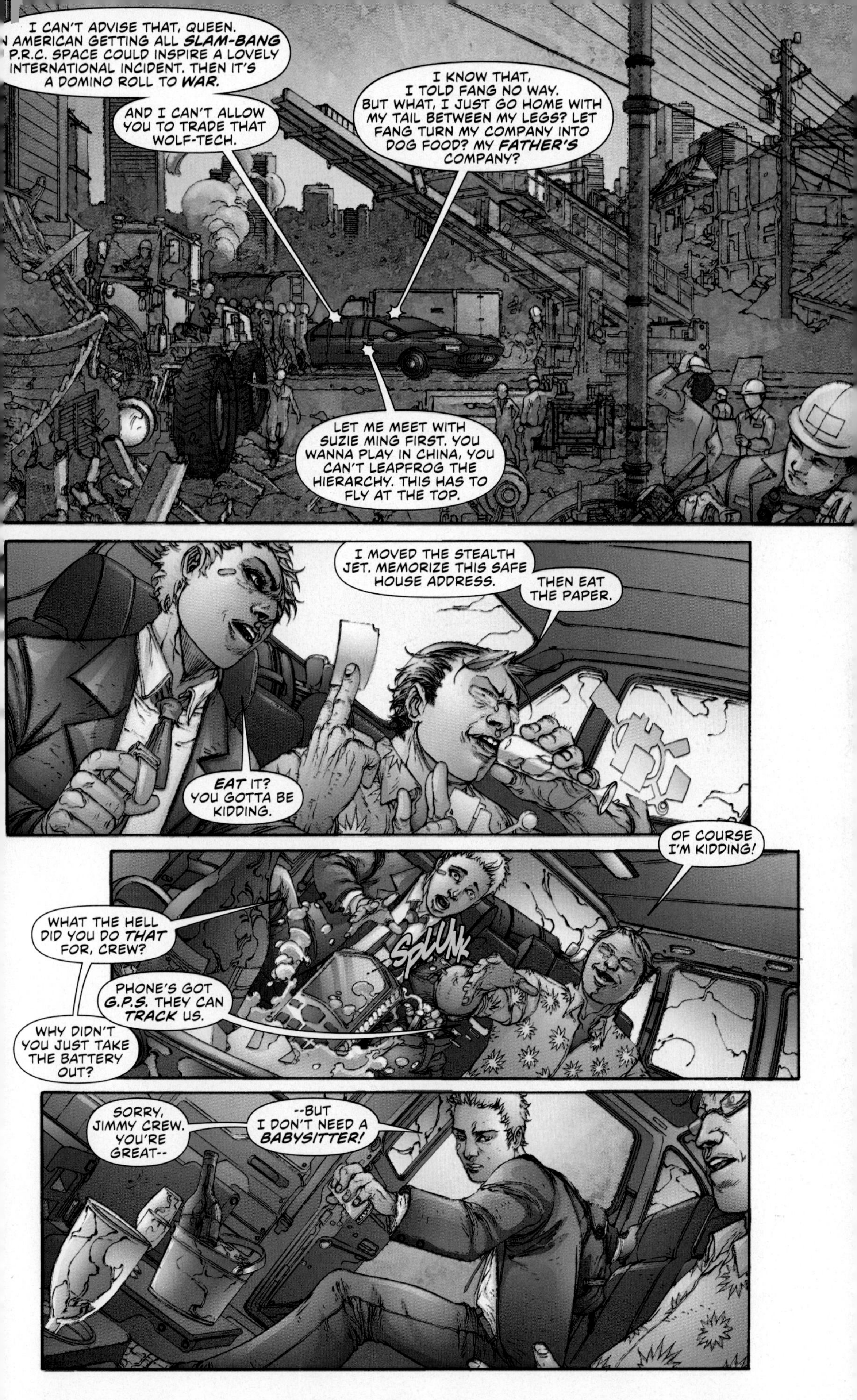
I CAN'T ADVISE THAT, QUEEN. AN AMERICAN GETTING ALL SLAM-BANG IN P.R.C. SPACE COULD INSPIRE A LOVELY INTERNATIONAL INCIDENT. THEN IT'S A DOMINO ROLL TO WAR.
AND I CAN'T ALLOW YOU TO TRADE THAT WOLF-TECH.
I KNOW THAT, I TOLD FANG NO WAY. BUT WHAT, I JUST GO HOME WITH MY TAIL BETWEEN MY LEGS? LET FANG TURN MY COMPANY INTO DOG FOOD? MY FATHER'S COMPANY?
LET ME MEET WITH SUZIE MING FIRST. YOU WANNA PLAY IN CHINA, YOU CAN'T LEAPFROG THE HIERARCHY. THIS HAS TO FLY AT THE TOP.
I MOVED THE STEALTH JET. MEMORIZE THIS SAFE HOUSE ADDRESS.
THEN EAT THE PAPER.
EAT IT? YOU GOTTA BE KIDDING.
OF COURSE I'M KIDDING!
SPLUNK
WHAT THE HELL DID YOU DO THAT FOR, CREW?
PHONE'S GOT G.P.S. THEY CAN TRACK US.
WHY DIDN'T YOU JUST TAKE THE BATTERY OUT?
SORRY, JIMMY CREW. YOU'RE GREAT--
--BUT I DON'T NEED A BABYSITTER!

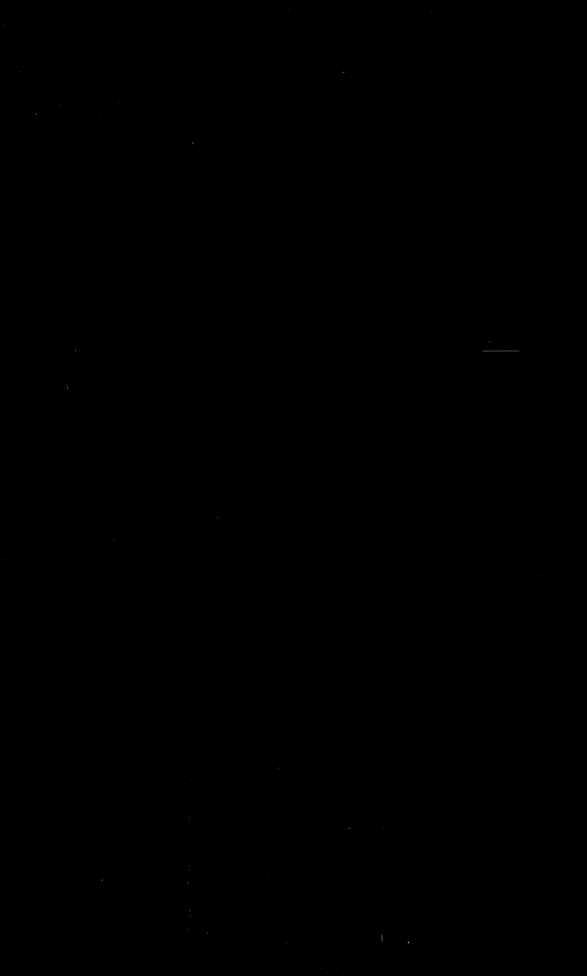

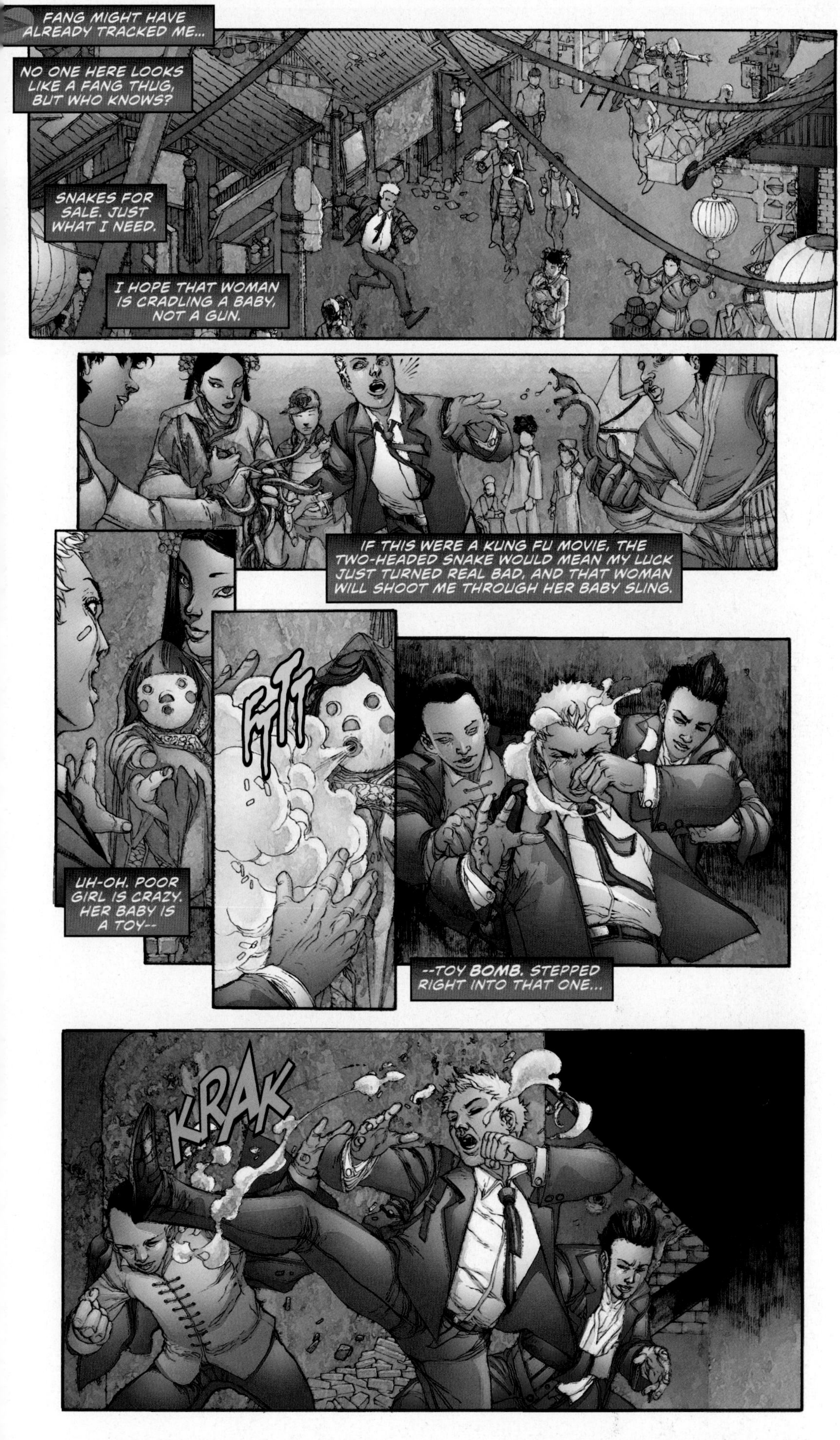

FANG MIGHT HAVE ALREADY TRACKED ME...
NO ONE HERE LOOKS LIKE A FANG THUG, BUT WHO KNOWS?
SNAKES FOR SALE. JUST WHAT I NEED.
I HOPE THAT WOMAN IS CRADLING A BABY, NOT A GUN.
IF THIS WERE A KUNG FU MOVIE, THE TWO-HEADED SNAKE WOULD MEAN MY LUCK JUST TURNED REAL BAD, AND THAT WOMAN WILL SHOOT ME THROUGH HER BABY SLING.
UH-OH. POOR GIRL IS CRAZY. HER BABY IS A TOY--
FTTT
--TOY BOMB. STEPPED RIGHT INTO THAT ONE...
KRAK

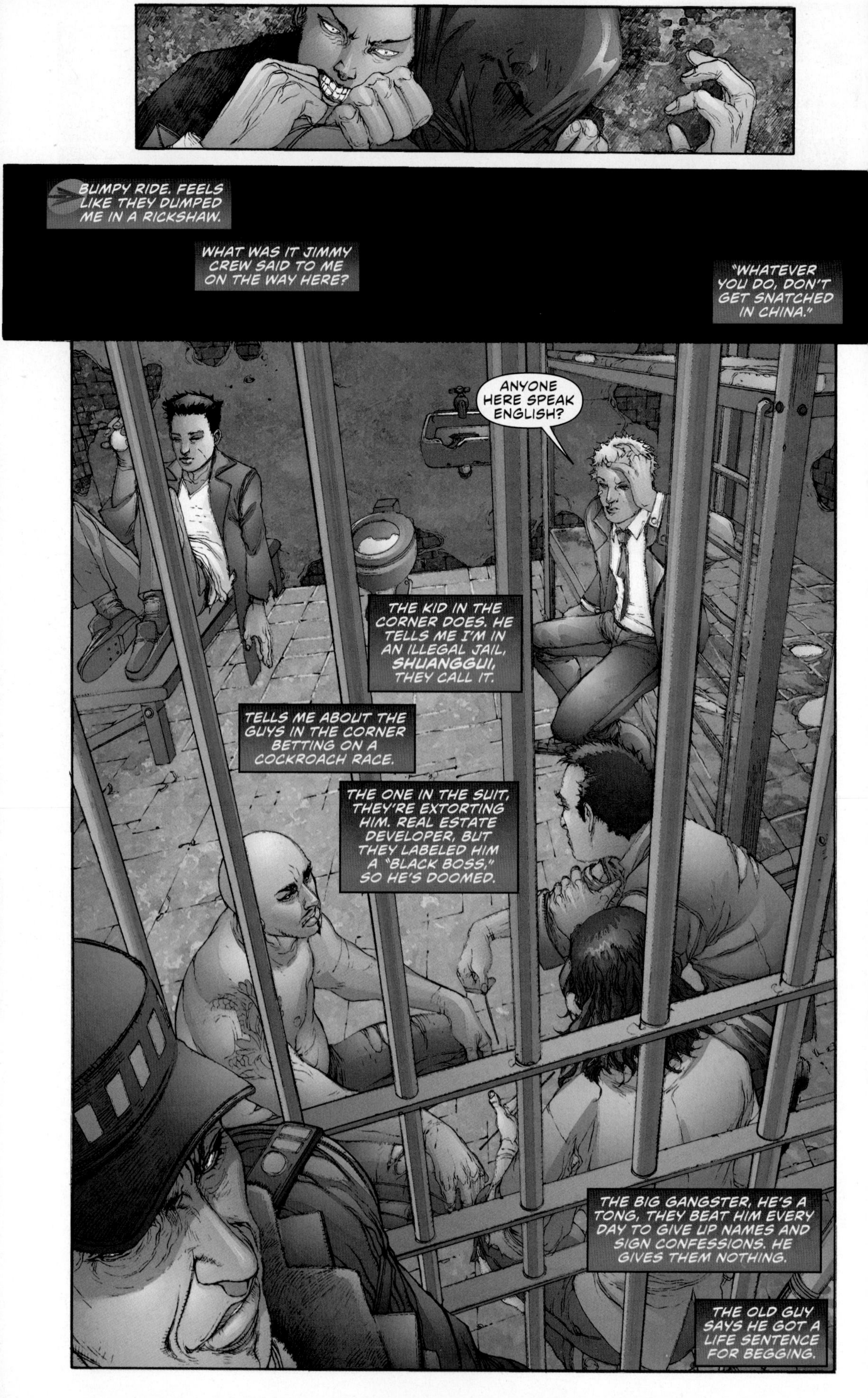

BUMPY RIDE. FEELS LIKE THEY DUMPED ME IN A RICKSHAW.
WHAT WAS IT JIMMY CREW SAID TO ME ON THE WAY HERE?
"WHATEVER YOU DO, DON'T GET SNATCHED IN CHINA."
ANYONE HERE SPEAK ENGLISH?
THE KID IN THE CORNER DOES. HE TELLS ME I'M IN AN ILLEGAL JAIL, SHUANGGUI, THEY CALL IT.
TELLS ME ABOUT THE GUYS IN THE CORNER BETTING ON A COCKROACH RACE.
THE ONE IN THE SUIT, THEY'RE EXTORTING HIM. REAL ESTATE DEVELOPER, BUT THEY LABELED HIM A "BLACK BOSS," SO HE'S DOOMED.
THE BIG GANGSTER, HE'S A TONG, THEY BEAT HIM EVERY DAY TO GIVE UP NAMES AND SIGN CONFESSIONS. HE GIVES THEM NOTHING.
THE OLD GUY SAYS HE GOT A LIFE SENTENCE FOR BEGGING.

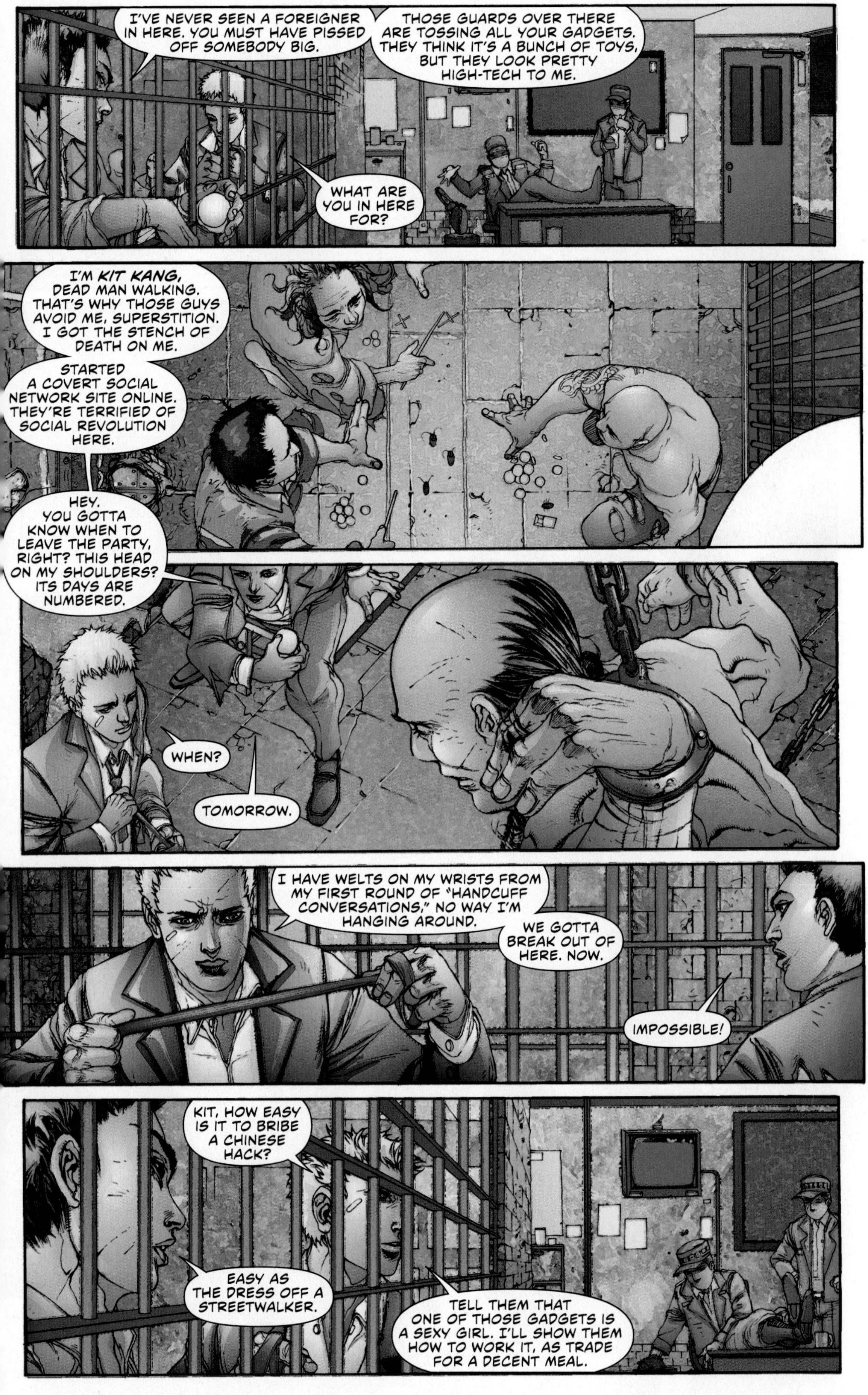

I'VE NEVER SEEN A FOREIGNER IN HERE. YOU MUST HAVE PISSED OFF SOMEBODY BIG.
THOSE GUARDS OVER THERE ARE TOSSING ALL YOUR GADGETS. THEY THINK IT'S A BUNCH OF TOYS, BUT THEY LOOK PRETTY HIGH-TECH TO ME.
WHAT ARE YOU IN HERE FOR?
I'M *KIT KANG,* DEAD MAN WALKING. THAT'S WHY THOSE GUYS AVOID ME, SUPERSTITION. I GOT THE STENCH OF DEATH ON ME.
STARTED A COVERT SOCIAL NETWORK SITE ONLINE. THEY'RE TERRIFIED OF SOCIAL REVOLUTION HERE.
HEY. YOU GOTTA KNOW WHEN TO LEAVE THE PARTY, RIGHT? THIS HEAD ON MY SHOULDERS? ITS DAYS ARE NUMBERED.
WHEN?
TOMORROW.
I HAVE WELTS ON MY WRISTS FROM MY FIRST ROUND OF "HANDCUFF CONVERSATIONS," NO WAY I'M HANGING AROUND.
WE GOTTA BREAK OUT OF HERE. NOW.
IMPOSSIBLE!
KIT, HOW EASY IS IT TO BRIBE A CHINESE HACK?
EASY AS THE DRESS OFF A STREETWALKER.
TELL THEM THAT ONE OF THOSE GADGETS IS A SEXY GIRL. I'LL SHOW THEM HOW TO WORK IT, AS TRADE FOR A DECENT MEAL.

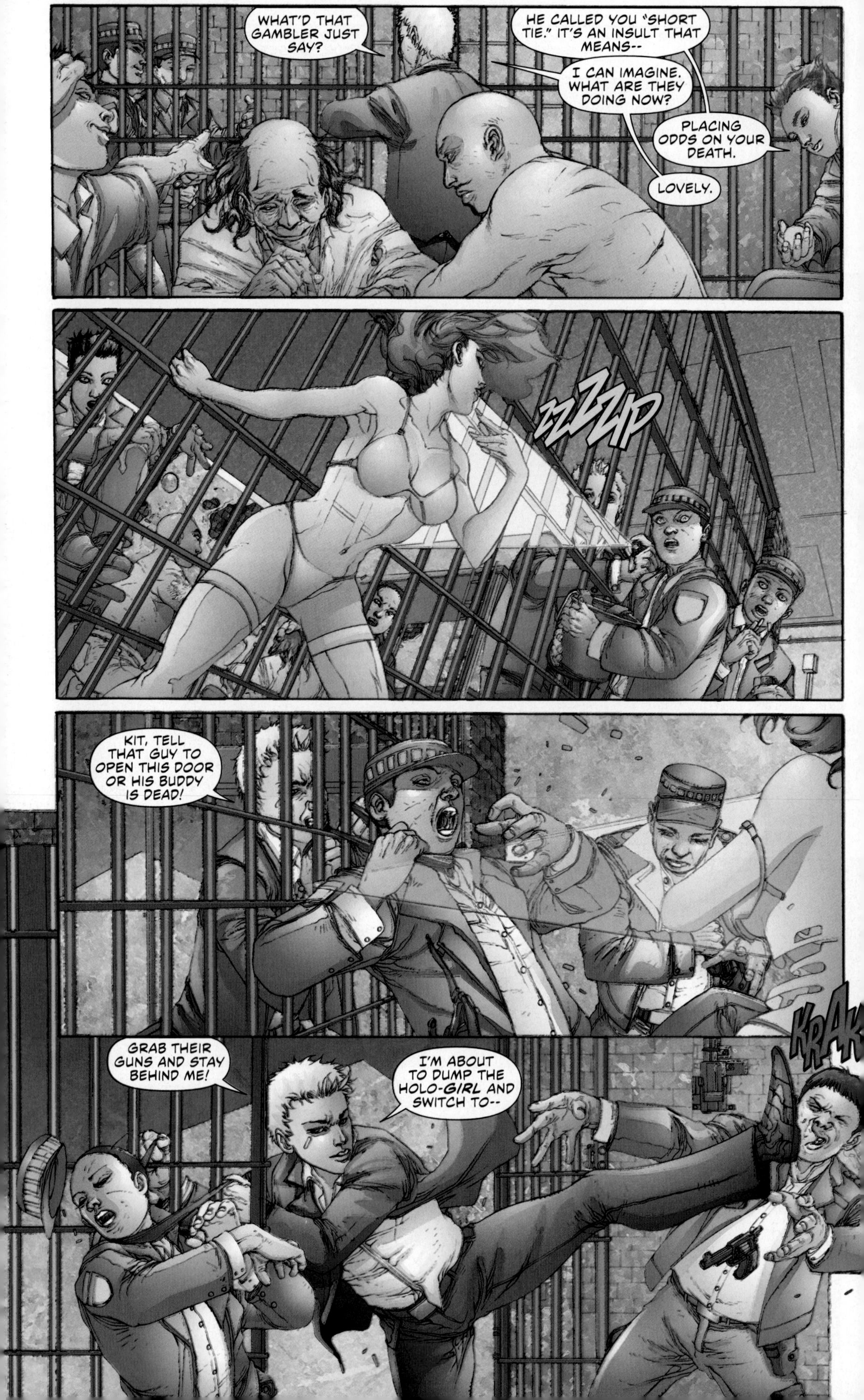
WHAT'D THAT GAMBLER JUST SAY?
HE CALLED YOU "SHORT TIE." IT'S AN INSULT THAT MEANS--
I CAN IMAGINE. WHAT ARE THEY DOING NOW?
PLACING ODDS ON YOUR DEATH.
LOVELY.
zzZZIP
KIT, TELL THAT GUY TO OPEN THIS DOOR OR HIS BUDDY IS DEAD!
GRAB THEIR GUNS AND STAY BEHIND ME!
I'M ABOUT TO DUMP THE HOLO-GIRL AND SWITCH TO--
KRAK

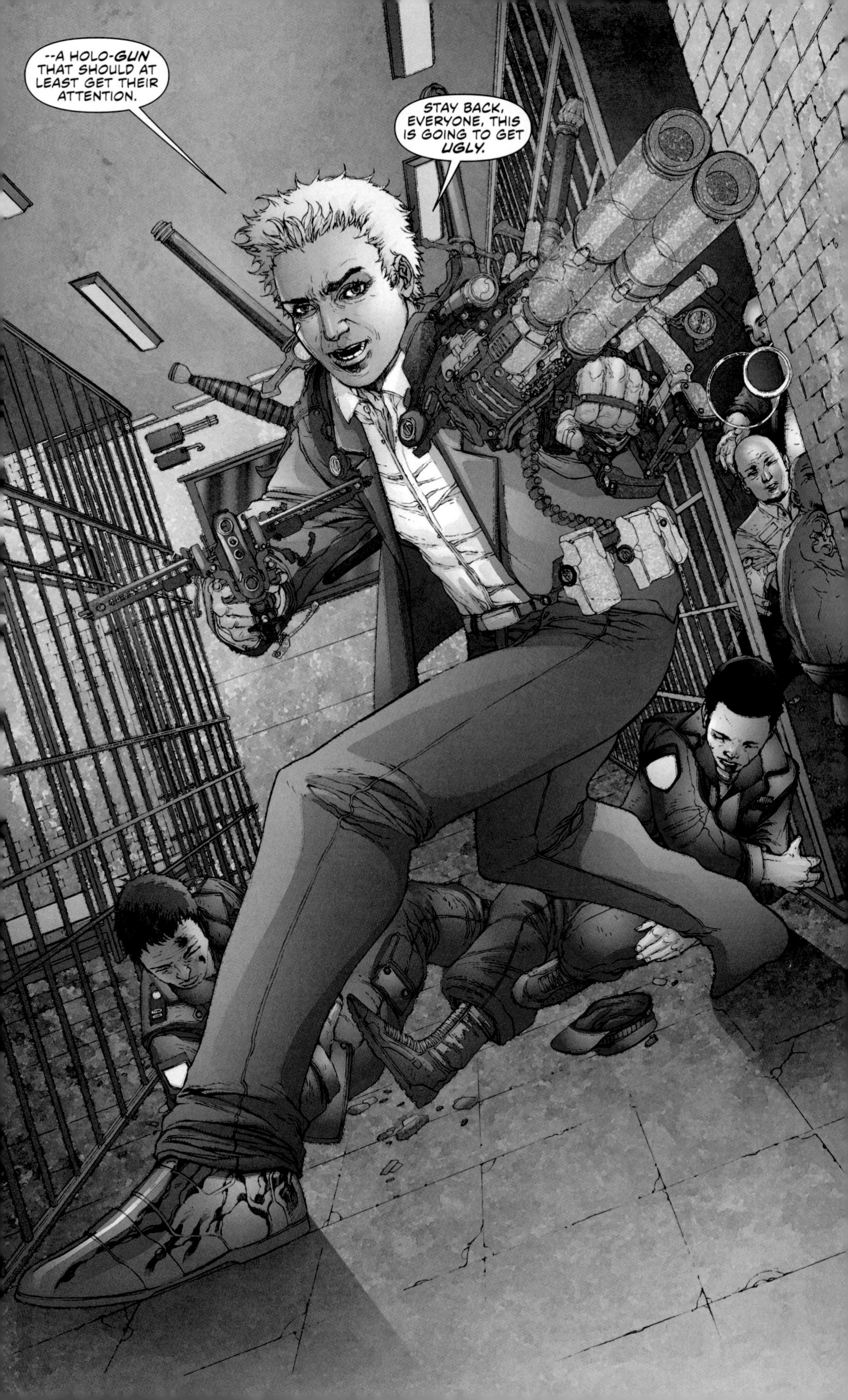
--A HOLO-GUN THAT SHOULD AT LEAST GET THEIR ATTENTION.
STAY BACK, EVERYONE, THIS IS GOING TO GET UGLY.

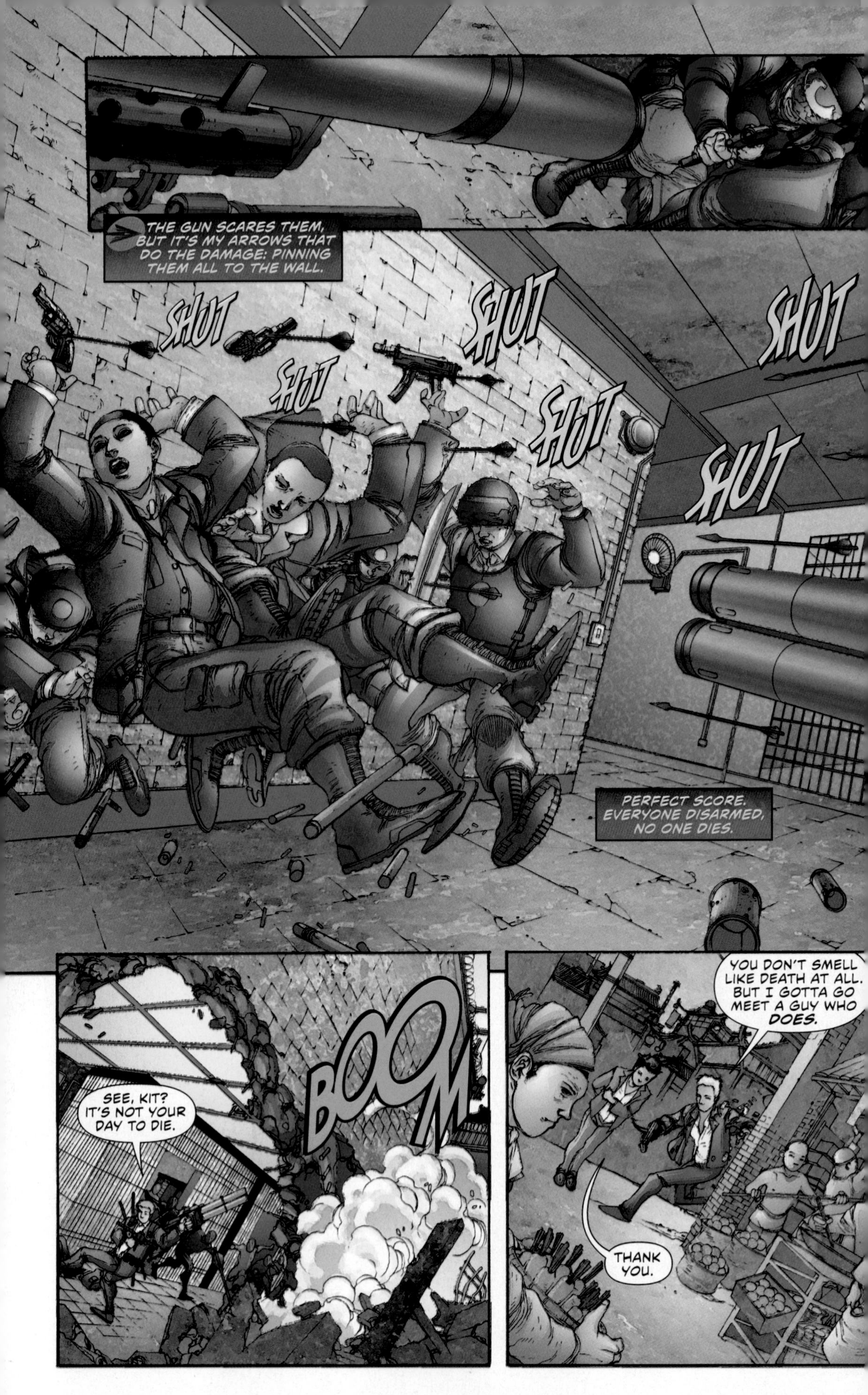
THE GUN SCARES THEM, BUT IT'S MY ARROWS THAT DO THE DAMAGE: PINNING THEM ALL TO THE WALL.
SHUT
SHUT
SHUT
SHUT
SHUT
SHUT
PERFECT SCORE. EVERYONE DISARMED, NO ONE DIES.
BOOM
SEE, KIT? IT'S NOT YOUR DAY TO DIE.
YOU DON'T SMELL LIKE DEATH AT ALL. BUT I GOTTA GO MEET A GUY WHO DOES.
THANK YOU.

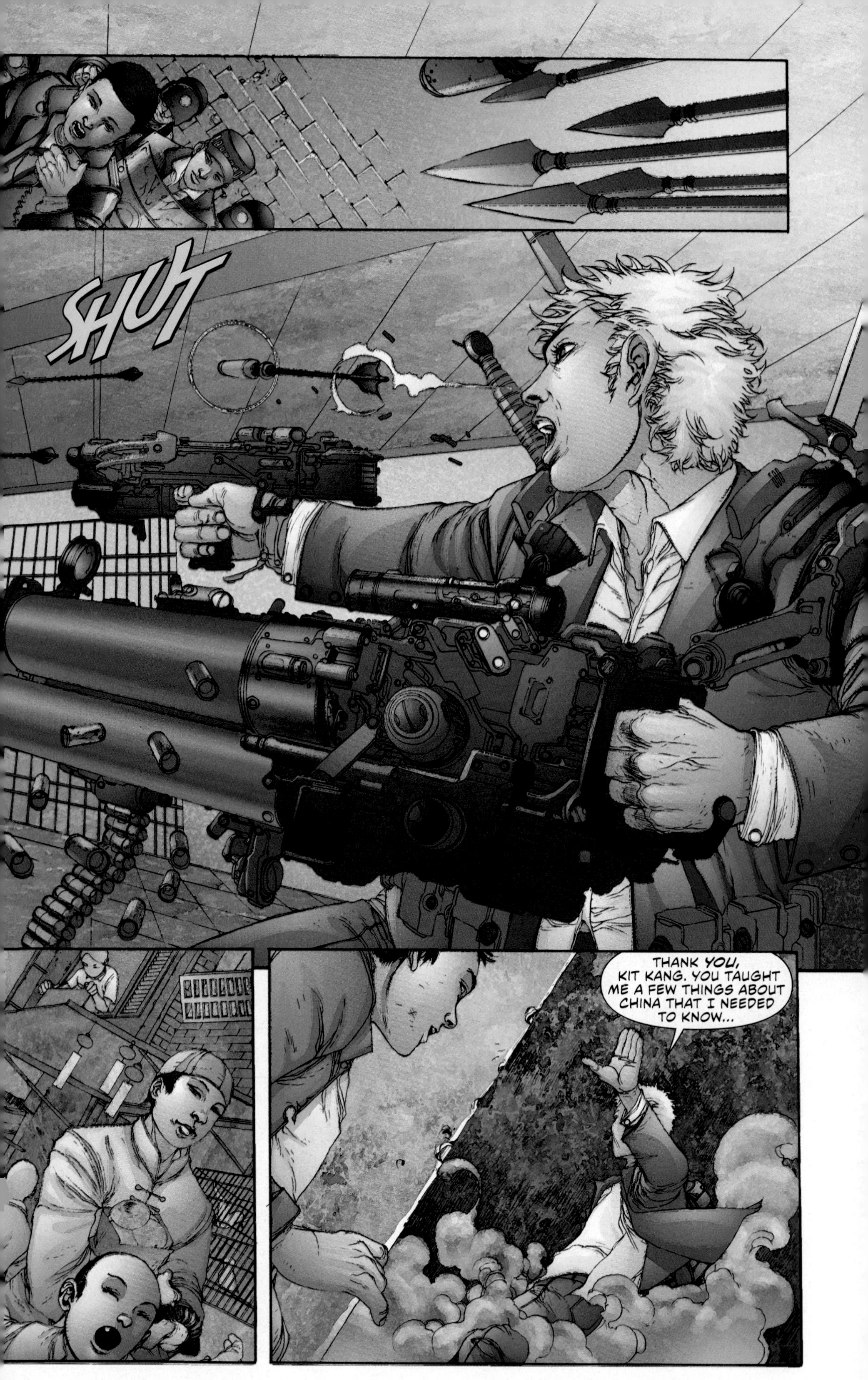
SHUT
THANK YOU, KIT KANG. YOU TAUGHT ME A FEW THINGS ABOUT CHINA THAT I NEEDED TO KNOW...

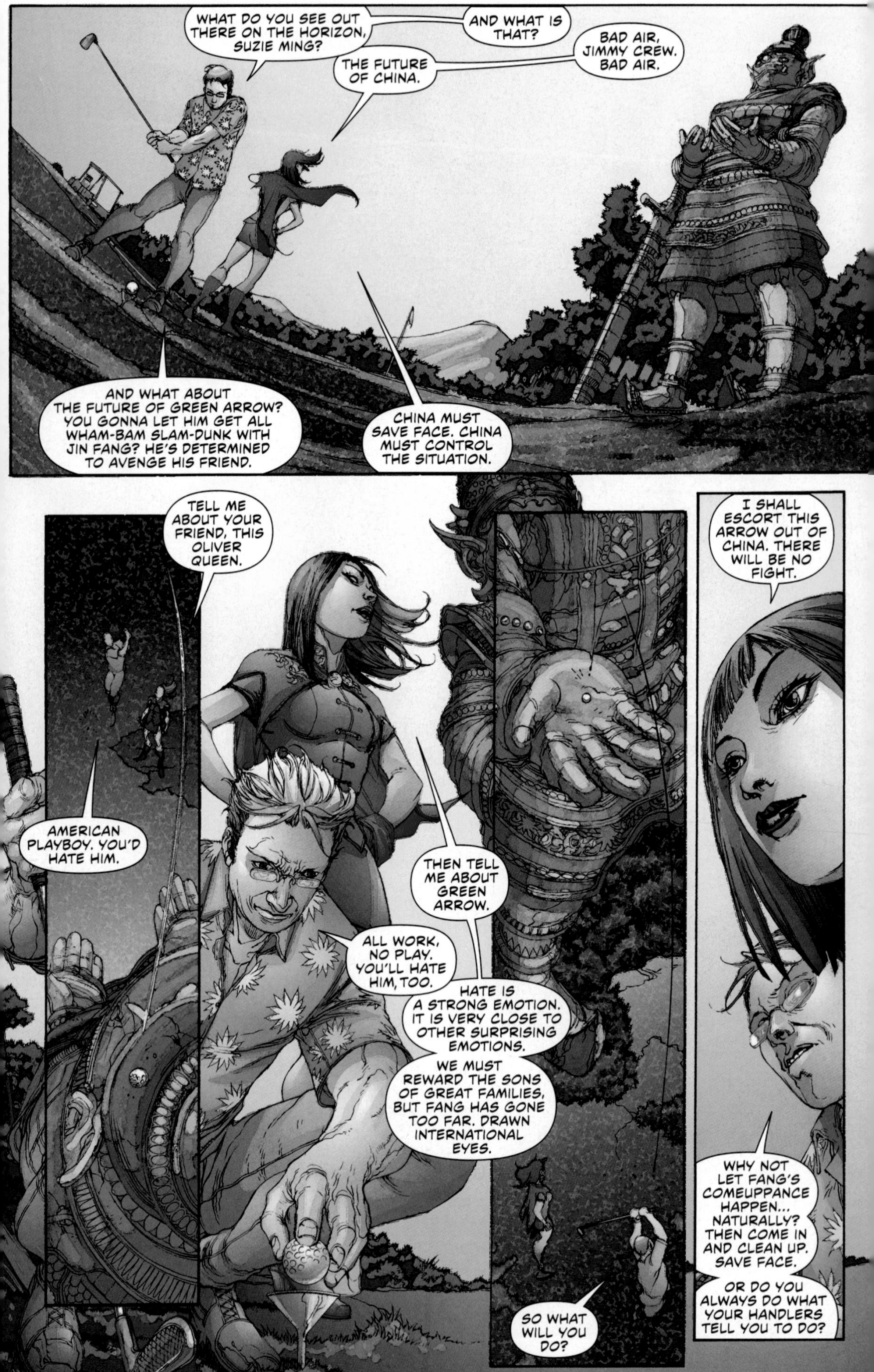

WHAT DO YOU SEE OUT THERE ON THE HORIZON, SUZIE MING?
THE FUTURE OF CHINA.
AND WHAT IS THAT?
BAD AIR, JIMMY CREW. BAD AIR.
AND WHAT ABOUT THE FUTURE OF GREEN ARROW? YOU GONNA LET HIM GET ALL WHAM-BAM SLAM-DUNK WITH JIN FANG? HE'S DETERMINED TO AVENGE HIS FRIEND.
CHINA MUST SAVE FACE. CHINA MUST CONTROL THE SITUATION.
TELL ME ABOUT YOUR FRIEND, THIS OLIVER QUEEN.
AMERICAN PLAYBOY. YOU'D HATE HIM.
THEN TELL ME ABOUT GREEN ARROW.
ALL WORK, NO PLAY. YOU'LL HATE HIM, TOO.
HATE IS A STRONG EMOTION. IT IS VERY CLOSE TO OTHER SURPRISING EMOTIONS.
WE MUST REWARD THE SONS OF GREAT FAMILIES, BUT FANG HAS GONE TOO FAR. DRAWN INTERNATIONAL EYES.
SO WHAT WILL YOU DO?
I SHALL ESCORT THIS ARROW OUT OF CHINA. THERE WILL BE NO FIGHT.
WHY NOT LET FANG'S COMEUPPANCE HAPPEN... NATURALLY? THEN COME IN AND CLEAN UP. SAVE FACE.
OR DO YOU ALWAYS DO WHAT YOUR HANDLERS TELL YOU TO DO?

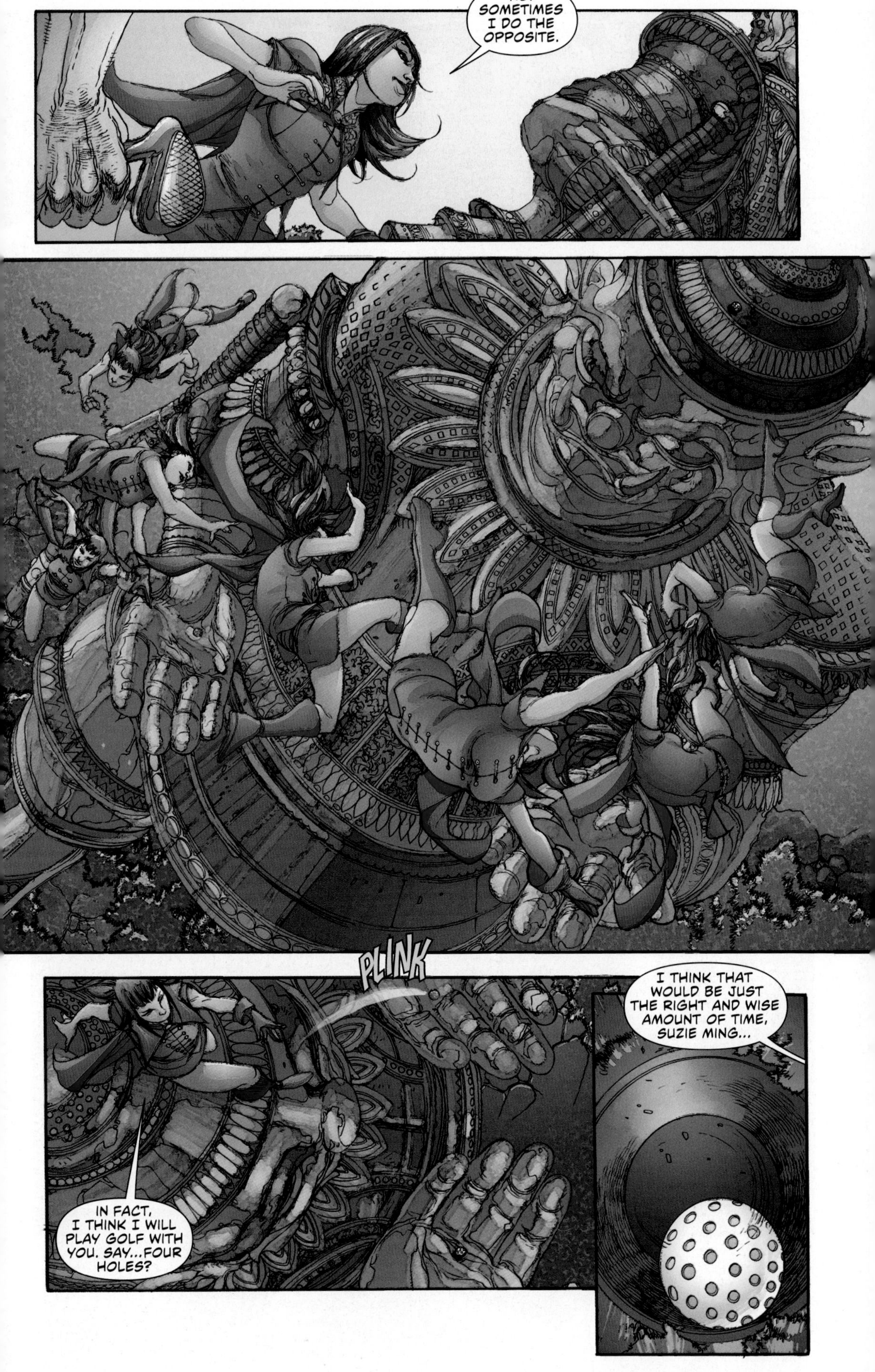
NO. SOMETIMES I DO THE OPPOSITE.
PLINK
IN FACT, I THINK I WILL PLAY GOLF WITH YOU. SAY...FOUR HOLES?
I THINK THAT WOULD BE JUST THE RIGHT AND WISE AMOUNT OF TIME, SUZIE MING...

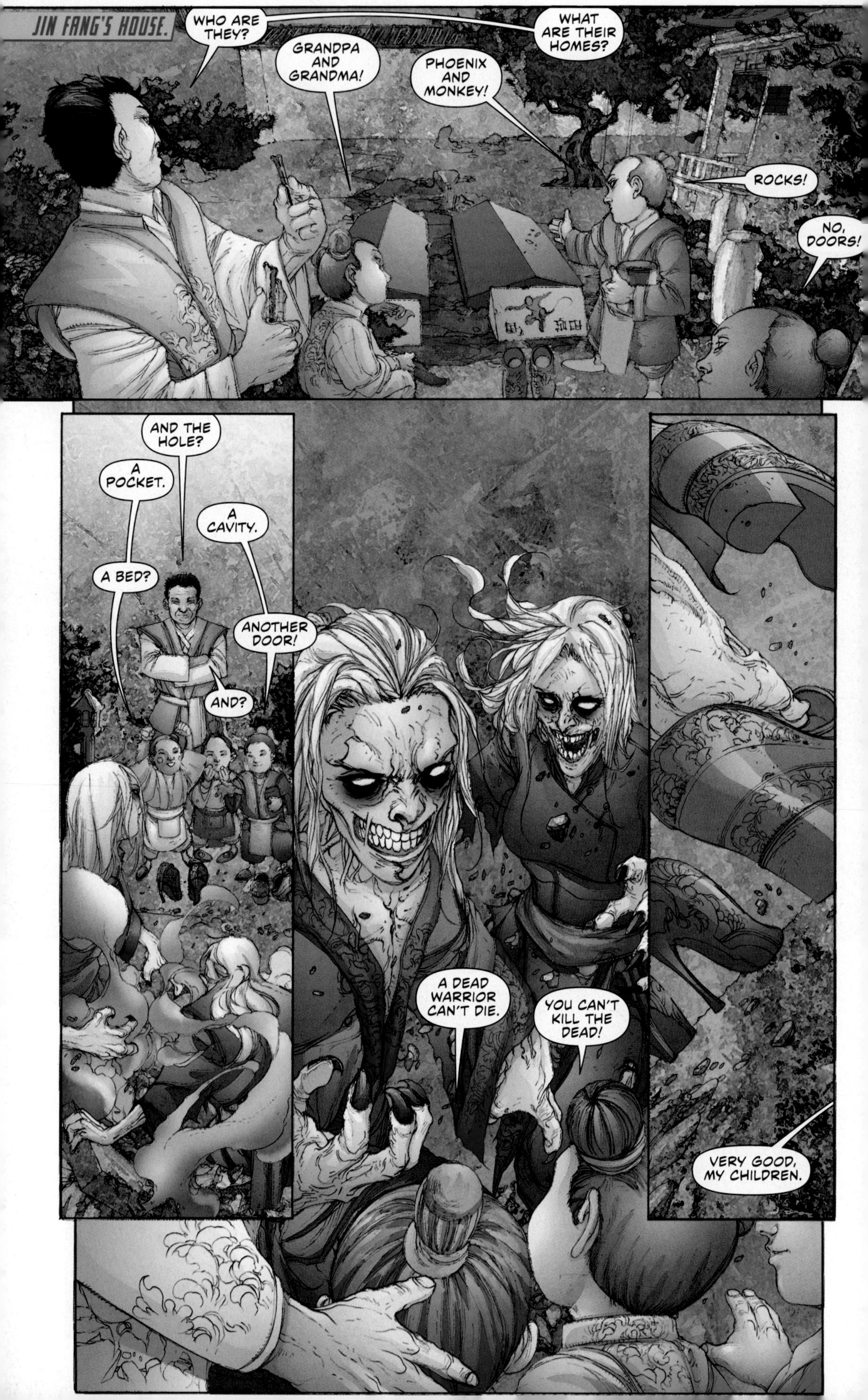
JIN FANG'S HOUSE.
WHO ARE THEY?
GRANDPA AND GRANDMA!
WHAT ARE THEIR HOMES?
PHOENIX AND MONKEY!
ROCKS!
NO, DOORS!
AND THE HOLE?
A POCKET.
A CAVITY.
A BED?
ANOTHER DOOR!
AND?
A DEAD WARRIOR CAN'T DIE.
YOU CAN'T KILL THE DEAD!
VERY GOOD, MY CHILDREN.

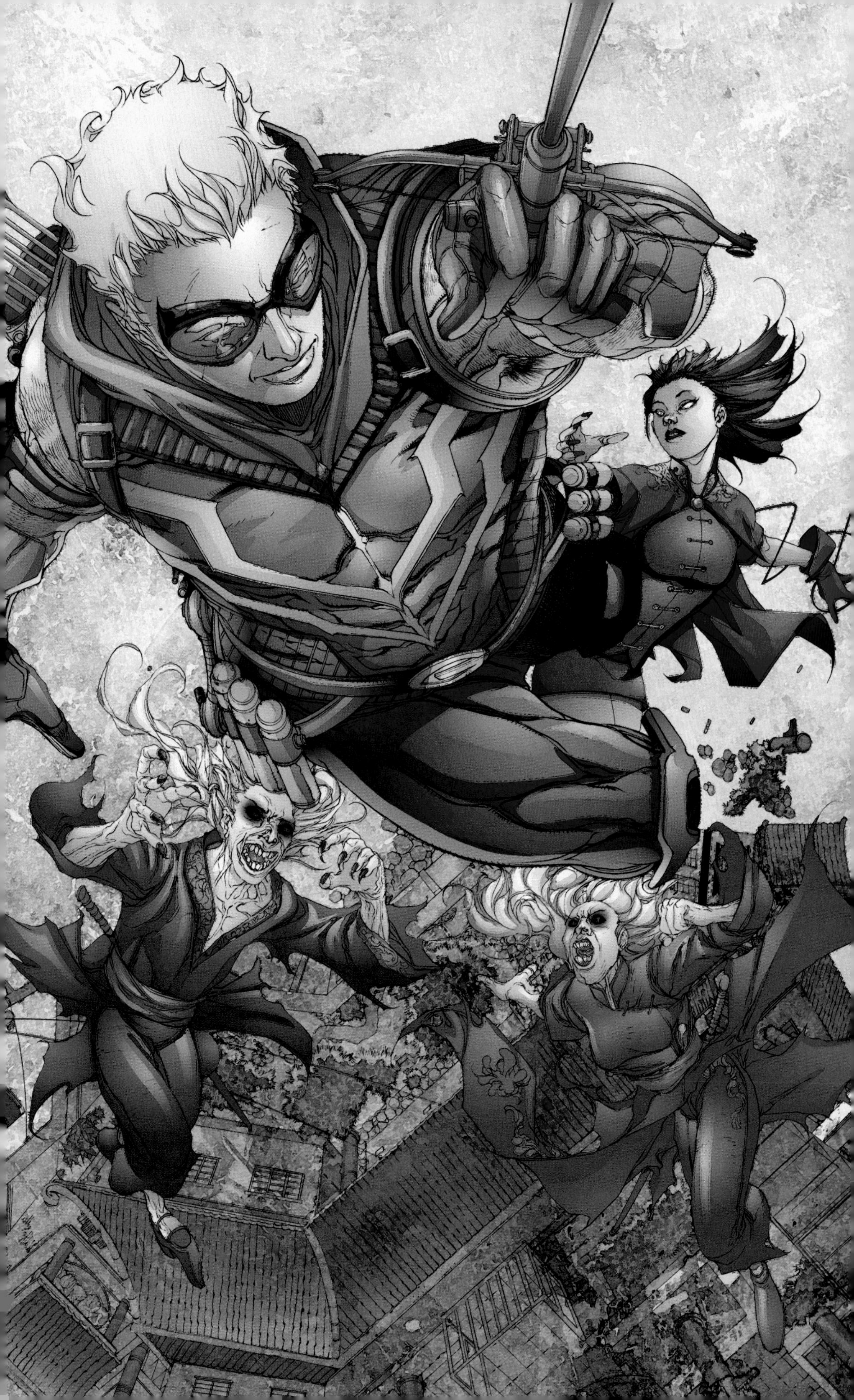

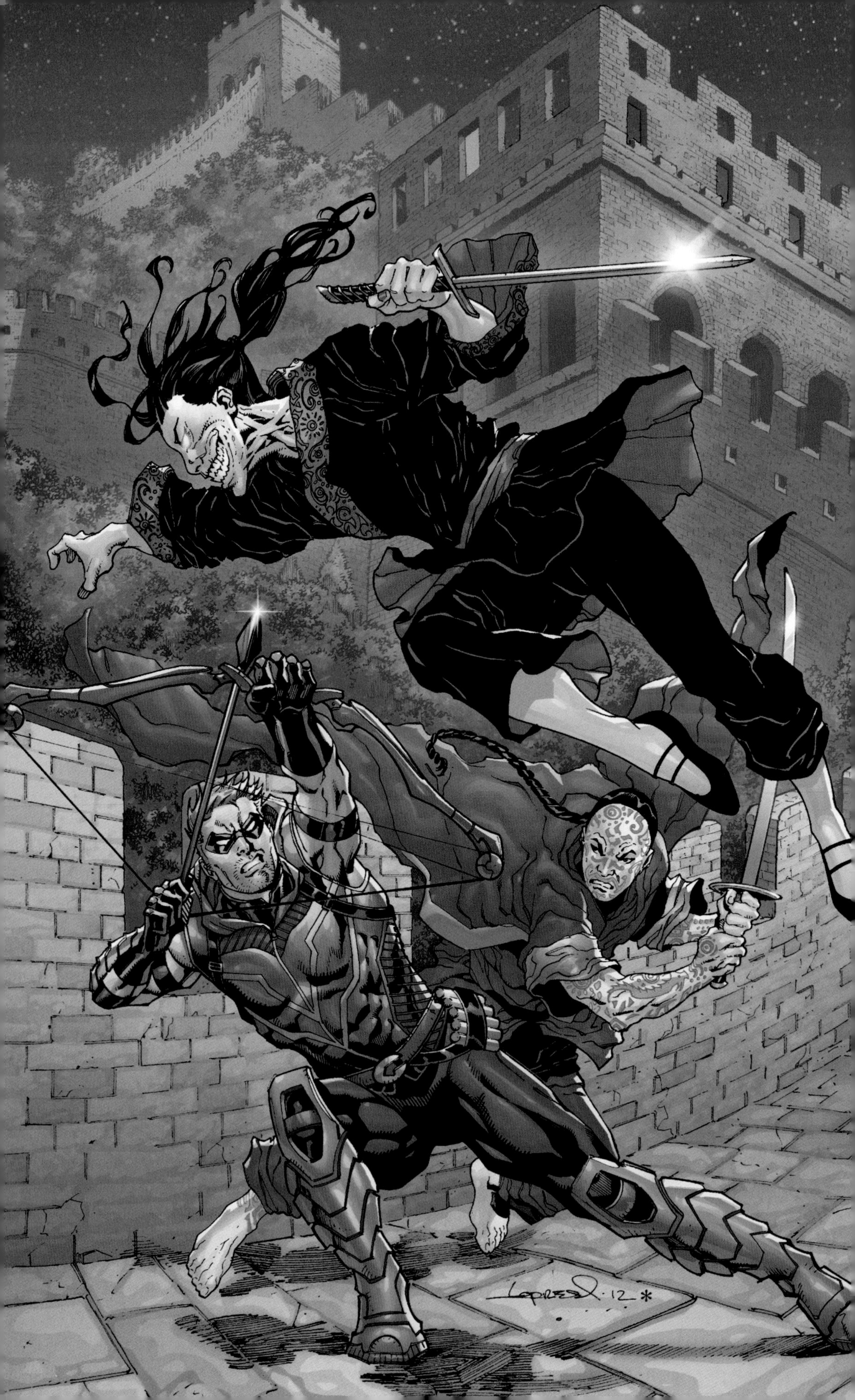

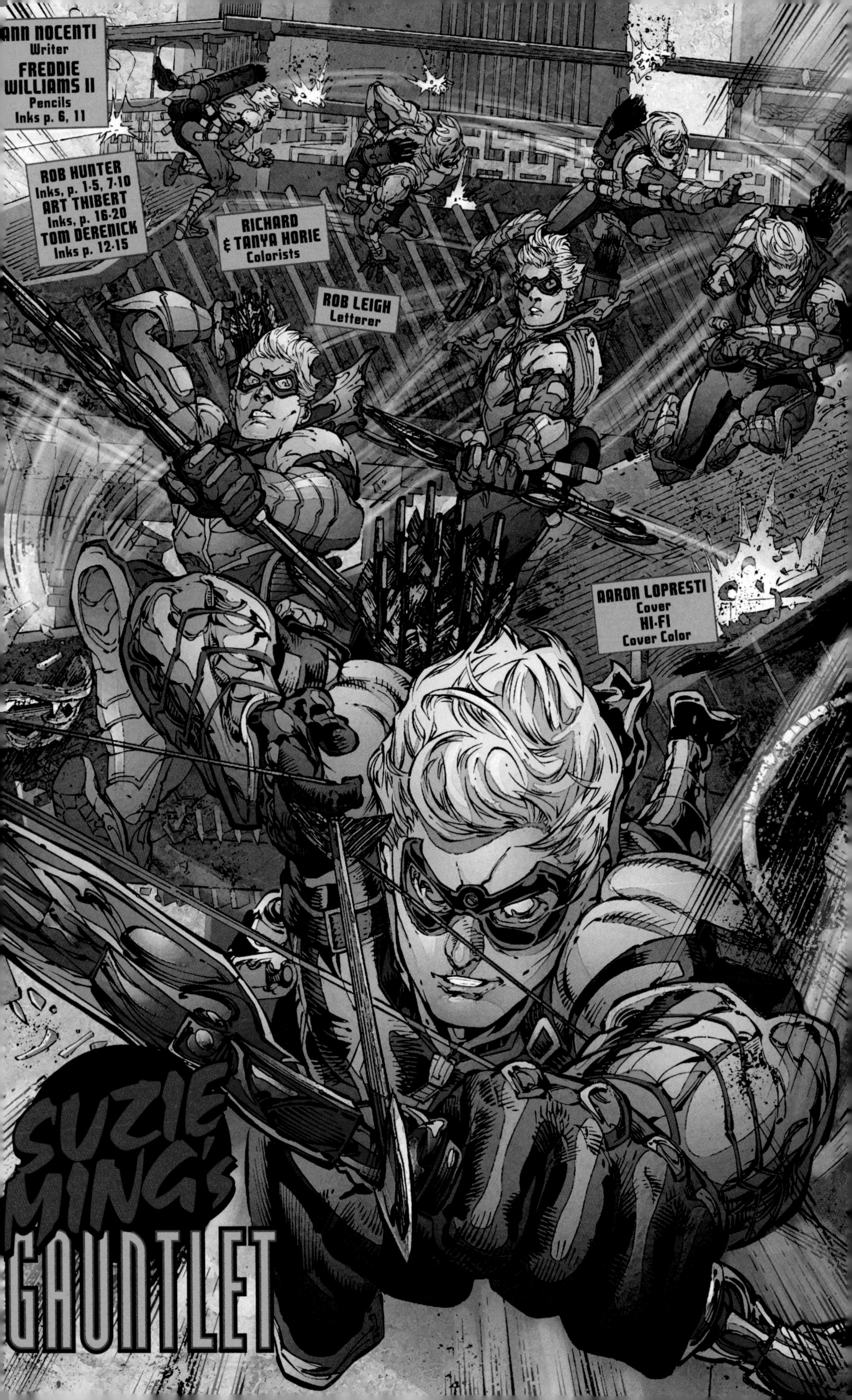
ANN NOCENTI
Writer
FREDDIE WILLIAMS II
Pencils
Inks p. 6, 11
ROB HUNTER
Inks, p. 1-5, 7-10
ART THIBERT
Inks, p. 16-20
TOM DERENICK
Inks p. 12-15
RICHARD & TANYA HORIE
Colorists
ROB LEIGH
Letterer
AARON LOPRESTI
Cover
HI-FI
Cover Color
SUZIE MING'S
GAUNTLET

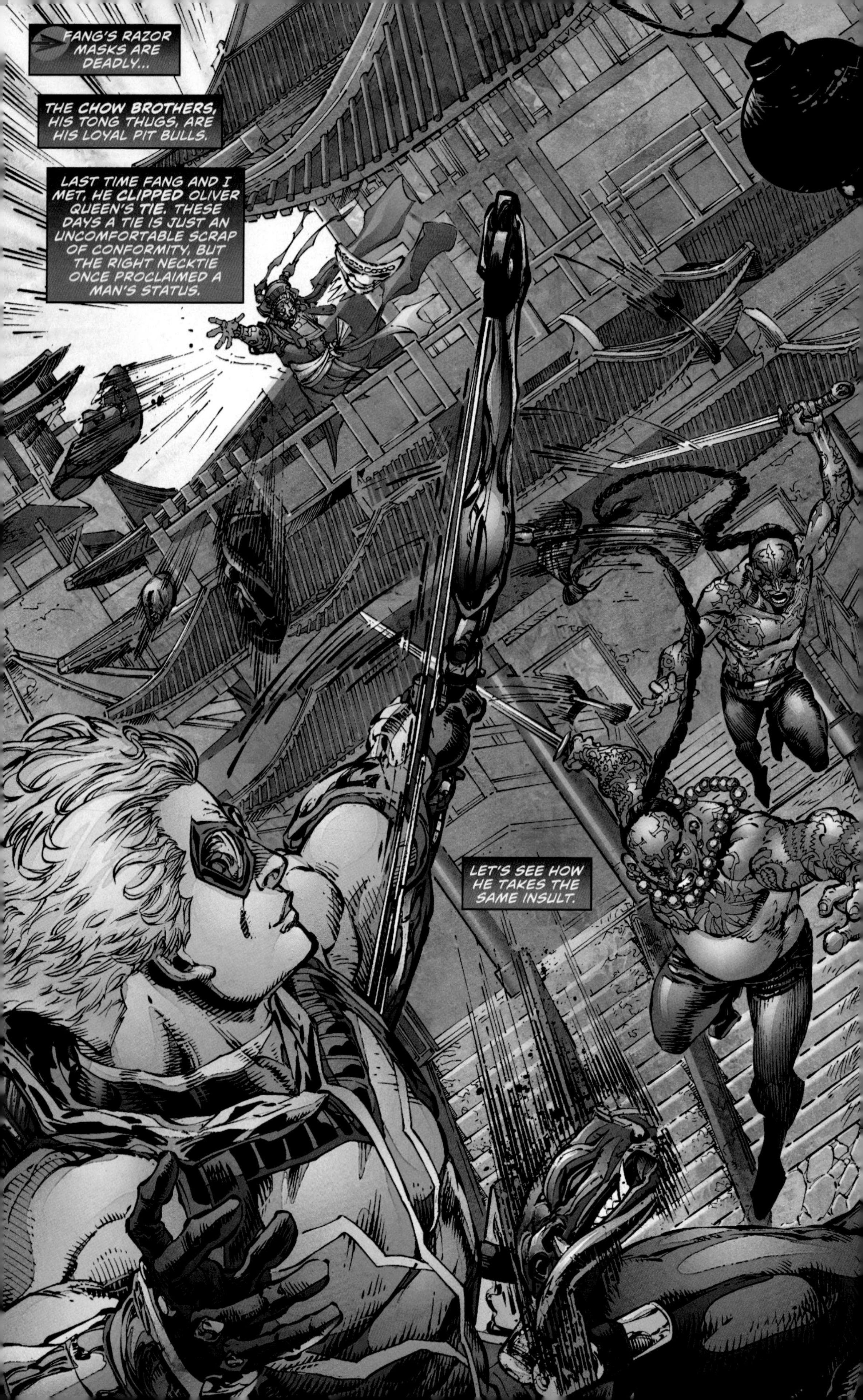
FANG'S RAZOR MASKS ARE DEADLY...
THE CHOW BROTHERS, HIS TONG THUGS, ARE HIS LOYAL PIT BULLS.
LAST TIME FANG AND I MET, HE CLIPPED OLIVER QUEEN'S TIE. THESE DAYS A TIE IS JUST AN UNCOMFORTABLE SCRAP OF CONFORMITY, BUT THE RIGHT NECKTIE ONCE PROCLAIMED A MAN'S STATUS.
LET'S SEE HOW HE TAKES THE SAME INSULT.

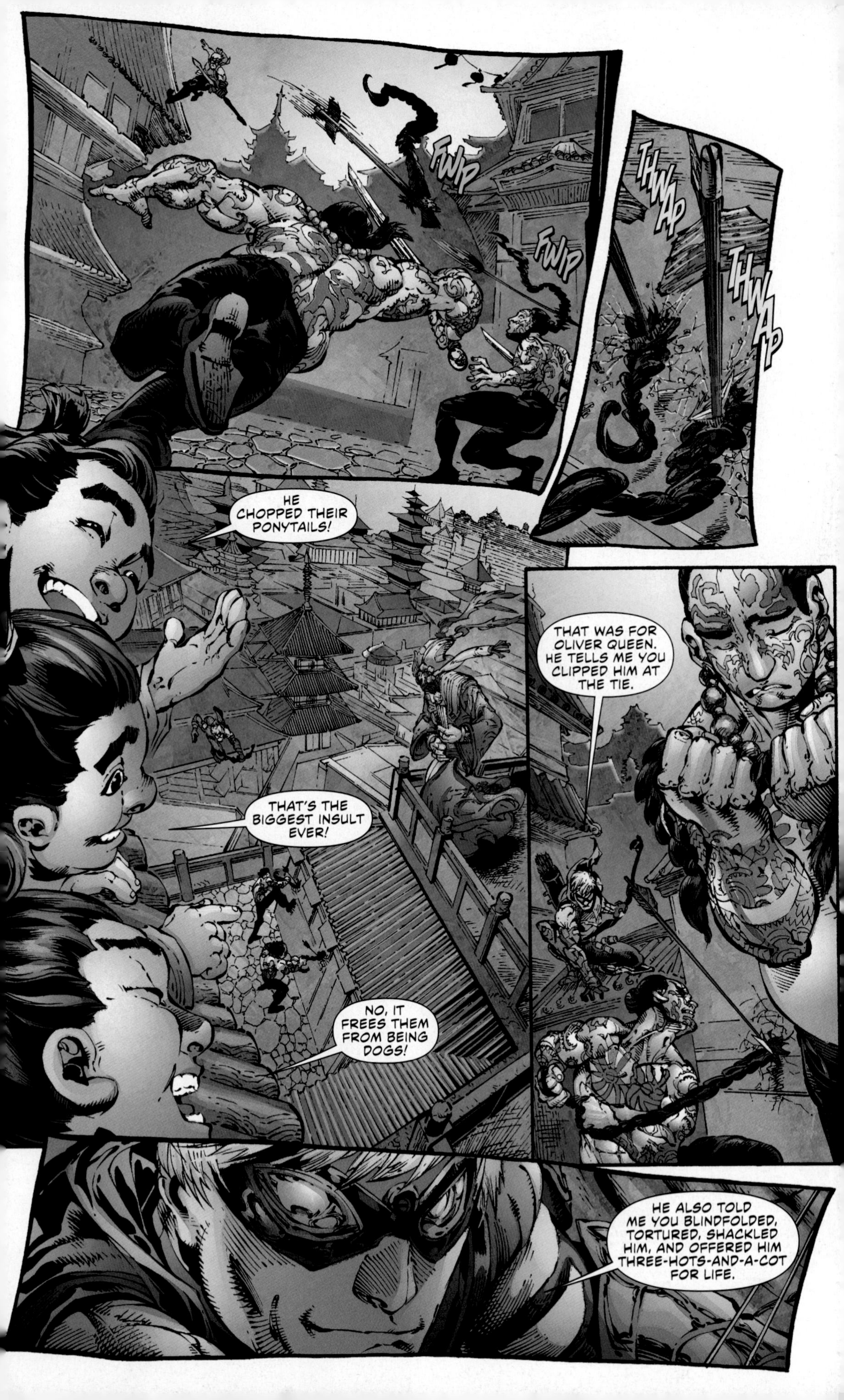
FWIP
FWIP
THWAP
THWAP
HE CHOPPED THEIR PONYTAILS!
THAT'S THE BIGGEST INSULT EVER!
NO, IT FREES THEM FROM BEING DOGS!
THAT WAS FOR OLIVER QUEEN. HE TELLS ME YOU CLIPPED HIM AT THE TIE.
HE ALSO TOLD ME YOU BLINDFOLDED, TORTURED, SHACKLED HIM, AND OFFERED HIM THREE-HOTS-AND-A-COT FOR LIFE.

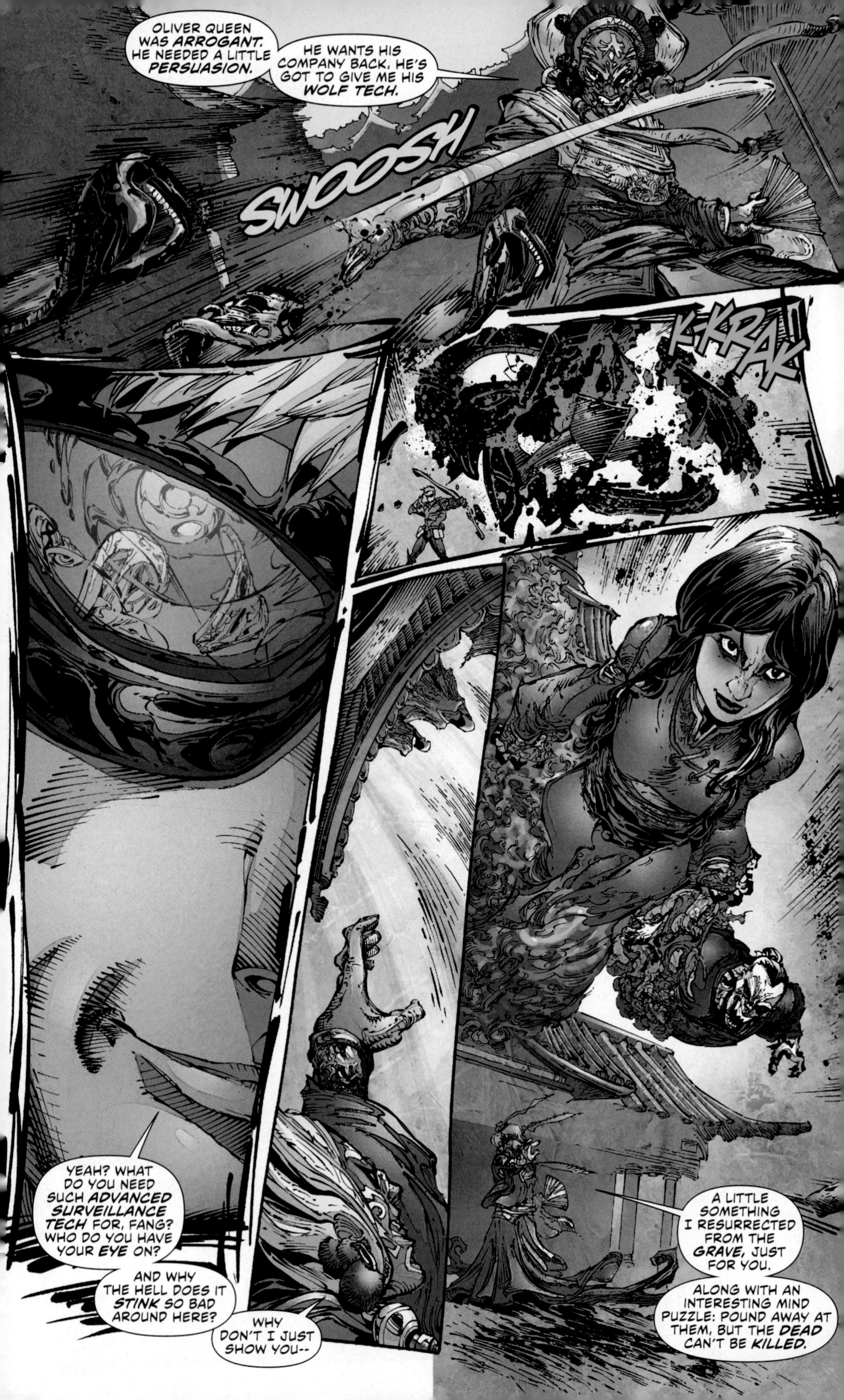
OLIVER QUEEN WAS ARROGANT. HE NEEDED A LITTLE PERSUASION.
HE WANTS HIS COMPANY BACK, HE'S GOT TO GIVE ME HIS WOLF TECH.
SWOOSH
K-KRAK
YEAH? WHAT DO YOU NEED SUCH ADVANCED SURVEILLANCE TECH FOR, FANG? WHO DO YOU HAVE YOUR EYE ON?
AND WHY THE HELL DOES IT STINK SO BAD AROUND HERE?
WHY DON'T I JUST SHOW YOU--
A LITTLE SOMETHING I RESURRECTED FROM THE GRAVE, JUST FOR YOU.
ALONG WITH AN INTERESTING MIND PUZZLE: POUND AWAY AT THEM, BUT THE DEAD CAN'T BE KILLED.

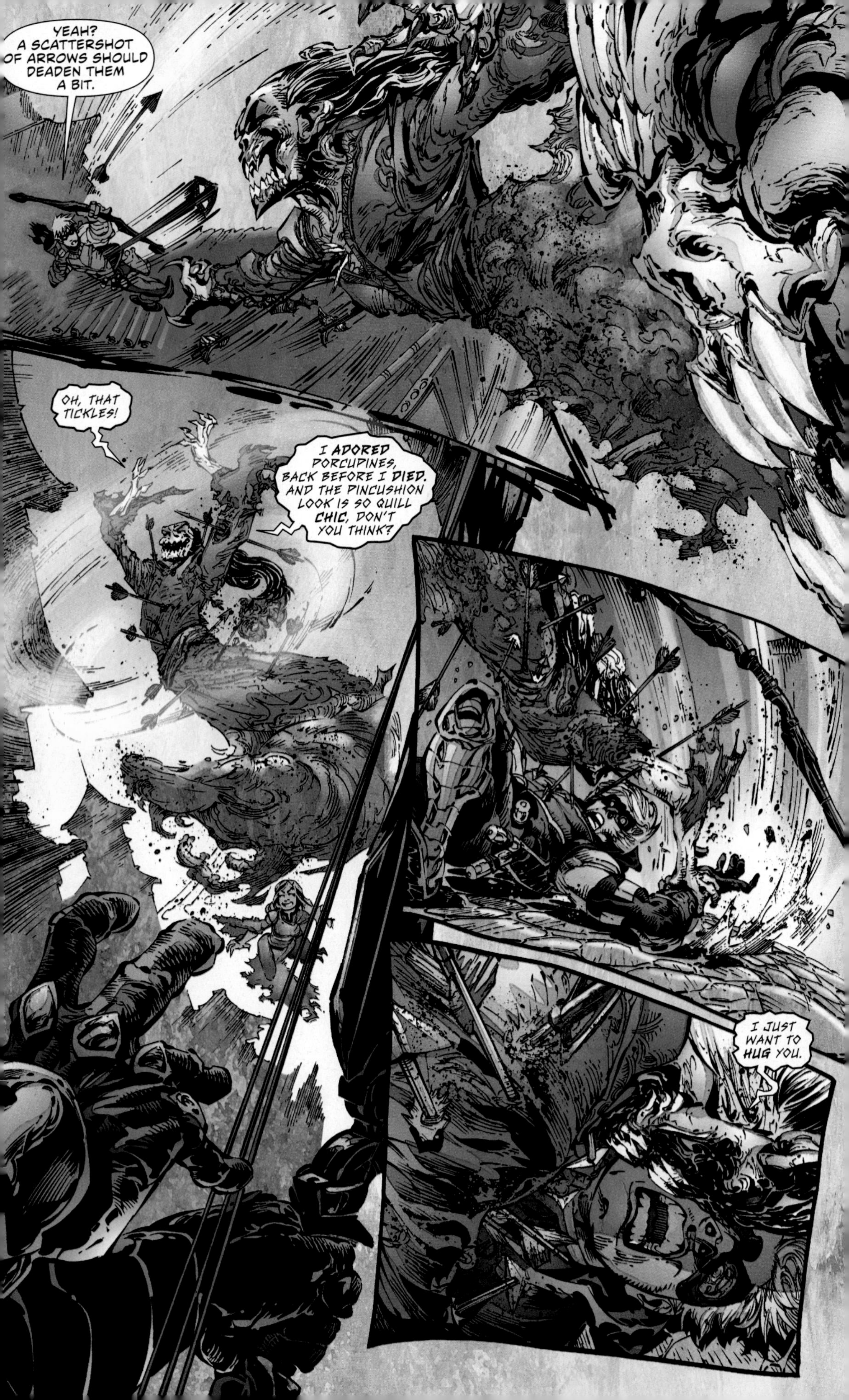
YEAH? A SCATTERSHOT OF ARROWS SHOULD DEADEN THEM A BIT.
OH, THAT TICKLES!
I ADORED PORCUPINES, BACK BEFORE I DIED. AND THE PINCUSHION LOOK IS SO QUILL CHIC, DON'T YOU THINK?
I JUST WANT TO HUG YOU.

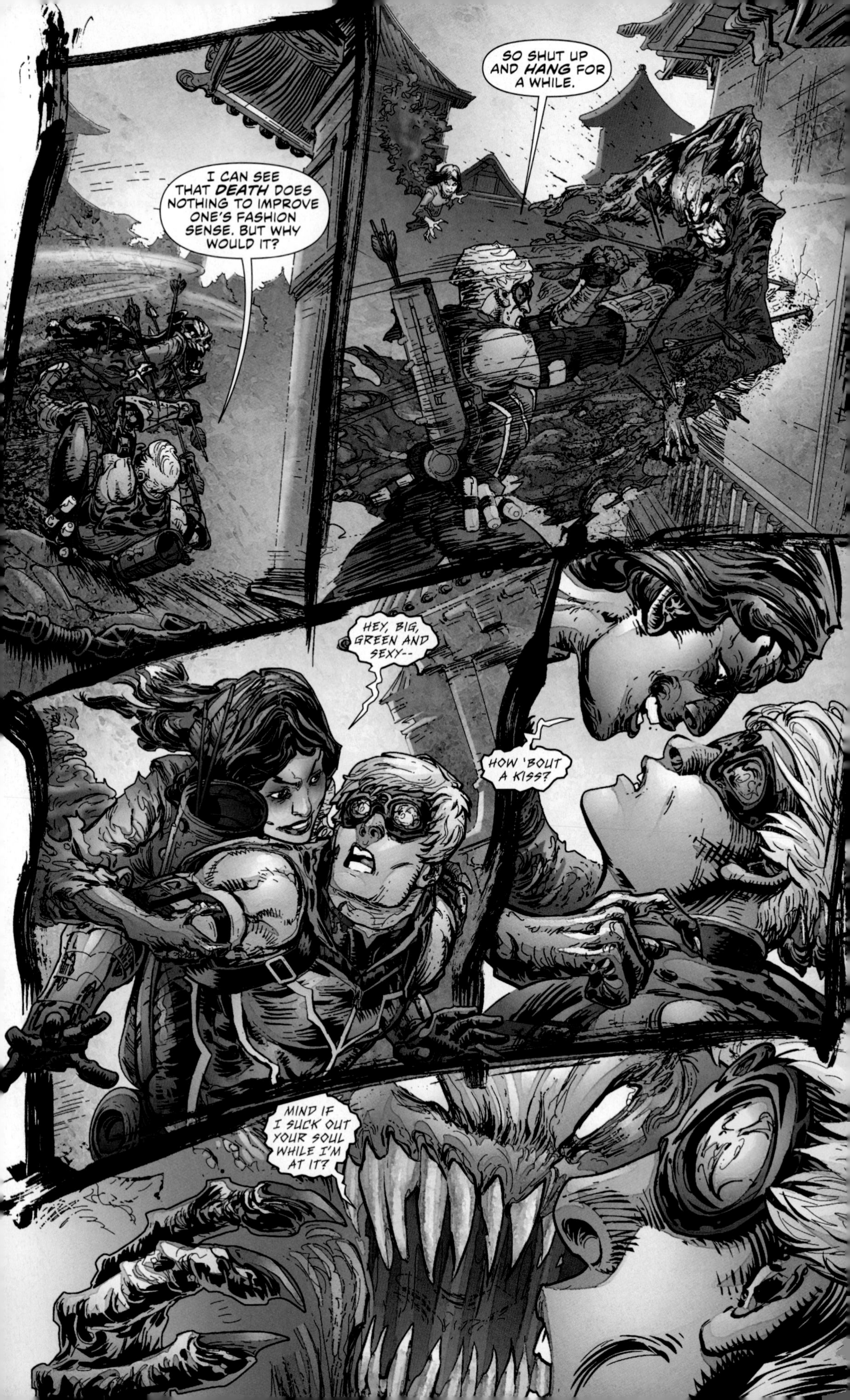
I CAN SEE THAT DEATH DOES NOTHING TO IMPROVE ONE'S FASHION SENSE. BUT WHY WOULD IT?
SO SHUT UP AND HANG FOR A WHILE.
HEY, BIG, GREEN AND SEXY--
HOW 'BOUT A KISS?
MIND IF I SUCK OUT YOUR SOUL WHILE I'M AT IT?

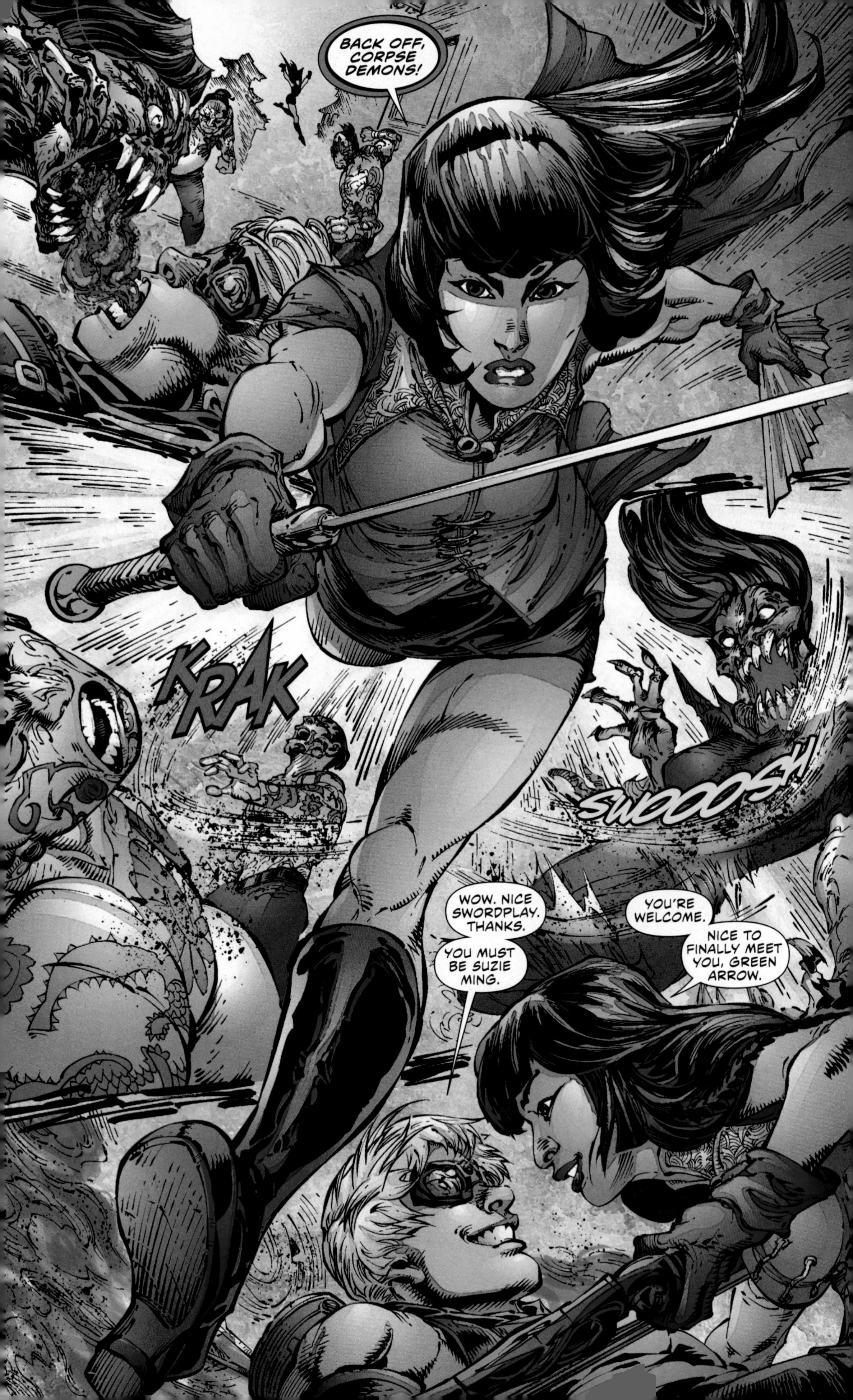

BACK OFF, CORPSE DEMONS!
KRAK
SWOOOOSH
WOW. NICE SWORDPLAY. THANKS.
YOU MUST BE SUZIE MING.
YOU'RE WELCOME.
NICE TO FINALLY MEET YOU, GREEN ARROW.

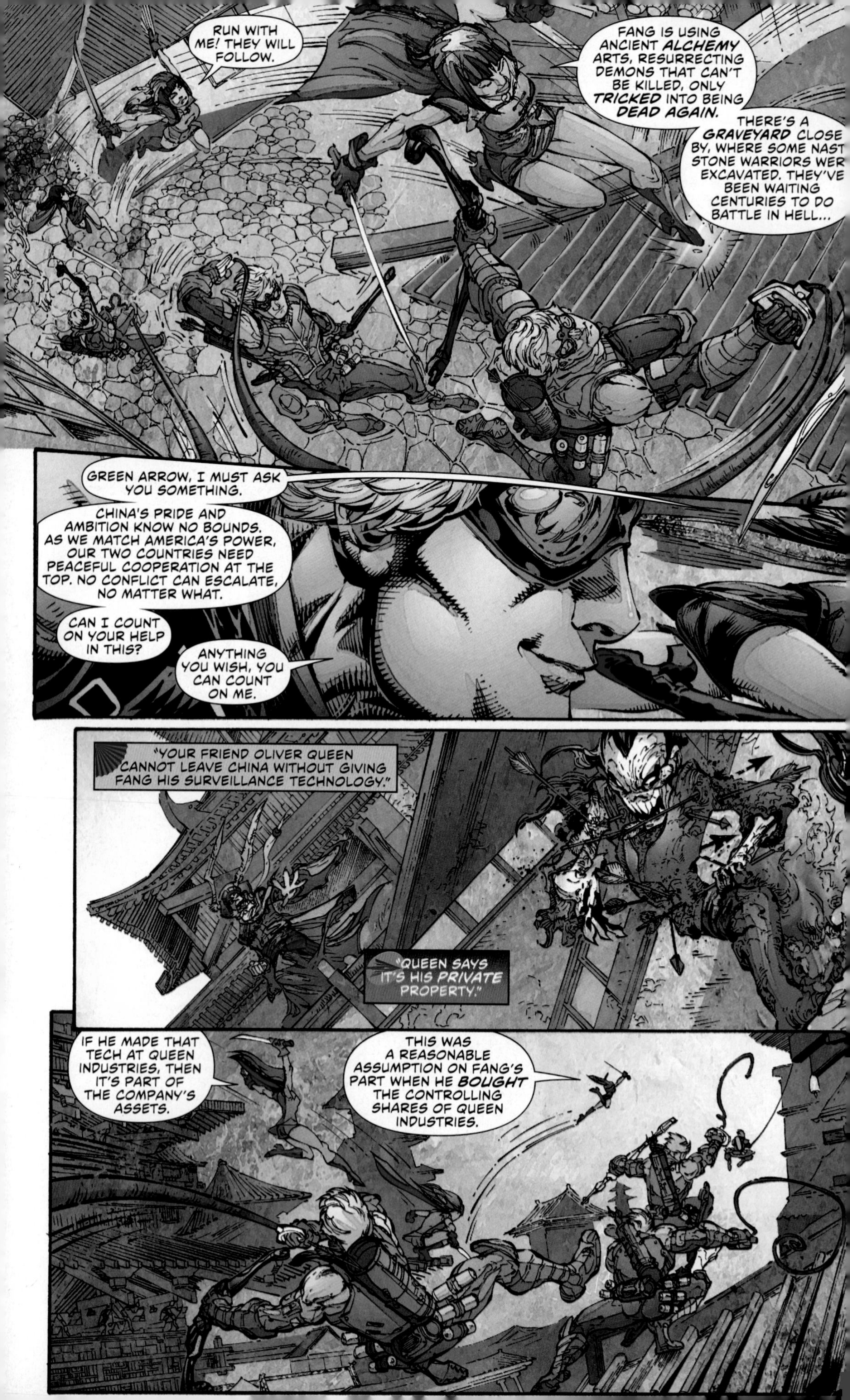
RUN WITH ME! THEY WILL FOLLOW.
FANG IS USING ANCIENT ALCHEMY ARTS, RESURRECTING DEMONS THAT CAN'T BE KILLED, ONLY TRICKED INTO BEING DEAD AGAIN.
THERE'S A GRAVEYARD CLOSE BY, WHERE SOME NAST STONE WARRIORS WER EXCAVATED. THEY'VE BEEN WAITING CENTURIES TO DO BATTLE IN HELL...
GREEN ARROW, I MUST ASK YOU SOMETHING.
CHINA'S PRIDE AND AMBITION KNOW NO BOUNDS. AS WE MATCH AMERICA'S POWER, OUR TWO COUNTRIES NEED PEACEFUL COOPERATION AT THE TOP. NO CONFLICT CAN ESCALATE, NO MATTER WHAT.
CAN I COUNT ON YOUR HELP IN THIS?
ANYTHING YOU WISH, YOU CAN COUNT ON ME.
"YOUR FRIEND OLIVER QUEEN CANNOT LEAVE CHINA WITHOUT GIVING FANG HIS SURVEILLANCE TECHNOLOGY."
"QUEEN SAYS IT'S HIS PRIVATE PROPERTY."
IF HE MADE THAT TECH AT QUEEN INDUSTRIES, THEN IT'S PART OF THE COMPANY'S ASSETS.
THIS WAS A REASONABLE ASSUMPTION ON FANG'S PART WHEN HE BOUGHT THE CONTROLLING SHARES OF QUEEN INDUSTRIES.

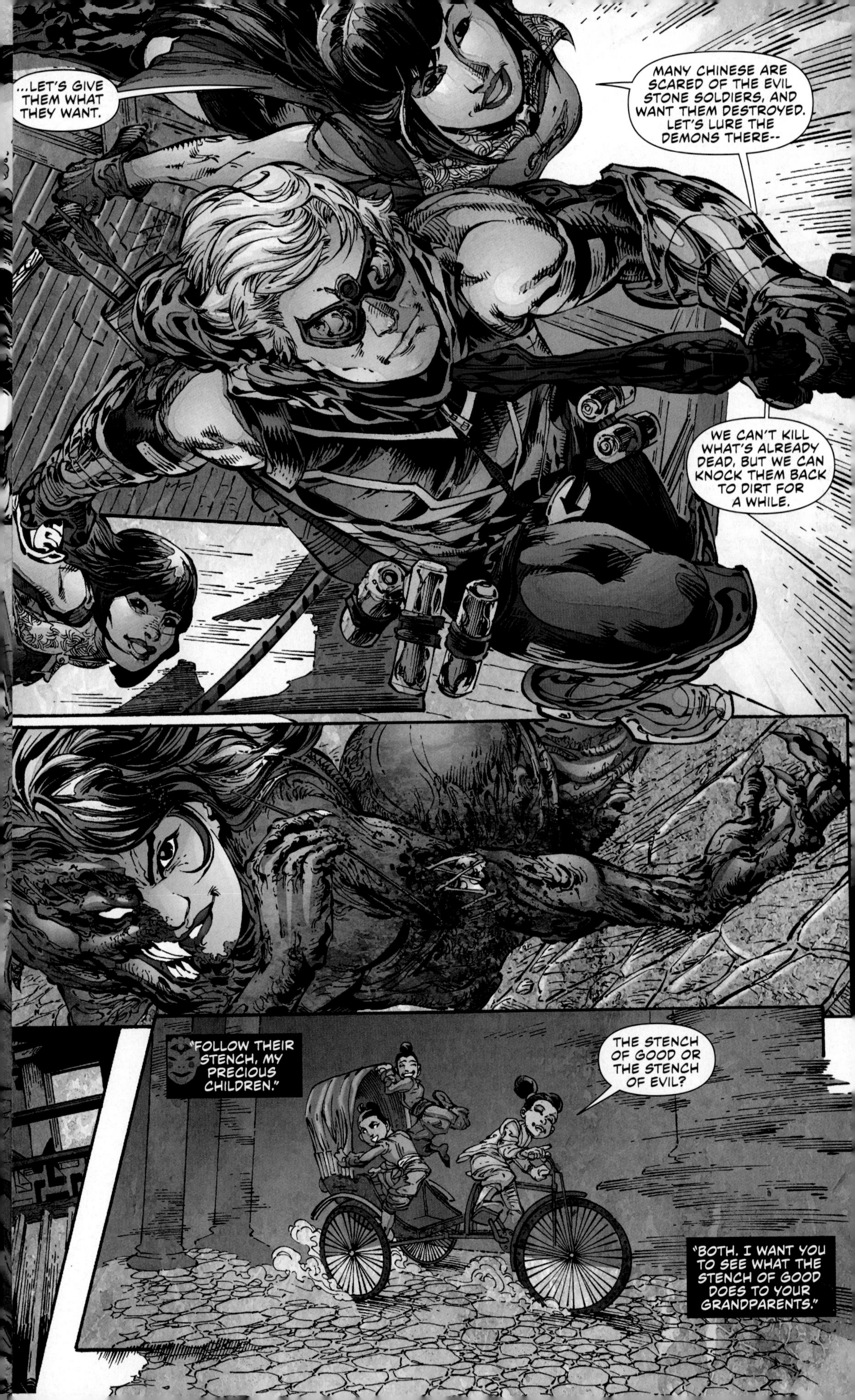
MANY CHINESE ARE SCARED OF THE EVIL STONE SOLDIERS, AND WANT THEM DESTROYED. LET'S LURE THE DEMONS THERE--
...LET'S GIVE THEM WHAT THEY WANT.
WE CAN'T KILL WHAT'S ALREADY DEAD, BUT WE CAN KNOCK THEM BACK TO DIRT FOR A WHILE.
"FOLLOW THEIR STENCH, MY PRECIOUS CHILDREN."
THE STENCH OF GOOD OR THE STENCH OF EVIL?
"BOTH. I WANT YOU TO SEE WHAT THE STENCH OF GOOD DOES TO YOUR GRANDPARENTS."

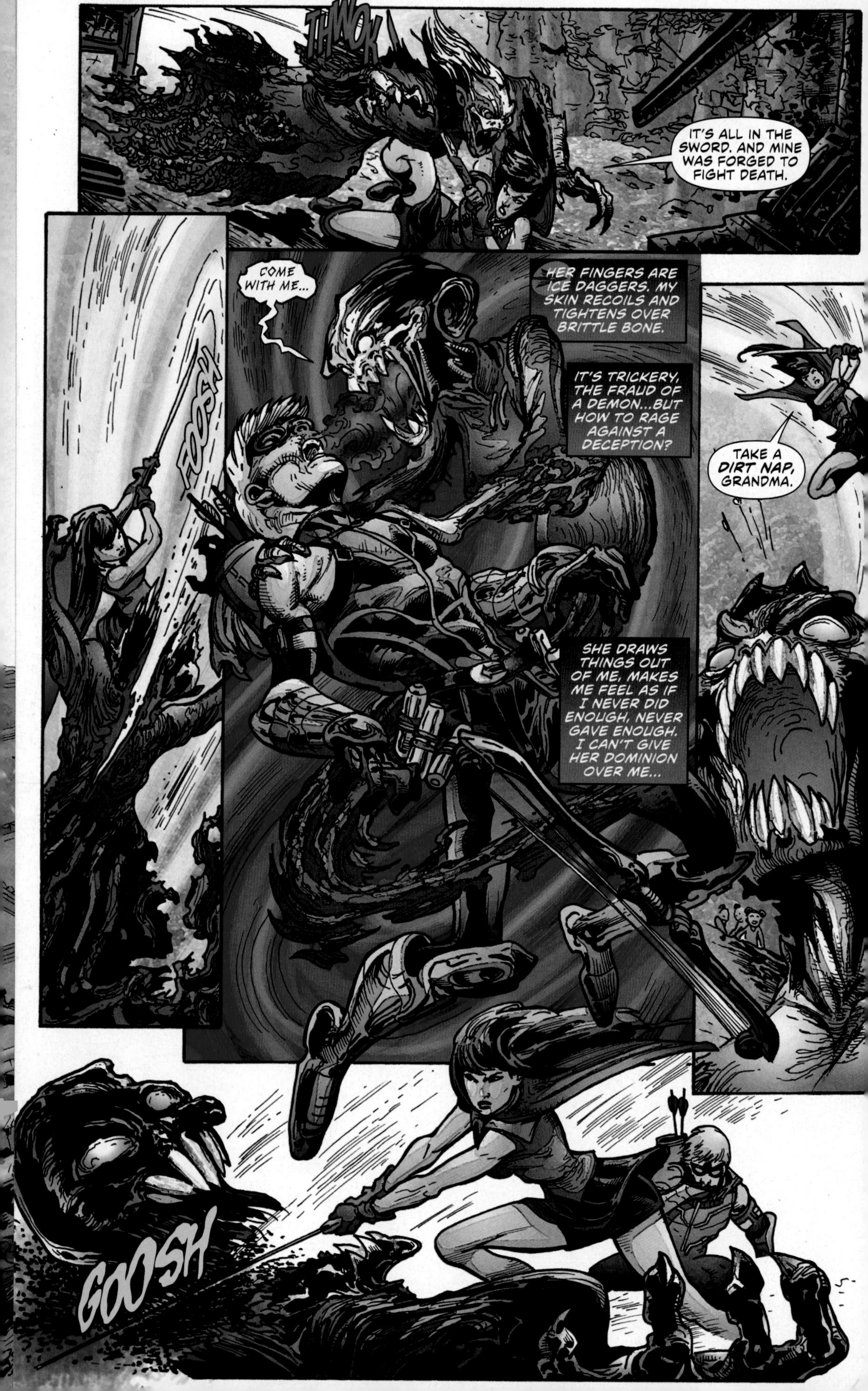
THWOK
IT'S ALL IN THE SWORD. AND MINE WAS FORGED TO FIGHT DEATH.
COME WITH ME...
HER FINGERS ARE ICE DAGGERS. MY SKIN RECOILS AND TIGHTENS OVER BRITTLE BONE.
IT'S TRICKERY, THE FRAUD OF A DEMON...BUT HOW TO RAGE AGAINST A DECEPTION?
FOOSH
TAKE A DIRT NAP, GRANDMA.
SHE DRAWS THINGS OUT OF ME, MAKES ME FEEL AS IF I NEVER DID ENOUGH, NEVER GAVE ENOUGH. I CAN'T GIVE HER DOMINION OVER ME...
GOOSH

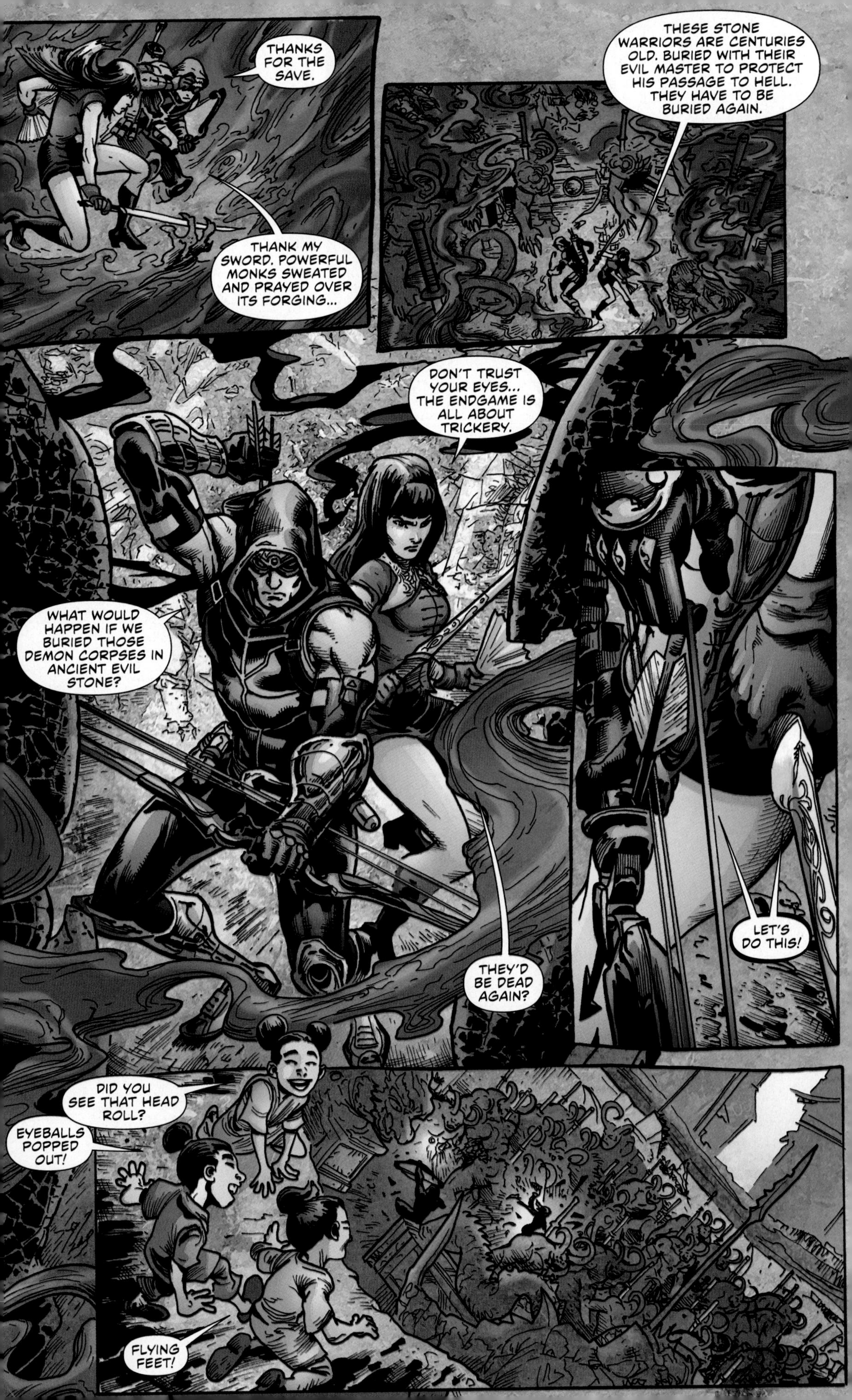
THANKS FOR THE SAVE.
THANK MY SWORD. POWERFUL MONKS SWEATED AND PRAYED OVER ITS FORGING...
THESE STONE WARRIORS ARE CENTURIES OLD. BURIED WITH THEIR EVIL MASTER TO PROTECT HIS PASSAGE TO HELL. THEY HAVE TO BE BURIED AGAIN.
DON'T TRUST YOUR EYES... THE ENDGAME IS ALL ABOUT TRICKERY.
WHAT WOULD HAPPEN IF WE BURIED THOSE DEMON CORPSES IN ANCIENT EVIL STONE?
THEY'D BE DEAD AGAIN?
LET'S DO THIS!
DID YOU SEE THAT HEAD ROLL?
EYEBALLS POPPED OUT!
FLYING FEET!

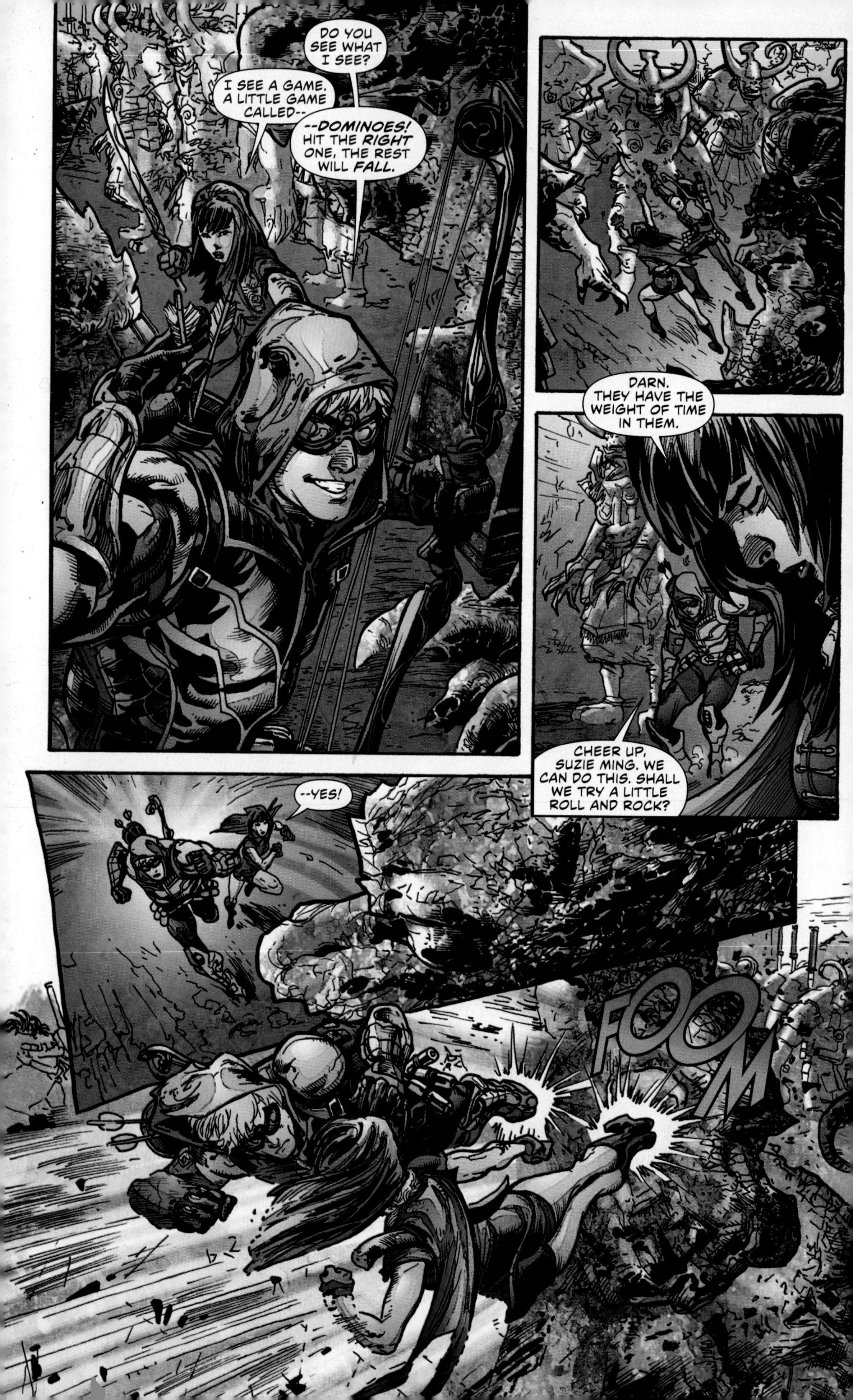
DO YOU SEE WHAT I SEE?
I SEE A GAME. A LITTLE GAME CALLED--
--DOMINOES! HIT THE RIGHT ONE, THE REST WILL FALL.
DARN. THEY HAVE THE WEIGHT OF TIME IN THEM.
CHEER UP, SUZIE MING. WE CAN DO THIS. SHALL WE TRY A LITTLE ROLL AND ROCK?
--YES!
FOOM

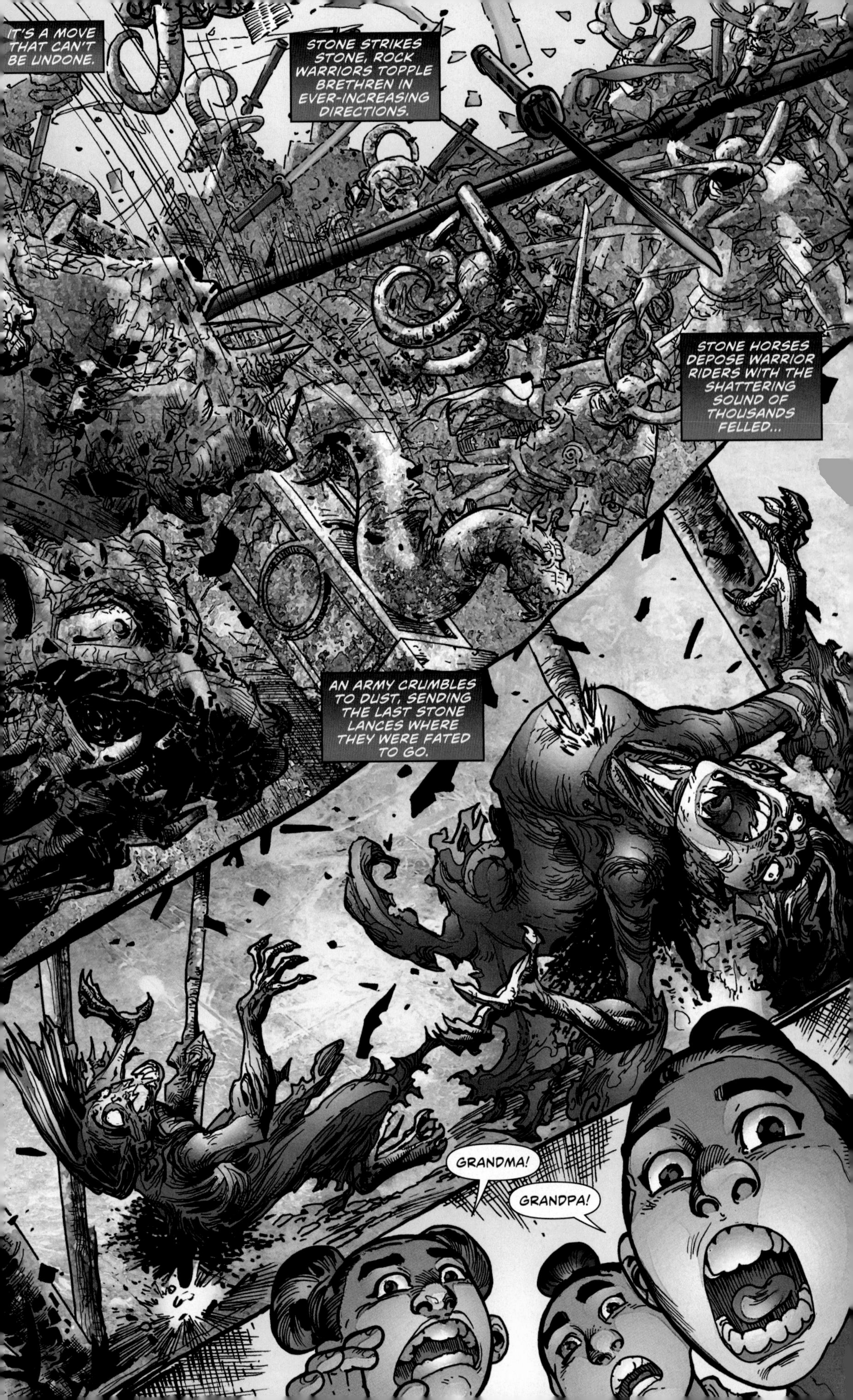
IT'S A MOVE THAT CAN'T BE UNDONE.
STONE STRIKES STONE, ROCK WARRIORS TOPPLE BRETHREN IN EVER-INCREASING DIRECTIONS.
STONE HORSES DEPOSE WARRIOR RIDERS WITH THE SHATTERING SOUND OF THOUSANDS FELLED...
AN ARMY CRUMBLES TO DUST, SENDING THE LAST STONE LANCES WHERE THEY WERE FATED TO GO.
GRANDMA!
GRANDPA!

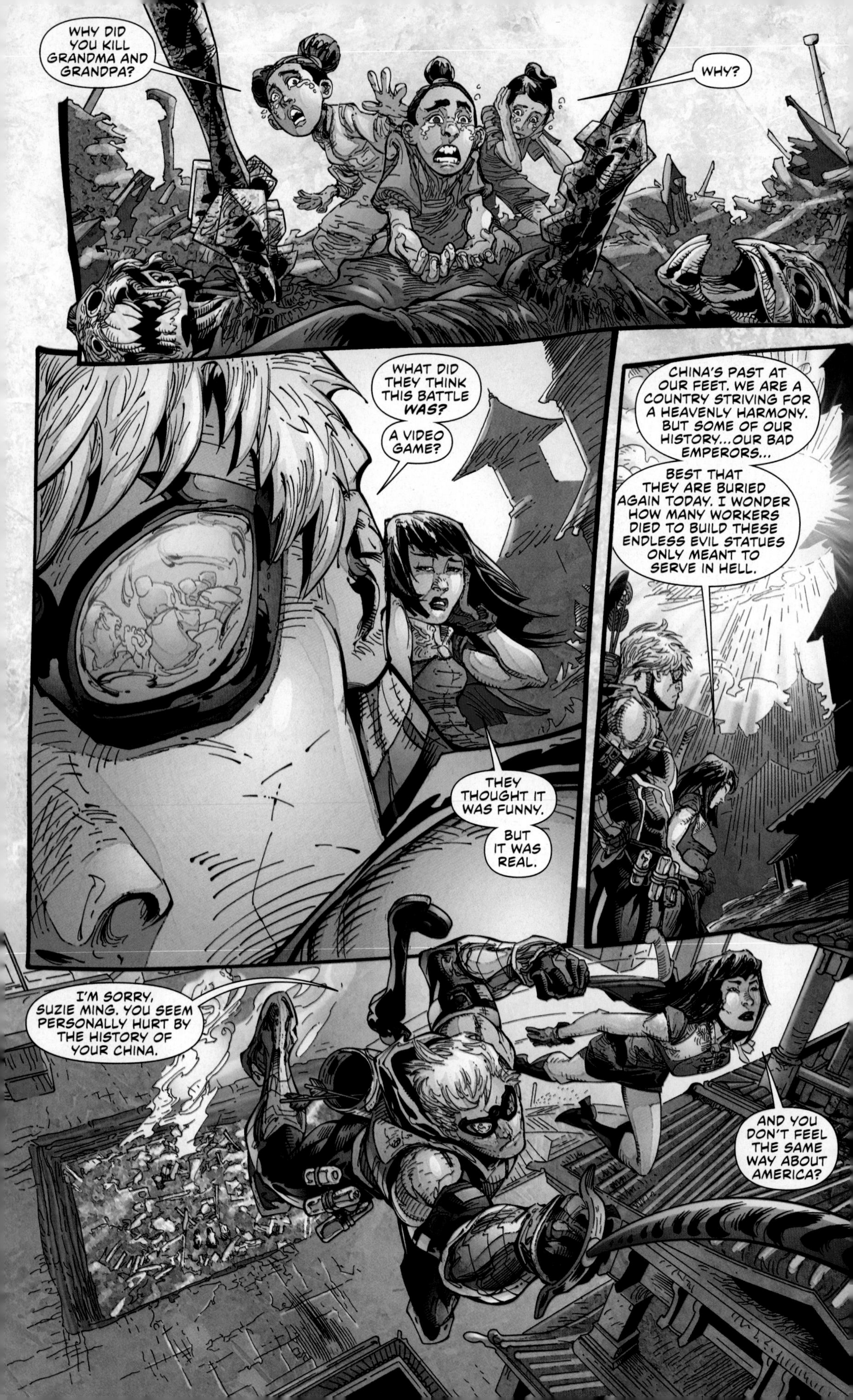
WHY DID YOU KILL GRANDMA AND GRANDPA?
WHY?
WHAT DID THEY THINK THIS BATTLE WAS?
A VIDEO GAME?
THEY THOUGHT IT WAS FUNNY.
BUT IT WAS REAL.
CHINA'S PAST AT OUR FEET. WE ARE A COUNTRY STRIVING FOR A HEAVENLY HARMONY. BUT SOME OF OUR HISTORY...OUR BAD EMPERORS...
BEST THAT THEY ARE BURIED AGAIN TODAY. I WONDER HOW MANY WORKERS DIED TO BUILD THESE ENDLESS EVIL STATUES ONLY MEANT TO SERVE IN HELL.
I'M SORRY, SUZIE MING. YOU SEEM PERSONALLY HURT BY THE HISTORY OF YOUR CHINA.
AND YOU DON'T FEEL THE SAME WAY ABOUT AMERICA?

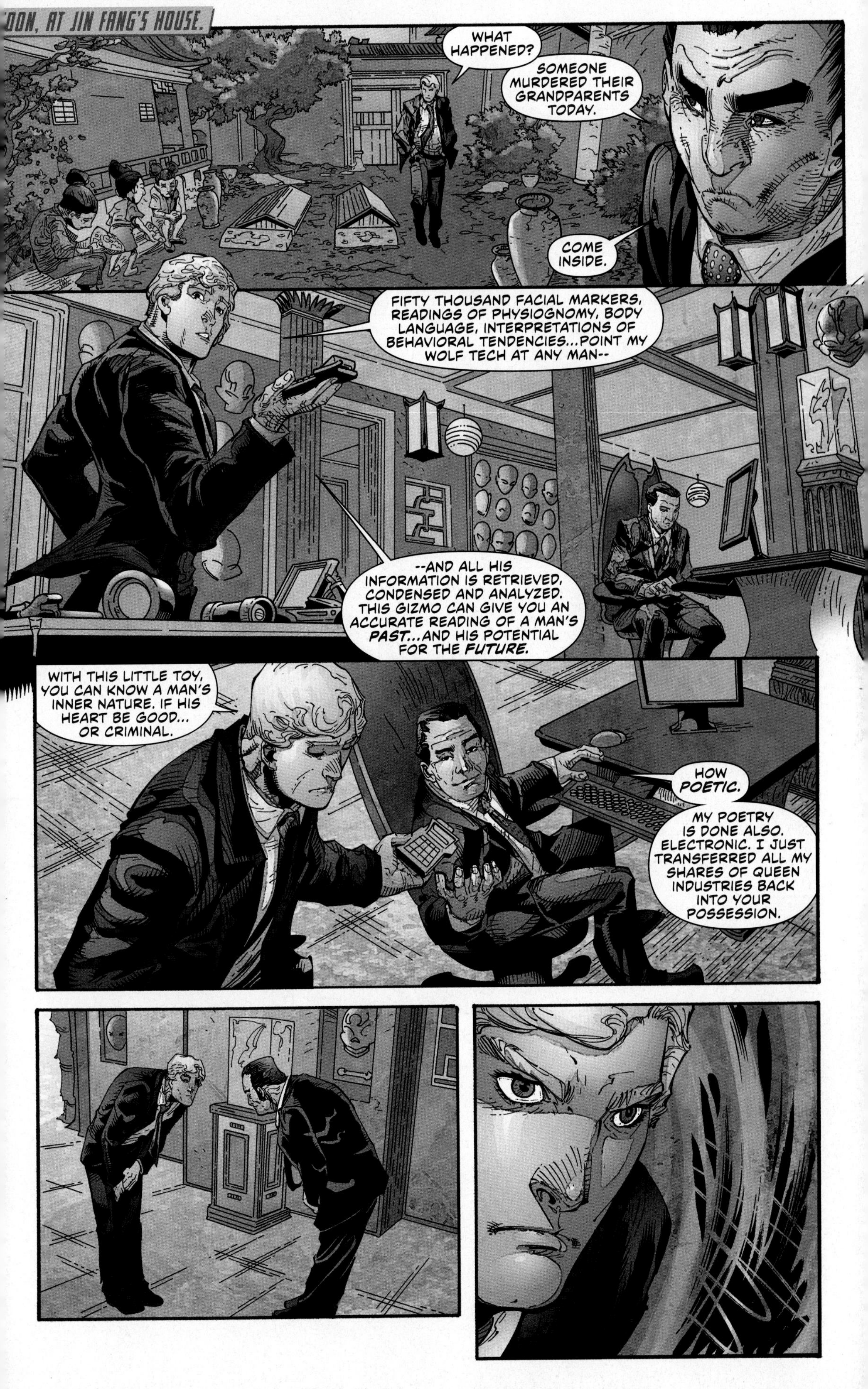
OON, AT JIN FANG'S HOUSE.
WHAT HAPPENED?
SOMEONE MURDERED THEIR GRANDPARENTS TODAY.
COME INSIDE.
FIFTY THOUSAND FACIAL MARKERS, READINGS OF PHYSIOGNOMY, BODY LANGUAGE, INTERPRETATIONS OF BEHAVIORAL TENDENCIES...POINT MY WOLF TECH AT ANY MAN--
--AND ALL HIS INFORMATION IS RETRIEVED, CONDENSED AND ANALYZED. THIS GIZMO CAN GIVE YOU AN ACCURATE READING OF A MAN'S PAST...AND HIS POTENTIAL FOR THE FUTURE.
WITH THIS LITTLE TOY, YOU CAN KNOW A MAN'S INNER NATURE. IF HIS HEART BE GOOD... OR CRIMINAL.
HOW POETIC.
MY POETRY IS DONE ALSO. ELECTRONIC. I JUST TRANSFERRED ALL MY SHARES OF QUEEN INDUSTRIES BACK INTO YOUR POSSESSION.

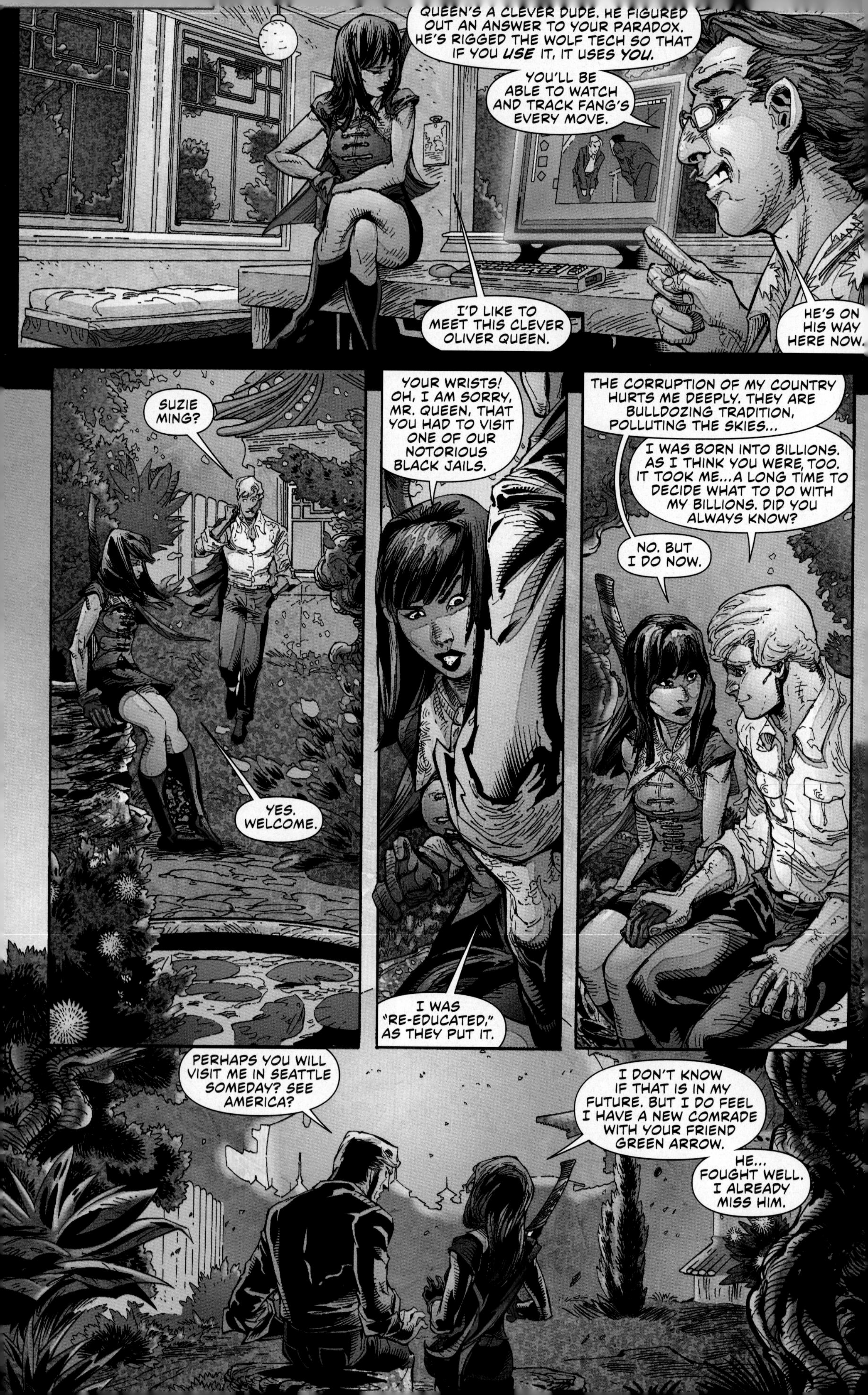
QUEEN'S A CLEVER DUDE. HE FIGURED OUT AN ANSWER TO YOUR PARADOX. HE'S RIGGED THE WOLF TECH SO THAT IF YOU USE IT, IT USES YOU.
YOU'LL BE ABLE TO WATCH AND TRACK FANG'S EVERY MOVE.
I'D LIKE TO MEET THIS CLEVER OLIVER QUEEN.
HE'S ON HIS WAY HERE NOW.
SUZIE MING?
YES. WELCOME.
YOUR WRISTS! OH, I AM SORRY, MR. QUEEN, THAT YOU HAD TO VISIT ONE OF OUR NOTORIOUS BLACK JAILS.
I WAS "RE-EDUCATED," AS THEY PUT IT.
THE CORRUPTION OF MY COUNTRY HURTS ME DEEPLY. THEY ARE BULLDOZING TRADITION, POLLUTING THE SKIES...
I WAS BORN INTO BILLIONS. AS I THINK YOU WERE, TOO. IT TOOK ME...A LONG TIME TO DECIDE WHAT TO DO WITH MY BILLIONS. DID YOU ALWAYS KNOW?
NO. BUT I DO NOW.
PERHAPS YOU WILL VISIT ME IN SEATTLE SOMEDAY? SEE AMERICA?
I DON'T KNOW IF THAT IS IN MY FUTURE. BUT I DO FEEL I HAVE A NEW COMRADE WITH YOUR FRIEND GREEN ARROW.
HE... FOUGHT WELL. I ALREADY MISS HIM.

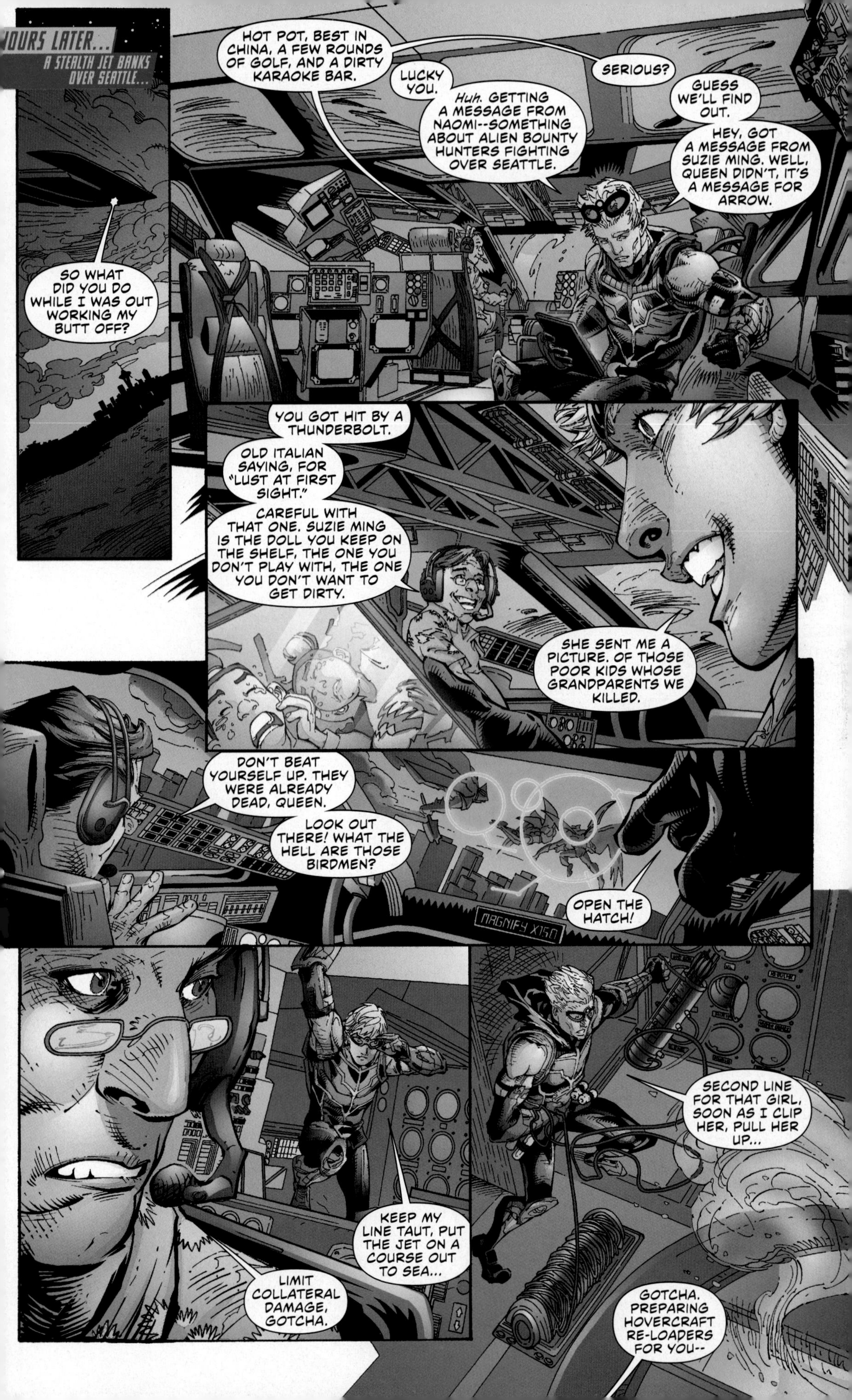
HOURS LATER...
A STEALTH JET BANKS OVER SEATTLE...
SO WHAT DID YOU DO WHILE I WAS OUT WORKING MY BUTT OFF?
HOT POT, BEST IN CHINA, A FEW ROUNDS OF GOLF, AND A DIRTY KARAOKE BAR.
SERIOUS?
LUCKY YOU.
Huh. GETTING A MESSAGE FROM NAOMI--SOMETHING ABOUT ALIEN BOUNTY HUNTERS FIGHTING OVER SEATTLE.
GUESS WE'LL FIND OUT.
HEY, GOT A MESSAGE FROM SUZIE MING. WELL, QUEEN DIDN'T, IT'S A MESSAGE FOR ARROW.
YOU GOT HIT BY A THUNDERBOLT.
OLD ITALIAN SAYING, FOR "LUST AT FIRST SIGHT."
CAREFUL WITH THAT ONE. SUZIE MING IS THE DOLL YOU KEEP ON THE SHELF, THE ONE YOU DON'T PLAY WITH, THE ONE YOU DON'T WANT TO GET DIRTY.
SHE SENT ME A PICTURE. OF THOSE POOR KIDS WHOSE GRANDPARENTS WE KILLED.
DON'T BEAT YOURSELF UP. THEY WERE ALREADY DEAD, QUEEN.
LOOK OUT THERE! WHAT THE HELL ARE THOSE BIRDMEN?
OPEN THE HATCH!
MAGNIFY X150
LIMIT COLLATERAL DAMAGE, GOTCHA.
KEEP MY LINE TAUT, PUT THE JET ON A COURSE OUT TO SEA...
SECOND LINE FOR THAT GIRL, SOON AS I CLIP HER, PULL HER UP...
GOTCHA. PREPARING HOVERCRAFT RE-LOADERS FOR YOU--

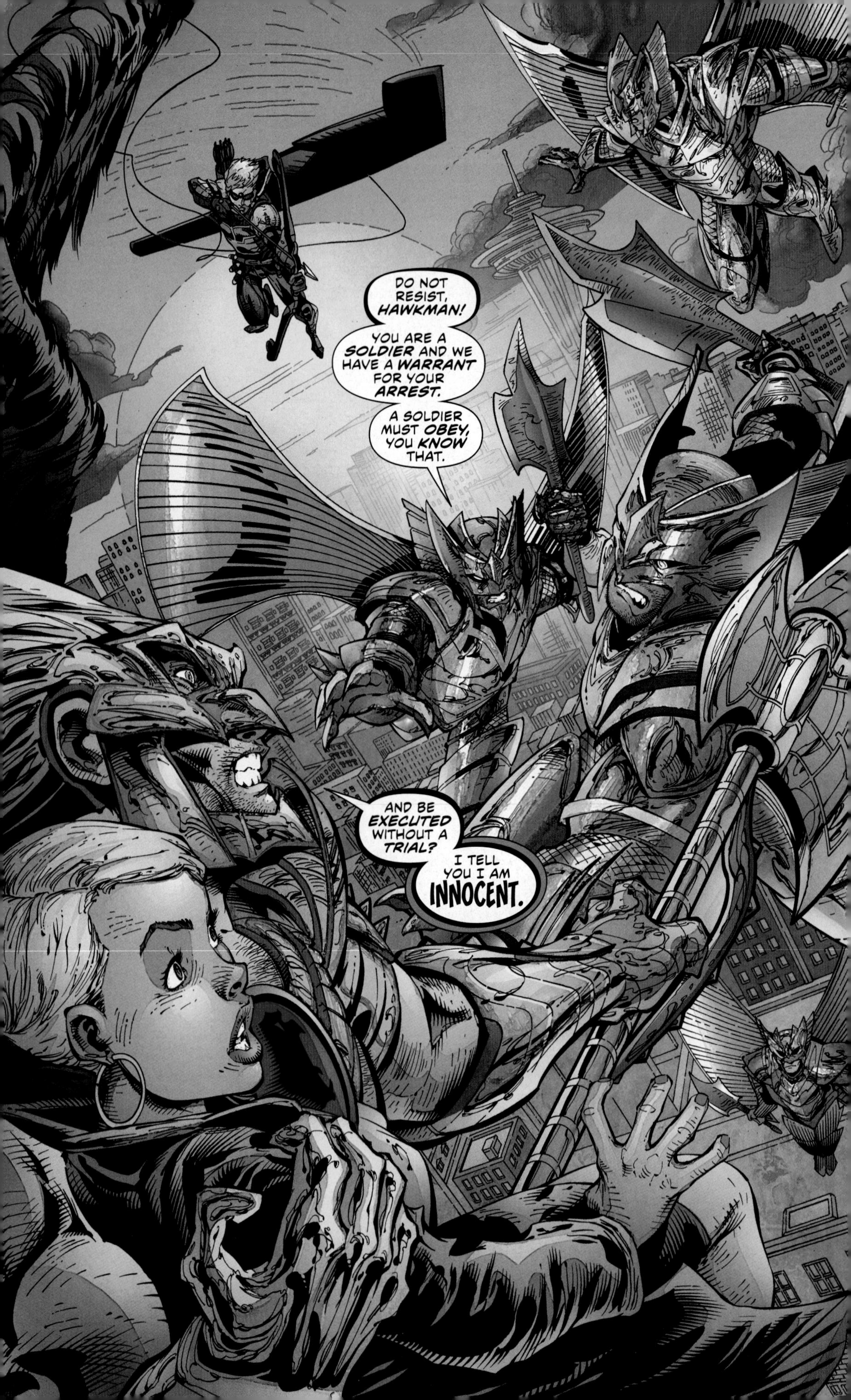
DO NOT RESIST, HAWKMAN!
YOU ARE A SOLDIER AND WE HAVE A WARRANT FOR YOUR ARREST.
A SOLDIER MUST OBEY, YOU KNOW THAT.
AND BE EXECUTED WITHOUT A TRIAL?
I TELL YOU I AM INNOCENT.

GREEN ARROW

CHARACTER SKETCH BY FREDDIE WILLIAMS II

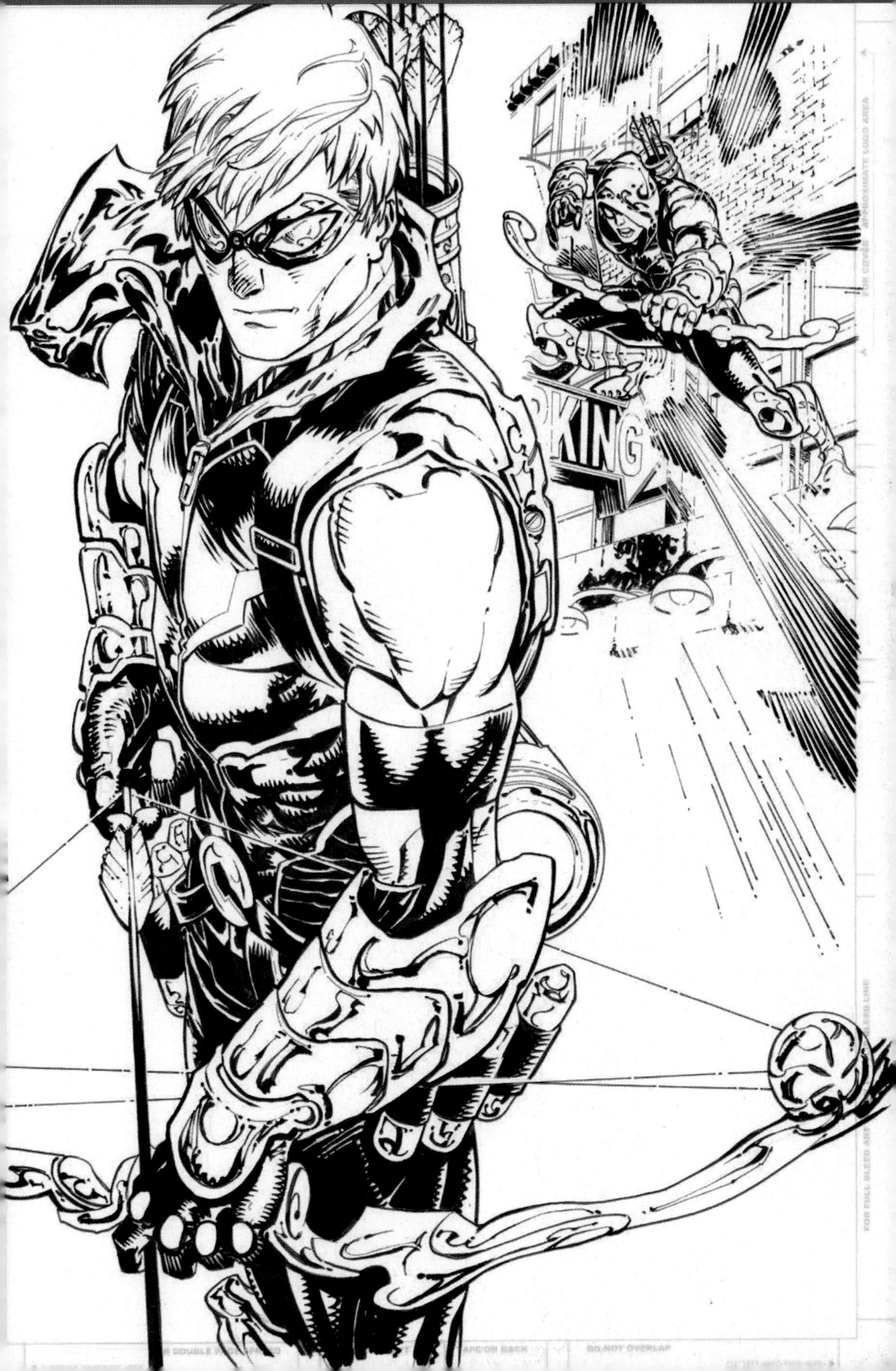

SKYLARK CHARACTER SKETCHES BY HARVEY TOLIBAO

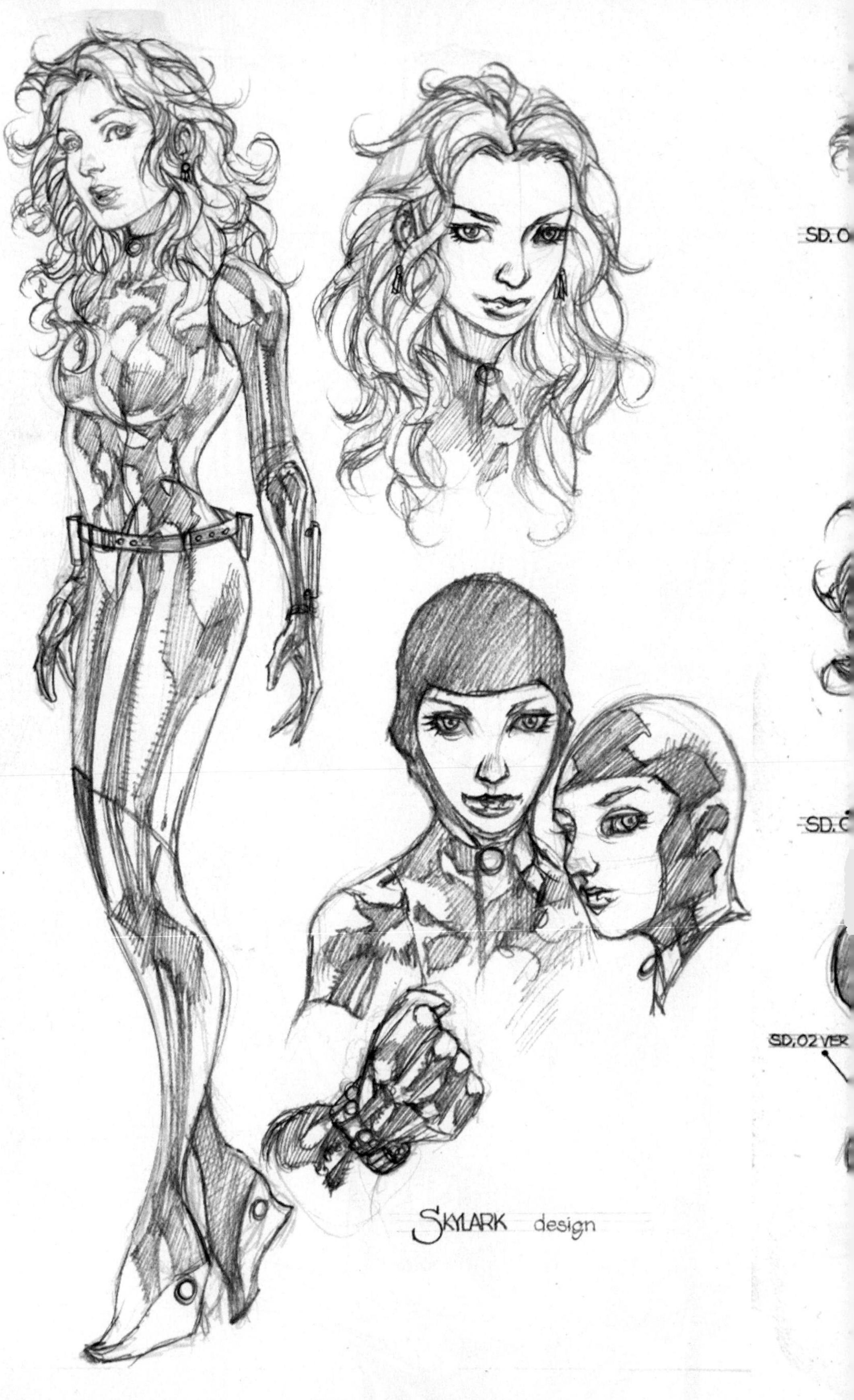
SKYLARK design
SD. O
SD. C
SD. 02 VER

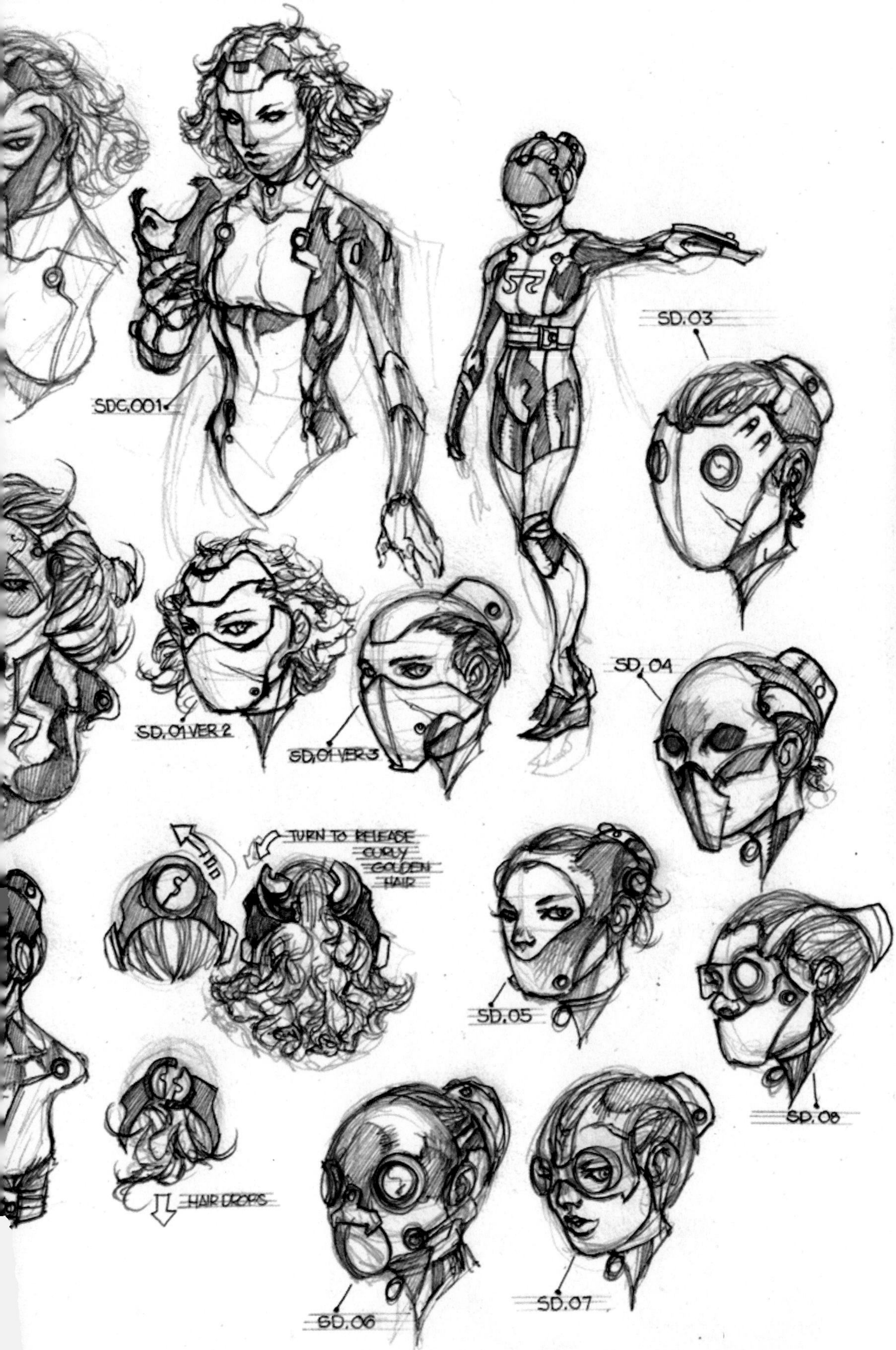
SDG.001
SD.03
SD.01 VER 2
SD.01 VER 3
SD.04
TURN TO RELEASE CURLY GOLDEN HAIR
SD.05
SD.08
HAIR DROPS
SD.06
SD.07

LEER CHARACTER SKETCHES BY HARVEY TOLIBAO

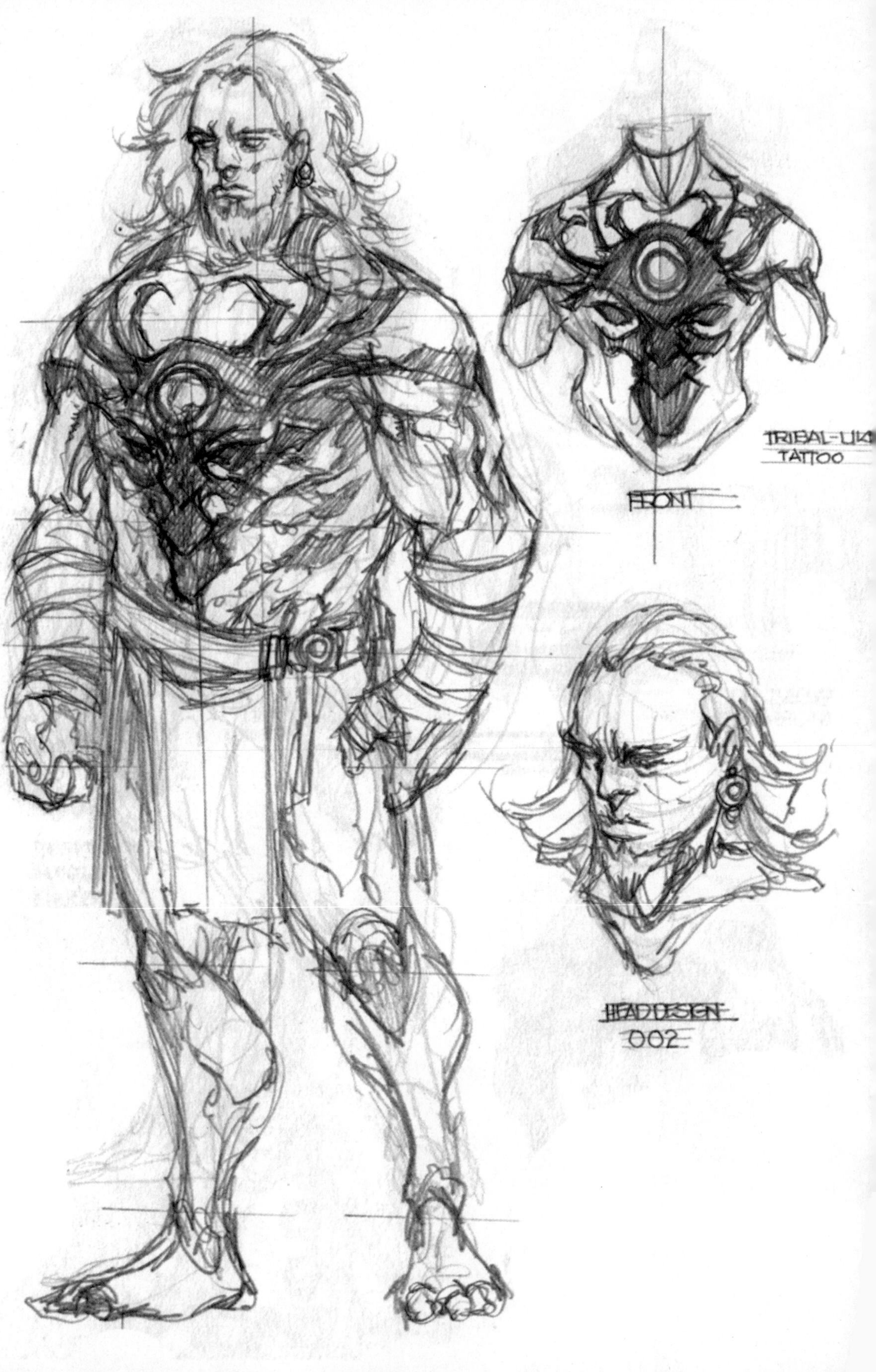
TRIBAL-LIK
TATTOO
FRONT
HEAD DESIGN
002

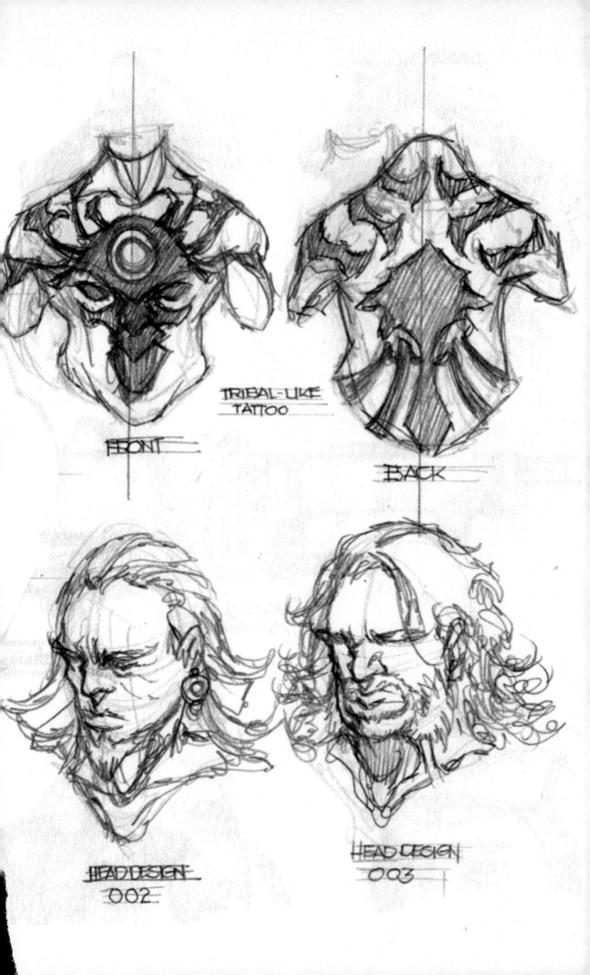

TRIBAL-LIKE
TATTOO

FRONT

BACK

HEAD DESIGN
002

HEAD DESIGN
003

SUZIE MING CHARACTER SKETCHES BY HARVEY TOLIBAO

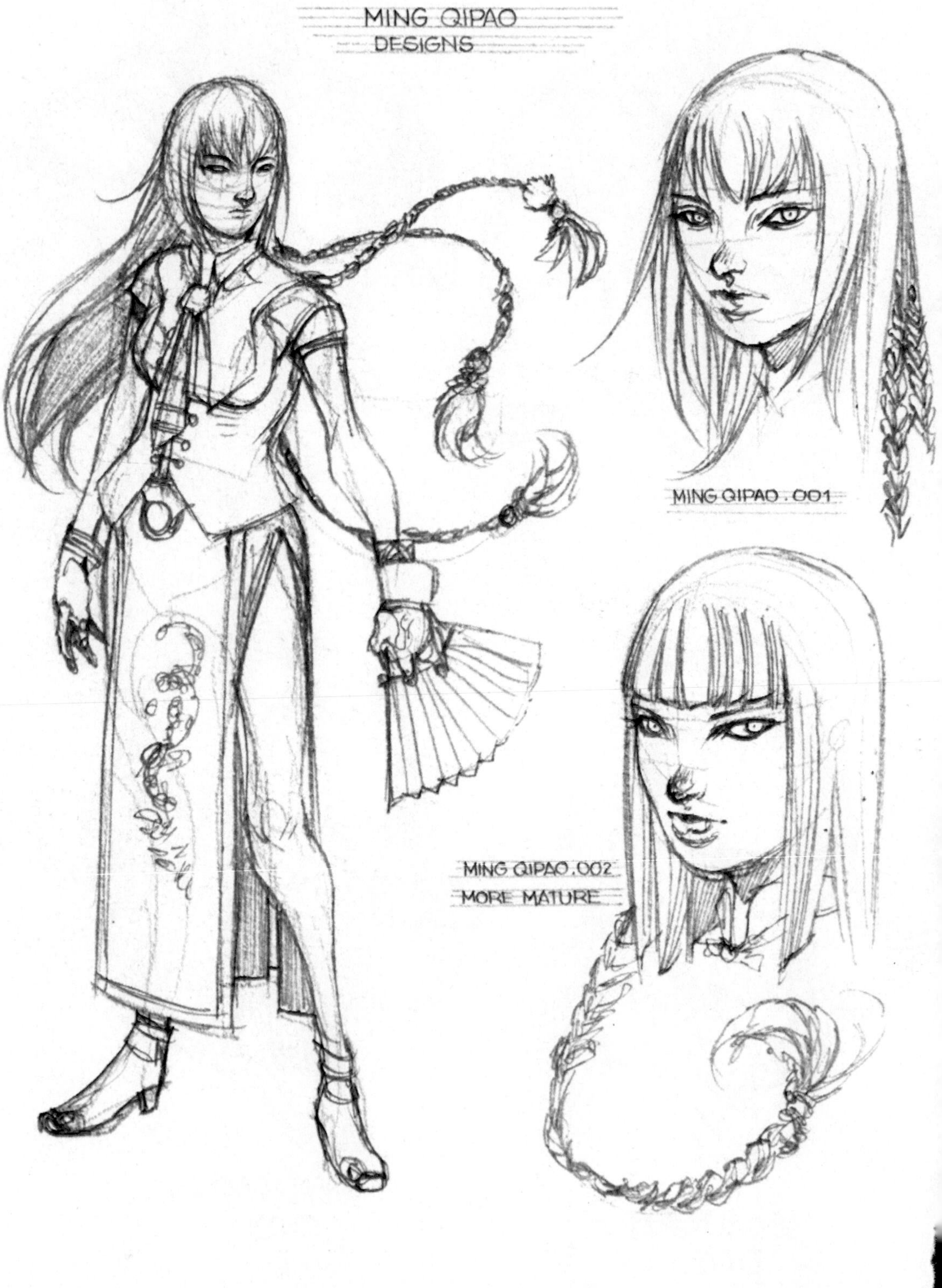
MING QIPAO
DESIGNS
MING QIPAO .001
MING QIPAO .002
MORE MATURE